THE AMERICAN YAWP

A Massively Collaborative Open U.S. History Textbook

VOL. I: TO 1877

EDITED BY JOSEPH L. LOCKE AND BEN WRIGHT

STANFORD UNIVERSITY PRESS • STANFORD, CALIFORNIA

Stanford University Press
Stanford, California

Printed in the United States of America on acid-free, archival-quality paper

Library of Congress Cataloging-in-Publication Data

Names: Locke, Joseph L., editor. | Wright, Ben, editor.
Title: The American yawp : a massively collaborative open U.S. history textbook / edited by Joseph L. Locke and Ben Wright.
Description: Stanford, California : Stanford University Press, 2019. | Includes bibliographical references and index.
Identifiers: LCCN 2018015206 (print) | LCCN 2018017638 (ebook) | ISBN 9781503608139 (e-book) | ISBN 9781503606715 | ISBN 9781503606715 (v. 1 :pbk. :alk. paper) | ISBN 9781503606883(v. 2 :pbk. :alk. paper) | ISBN 9781503608139(v. 1 :ebook) | ISBN 9781503608146(v. 2 :ebook)
Subjects: LCSH: United States—History—Textbooks.
Classification: LCC E178.1 (ebook) | LCC E178.1 .A493673 2019 (print) | DDC 973—dc23
LC record available at https://lccn.loc.gov/2018015206

Typeset by Newgen in Sabon LT 11/15
Cover illustration: Detail from "Grand Democratic Free Soil Banner," by N. Currier and John Plumbe Jr., 1848. Source: Susan H. Douglas Political Americana Collection, Division of Rare and Manuscript Collections, Cornell University Library.

THE AMERICAN YAWP

Yawp \yôp\ *n*: 1: a raucous noise 2: rough vigorous language
"I sound my barbaric yawp over the roofs of the world."
Walt Whitman, 1854

Contents

Preface

We are the heirs of our history. Our communities, our politics, our culture: it is all a product of the past. As William Faulkner wrote, "The past is never dead. It's not even past."[1] To understand who we are, we must therefore understand our history.

But what *is* history? What does it mean to study the past? History can never be the simple memorizing of names and dates (how would we even know what names and dates are worth studying?). It is too complex a task and too dynamic a process to be reduced to that. It must be something more because, in a sense, it is we who give life to the past. Historians ask historical questions, weigh evidence from primary sources (material produced in the era under study), grapple with rival interpretations, and argue for their conclusions. History, then, is our ongoing conversation about the past.

Every generation must write its own history. Old conclusions—say, about the motives of European explorers or the realities of life on slave plantations—fall before new evidence and new outlooks. Names of leaders and dates of events may not change, but the weight we give them and the context with which we frame them invariably evolves. History is a conversation between the past and the present. To understand a global society, we must explore a history of transnational forces. To understand the lived experiences of ordinary Americans, we must look beyond the elites who framed older textbooks and listen to the poor and disadvantaged from all generations.

But why study history in the first place? History can cultivate essential and relevant—or, in more utilitarian terms, "marketable"—skills: careful reading, creative thinking, and clear communication. Many are familiar with a famous quote of philosopher George Santayana: "Those who fail to learn from history are doomed to repeat it."[2] The role of history in shaping current events is more complicated than this quote implies, but Santayana was right in arguing that history offers important lessons. The historical sensibility yields perspective and context and broader awareness. It liberates us from our narrow experiences and pulls us into, in the words of historian Peter Stearns, "the laboratory of human experience."[3] Perhaps a better way to articulate the importance of studying history would be, "Those who fail to understand their history will fail to understand themselves."

Historical interpretation is never wholly subjective: it requires method, rigor, and perspective. The open nature of historical discourse does not mean that all arguments—and certainly not all "opinions"—about the past are equally valid. Some are simply wrong. And yet good historical questions will not always have easy answers. Asking "When did Christopher Columbus first sail across the Atlantic?" will tell us far less than "What inspired Columbus to attempt his voyage?" or "How did Native Americans interpret the arrival of Europeans?" Crafting answers to these questions reveals far greater insights into our history.

But how can any textbook encapsulate American history? Should it organize around certain themes or surrender to the impossibility of synthesis and retreat toward generality? In the oft-cited lines of the American poet Walt Whitman, we found as good an organizing principle as any other: "I too am not a bit tamed—I too am untranslatable," he wrote, "I sound my barbaric yawp over the roofs of the world."[4] Long before Whitman and long after, Americans have sung something collectively amid the deafening roar of their many individual voices. Here we find both chorus and cacophony together, as one. This textbook therefore offers the story of that barbaric, untranslatable American yawp by constructing a coherent and accessible narrative from all the best of recent historical scholarship. Without losing sight of politics and power, it incorporates transnational perspectives, integrates diverse voices, recovers narratives of resistance, and explores the complex process of cultural creation. It looks for America in crowded slave cabins, bustling markets, congested tenements, and marbled halls. It navigates between maternity wards, prisons, streets, bars, and boardrooms. Whitman's America, like ours, cut across the narrow boundaries that can strangle narratives of American history.

We have produced *The American Yawp* to help guide students in their encounter with American history. *The American Yawp* is a collaboratively built, open American history textbook designed for general readers and college-level history courses. Over three hundred academic historians—scholars and experienced college-level instructors—have come together and freely volunteered their expertise to help democratize the American past for twenty-first century readers. The project is freely accessible online at www.AmericanYawp.com, and in addition to providing a peer review of the text, Stanford University Press has partnered with *The American Yawp* to publish a print edition. Furthermore, *The American Yawp* remains an evolving, collaborative text: you are encouraged to help us improve by offering comments on our feedback page, available through AmericanYawp.com.

The American Yawp is a fully open resource: you are encouraged to use it, download it, distribute it, and modify it as you see fit. The project is formally operated under a Creative Commons Attribution-Share Alike 4.0 International (CC-BY-SA) License and is designed to meet the standards of a "Free Cultural Work." We are happy to share it and we hope you will do the same.

A Note on Updates

The American Yawp was designed to capture the cutting edge of historical scholarship.

It is, above all else, a collaborative project, and we follow the advice of content experts. On our website, scholars provide detailed feedback on our content. We have received hundreds of smart, helpful suggestions from trained, academic historians. Each summer, we have made small changes based on this feedback. This print edition incorporates some of the updates that had appeared online before January 2023.

Most of our changes have been minor. Several chapters have new names. For example, we now begin the text with "Indigenous America." Some changes are more substantial. Our discussion of the New Deal, for instance, has changed considerably to reflect new perspectives on how Americans reckoned with the Great Depression. Moreover, we have updated the text to reflect our own momentous times. Our final chapter, on the "Recent Past," now includes discussions of the COVID-19 pandemic, the Black Lives Matter movement, the January 6 insurrection, and more. We do not believe these changes are substantial enough to merit a new edition, but we nevertheless want to ensure that print readers have access to these updates. A comprehensive list of our annual updates is available online at http://americanyawp.com/text/updates.

History, as we write in our text, is an ongoing conversation between the present and the past. *The American Yawp* remains committed to capturing the current state of that conversation.

Joseph Locke & Ben Wright, editors

NOTES TO PREFACE

1. William Faulkner, *Requiem for a Nun* (New York: Random House, 1954), 73.

2. George Santayana, *The Life of Reason: Or the Phases of Human Progress, Volume I* (New York: Scribner, 1905), 284.

3. Peter N. Stearns, "Why Study History," *American Historical Association* (July 11, 2008). https://www.historians.org/about-aha-and-membership/aha-history-and-archives/archives/why-study-history-(1998.

4. Walt Whitman, *Leaves of Grass* (Brooklyn: Rome, 1855), 55.

THE AMERICAN YAWP

1

Indigenous America

I. Introduction

Europeans called the Americas "the New World." But for the millions of Native Americans they encountered, it was anything but. Humans have lived in the Americas for over ten thousand years. Dynamic and diverse, they spoke hundreds of languages and created thousands of distinct cultures. Native Americans built settled communities and followed seasonal migration patterns, maintained peace through alliances and warred with their neighbors, and developed self-sufficient economies and maintained vast trade networks. They cultivated distinct art forms and spiritual values. Kinship ties knit their communities together. But the arrival of Europeans and the resulting global exchange of people, animals, plants, and microbes—what scholars benignly call the Columbian Exchange—bridged more than ten thousand years of geographic separation, inaugurated centuries of violence, unleashed the greatest biological terror the world had ever seen, and revolutionized the history of the world. It began one of the most consequential developments in all of human history and the first chapter in the long American yawp.

Cahokia, as it may have appeared around 1150 CE. Painting by Michael Hampshire for the Cahokia Mounds State Historic Site.

II. The First Americans

American history begins with the first Americans. But where do their stories start? Native Americans passed stories down through the millennia that tell of their creation and reveal the contours of Indigenous belief. The Salinan people of present-day California, for example, tell of a bald eagle that formed the first man out of clay and the first woman out of a feather.[1] According to a Lenape tradition, the earth was made when Sky Woman fell into a watery world and, with the help of muskrat and beaver, landed safely on a turtle's back, thus creating Turtle Island, or North America. A Choctaw tradition locates southeastern peoples' beginnings inside the great Mother Mound earthwork, Nunih Waya, in the lower Mississippi Valley.[2] Nahua people trace their beginnings to the place of the Seven Caves, from which their ancestors emerged before they migrated to what is now central Mexico.[3] America's Indigenous peoples have passed down many accounts of their origins, written and oral, which share creation and migration histories.

Archaeologists and anthropologists, meanwhile, focus on migration histories. Studying artifacts, bones, and genetic signatures, these scholars have pieced together a narrative that claims that the Americas were once a "new world" for Native Americans as well.

The last global ice age trapped much of the world's water in enormous continental glaciers. Twenty thousand years ago, ice sheets, some a mile thick, extended across North America as far south as modern-day Illinois. With so much of the world's water captured in these massive ice sheets, global sea levels were much lower, and a land bridge connected Asia and North America across the Bering Strait. Between twelve and twenty thousand years ago, Native ancestors crossed the ice, waters, and exposed lands between the continents of Asia and America. These mobile hunter-gatherers traveled in small bands, exploiting vegetable, animal, and marine resources into the Beringian tundra at the northwestern edge of North America. DNA evidence suggests that these ancestors paused— for perhaps fifteen thousand years—in the expansive region between Asia and America.[4] Other ancestors crossed the seas and voyaged along the Pacific coast, traveling along riverways and settling where local ecosystems permitted.[5] Glacial sheets receded around fourteen thousand years ago, opening a corridor to warmer climates and new resources. Some ancestral communities migrated southward and eastward. Evidence found at Monte Verde, a site in modern-day Chile, suggests that human activity began there at least 14,500 years ago. Similar evidence hints at human settlement in the Florida panhandle and in central Texas at the same time.[6] On many points, archaeological and traditional knowledge sources converge: the dental, archaeological, linguistic, oral, ecological, and genetic evidence illustrates a great deal of diversity, with numerous groups settling and migrating over thousands of years, potentially from many different points of origin.[7] Whether emerging from the earth, water, or sky; being made by a creator; or migrating to their homelands, modern Native American communities recount histories in America that date long before human memory.

In the Northwest, Native groups exploited the great salmon-filled rivers. On the plains and prairie lands, hunting communities followed bison herds and moved according to seasonal patterns. In mountains, prairies, deserts, and forests, the cultures and ways of life of paleo-era ancestors were as varied as the geography. These groups spoke hundreds of languages and adopted distinct cultural practices. Rich and diverse diets fueled massive population growth across the continent.

Prehistoric settlement in Warren County, Mississippi. Mural by Robert Dafford, depicting the Kings Crossing archaeological site as it may have appeared in 1000 CE. Vicksburg Riverfront Murals.

Agriculture arose sometime between nine thousand and five thousand years ago, almost simultaneously in the Eastern and Western Hemispheres. Mesoamericans in modern-day Mexico and Central America relied on domesticated maize (corn) to develop the hemisphere's first

settled population around 1200 BCE.[8] Corn was high in caloric content, easily dried and stored, and, in Mesoamerica's warm and fertile Gulf Coast, could sometimes be harvested twice in a year. Corn—as well as other Mesoamerican crops—spread across North America and continues to hold an important spiritual and cultural place in many Native communities.

Agriculture flourished in the fertile river valleys between the Mississippi River and the Atlantic Ocean, an area known as the Eastern Woodlands. There, three crops in particular—corn, beans, and squash, known as the Three Sisters—provided nutritional needs necessary to sustain cities and civilizations. In Woodland areas from the Great Lakes and the Mississippi River to the Atlantic coast, Native communities managed their forest resources by burning underbrush to create vast parklike hunting grounds and to clear the ground for planting the Three Sisters. Many groups used shifting cultivation, in which farmers cut the forest, burned the undergrowth, and then planted seeds in the nutrient-rich ashes. When crop yields began to decline, farmers moved to another field and allowed the land to recover and the forest to regrow before again cutting the forest, burning the undergrowth, and restarting the cycle. This technique was particularly useful in areas with difficult soil. In the fertile regions of the Eastern Woodlands, Native American farmers engaged in permanent, intensive agriculture, using hand tools. The rich soil and use of hand tools enabled effective and sustainable farming practices, producing high yields without overburdening the soil.[9] Typically in Woodland communities, women practiced agriculture while men hunted and fished.

Agriculture allowed for dramatic social change, but for some, it also may have accompanied a decline in health. Analysis of remains reveals that societies transitioning to agriculture often experienced weaker bones and teeth.[10] But despite these possible declines, agriculture brought important benefits. Farmers could produce more food than hunters, enabling some members of the community to pursue other skills. Religious leaders, skilled soldiers, and artists could devote their energy to activities other than food production.

North America's Indigenous peoples shared some broad traits. Spiritual practices, understandings of property, and kinship networks differed markedly from European arrangements. Most Native Americans did not neatly distinguish between the natural and the supernatural. Spiritual power permeated their world and was both tangible and accessible. It could be appealed to and harnessed. Kinship bound most Native North

American people together. Most people lived in small communities tied by kinship networks. Many Native cultures understood ancestry as matrilineal: family and clan identity proceeded along the female line, through mothers and daughters, rather than fathers and sons. Fathers, for instance, often joined mothers' extended families, and sometimes even a mother's brothers took a more direct role in child-raising than biological fathers. Therefore, mothers often wielded enormous influence at local levels, and men's identities and influence often depended on their relationships to women. Native American culture, meanwhile, generally afforded greater sexual and marital freedom than European cultures.[11] Women, for instance, often chose their husbands, and divorce often was a relatively simple and straightforward process. Moreover, most Native peoples' notions of property rights differed markedly from those of Europeans. Native Americans generally felt a personal ownership of tools, weapons, or other items that were actively used, and this same rule applied to land and crops. Groups and individuals exploited particular pieces of land and used violence or negotiation to exclude others. But the right to the use of land did not imply the right to its permanent possession.

Native Americans had many ways of communicating, including graphic ones, and some of these artistic and communicative technologies are still used today. For example, Algonquian-speaking Ojibwes used birch-bark scrolls to record medical treatments, recipes, songs, stories, and more. Other Eastern Woodland peoples wove plant fibers, embroidered skins with porcupine quills, and modeled the earth to make sites of complex ceremonial meaning. On the Plains, artisans wove buffalo hair and painted on buffalo skins; in the Pacific Northwest, after the arrival of the Europeans, weavers wove goat hair into soft textiles with particular patterns. Maya, Zapotec, and Nahua ancestors in Mesoamerica painted their histories on plant-derived textiles and carved them into stone. In the Andes, Inca recorders noted information in the form of knotted strings, or *khipu*.[12]

Two thousand years ago, some of the largest culture groups in North America were the Puebloan groups, centered in the current-day Greater Southwest (the southwestern United States and northwestern Mexico), the Mississippian groups located along the Great River and its tributaries, and the Mesoamerican groups of the areas now known as central Mexico and the Yucatán. Previous developments in agricultural technology enabled the explosive growth of the large early societies, such as that at Tenochtitlán in the Valley of Mexico, Cahokia along the Mississippi River, and in the desert oasis areas of the Greater Southwest.

Native peoples in the Southwest began constructing these highly defensible cliff dwellings in 1190 CE and continued expanding and refurbishing them until 1260 CE before abandoning them around 1300 CE. Andreas F. Borchert, "Mesa Verde National Park Cliff Palace." Wikimedia. Creative Commons Attribution-Share Alike 3.0 Germany.

Chaco Canyon in northern New Mexico was home to ancestral Puebloan peoples between 900 and 1300 CE. As many as fifteen thousand individuals lived in the Chaco Canyon complex in present-day New Mexico.[13] Sophisticated agricultural practices, extensive trading networks, and even the domestication of animals like turkeys allowed the population to swell. Massive residential structures, built from sandstone blocks and lumber carried across great distances, housed hundreds of Puebloan people. One building, Pueblo Bonito, stretched over two acres and rose five stories. Its six hundred rooms were decorated with copper bells, turquoise decorations, and bright macaws.[14] Homes like those at Pueblo Bonito included a small dugout room, or *kiva*, which played an important role in a variety of ceremonies and served as an important center for Puebloan life and culture. Puebloan spirituality was tied both to the earth and the heavens, as generations carefully charted the stars and designed homes in line with the path of the sun and moon.[15]

The Puebloan people of Chaco Canyon faced several ecological challenges, including deforestation and overirrigation, which ultimately caused the community to collapse and its people to disperse to smaller settlements. An extreme fifty-year drought began in 1130. Shortly thereafter, Chaco Canyon was deserted. New groups, including the Apache and Navajo, entered the vacated territory and adopted several Puebloan customs. The same drought that plagued the Pueblo also likely affected the Mississippian peoples of the American Midwest and South. The Mississippians developed one of the largest civilizations north of modern-day Mexico. Roughly one thousand years ago, the largest Mississippian settlement, Cahokia, located just east of modern-day St. Louis, peaked at a population of between ten thousand and thirty thousand. It rivaled contemporary European cities in size. No city north of modern Mexico, in fact, would match Cahokia's peak population levels until after the American Revolution. The city itself spanned two thousand acres and centered on Monks Mound, a large earthen hill that rose ten stories and was larger at its base than the pyramids of Egypt. As with many of the peoples who lived in the Woodlands, life and death in Cahokia were linked to the movement of the stars, sun, and moon, and their ceremonial earthwork structures reflect these important structuring forces.

Cahokia was politically organized around chiefdoms, a hierarchical, clan-based system that gave leaders both secular and sacred authority. The size of the city and the extent of its influence suggest that the city relied on a number of lesser chiefdoms under the authority of a paramount leader. Social stratification was partly preserved through frequent warfare. War captives were enslaved, and these captives formed an important part of the economy in the North American Southeast. Native American slavery was not based on holding people as property. Instead, Native Americans understood the enslaved as people who lacked kinship networks. Slavery, then, was not always a permanent condition. Very often, a formerly enslaved person could become a fully integrated member of the community. Adoption or marriage could enable an enslaved person to enter a kinship network and join the community. Slavery and captive trading became an

An artist's rendering of Cahokia as it may have appeared in 1150 CE. Prepared by Bill Isminger and Mark Esarey with artwork by Greg Harlin. From the Cahokia Mounds State Historic Site.

important way that many Native communities regrew and gained or maintained power.

Around 1050, Cahokia experienced what one archaeologist has called a "big bang," which included "a virtually instantaneous and pervasive shift in all things political, social, and ideological."[16] The population grew almost 500 percent in only one generation, and new people groups were absorbed into the city and its supporting communities. By 1300, the once-powerful city had undergone a series of strains that led to collapse. Scholars previously pointed to ecological disaster or slow depopulation through emigration, but new research instead emphasizes mounting warfare, or internal political tensions. Environmental explanations suggest that population growth placed too great a burden on the arable land. Others suggest that the demand for fuel and building materials led to deforestation, erosion, and perhaps an extended drought. Recent evidence, including defensive stockades, suggests that political turmoil among the ruling elite and threats from external enemies may explain the end of the once-great civilization.[17]

North American communities were connected by kin, politics, and culture and sustained by long-distance trading routes. The Mississippi River served as an important trade artery, but all of the continent's waterways were vital to transportation and communication. Cahokia became a key trading center partly because of its position near the Mississippi, Illinois, and Missouri Rivers. These rivers created networks that stretched from the Great Lakes to the American Southeast. Archaeologists can identify materials, like seashells, that traveled over a thousand miles to reach the center of this civilization. At least 3,500 years ago, the community at what is now Poverty Point, Louisiana, had access to copper from present-day Canada and flint from modern-day Indiana. Sheets of mica found at the sacred Serpent Mound site near the Ohio River came from the Allegheny Mountains, and obsidian from nearby earthworks came from Mexico. Turquoise from the Greater Southwest was used at Teotihuacan 1200 years ago.

In the Eastern Woodlands, many Native American societies lived in smaller, dispersed communities to take advantage of rich soils and abundant rivers and streams. The Lenapes, also known as Delawares, farmed the bottomlands throughout the Hudson and Delaware River watersheds in New York, Pennsylvania, New Jersey, and Delaware. Their hundreds of settlements, stretching from southern Massachusetts through Delaware, were loosely bound together by political, social, and spiritual connections.

Dispersed and relatively independent, Lenape communities were bound together by oral histories, ceremonial traditions, consensus-based political organization, kinship networks, and a shared clan system. Kinship tied the various Lenape communities and clans together, and society was organized along matrilineal lines. Marriage occurred between clans, and a married man joined the clan of his wife. Lenape women wielded authority over marriages, households, and agricultural production and may even have played a significant part in determining the selection of leaders, called sachems. Dispersed authority, small settlements, and kin-based organization contributed to the long-lasting stability and resilience of Lenape communities.[18] One or more sachems governed Lenape communities by the consent of their people. Lenape sachems acquired their authority by demonstrating wisdom and experience. This differed from the hierarchical organization of many Mississippian cultures. Large gatherings did exist, however, as dispersed communities and their leaders gathered for ceremonial purposes or to make big decisions. Sachems spoke for their people in larger councils that included men, women, and elders. The Lenapes experienced occasional tensions with other Indigenous groups like the Iroquois to the north or the Susquehannock to the south, but the lack of defensive fortifications near Lenape communities convinced archaeologists that the Lenapes avoided large-scale warfare.

The continued longevity of Lenape societies, which began centuries before European contact, was also due to their skills as farmers and fishers. Along with the Three Sisters, Lenape women planted tobacco, sunflowers, and gourds. They harvested fruits and nuts from trees and cultivated numerous medicinal plants, which they used with great proficiency. The Lenapes organized their communities to take advantage of growing seasons and the migration patterns of animals and fowl that were a part of their diet. During planting and harvesting seasons, Lenapes gathered in larger groups to coordinate their labor and take advantage of local abundance. As proficient fishers, they organized seasonal fish camps to net shellfish and catch shad. Lenapes wove nets, baskets, mats, and a variety of household materials from the rushes found along the streams, rivers, and coasts. They made their homes in some of the most fertile and abundant lands in the Eastern Woodlands and used their skills to create a stable and prosperous civilization. The first Dutch and Swedish settlers who encountered the Lenapes in the seventeenth century recognized Lenape prosperity and quickly sought their friendship. Their lives came to depend on it.

In the Pacific Northwest, the Kwakwaka'wakw, Tlingits, Haidas, and hundreds of other peoples, speaking dozens of languages, thrived in a land with a moderate climate, lush forests, and many rivers. The peoples of this region depended on salmon for survival and valued it accordingly. Images of salmon decorated totem poles, baskets, canoes, oars, and other tools. The fish was treated with spiritual respect and its image represented prosperity, life, and renewal. Sustainable harvesting practices ensured the survival of salmon populations. The Coast Salish people and several others celebrated the First Salmon Ceremony when the first migrating salmon was spotted each season. Elders closely observed the size of the salmon run and delayed harvesting to ensure that a sufficient number survived to spawn and return in the future.[19] Men commonly used nets, hooks, and other small tools to capture salmon as they migrated upriver to spawn. Massive cedar canoes, as long as fifty feet and carrying as many as twenty men, also enabled extensive fishing expeditions in the Pacific Ocean, where skilled fishermen caught halibut, sturgeon, and other fish, sometimes hauling thousands of pounds in a single canoe.[20]

Food surpluses enabled significant population growth, and the Pacific Northwest became one of the most densely populated regions of North America. The combination of population density and surplus food created a unique social organization centered on elaborate feasts, called potlatches. These potlatches celebrated births and weddings and determined social status. The party lasted for days and hosts demonstrated their wealth and power by entertaining guests with food, artwork, and performances. The more the hosts gave away, the more prestige and power they had within the group. Some men saved for decades to host an extravagant potlatch that would in turn give him greater respect and power within the community.

Many peoples of the Pacific Northwest built elaborate plank houses out of the region's abundant cedar trees. The five-hundred-foot-long Suquamish Oleman House (or Old Man House), for instance, rested on the banks of Puget Sound.[21] Giant cedar trees were also carved and painted in the shape of animals or other figures to tell stories and express identities. These totem poles became the most recognizable artistic form of the Pacific Northwest, but people also carved masks and other wooden items, such as hand drums and rattles, out of the region's great trees.

Despite commonalities, Native cultures varied greatly. The New World was marked by diversity and contrast. By the time Europeans were poised to cross the Atlantic, Native Americans spoke hundreds of lan-

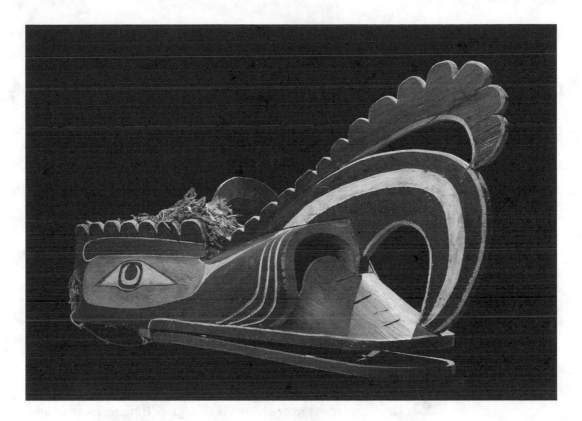

guages and lived in keeping with the hemisphere's many climates. Some lived in cities, others in small bands. Some migrated seasonally; others settled permanently. All Native peoples had long histories and well-formed, unique cultures that developed over millennia. But the arrival of Europeans changed everything.

III. European Expansion

Scandinavian seafarers reached the New World long before Columbus. At their peak they sailed as far east as Constantinople and raided settlements as far south as North Africa. They established limited colonies in Iceland and Greenland and, around the year 1000, Leif Erikson reached Newfoundland in present-day Canada. But the Norse colony failed. Culturally and geographically isolated, the Norse were driven back to the sea by some combination of limited resources, inhospitable weather, food shortages, and Native resistance.

Then, centuries before Columbus, the Crusades linked Europe with the wealth, power, and knowledge of Asia. Europeans rediscovered or adopted Greek, Roman, and Muslim knowledge. The hemispheric dissemination of goods and knowledge not only sparked the Renaissance

Intricately carved masks, like the Crooked Beak of Heaven Mask, used natural elements such as animals to represent supernatural forces during ceremonial dances and festivals. Nineteenth-century brooked beak of heaven mask from the Kwakwaka'wakw. Wikimedia. Creative Commons Attribution 3.0 Unported.

but fueled long-term European expansion. Asian goods flooded European markets, creating a demand for new commodities. This trade created vast new wealth, and Europeans battled one another for trade supremacy.

European nation-states consolidated under the authority of powerful kings. A series of military conflicts between England and France—the Hundred Years' War—accelerated nationalism and cultivated the financial and military administration necessary to maintain nation-states. In Spain, the marriage of Ferdinand of Aragon and Isabella of Castile consolidated the two most powerful kingdoms of the Iberian peninsula. The Crusades had never ended in Iberia: the Spanish crown concluded centuries of intermittent warfare—the Reconquista—by expelling Muslim Moors and Iberian Jews from the Iberian peninsula in 1492, just as Christopher Columbus sailed west. With new power, these new nations—and their newly empowered monarchs—yearned to access the wealth of Asia.

Seafaring Italian traders commanded the Mediterranean and controlled trade with Asia. Spain and Portugal, at the edges of Europe, relied on middlemen and paid higher prices for Asian goods. They sought a more direct route. And so they looked to the Atlantic. Portugal invested heavily in exploration. From his estate on the Sagres Peninsula of Portugal, a rich sailing port, Prince Henry the Navigator (Infante Henry, Duke of Viseu) invested in research and technology and underwrote many technological breakthroughs. His investments bore fruit. In the fifteenth century, Portuguese sailors perfected the astrolabe, a tool to calculate latitude, and the caravel, a ship well suited for ocean exploration. Both were technological breakthroughs. The astrolabe allowed for precise navigation, and the caravel, unlike more common vessels designed for trading on the relatively placid Mediterranean, was a rugged ship with a deep draft capable of making lengthy voyages on the open ocean and, equally important, carrying large amounts of cargo while doing so.

Blending economic and religious motivations, the Portuguese established forts along the Atlantic coast of Africa during the fifteenth century, inaugurating centuries of European colonization there. Portuguese trading posts generated new profits that funded further trade and further colonization. Trading posts spread across the vast coastline of Africa, and by the end of the fifteenth century, Vasco da Gama leapfrogged his way around the coasts of Africa to reach India and other lucrative Asian markets.

The vagaries of ocean currents and the limits of contemporary technology forced Iberian sailors to sail west into the open sea before cutting back east to Africa. So doing, the Spanish and Portuguese stumbled on several islands off the coast of Europe and Africa, including the Azores,

the Canary Islands, and the Cape Verde Islands. They became training grounds for the later colonization of the Americas and saw the first large-scale cultivation of sugar by enslaved laborers.

Sugar was originally grown in Asia but became a popular, widely profitable luxury item consumed by the nobility of Europe. The Portuguese learned the sugar-growing process from Mediterranean plantations started by Muslims, using imported enslaved labor from southern Russia and Islamic countries. Sugar was a difficult crop. It required tropical temperatures, daily rainfall, unique soil conditions, and a fourteen-month growing season. But on the newly discovered, mostly uninhabited Atlantic islands, the Portuguese had found new, defensible land to support sugar production. New patterns of human and ecological destruction followed. Isolated from the mainlands of Europe and Africa for millennia, Canary Island natives—known as the Guanches—were enslaved or perished soon after Europeans arrived. This demographic disaster presaged the demographic results for the Native American populations upon the arrival of the Spanish.

Portugal's would-be planters needed workers to cultivate the difficult, labor-intensive crop. They first turned to the trade relationships that Portuguese merchants established with African city-states in Senegambia, along the Gold Coast, as well as the kingdoms of Benin, Kongo, and Ndongo.[22] The Portuguese turned to enslaved Africans from the mainland as a labor source for these island plantations. At the beginning of this Euroafrican slave-trading system, African leaders traded war captives—who by custom forfeited their freedom if captured during battle—for Portuguese guns, iron, and manufactured goods. It is important to note that slaving in Africa, like slaving among Indigenous Americans, bore little resemblance to the chattel slavery of the antebellum United States.[23]

Engraving of sixteenth-century Lisbon from Civitatis Orbis Terrarum, *The Cities of the World*, ed. Georg Braun (Cologne: 1572). Wikimedia.

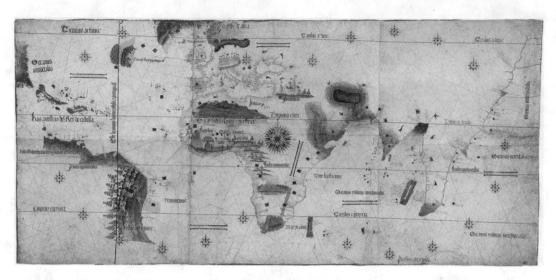

By the fifteenth century, the Portuguese had established forts and colonies on islands and along the rim of the Atlantic Ocean; other major European countries soon followed in step. An anonymous cartographer created this map known as the Cantino Map, the earliest known map of European exploration in the New World, to depict these holdings and argue for the greatness of his native Portugal. *Cantino planisphere* (1502), Biblioteca Estense, Modena, Italy. Wikimedia.

From bases along the Atlantic coast, the Portuguese began purchasing enslaved people for export to the Atlantic islands of Madeira, the Canaries, and the Cape Verdes to work the sugar fields. Thus were born the first great Atlantic plantations. A few decades later, at the end of the fifteenth century, the Portuguese plantation system developed on the island of São Tomé became a model for the plantation system as it was expanded across the Atlantic.

Spain, too, stood on the cutting edge of maritime technology. Spanish sailors had become masters of the caravels. As Portugal consolidated control over African trading networks and the circuitous eastbound sea route to Asia, Spain yearned for its own path to empire. Christopher Columbus, a skilled Italian-born sailor who had studied under Portuguese navigators, promised just that opportunity.

Educated Asians and Europeans of the fifteenth century knew the world was round. They also knew that while it was therefore technically possible to reach Asia by sailing west from Europe—thereby avoiding Italian or Portuguese middlemen—the earth's vast size would doom even the greatest caravels to starvation and thirst long before they ever reached their destination. But Columbus underestimated the size of the globe by a full two thirds and therefore believed it was possible. After unsuccessfully shopping his proposed expedition in several European courts, he convinced Queen Isabella and King Ferdinand of Spain to provide him three small ships, which set sail in 1492. Columbus was both confoundingly wrong about the size of the earth and spectacularly lucky that two large continents lurked in his path. On October 12, 1492, after two months at sea, the *Niña*, *Pinta*, and *Santa María* and their ninety men landed in the modern-day Bahamas.

The Indigenous Arawaks, or Taíno, populated the Caribbean islands. They fished and grew corn, yams, and cassava. Columbus described them as innocents. "They are very gentle and without knowledge of what is evil; nor the sins of murder or theft," he reported to the Spanish crown. "Your highness may believe that in all the world there can be no better people. . . . They love their neighbors as themselves, and their speech is the sweetest and gentlest in the world, and always with a smile." But Columbus had come for wealth and he could find little. The Arawaks, however, wore small gold ornaments. Columbus left thirty-nine Spaniards at a military fort on Hispaniola to find and secure the source of the gold while he returned to Spain with a dozen captured and branded Arawaks. Columbus arrived to great acclaim and quickly worked to outfit a return voyage. Spain's New World motives were clear from the beginning. If outfitted for a return voyage, Columbus promised the Spanish crown gold and enslaved laborers. Columbus reported, "With fifty men they can all be subjugated and made to do what is required of them."[24]

Columbus was outfitted with seventeen ships and over one thousand men to return to the West Indies (Columbus made four voyages to the New World). Still believing he had landed in the East Indies, he promised to reward Isabella and Ferdinand's investment. But when material wealth proved slow in coming, the Spanish embarked on a vicious campaign to extract every possible ounce of wealth from the Caribbean. The Spanish decimated the Arawaks. Bartolomé de Las Casas traveled to the New World in 1502 and later wrote, "I saw with these Eyes of mine the Spaniards for no other reason, but only to gratify their bloody mindedness, cut off the Hands, Noses, and Ears, both of Indians and Indianesses." When the enslaved laborers exhausted the islands' meager gold reserves, the Spaniards forced them to labor on their huge new estates, the *encomiendas*. Las Casas described European barbarities in cruel detail. By presuming the natives had no humanity, the Spaniards utterly abandoned theirs. Casual violence and dehumanizing exploitation ravaged the Arawaks. The Indigenous population collapsed. Within a few generations the whole island of Hispaniola had been depopulated and a whole people exterminated. Historians' estimates of the island's pre-contact population range from fewer than one million to as many as eight million (Las

Casas estimated it at three million). In a few short years, they were gone. "Who in future generations will believe this?" Las Casas wondered. "I myself writing it as a knowledgeable eyewitness can hardly believe it."[25]

Despite the diversity of Native populations and the existence of several strong empires, Native Americans were wholly unprepared for the arrival of Europeans. Biology magnified European cruelties. Cut off from what Europeans called "the Old World," its domesticated animals, and its immunological history, Native Americans lived free from the terrible diseases that ravaged populations in Asia, Europe and Africa. But their blessing now became a curse. Native Americans lacked the immunities that Europeans and Africans had developed over centuries of deadly epidemics, and so when Europeans arrived, carrying smallpox, typhus, influenza, diphtheria, measles, and hepatitis, plagues decimated Native communities.[26] Many died in war and slavery, but millions died in epidemics. All told, in fact, some scholars estimate that as much as 90 percent of the population of the Americas perished within the first century and a half of European contact.[27]

Though ravaged by disease and warfare, Native Americans forged middle grounds, resisted with violence, accommodated and adapted to the challenges of colonialism, and continued to shape the patterns of life throughout the New World for hundreds of years. But the Europeans kept coming.

IV. Spanish Exploration and Conquest

As news of the Spanish conquest spread, wealth-hungry Spaniards poured into the New World seeking land, gold, and titles. A New World empire spread from Spain's Caribbean foothold. Motives were plain: said one soldier, "we came here to serve God and the king, and also to get rich."[28] Mercenaries joined the conquest and raced to capture the human and material wealth of the New World.

The Spanish managed labor relations through a legal system known as the *encomienda*, an exploitive feudal arrangement in which Spain tied Indigenous laborers to vast estates. In the *encomienda*, the Spanish crown granted a person not only land but a specified number of natives as well. *Encomenderos* brutalized their laborers. After Bartolomé de Las Casas published his incendiary account of Spanish abuses (*The Destruction of the Indies*), Spanish authorities abolished the *encomienda* in 1542 and replaced it with the *repartimiento*. Intended as a milder system, the *repartimiento* nevertheless replicated many of the abuses of the older sys-

tem, and the rapacious exploitation of the Native population continued as Spain spread its empire over the Americas.

As Spain's New World empire expanded, Spanish conquerors met the massive empires of Central and South America, civilizations that dwarfed anything found in North America. In Central America the Maya built massive temples, sustained large populations, and constructed a complex and long-lasting civilization with a written language, advanced mathematics, and stunningly accurate calendars. But Maya civilization, although it had not disappeared, nevertheless collapsed before European arrival, likely because of droughts and unsustainable agricultural practices. But the eclipse of the Maya only heralded the later rise of the most powerful Native civilization ever seen in the Western Hemisphere: the Aztecs.

Militaristic migrants from northern Mexico, the Aztecs moved south into the Valley of Mexico, conquered their way to dominance, and built the largest empire in the New World. When the Spaniards arrived in Mexico they found a sprawling civilization centered around Tenochtitlán, an awe-inspiring city built on a series of natural and man-made islands in the middle of Lake Texcoco, located today within modern-day Mexico City. Tenochtitlán, founded in 1325, rivaled the world's largest cities in size and grandeur.[29]

Much of the city was fed by crops grown on large artificial islands called *chinampas*, which the Aztecs constructed by dredging mud and rich sediment from the bottom of the lake and depositing it over time to form new landscapes. A massive pyramid temple, the Templo Mayor, was

El Castillo (pyramid of Kukulcán) in Chichén Itzá. Photograph by Daniel Schwen. Wikimedia. Creative Commons Attribution-Share Alike 4.0 International.

located at the city center (its ruins can still be found in the center of Mexico City). When the Spaniards arrived, they could scarcely believe what they saw: 70,000 buildings, housing perhaps 200,000–250,000 people, all built on a lake and connected by causeways and canals. Bernal Díaz del Castillo, a Spanish soldier, later recalled, "When we saw so many cities and villages built in the water and other great towns on dry land, we were amazed and said that it was like the enchantments. . . . Some of our soldiers even asked whether the things that we saw were not a dream? . . . I do not know how to describe it, seeing things as we did that had never been heard of or seen before, not even dreamed about."[30]

From their island city the Aztecs dominated an enormous swath of central and southern Mesoamerica. They ruled their empire through a decentralized network of subject peoples that paid regular tribute—including everything from the most basic items, such as corn, beans, and other foodstuffs, to luxury goods such as jade, cacao, and gold—and provided troops for the empire. But unrest festered beneath the Aztecs' imperial power, and European conquerors lusted after its vast wealth.

Hernán Cortés, an ambitious, thirty-four-year-old Spaniard who had won riches in the conquest of Cuba, organized an invasion of Mexico in 1519. Sailing with six hundred men, horses, and cannon, he landed on the coast of Mexico. Relying on a Native translator, whom he called Doña Marina, and whom Mexican folklore denounces as La Malinche, Cortés

This sixteenth-century map of Tenochtitlán shows the aesthetic beauty and advanced infrastructure of this great Aztec city. Map, c. 1524. Wikimedia.

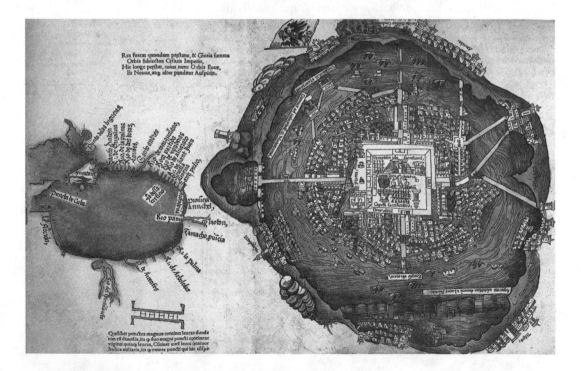

gathered information and allies in preparation for conquest. Through
intrigue, brutality, and the exploitation of endemic political divisions, he
enlisted the aid of thousands of Native allies, defeated Spanish rivals, and
marched on Tenochtitlán.

Aztec dominance rested on fragile foundations and many of the region's semi-independent city-states yearned to break from Aztec rule.
Nearby kingdoms, including the Tarascans to the north and the remains
of Maya city-states on the Yucatán peninsula, chafed at Aztec power.

Through persuasion, the Spaniards entered Tenochtitlán peacefully.
Cortés then captured the emperor Montezuma and used him to gain control of the Aztecs' gold and silver reserves and their network of mines.
Eventually, the Aztecs revolted. Montezuma was branded a traitor, and
uprising ignited the city. Montezuma was killed along with a third of

The Spanish relied on Indigenous allies. The Tlaxcala were among the most important Spanish allies in their
conquest. This sixteenth-century drawing depicts the Spanish and their Tlaxcalan allies fighting against the
Purépecha. Wikimedia.

Cortés's men in *la noche triste*, the "night of sorrows." The Spanish fought through thousands of Indigenous insurgents and across canals to flee the city, where they regrouped, enlisted more Native allies, captured Spanish reinforcements, and, in 1521, besieged the island city. The Spaniards' eighty-five-day siege cut off food and fresh water. Smallpox ravaged the city. One Spanish observer said it "spread over the people as great destruction. Some it covered on all parts—their faces, their heads, their breasts, and so on. There was great havoc. Very many died of it. . . . They could not move; they could not stir."[31] Cortés, the Spaniards, and their Native allies then sacked the city. The temples were plundered and fifteen thousand died. After two years of conflict, a million-person-strong empire was toppled by disease, dissension, and a thousand European conquerors.

Farther south, along the Andes Mountains in South America, the Quechuas, or Incas, managed a vast mountain empire. From their capital of Cuzco in the Andean highlands, through conquest and negotiation, the Incas built an empire that stretched around the western half of the South American continent from present day Ecuador to central Chile and Argentina. They cut terraces into the sides of mountains to farm fertile soil, and by the 1400s they managed a thousand miles of Andean roads that tied together perhaps twelve million people. But like the Aztecs, unrest between the Incas and conquered groups created tensions and left the empire vulnerable to invaders. Smallpox spread in advance of Spanish conquerors and hit the Incan empire in 1525. Epidemics ravaged the population, cutting the empire's population in half and killing the Incan emperor Huayna Capac and many members of his family. A bloody war of succession ensued. Inspired by Cortés's conquest of Mexico, Francisco Pizarro moved south and found an empire torn by chaos. With 168 men, he deceived Incan rulers, took control of the empire, and seized the capital city, Cuzco, in 1533. Disease, conquest, and slavery ravaged the remnants of the Incan empire.

After the conquests of Mexico and Peru, Spain settled into its new empire. A vast administrative hierarchy governed the new holdings: royal appointees oversaw an enormous territory of landed estates, and Indigenous laborers and administrators regulated the extraction of gold and silver and oversaw their transport across the Atlantic in Spanish galleons. Meanwhile Spanish migrants poured into the New World. During the sixteenth century alone, 225,000 migrated, and 750,000 came during the entire three centuries of Spanish colonial rule. Spaniards, often single, young, and male, emigrated for the various promises of land, wealth, and social advancement. Laborers, craftsmen, soldiers, clerks, and priests all crossed the Atlantic in large numbers. Indigenous people, however, al-

Casta paintings illustrated the varying degrees of intermixture between colonial subjects, defining them for Spanish officials. Unknown artist, *Las Castas*, Museo Nacional del Virreinato, Tepotzotlan, Mexico. Wikimedia.

ways outnumbered the Spanish, and the Spaniards, by both necessity and design, incorporated Native Americans into colonial life. This incorporation did not mean equality, however.

An elaborate racial hierarchy marked Spanish life in the New World. Regularized in the mid-1600s but rooted in medieval practices, the Sistema de Castas organized individuals into various racial groups based on their supposed "purity of blood." Elaborate classifications became almost prerequisites for social and political advancement in Spanish colonial society. *Peninsulares*—Iberian-born Spaniards, or *españoles*—occupied the highest levels of administration and acquired the greatest estates. Their descendants, New World-born Spaniards, or *criollos*, occupied the next rung and rivaled the *peninsulares* for wealth and opportunity. *Mestizos*—a term used to describe those of mixed Spanish and Indigenous heritage—followed.

Like the French later in North America, the Spanish tolerated and sometimes even supported interracial marriage. There were simply too few Spanish women in the New World to support the natural growth of a purely Spanish population. The Catholic Church endorsed interracial marriage as a moral bulwark against bastardy and rape. By 1600, mestizos made up a large portion of the colonial population.[32] By the early 1700s, more than one third of all marriages bridged the Spanish-Indigenous divide. Separated by wealth and influence from the *peninsulares* and *criollos*, mestizos typically occupied a middling social position in Spanish New World society. They were not quite *Indios*, or Indigenous people, but their lack of *limpieza de sangre*, or "pure blood," removed them from the privileges of full-blooded Spaniards. Spanish fathers of sufficient wealth and influence might shield their mestizo children from racial prejudice, and a number of wealthy mestizos married *españoles* to "whiten" their family lines, but more often mestizos were confined to a middle station in the Spanish New World. Enslaved and Indigenous people occupied the lowest rungs of the social ladder.

Many manipulated the Sistema de Castas to gain advantages for themselves and their children. Mestizo mothers, for instance, might insist that their mestizo daughters were actually *castizas*, or quarter-Indigenous, who, if they married a Spaniard, could, in the eyes of the law, produce "pure" *criollo* children entitled to the full rights and opportunities of Spanish citizens. But "passing" was an option only for the few. Instead, the massive Native populations within Spain's New World Empire

Our Lady of Guadalupe is perhaps the most culturally important and extensively reproduced Mexican-Catholic image. In the iconic depiction, Mary stands atop the tilma (peasant cloak) of Juan Diego, on which according to his story appeared the image of the Virgin of Guadalupe. Throughout Mexican history, the story and image of Our Lady of Guadalupe has been a unifying national symbol. Mexican *retablo* of *Our Lady of Guadalupe*, nineteenth century, in El Paso Museum of Art. Wikimedia.

ensured a level of cultural and racial mixture—or *mestizaje*—unparalleled in British North America. Spanish North America wrought a hybrid culture that was neither fully Spanish nor Indigenous. The Spanish not only built Mexico City atop Tenochtitlán, but food, language, and families were also constructed on Indigenous foundations. In 1531, a poor Indigenous man named Juan Diego reported that he was visited by the Virgin Mary, who came as a dark-skinned Nahuatl-speaking Indigenous woman.[33] Reports of miracles spread across Mexico and the Virgen de Guadalupe became a national icon for a new mestizo society.

From Mexico, Spain expanded northward. Lured by the promises of gold and another Tenochtitlán, Spanish expeditions scoured North America for another wealthy Indigenous empire. Huge expeditions, resembling vast moving communities, composed of hundreds of soldiers, settlers, priests, and enslaved people, with enormous numbers of livestock, moved across the continent. Juan Ponce de León, the conqueror of Puerto Rico, landed in Florida in 1513 in search of wealth and enslaved laborers. Álvar Núñez Cabeza de Vaca joined the Narváez expedition to Florida a decade later but was shipwrecked and forced to embark on a remarkable multiyear odyssey along the coast of the Gulf of Mexico and Texas into Mexico. Pedro Menéndez de Avilés founded St. Augustine, Florida, in 1565, and it remains the oldest continuously occupied European settlement in the present-day United States.

But without the rich gold and silver mines of Mexico, the plantation-friendly climate of the Caribbean, or the exploitive potential of large Indigenous empires, North America offered little incentive for Spanish officials. Still, Spanish expeditions combed North America. Francisco Vázquez de Coronado pillaged his way across the Southwest. Hernando de Soto tortured and raped and enslaved his way across the Southeast. Soon Spain had footholds—however tenuous—across much of the continent.

V. Conclusion

The "discovery" of America unleashed horrors. Europeans embarked on a debauching path of death and destructive exploitation that wrought murder and greed and slavery. But disease was deadlier than any weapon in the European arsenal. It unleashed death on a scale never before seen in human history. Estimates of the population of pre-Columbian America range wildly. Some argue for as much as 100 million, some as low as 2 million. In 1983, Henry Dobyns put the number at 18 million. Whatever the precise estimates, nearly all scholars tell of the utter devastation wrought by European disease. Dobyns estimated that in the first 130 years following European contact, 95 percent of Native Americans perished.[34] (At its worst, Europe's Black Death peaked at death rates of 25 to 35 percent. Nothing else in history rivals the American demographic disaster.) A ten-thousand-year history of disease hit the New World in an instant. Smallpox, typhus, bubonic plague, influenza, mumps, measles: pandemics ravaged populations up and down the continents. Wave after wave of disease crashed relentlessly. Disease flung whole communities into chaos. Others it destroyed completely.

Disease was only the most terrible in a cross-hemispheric exchange of violence, culture, trade, and peoples—the so-called Columbian Exchange—that followed in Columbus's wake. Global diets, for instance, were transformed. The Americas' calorie-rich crops revolutionized Old World agriculture and spawned a worldwide population boom. Many modern associations between food and geography are by-products of the Columbian Exchange: potatoes in Ireland, tomatoes in Italy, chocolate in Switzerland, peppers in Thailand, and oranges in Florida are all manifestations of the new global exchange. Europeans, for their part, introduced their domesticated animals to the New World. Pigs ran rampant through the Americas, transforming the landscape as they spread throughout both continents. Horses spread as well, transforming the Native American cultures who adapted to the newly introduced animal. Partly from trade, partly from the remnants of failed European expeditions, and partly from theft, Indigenous people acquired horses and transformed Native American life in the vast North American plains.

The Europeans' arrival bridged two worlds and ten thousand years of history largely separated from each other since the closing of the Bering Strait. Both sides of the world had been transformed. And neither would ever again be the same.

VI. Reference Material

This chapter was edited by Joseph Locke and Ben Wright, with content contributions by L. D. Burnett, Michelle Cassidy, D. Andrew Johnson, Joseph Locke, Dawn Marsh, Christen Mucher, Cameron Shriver, Ben Wright, and Garrett Wright.

Recommended citation: L. D. Burnett et al., "The New World," in *The American Yawp*, eds. Joseph Locke and Ben Wright (Stanford, CA: Stanford University Press, 2019).

NOTES TO CHAPTER 1

1. A. L. Kroeber, ed., *University of California Publications: American Archaeology and Ethnology*, Vol. 10 (Berkeley: University of California Press, 1911–1914), 191–192.

2. James F. Barnett Jr., *Mississippi's American Indians* (Jackson: University Press of Mississippi, 2012), 90.

3. Edward W. Osowski, *Indigenous Miracles: Nahua Authority in Colonial Mexico* (Tucson: University of Arizona Press, 2010), 25.

4. David J. Meltzer, *First Peoples in a New World: Colonizing Ice Age America* (Berkeley: University of California Press, 2010), 170.

5. Knut R. Fladmark, "Routes: Alternate Migration Corridors for Early Man in North America," *American Antiquity* 44, no. 1 (1979): 55–69.

6. Jessi J. Halligan et al., "Pre-Clovis Occupation 14,550 Years Ago at the Page-Ladson Site, Florida, and the People of the Americas," *Science Advances* 2, no. 5 (May 13, 2016) and Michael R. Waters et al., "The Buttermilk Creek Complex and the Origins of Clovis at the Debra L. Friedkin Site, Texas," *Science* 331 (March 25, 2011), 15991603.

7. Tom D. Dillehay, *The Settlement of the Americas: A New Prehistory* (New York: Basic Books, 2000).

8. Richard A. Diehl, *The Olmecs: America's First Civilization* (London: Thames and Hudson, 2004), 25.

9. Jane Mt. Pleasant, "A New Paradigm for Pre-Columbian Agriculture in North America," *Early American Studies* 13, no. 2 (Spring 2015): 374–412.

10. Richard H. Steckel, "Health and Nutrition in Pre-Columbian America: The Skeletal Evidence," *Journal of Interdisciplinary History* 36, no. 1 (Summer 2005): 19–21.

11. Traci Ardren, "Studies of Gender in the Prehispanic Americas," *Journal of Archaeological Research* Vol. 16, No. 1 (March 2008), 1–35.

12. Elizabeth Hill Boone and Walter D. Mignolo, eds., *Writing Without Words: Alternative Literacies in Mesoamerica and the Andes* (Durham, NC: Duke University Press, 1994).

13. Stuart J. Fiedel, *Prehistory of the Americas* (New York: Cambridge University Press, 1992), 217.

14. H. Wolcott Toll, "Making and Breaking Pots in the Chaco World," *American Antiquity* 66, no. 1 (January 2001): 65.

15. Anna Sofaer, "The Primary Architecture of the Chacoan Culture: A Cosmological Expression," in *Anasazi Architecture and American Design*, ed. Baker H. Morrow and V. B. Price (Albuquerque: University of New Mexico Press, 1997).

16. Timothy R. Pauketat and Thomas E. Emerson, eds., *Cahokia: Domination and Ideology in the Mississippian World* (Lincoln: University of Nebraska Press, 1997), 31.

17. Thomas E. Emerson, "An Introduction to Cahokia 2002: Diversity, Complexity, and History," *Midcontinental Journal of Archaeology* 27, no. 2 (Fall 2002): 137–139.

18. Amy Schutt, *Peoples of the River Valleys: The Odyssey of the Delaware Indians* (Philadelphia: University of Pennsylvania Press, 2007), 7–30.

19. Erna Gunther, "An Analysis of the First Salmon Ceremony," *American Anthropologist* 28, no. 4 (October–December 1926): 605–617.

20. Gary E. Moulton, ed., *The Journals of the Lewis and Clark Expedition*, Vol. 6 (Lincoln: University of Nebraska Press, 1983), https://www.loc.gov/exhib its/lewisandclark/transcript68.html.

21. Coll Thrush, *Native Seattle: Histories from the Crossing-Over Place*, 2nd ed. (Seattle: University of Washington Press, 2007), 126.

22. Walter Rodney, *A History of the Upper Guinea Coast: 1545–1800* (Bungay, Suffolk: Clarendon Press, 1970); Ivor Wilks, "Land, Labour, Capital, and the Forest Kingdoms of Asante: A Model of Early Change," in *The Evolution of Social Systems*, ed. J. F. Friedman and M. J. Rowlands (London: Duckworth, 1977), 487–534; Walter Rodney, "Gold and Slaves on the Gold Coast," *Transactions of the Historical Society of Ghana* 10 (1969): 13–28; Alan F. C. Ryder, *Benin and the Europeans, 1485–1897* (London: Longman, 1969); John Thornton, "Early Kongo-Portuguese Relations, 1483–1575: A New Interpretation," *History in Africa* 8 (1981): 183–204. French translation in *Cahiers des Anneaux de la Mémoire* 3 (2001); "The Portuguese in Africa," in *Portuguese Oceanic Expansion, 1400–1800*, ed. Francisco Bethencourt and Diogo Ramada Curto (Cambridge and New York: Cambridge University Press, 2007), 138–160; and Linda Heywood, "Slavery and Its Transformation in the Kingdom of Kongo: 1491–1800," *Journal of African History* 50 (2009): 1–22.

23. Joseph C. Miller, *The Problem of Slavery as History: A Global Approach* (New Haven: Yale University Press, 2012).

24. Clements R. Markham, ed. and trans., *The Journal of Christopher Columbus (During His First Voyage), and Documents Relating to the Voyages of John Cabot and Gaspar Corte Real* (London: Hakluyt Society, 1893), 73, 135, 41.

25. Bartolomé de Las Casas, *A Brief Account of the Destruction of the Indies . . .* (1552; Project Gutenberg, 2007), 147. http://www.gutenberg.org/ebooks /20321, accessed June 11, 2018.

26. Dean R. Snow, "Microchronology and Demographic Evidence Relating to the Size of Pre-Columbian North American Indian Populations," *Science* 268, no. 5217 (June 16, 1995): 1601.

27. Jack Weatherford, *Indian Givers: How the Indians of the Americas Transformed the World* (New York: Random House, 1988), 195.

28. J. H. Elliott, *Imperial Spain 1469–1716* (London: Edward Arnold, 1963), 53.

29. Victor Butler-Thomas et al., *The Cambridge Economic History of Latin America: Volume 1, The Colonial Era and the Short Nineteenth Century* (New York: Cambridge University Press, 2005).

30. Bernal Díaz del Castillo, *The Discovery and Conquest of Mexico, 1517–1521*, trans. A. P. Maudslay (New York: Da Capo Press, 1996), 190–191.

31. Bernardino de Sahagún, *Florentine Codex: General History of the Things of New Spain* (Salt Lake City: University of Utah Press, 1970).

32. Suzanne Bost, *Mulattas and Mestizas: Representing Mixed Identities in the Americas, 1850–2000* (Athens: University of Georgia Press, 2003), 27.

33. Stafford Poole, C. M., *Our Lady of Guadalupe: The Origins and Sources of a Mexican National Symbol, 1531–1797* (Tucson: University of Arizona Press, 1995).

34. Henry F. Dobyns, *Their Number Become Thinned: Native American Population Dynamics in Eastern North America* (Knoxville: University of Tennessee Press, 1983).

RECOMMENDED READING

Alt, Susan, ed. *Ancient Complexities: New Perspectives in Pre-Columbian North America.* Salt Lake City: University of Utah Press, 2010.

Bruhns, Karen Olsen. *Ancient South America.* New York: Cambridge University Press, 1994.

Claasen, Cheryl, and Rosemary A. Joyce, eds. *Women in Prehistory: North America and Mesoamerica.* Philadelphia: University of Pennsylvania Press, 1994.

Cook, Noble David. *Born to Die: Disease and New World Conquest, 1492–1650.* New York: Cambridge University Press, 1998.

Crosby, Alfred W. *The Columbian Exchange: Biological and Cultural Consequences of 1492.* New York: Praeger, 2003.

Dewar, Elaine. *Bones.* Toronto: Vintage Canada, 2001.

Dye, David. *War Paths, Peace Paths: An Archaeology of Cooperation and Conflict in Native Eastern North America.* Lanham, MD: AltaMira Press, 2009.

Fenn, Elizabeth A. *Encounters at the Heart of the World: A History of the Mandan People.* New York: Hill and Wang, 2014.

Jablonski, Nina G. *The First Americans: The Pleistocene Colonization of the New World.* Berkeley: University of California Press, 2002.

John, Elizabeth A. H. *Storms Brewed in Other Men's Worlds: The Confrontation of Indians, Spanish, and French in the Southwest, 1540–1795*, 2nd ed. Norman: University of Oklahoma Press, 1996.

Kehoe, Alice Beck. *America Before the European Invasions.* New York: Routledge, 2002.

Leon-Portilla, Miguel. *The Broken Spears: The Aztec Account of the Conquest of Mexico.* Boston: Beacon Books, 1992.

Mann, Charles C. *1491: New Revelations of the Americas Before Columbus.* New York: Vintage Books, 2006.

Meltzer, David J. *First Peoples in a New World: Colonizing Ice Age America.* Berkeley: University of California Press, 2010.

Mt. Pleasant, Jane. "A New Paradigm for Pre-Columbian Agriculture in North America." *Early American Studies* 13, no. 2 (Spring 2015): 374–412.

Oswalt, Wendell H. *This Land Was Theirs: A Study of Native North Americans.* New York: Oxford University Press, 2009.

Pauketat, Timothy R. *Cahokia: Ancient America's Great City on the Mississippi.* New York: Penguin, 2010.

Pringle, Heather. *In Search of Ancient North America: An Archaeological Journey to Forgotten Cultures*. New York: Wiley, 1996.

Reséndez, Andrés. *A Land So Strange: The Epic Journey of Cabeza de Vaca*. New York: Basic Books, 2009.

Restall, Matthew. *Seven Myths of the Spanish Conquest*. New York: Oxford University Press, 2004.

Scarry, C. Margaret. *Foraging and Farming in the Eastern Woodlands*. Gainesville: University Press of Florida, 1993.

Schwartz, Stuart B. *Victors and Vanquished: Spanish and Nahua Views of the Conquest of Mexico*. New York: Bedford St. Martin's, 2000.

Seed, Patricia. *Ceremonies of Possession: Europe's Conquest of the New World, 1492–1640*. New York: Cambridge University Press, 1995.

Townsend, Camilla. *Malintzin's Choices: An Indian Woman in the Conquest of Mexico*. Albuquerque: University of New Mexico Press, 2006.

Weatherford, Jack. *Indian Givers: How the Indians of the Americas Transformed the World*. New York: Random House, 1988.

2

Colliding Cultures

I. Introduction

The Columbian Exchange transformed both sides of the Atlantic, but with dramatically disparate outcomes. New diseases wiped out entire civilizations in the Americas, while newly imported nutrient-rich foodstuffs enabled a European population boom. Spain benefited most immediately as the wealth of the Aztec and Incan Empires strengthened the Spanish monarchy. Spain used its new riches to gain an advantage over other European nations, but this advantage was soon contested.

Portugal, France, the Netherlands, and England all raced to the New World, eager to match the gains of the Spanish. Native peoples greeted the new visitors with responses ranging from welcoming cooperation to aggressive violence, but the ravages of disease and the possibility of new trading relationships enabled Europeans to create settlements all along the western rim of the Atlantic world. New empires would emerge from

Theodor de Bry, "Negotiating Peace with the Indians," 1634. Virginia Historical Society.

these tenuous beginnings, and by the end of the seventeenth century, Spain would lose its privileged position to its rivals. An age of colonization had begun and, with it, a great collision of cultures commenced.

II. Spanish America

Spain extended its reach in the Americas after reaping the benefits of its colonies in Mexico, the Caribbean, and South America. Expeditions slowly began combing the continent and bringing Europeans into the modern-day United States in the hopes of establishing religious and economic dominance in a new territory.

Juan Ponce de León arrived in the area named La Florida in 1513. He found between 150,000 and 300,000 Native Americans. But then two and a half centuries of contact with European and African peoples— whether through war, slave raids, or, most dramatically, foreign disease—decimated Florida's Indigenous population. European explorers, meanwhile, had hoped to find great wealth in Florida, but reality never aligned with their imaginations.

In the first half of the sixteenth century, Spanish colonizers fought frequently with Florida's Native peoples as well as with other Europeans. In the 1560s Spain expelled French Protestants, called Huguenots, from the

1513 Atlantic map from cartographer Martin Waldseemuller. Wikimedia.

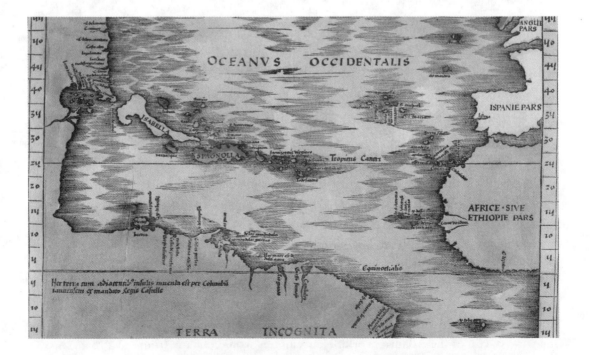

area near modern-day Jacksonville in northeast Florida. In 1586 English privateer Sir Francis Drake burned the wooden settlement of St. Augustine. At the dawn of the seventeenth century, Spain's reach in Florida extended from the mouth of the St. Johns River south to the environs of St. Augustine—an area of roughly 1,000 square miles. The Spaniards attempted to duplicate methods for establishing control used previously in Mexico, the Caribbean, and the Andes. The Crown granted missionaries the right to live among Timucua and Guale villagers in the late 1500s and early 1600s and encouraged settlement through the *encomienda* system (grants of Native labor).[1]

In the 1630s, the mission system extended into the Apalachee district in the Florida panhandle. The Apalachee, one of the most powerful tribes in Florida at the time of contact, claimed the territory from the modern Florida-Georgia border to the Gulf of Mexico. Apalachee farmers grew an abundance of corn and other crops. Native American traders carried surplus products east along the Camino Real (the royal road) that connected the western anchor of the mission system with St. Augustine. Spanish settlers drove cattle eastward across the St. Johns River and established ranches as far west as Apalachee. Still, Spain held Florida tenuously.

Farther west, in 1598, Juan de Oñate led four hundred settlers, soldiers, and missionaries from Mexico into New Mexico. The Spanish Southwest had brutal beginnings. When Oñate sacked the Pueblo city of Acoma, the "sky city," the Spaniards slaughtered nearly half of its roughly 1,500 inhabitants, including women and children. Oñate ordered one foot cut off every surviving male over age fifteen, and he enslaved the remaining women and children.[2]

Santa Fe, the first permanent European settlement in the Southwest, was established in 1610. Few Spaniards relocated to the Southwest because of the distance from Mexico City and the dry and hostile environment. Thus, the Spanish never achieved a commanding presence in the region. By 1680, only about three thousand colonists called Spanish New Mexico home.[3] There, they traded with and exploited the local Puebloan peoples. The region's Puebloan population had plummeted from as many as sixty thousand in 1600 to about seventeen thousand in 1680.[4]

Spain shifted strategies after the military expeditions wove their way through the southern and western half of North America. Missions became the engine of colonization in North America. Missionaries, most of whom were members of the Franciscan religious order, provided Spain with an advance guard in North America. Catholicism had always justified Spanish conquest, and colonization always carried religious imperatives. By the early seventeenth century, Spanish friars had established dozens of missions along the Rio Grande and in California.

III. Spain's Rivals Emerge

While Spain plundered the New World, unrest plagued Europe. The Reformation threw England and France, the two European powers capable of contesting Spain, into turmoil. Long and expensive conflicts drained time, resources, and lives. Millions died from religious violence in France alone. As the violence diminished in Europe, however, religious and political rivalries continued in the New World.

The Spanish exploitation of New Spain's riches inspired European monarchs to invest in exploration and conquest. Reports of Spanish atrocities spread throughout Europe and provided a humanitarian justification for European colonization. An English reprint of the writings of Bartolomé de Las Casas bore the sensational title "Popery Truly Display'd in its Bloody Colours: Or, a Faithful Narrative of the Horrid and Unexampled Massacres, Butcheries, and all manners of Cruelties that Hell and Malice could invent, committed by the Popish Spanish." An English writer explained

The earliest plan of New Amsterdam (now Manhattan), 1660. Wikimedia.

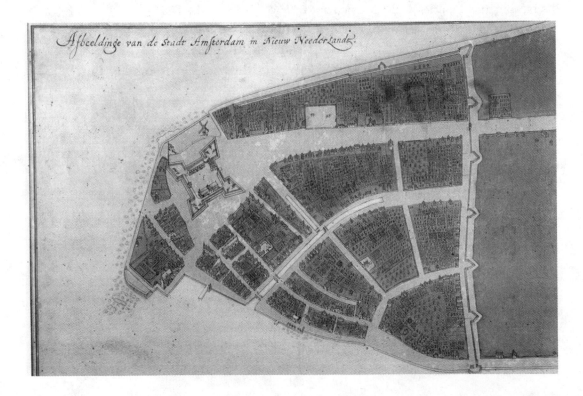

that the Native Americans "were simple and plain men, and lived without great labour," but in their lust for gold the Spaniards "forced the people (that were not used to labour) to stand all the daie in the hot sun gathering gold in the sand of the rivers. By this means a great number of them (not used to such pains) died, and a great number of them (seeing themselves brought from so quiet a life to such misery and slavery) of desperation killed themselves. And many would not marry, because they would not have their children slaves to the Spaniards."[5] The Spanish accused their critics of fostering a "Black Legend." The Black Legend drew on religious differences and political rivalries. Spain had successful conquests in France, Italy, Germany, and the Netherlands and left many in those nations yearning to break free from Spanish influence. English writers argued that Spanish barbarities were foiling a tremendous opportunity for the expansion of Christianity across the globe and that a benevolent conquest of the New World by non-Spanish monarchies offered the surest salvation of the New World's pagan masses. With these religious justifications, and with obvious economic motives, Spain's rivals arrived in the New World.

THE FRENCH

The French crown subsidized exploration in the early sixteenth century. Early French explorers sought a fabled Northwest Passage, a mythical waterway passing through the North American continent to Asia. Despite the wealth of the New World, Asia's riches still beckoned to Europeans. Canada's St. Lawrence River appeared to be such a passage, stretching deep into the continent and into the Great Lakes. French colonial possessions centered on these bodies of water (and, later, down the Mississippi River to the port of New Orleans).

French colonization developed through investment from private trading companies. Traders established Port Royal in Acadia (Nova Scotia) in 1603 and launched trading expeditions that stretched down the Atlantic coast as far as Cape Cod. The needs of the fur trade set the future pattern of French colonization. Founded in 1608 under the leadership of Samuel de Champlain, Quebec provided the foothold for what would become New France. French fur traders placed a higher value on cooperating with the Indigenous people than on establishing a successful French colonial footprint. Asserting dominance in the region could have been to their own detriment, as it might have compromised their access to skilled Native American trappers, and therefore wealth. Few Frenchmen traveled to the New World to settle permanently. In fact, few traveled at

A depiction of New Orleans in 1726, when it was an eight-year-old French frontier settlement. Jean-Pierre Lassus, *Veüe et Perspective de la Nouvelle Orleans*, 1726, Centre des archives d'outre-mer, France. Wikimedia.

all. Many persecuted French Protestants (Huguenots) sought to emigrate after France criminalized Protestantism in 1685, but all non-Catholics were forbidden in New France.[6]

The French preference for trade over permanent settlement fostered more cooperative and mutually beneficial relationships with Native Americans than was typical among the Spanish and English. Perhaps eager to debunk the anti-Catholic elements of the Black Legend, the French worked to cultivate cooperation with Native Americans. Jesuit missionaries, for instance, adopted different conversion strategies than the Spanish Franciscans. Spanish missionaries brought Natives into enclosed missions, whereas Jesuits more often lived with or alongside Indigenous people. Many French fur traders married Native American women.[7] The offspring of Native American women and French men were so common in New France that the French developed a word for these children, *Métis(sage)*. The Huron people developed a particularly close relationship with the French, and many converted to Christianity and engaged in the fur trade. But close relationships with the French would come at a high cost. The Huron were decimated by the ravages of European disease, and entanglements in French and Dutch conflicts proved disastrous.[8] Despite this, some Native peoples maintained alliances with the French.

Pressure from the powerful Iroquois in the East pushed many Algonquian-speaking peoples toward French territory in the midseventeenth century, and together they crafted what historians have called a "middle ground," a kind of cross-cultural space that allowed for Native and European interaction, negotiation, and accommodation. French traders adopted—sometimes clumsily—the gift-giving and mediation strategies expected of Native leaders. Natives similarly engaged the impersonal European market and adapted—often haphazardly—to European laws. The Great Lakes "middle ground" experienced tumultuous success throughout the late seventeenth and early eighteenth centuries until English colonial officials and American settlers swarmed the region. The pressures of European expansion strained even the closest bonds.[9]

THE DUTCH

The Netherlands, a small maritime nation with great wealth, achieved considerable colonial success. In 1581, the Netherlands had officially broken away from the Hapsburgs and won a reputation as the freest of the new European nations. Dutch women maintained separate legal identities from their husbands and could therefore hold property and inherit full estates.

Ravaged by the turmoil of the Reformation, the Dutch embraced greater religious tolerance and freedom of the press than other European nations.[10] Radical Protestants, Catholics, and Jews flocked to the Netherlands. The English Pilgrims, for instance, fled first to the Netherlands before sailing to the New World years later. The Netherlands built its colonial empire through the work of experienced merchants and skilled sailors. The Dutch were the most advanced capitalists in the modern world and marshaled extensive financial resources by creating innovative financial organizations such as the Amsterdam Stock Exchange and the Dutch East India Company. Although the Dutch offered liberties, they offered very little democracy—power remained in the hands of only a few. And Dutch liberties certainly had their limits. The Dutch advanced the slave trade and brought enslaved Africans with them to the New World. Slavery was an essential part of Dutch capitalist triumphs.

Sharing the European hunger for access to Asia, in 1609 the Dutch commissioned the Englishman Henry Hudson to discover the fabled Northwest Passage through North America. He failed, of course, but nevertheless found the Hudson River and claimed modern-day New York for the Dutch. There they established New Netherland, an essential part of the Dutch New World empire. The Netherlands chartered the Dutch West India Company in 1621 and established colonies in Africa, the Caribbean, and North America. The island of Manhattan provided a launching pad to support its Caribbean colonies and attack Spanish trade.

Spiteful of the Spanish and mindful of the Black Legend, the Dutch were determined not to repeat Spanish atrocities. They fashioned guidelines for New Netherland that conformed to the ideas of Hugo Grotius, a legal philosopher who believed that Native peoples possessed the same natural rights as Europeans. Colony leaders insisted that land be purchased; in 1626 Peter Minuit therefore "bought" Manhattan from Munsee people.[11] Despite the seemingly honorable intentions, it is likely the Dutch paid the wrong people for the land (either intentionally or unintentionally) or that the Munsee and the Dutch understood the transaction in very different terms. Transactions like these illustrated both the Dutch attempt to find a more peaceful process of colonization and the inconsistency between European and Native American understandings of property.

Like the French, the Dutch sought to profit, not to conquer. Trade with Native peoples became New Netherland's central economic activity. Dutch traders carried wampum along Native trade routes and exchanged it for beaver pelts. Wampum consisted of shell beads fashioned by Algonquians on the southern New England coast and was valued as a ceremonial and diplomatic commodity among the Iroquois. Wampum became a currency that could buy anything from a loaf of bread to a plot of land.[12]

In addition to developing these trading networks, the Dutch also established farms, settlements, and lumber camps. The West India Company directors implemented the patroon system to encourage colonization. The patroon system granted large estates to wealthy landlords, who subsequently paid passage for the tenants to work their land. Expanding Dutch settlements correlated with deteriorating relations with local Native Americans. In the interior of the continent, the Dutch retained valuable alliances with the Iroquois to maintain Beverwijck, modern-day Albany, as a hub for the fur trade.[13] In the places where the Dutch built permanent settlements, the ideals of peaceful colonization succumbed to the settlers' increasing demand for land. Armed conflicts erupted as colonial settlements encroached on Native villages and hunting lands. Profit and peace, it seemed, could not coexist.

Labor shortages, meanwhile, crippled Dutch colonization. The patroon system failed to bring enough tenants, and the colony could not attract a sufficient number of indentured servants to satisfy the colony's backers. In response, the colony imported eleven enslaved people owned by the company in 1626, the same year that Minuit purchased Manhattan. Enslaved laborers were tasked with building New Amsterdam (modern-day New York City), including a defensive wall along the northern edge of the colony (the site of modern-day Wall Street). They created its roads and maintained its all-important port. Fears of racial mixing led the Dutch to import enslaved women, enabling the formation of African

Dutch families. The colony's first African marriage occurred in 1641, and by 1650 there were at least five hundred enslaved Africans in the colony. By 1660, New Amsterdam had the largest urban enslaved population on the continent.[14]

As was typical of the practice of African slavery in much of the early seventeenth century, Dutch slavery in New Amsterdam was less comprehensively exploitative than later systems of American slavery. Some enslaved Africans, for instance, successfully sued for back wages. When several enslaved people owned by the company fought for the colony against the Munsee, they petitioned for their freedom and won a kind of "half freedom" that allowed them to work their own land in return for paying a large tithe, or tax, to their enslavers. The children of these "half-free" laborers remained held in bondage by the West India Company, however. The Dutch, who so proudly touted their liberties, grappled with the reality of African slavery, and some New Netherlanders protested the enslavement of Christianized Africans. The economic goals of the colony slowly crowded out these cultural and religious objections, and the much-boasted liberties of the Dutch came to exist alongside increasingly brutal systems of slavery.

THE PORTUGUESE

The Portuguese had been leaders in Atlantic navigation well ahead of Columbus's voyage. But the incredible wealth flowing from New Spain piqued the rivalry between the two Iberian countries, and accelerated Portuguese colonization efforts. This rivalry created a crisis within the Catholic world as Spain and Portugal squared off in a battle for colonial supremacy. The pope had earlier intervened and divided the New World with the Treaty of Tordesillas in 1494. Land east of the Tordesillas Meridian, an imaginary line dividing South America, would be given to Portugal, whereas land west of the line was reserved for Spanish conquest. In return for the license to conquer, both Portugal and Spain were instructed to treat the natives with Christian compassion and to bring them under the protection of the Church.

Lucrative colonies in Africa and India initially preoccupied Portugal, but by 1530 the Portuguese turned their attention to the land that would become Brazil, driving out French traders and establishing permanent settlements. Gold and silver mines dotted the interior of the colony, but two industries powered early colonial Brazil: sugar and the slave trade. In fact, over the entire history of the Atlantic slave trade, more Africans were enslaved in Brazil than in any other colony in the Atlantic World. Gold mines emerged in greater numbers throughout the eighteenth century but still never rivaled the profitability of sugar or slave trading.

Jesuit missionaries brought Christianity to Brazil, but strong elements of African and Native spirituality mixed with orthodox Catholicism to create a unique religious culture. This culture resulted from the demographics of Brazilian slavery. High mortality rates on sugar plantations required a steady influx of new enslaved laborers, thus perpetuating the cultural connection between Brazil and Africa. The reliance on new imports of enslaved laborers increased the likelihood of resistance, however, and those who escaped slavery managed to create several free settlements, called *quilombos*. These settlements drew from both enslaved Africans and Natives, and despite frequent attacks, several endured throughout the long history of Brazilian slavery.[15]

Despite the arrival of these new Europeans, Spain continued to dominate the New World. The wealth flowing from the exploitation of the Aztec and Incan Empires greatly eclipsed the profits of other European nations. But this dominance would not last long. By the end of the sixteenth century, the powerful Spanish Armada would be destroyed, and the English would begin to rule the waves.

IV. English Colonization

Spain had a one-hundred-year head start on New World colonization, and a jealous England eyed the enormous wealth that Spain gleaned. The Protestant Reformation had shaken England, but Elizabeth I assumed the English crown in 1558. Elizabeth oversaw England's so-called golden age, which included both the expansion of trade and exploration and the literary achievements of Shakespeare and Marlowe. English mercantilism, a state-assisted manufacturing and trading system, created and maintained markets. The markets provided a steady supply of consumers and laborers, stimulated economic expansion, and increased English wealth.

However, wrenching social and economic changes unsettled the English population. The island's population increased from fewer than three million in 1500 to over five million by the middle of the seventeenth century.[16] The skyrocketing cost of land coincided with plummeting farming income. Rents and prices rose but wages stagnated. Moreover, movements to enclose public land—sparked by the transition of English

landholders from agriculture to livestock raising—evicted tenants from the land and created hordes of landless, jobless peasants that haunted the cities and countryside. One quarter to one half of the population lived in extreme poverty.[17]

Nicholas Hilliard, *The Battle of Gravelines*, 1588. Wikimedia.

New World colonization won support in England amid a time of rising English fortunes among the wealthy, a tense Spanish rivalry, and mounting internal social unrest. But supporters of English colonization always touted more than economic gains and mere national self-interest. They claimed to be doing God's work. Many claimed that colonization would glorify God, England, and Protestantism by Christianizing the New World's pagan peoples. Advocates such as Richard Hakluyt the Younger and John Dee, for instance, drew upon *The History of the Kings of Britain*, written by the twelfth-century monk Geoffrey of Monmouth, and its mythical account of King Arthur's conquest and Christianization of pagan lands to justify American conquest.[18] Moreover, promoters promised that the conversion of New World Native Americans would satisfy God and glorify England's "Virgin Queen," Elizabeth I, who was seen as nearly divine by some in England. The English—and other European Protestant colonizers—imagined themselves superior to the Spanish, who still bore the Black Legend of inhuman cruelty. English colonization, supporters argued, would prove that superiority.

In his 1584 "Discourse on Western Planting," Richard Hakluyt amassed the supposed religious, moral, and exceptional economic benefits of colonization. He repeated the Black Legend of Spanish New World terrorism and attacked the sins of Catholic Spain. He promised that English colonization could strike a blow against Spanish heresy and bring Protestant religion to the New World. English interference, Hakluyt suggested, might provide the only salvation from Catholic rule in the New World. The New World, too, he said, offered obvious economic advantages. Trade and resource extraction would enrich the English treasury. England, for instance, could find plentiful materials to outfit a world-class navy. Moreover, he said, the New World could provide an escape for England's vast armies of landless "vagabonds." Expanded trade, he argued, would not only bring profit but also provide work for England's jobless poor. A Christian enterprise, a blow against Spain, an economic stimulus, and a social safety valve all beckoned the English toward a commitment to colonization.[19]

This noble rhetoric veiled the coarse economic motives that brought England to the New World. New economic structures and a new merchant class paved the way for colonization. England's merchants lacked estates, but they had new plans to build wealth. By collaborating with new government-sponsored trading monopolies and employing financial innovations such as joint-stock companies, England's merchants sought to improve on the Dutch economic system. Spain was extracting enormous material wealth from the New World; why shouldn't England? Joint-stock companies, the ancestors of modern corporations, became the initial instruments of colonization. With government monopolies, shared profits, and managed risks, these money-making ventures could attract and manage the vast capital needed for colonization. In 1606 James I approved the formation of the Virginia Company (named after Elizabeth, the Virgin Queen).

Rather than formal colonization, however, the most successful early English ventures in the New World were a form of state-sponsored piracy known as privateering. Queen Elizabeth sponsored sailors, or "Sea Dogges," such as John Hawkins and Francis Drake, to plunder Spanish ships and towns in the Americas. Privateers earned a substantial

profit both for themselves and for the English crown. England practiced piracy on a scale, one historian wrote, "that transforms crime
into politics."[20] Francis Drake harried Spanish ships throughout the
Western Hemisphere and raided Spanish caravans as far away as the
coast of Peru on the Pacific Ocean. In 1580 Elizabeth rewarded her
skilled pirate with knighthood. But Elizabeth walked a fine line. With
Protestant-Catholic tensions already running high, English privateering provoked Spain. Tensions worsened after the execution of Mary,
Queen of Scots, a Catholic. In 1588, King Philip II of Spain unleashed
the fabled Armada. With 130 ships, 8,000 sailors, and 18,000 soldiers,
Spain launched the largest invasion in history to destroy the British
navy and depose Elizabeth.

An island nation, England depended on a robust navy for trade and
territorial expansion. England had fewer ships than Spain, but they were
smaller and swifter. They successfully harassed the armada, forcing it to
retreat to the Netherlands for reinforcements. But then a fluke storm, celebrated in England as the "Protestant wind," annihilated the remainder
of the fleet.[21] The destruction of the armada changed the course of world
history. It not only saved England and secured English Protestantism,
but it also opened the seas to English expansion and paved the way for
England's colonial future. By 1600, England stood ready to embark on its
dominance over North America.

English colonization would look very different from Spanish or
French colonization. England had long been trying to conquer Catholic Ireland. Rather than integrating with the Irish and trying to convert
them to Protestantism, England more often simply seized land through
violence and pushed out the former inhabitants, leaving them to move
elsewhere or to die. These same tactics would later be deployed in North
American invasions.

English colonization, however, began haltingly. Sir Humphrey Gilbert
labored throughout the late sixteenth century to establish a colony in
Newfoundland but failed. In 1587, with a predominantly male cohort of
150 English colonizers, John White reestablished an abandoned settlement on North Carolina's Roanoke Island. Supply shortages prompted
White to return to England for additional support, but the Spanish Armada and the mobilization of British naval efforts stranded him in Britain
for several years. When he finally returned to Roanoke, he found the
colony abandoned. What befell the failed colony? White found the word
Croatan carved into a tree or a post in the abandoned colony. Historians

presume the colonists, short of food, may have fled for a nearby island of that name and encountered its settled native population. Others offer violence as an explanation. Regardless, the English colonists were never heard from again. When Queen Elizabeth died in 1603, no Englishmen had yet established a permanent North American colony.

After King James made peace with Spain in 1604, privateering no longer held out the promise of cheap wealth. Colonization assumed a new urgency. The Virginia Company, established in 1606, drew inspiration from Cortés and the Spanish conquests. It hoped to find gold and silver as well as other valuable trading commodities in the New World: glass, iron, furs, pitch, tar, and anything else the country could supply. The company planned to identify a navigable river with a deep harbor, away from the eyes of the Spanish. There they would find a Native American trading network and extract a fortune from the New World.

V. Jamestown

Incolarum Virginiae piscandi ratio (The Method of Fishing of the Inhabitants of Virginia), c. 1590. *The Encyclopedia Virginia.*

In April 1607 Englishmen aboard three ships—the *Susan Constant*, the *Godspeed*, and the *Discovery*—sailed forty miles up the James River (named for the English king) in present-day Virginia (named for Elizabeth I, the Virgin Queen) and settled on just such a place. The uninhabited peninsula they selected was upriver and out of sight of Spanish patrols. It offered easy defense against ground assaults and was both

uninhabited and located close to many Native American villages and their potentially lucrative trade networks. But the location was a disaster. Indigenous people had ignored the peninsula for two reasons: terrible soil hampered agriculture, and brackish tidal water led to debilitating disease. Despite these setbacks, the English built Jamestown, the first permanent English colony in the present-day United States.

The English had not entered a wilderness but had arrived amid a people they called the Powhatan Confederacy. Powhatan, or Wahunsena-cawh, as he called himself, led nearly ten thousand Algonquian-speaking people in the Chesapeake. They burned vast acreage to clear brush and create sprawling artificial parklike grasslands so they could easily hunt deer, elk, and bison. The Powhatan raised corn, beans, squash, and possibly sunflowers, rotating acreage throughout the Chesapeake. Without plows, manure, or draft animals, the Powhatan produced a remarkable number of calories cheaply and efficiently.

Jamestown was a profit-seeking venture backed by investors. The colonists were mostly gentlemen and proved entirely unprepared for the challenges ahead. They hoped for easy riches but found none. As John Smith later complained, they "would rather starve than work."[22] And so they did. Disease and starvation ravaged the colonists, thanks in part to the peninsula's unhealthy location and the fact that supplies from England arrived sporadically or spoiled. Fewer than half of the original colonists survived the first nine months.

John Smith, a yeoman's son and capable leader, took command of the crippled colony and promised, "He that will not work shall not eat." He navigated Native American diplomacy, claiming that he was captured and sentenced to death but Powhatan's daughter, Pocahontas, intervened to save his life. She would later marry another colonist, John Rolfe, and die in England.

Powhatan kept the English alive that first winter. The Powhatan had welcomed the English and placed a high value on metal ax-heads, kettles, tools, and guns and eagerly traded furs and other abundant goods for them. With ten thousand confederated natives and with food in abundance, the Indigenous people had little to fear and much to gain from the isolated outpost of sick and dying Englishmen.

Despite reinforcements, the English continued to die. Four hundred settlers arrived in 1609, but the overwhelmed colony entered a desperate "starving time" in the winter of 1609–1610. Supplies were lost at sea. Relations with the Native Americans deteriorated and the colonists

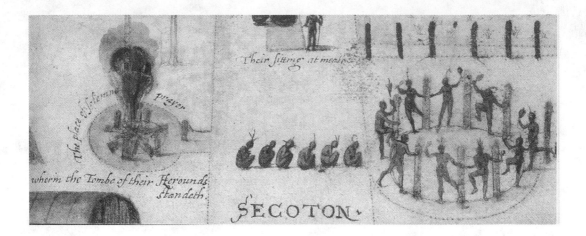

John White,
*Village of the
Secotan*, 1585.
Wikimedia.

fought a kind of slow-burning guerrilla war with the Powhatan. Disaster loomed for the colony. The settlers ate everything they could, roaming the woods for nuts and berries. They boiled leather. They dug up graves to eat the corpses of their former neighbors. One man was executed for killing and eating his wife. Some years later, George Percy recalled the colonists' desperation during these years, when he served as the colony's president: "Having fed upon our horses and other beasts as long as they lasted, we were glad to make shift with vermin as dogs, cats, rats and mice . . . as to eat boots shoes or any other leather. . . . And now famine beginning to look ghastly and pale in every face, that nothing was spared to maintain life and to do those things which seem incredible, as to dig up dead corpses out of graves and to eat them."[23] Archaeological excavations in 2012 exhumed the bones of a fourteen-year-old girl that exhibited signs of cannibalism.[24] All but sixty settlers would die by the summer of 1610.

Little improved over the next several years. By 1616, 80 percent of all English immigrants who had arrived in Jamestown had perished. England's first American colony was a catastrophe. The colony was reorganized, and in 1614 the marriage of Pocahontas to John Rolfe eased relations with the Powhatan, though the colony still limped along as a starving, commercially disastrous tragedy. The colonists were unable to find any profitable commodities and remained dependent on the Native Americans and sporadic shipments from England for food. But then tobacco saved Jamestown.

By the time King James I described tobacco as a "noxious weed, . . . loathsome to the eye, hateful to the nose, harmful to the brain, and dangerous to the lungs," it had already taken Europe by storm. In 1616 John Rolfe crossed tobacco strains from Trinidad and Guiana and planted

Virginia's first tobacco crop. In 1617 the colony sent its first cargo of to-bacco back to England. The "noxious weed," a native of the New World, fetched a high price in Europe and the tobacco boom began in Virginia and then later spread to Maryland. Within fifteen years American colo-nists were exporting over five hundred thousand pounds of tobacco per year. Within forty years, they were exporting fifteen million.[25]

Tobacco changed everything. It saved Virginia from ruin, incentivized further colonization, and laid the groundwork for what would become the United States. With a new market open, Virginia drew not only mer-chants and traders but also settlers. Colonists came in droves. They were mostly young, mostly male, and mostly indentured servants who signed contracts called indentures that bonded them to employers for a period of years in return for passage across the ocean. But even the rough terms of servitude were no match for the promise of land and potential profits that beckoned English farmers. But still there were not enough of them. Tobacco was a labor-intensive crop and ambitious planters, with seem-ingly limitless land before them, lacked only laborers to escalate their wealth and status. The colony's great labor vacuum inspired the creation of the "headright policy" in 1618: any person who migrated to Virginia would automatically receive fifty acres of land and any immigrant whose passage they paid would entitle them to fifty acres more.

In 1619, the Virginia Company established the House of Burgesses, a limited representative body composed of white landowners that first met in Jamestown. That same year, a Dutch slave ship sold twenty Africans to the Virginia colonists. Southern slavery was born.

Soon the tobacco-growing colonists expanded beyond the bounds of Jamestown's deadly peninsula. When it became clear that the English were not merely intent on maintaining a small trading post but sought a permanent ever-expanding colony, conflict with the Powhatan Confeder-acy became almost inevitable. Powhatan died in 1622 and was succeeded by his brother, Opechancanough, who promised to drive the land-hungry colonists back into the sea. He launched a surprise attack and in a single day (March 22, 1622) killed over 350 colonists, or one third of all the colonists in Virginia.[26] The colonists retaliated and revisited the massa-cres on Indigenous settlements many times over. The massacre freed the colonists to drive Native Americans off their land. The governor of Vir-ginia declared it colonial policy to achieve the "expulsion of the savages to gain the free range of the country."[27] War and disease tilted the bal-ance of power decisively toward the English colonizers.

English colonists brought to the New World particular visions of racial, cultural, and religious supremacy. Despite starving in the shadow of the Powhatan Confederacy, English colonists nevertheless judged themselves physically, spiritually, and technologically superior to Native peoples in North America. Christianity, metallurgy, intensive agriculture, transatlantic navigation, and even wheat all magnified the English sense of superiority. This sense of superiority, when coupled with outbreaks of violence, left the English feeling entitled to Indigenous lands and resources.

Spanish conquerors established the framework for the Atlantic slave trade over a century before the first chained Africans arrived at Jamestown. Even Bartolomé de Las Casas, celebrated for his pleas to save Native Americans from colonial butchery, for a time recommended that Indigenous labor be replaced by importing Africans. Early English settlers from the Caribbean and Atlantic coast of North America mostly imitated European ideas of African inferiority. "Race" followed the expansion of slavery across the Atlantic world. Skin color and race suddenly seemed fixed. Englishmen equated Africans with categorical blackness and blackness with sin, "the handmaid and symbol of baseness."[28] An English essayist in 1695 wrote that "a negro will always be a negro, carry him to Greenland, feed him chalk, feed and manage him never so many ways."[29] More and more Europeans embraced the notions that Europeans and Africans were of distinct races. Others now preached that the Old Testament God cursed Ham, the son of Noah, and doomed Black people to perpetual enslavement.

And yet in the early years of American slavery, ideas about race were not yet fixed and the practice of slavery was not yet codified. The first generations of Africans in English North America faced miserable conditions, but, in contrast to later American history, their initial servitude was not necessarily permanent, heritable, or even particularly disgraceful. Africans were definitively set apart as fundamentally different from their white counterparts and faced longer terms of service and harsher punishments, but, like the indentured white servants whisked away from English slums, these first Africans in North America could also work for only a set number of years before becoming free landowners themselves. The Angolan Anthony Johnson, for instance, was sold into servitude but fulfilled his indenture and became a prosperous tobacco planter himself.[30]

In 1622, at the dawn of the tobacco boom, Jamestown had still seemed a failure. But the rise of tobacco and the destruction of the Powhatan turned the tide. Colonists escaped the deadly peninsula and immigrants poured into the colony to grow tobacco and turn a profit for the Crown.

VI. New England

The English colonies in New England established from 1620 onward were founded with loftier goals than those in Virginia. Although migrants to New England expected economic profit, religious motives directed the rhetoric and much of the reality of these colonies. Not every English person who moved to New England during the seventeenth century was a Puritan, but Puritans dominated the politics, religion, and culture of New England. Even after 1700, the region's Puritan inheritance shaped many aspects of its history.

The term *Puritan* began as an insult, and its recipients usually referred to each other as "the godly" if they used a specific term at all. Puritans believed that the Church of England did not distance itself far enough from Catholicism after Henry VIII broke with Rome in the 1530s. They largely agreed with European Calvinists—followers of theologian John Calvin—on matters of religious doctrine. Calvinists (and Puritans) believed that humankind was redeemed by God's grace alone, and that the fate of an individual's immortal soul was predestined. The happy minority that God had already chosen to save were known among English Puritans as the Elect. Calvinists also argued that the decoration of churches, reliance

Seal of the Massachusetts Bay Colony. The History Project (UC Davis).

on ornate ceremony, and corrupt priesthood obscured God's message. They believed that reading the Bible was the best way to understand God.

Puritans were stereotyped by their enemies as dour killjoys, and the exaggeration has endured. It is certainly true that the Puritans' disdain for excess and opposition to many holidays popular in Europe (including Christmas, which, as Puritans never tired of reminding everyone, the Bible never told anyone to celebrate) lent themselves to caricature. But Puritans understood themselves as advocating a reasonable middle path in a corrupt world. It would never occur to a Puritan, for example, to abstain from alcohol or sex.

During the first century after the English Reformation (c. 1530–1630) Puritans sought to "purify" the Church of England of all practices that smacked of Catholicism, advocating a simpler worship service, the abolition of ornate churches, and other reforms. They had some success in pushing the Church of England in a more Calvinist direction, but with the coronation of King Charles I (r. 1625–1649), the Puritans gained an implacable foe that cast English Puritans as excessive and dangerous. Facing growing persecution, the Puritans began the Great Migration, during which about twenty thousand people traveled to New England between 1630 and 1640. The Puritans (unlike the small band of separatist "Pilgrims" who founded Plymouth Colony in 1620) remained committed to reforming the Church of England but temporarily decamped to North America to accomplish this task. Leaders like John Winthrop insisted they were not separating from, or abandoning, England but were rather forming a godly community in America that would be a "City on a Hill" and an example for reformers back home.[31] The Puritans did not seek to create a haven of religious toleration, a notion that they—along with nearly all European Christians—regarded as ridiculous at best and dangerous at worst.

While the Puritans did not succeed in building a godly utopia in New England, a combination of Puritan traits with several external factors created colonies wildly different from any other region settled by English people. Unlike those heading to Virginia, colonists in New England (Plymouth [1620], Massachusetts Bay [1630], Connecticut [1636], and Rhode Island [1636]) generally arrived in family groups. Most New England immigrants were small landholders in England, a class contemporary English called the "middling sort." When they arrived in New England they tended to replicate their home environments, founding towns composed of independent landholders. The New England climate and soil made large-scale plantation agriculture impractical, so the system of large landholders using masses of enslaved laborers or indentured servants to grow labor-intensive crops never took hold.

There is no evidence that the New England Puritans would have opposed such a system were it possible; other Puritans made their fortunes on the Caribbean sugar islands, and New England merchants profited as suppliers of provisions and enslaved laborers to those colonies. By accident of geography as much as by design, New England society was much less stratified than any of Britain's other seventeenth-century colonies.

Although New England colonies could boast wealthy landholding elites, the disparity of wealth in the region remained narrow compared to the Chesapeake, Carolina, or the Caribbean. Instead, seventeenth-century New England was characterized by a broadly shared modest prosperity based on a mixed economy dependent on small farms, shops, fishing, lumber, shipbuilding, and trade with the Atlantic World.

A combination of environmental factors and the Puritan social ethos produced a region of remarkable health and stability during the seventeenth century. New England immigrants avoided most of the deadly outbreaks of tropical disease that turned the Chesapeake colonies into graveyards. Disease, in fact, only aided English settlement and relations to Native Americans. In contrast to other English colonists who had to contend with powerful Native American neighbors, the Puritans confronted the stunned survivors of a biological catastrophe. A lethal pandemic of smallpox during the 1610s swept away as much as 90 percent of the region's Native American population. Many survivors welcomed the English as potential allies against rival tribes who had escaped the catastrophe. The relatively healthy environment coupled with political stability and the predominance of family groups among early immigrants allowed the New England population to grow to 91,000 people by 1700 from only 21,000 immigrants. In contrast, 120,000 English went to the Chesapeake, and only 85,000 white colonists remained in 1700.[32]

The New England Puritans set out to build their utopia by creating communities of the godly. Groups of men, often from the same region of England, applied to the colony's General Court for land grants.[33] They generally divided part of the land for immediate use while keeping much of the rest as "commons" or undivided land for future generations. The town's inhabitants collectively decided the size of each settler's home lot based on their current wealth and status. Besides oversight of property, the town restricted membership, and new arrivals needed to apply for admission. Those who gained admittance could participate in town governments that, while not democratic by modern standards, nevertheless had broad popular involvement. All male property holders could vote in town meetings and choose the selectmen, assessors, constables, and other officials from among themselves to conduct the daily affairs of government. Upon their founding, towns wrote covenants, reflecting the Puritan belief in God's covenant with his people. Towns sought to arbitrate disputes and contain strife, as did the Church. Wayward or divergent individuals were persuaded, corrected, or coerced. Popular conceptions of Puritans as hardened authoritarians are exaggerated, but if persuasion and arbitration failed, people who did not conform to community norms were punished or removed. Massachusetts banished Anne Hutchinson, Roger Williams, and other religious dissenters like the Quakers.

Although by many measures colonization in New England succeeded, its Puritan leaders failed in their own mission to create a utopian community that would inspire their fellows back in England. They tended to focus their disappointment on the younger generation. "But alas!" Increase Mather lamented, "That so many of the younger Generation have so early corrupted their [the founders'] doings!"[34] The jeremiad, a sermon lamenting the fallen state of New England due to its straying from its early virtuous path, became a staple of late-seventeenth-century Puritan literature.

Yet the jeremiad could not stop the effects of prosperity. The population spread and grew more diverse. Many, if not most, New Englanders retained strong ties to their Calvinist roots into the eighteenth century, but the Puritans (who became Congregationalists) struggled against a rising tide of religious pluralism. On December 25, 1727, Judge Samuel Sewell noted in his diary that a new Anglican minister "keeps the day in his new Church at Braintrey: people flock thither."[35] Previously forbidden holidays like Christmas were celebrated publicly in church and privately in homes. Puritan divine Cotton Mather discovered on Christmas 1711 that "a number of young people of both sexes, belonging, many of them, to my flock, had . . . a Frolick, a reveling Feast, and a Ball, which discovers their Corruption."[36]

Despite the lamentations of the Mathers and other Puritan leaders of their failure, they left an enduring mark on New England culture and society that endured long after the region's residents ceased to be called "Puritan."

VII. Conclusion

The fledgling settlements in Virginia and Massachusetts paled in importance when compared to the sugar colonies of the Caribbean. Valued more as marginal investments and social safety valves where the poor could be released, these colonies nonetheless created a foothold for Britain on a vast North American continent. And although the seventeenth century would be fraught for Britain—religious, social, and political upheavals would behead one king and force another to flee his throne—settlers in Massachusetts and Virginia were nonetheless tied together by the emerging Atlantic economy. While commodities such as tobacco and sugar fueled new markets in Europe, the economy grew increasingly dependent on slave labor. Enslaved Africans transported across the Atlantic would further complicate the collision of cultures in the Americas. The creation and maintenance of a slave system would spark new understandings of human difference and new modes of social control. The economic exchanges of the new Atlantic economy would not only generate great wealth and exploitation, they would also lead to new cultural systems and new identities for the inhabitants of at least four continents.

VIII. Reference Materials

This chapter was edited by Ben Wright and Joseph Locke, with content contributions by Erin Bonuso, L. D. Burnett, Jon Grandage, Joseph Locke, Lisa Mercer, Maria Montalvo, Ian Saxine, Jennifer Tellman, Luke Willert, and Ben Wright.

Recommended citation: Erin Bonuso et al., "Colliding Cultures," Ben Wright and Joseph L. Locke, eds., in *The American Yawp*, eds. Joseph L. Locke and Ben Wright (Stanford, CA: Stanford University Press, 2019).

NOTES TO CHAPTER 2

1. Stanley L. Engerman and Robert E. Gallman, eds., *The Cambridge Economic History of the United States, Vol. I: The Colonial Era* (New York: Cambridge University Press, 1996), 21.

2. Andrew L. Knaut, *The Pueblo Revolt of 1680: Conquest and Resistance in Seventeenth Century New Mexico* (Norman: University of Oklahoma Press, 2015), 46.

3. John E. Kicza and Rebecca Horn, *Resilient Cultures: America's Native Peoples Confront European Colonization, 1500–1800* (New York: Routledge, 2013), 122.

4. Knaut, *Pueblo Revolt of 1680*, 155.

5. John Ponet, *A Short Treatise on Political Power: And of the True Obedience Which Subjects Owe to Kings, and Other Civil Governors* (London: s.n.), 43–44.

6. Alan Greer, *The People of New France* (Toronto: University of Toronto Press, 1997).

7. Susan Sleeper-Smith, *Indian Women and French Men: Rethinking Cul-

tural Encounter in the Western Great Lakes (Amherst: University of Massachusetts Press, 2001).

8. Carole Blackburn, *Harvest of Souls: The Jesuit Missions and Colonialism in North America, 1632–1659* (Montreal: McGill-Queen's University Press, 2000), 116.

9. Richard White, *The Middle Ground: Indians, Empires, and Republics in the Great Lakes Region, 1650–1815* (New York: Cambridge University Press, 1991).

10. Evan Haefeli, *New Netherland and the Dutch Origins of American Religious Liberty* (Philadelphia: University of Pennsylvania Press, 2012), 20–53.

11. Allen W. Trelease, *Indian Affairs in Colonial New York: The Seventeenth Century* (Lincoln: University of Nebraska Press, 1997), 36.

12. Daniel K. Richter, *Trade, Land, Power: The Struggle for Eastern North America* (Philadelphia: University of Pennsylvania Press, 2013), 101.

13. Janny Venema, *Beverwijck: A Dutch Village on the American Frontier, 1652–1664* (Albany: SUNY Press, 2003).

14. Leslie M. Harris, *In the Shadow of Slavery: African Americans in New York City, 1626–1863* (Chicago: University of Chicago Press, 2003), 21.

15. Alida C. Metcalf, *Go-betweens and the Colonization of Brazil: 1500–1600* (Austin: University of Texas Press, 2005). See also James H. Sweet, *Recreating Africa: Culture, Kinship, and Religion in the African-Portuguese World, 1441–1770* (Chapel Hill: University of North Carolina Press, 2003.

16. Edmund S. Morgan, *American Slavery, American Freedom: The Ordeal of Colonial Virginia* (New York: Norton, 1975), 30.

17. John Walter, *Crowds and Popular Politics in Early Modern England* (Manchester, UK: Manchester University Press, 2006), 131–135.

18. Christopher Hodgkins, *Reforming Empire: Protestant Colonialism and Conscience in British Literature* (Columbia: University of Missouri Press, 2002), 15.

19. Richard Hakluyt, *Discourse on Western Planting* (1584). https://archive .org/details/discourseonweste02hakl_0.

20. Morgan, *American Slavery, American Freedom*, 9.

21. Felipe Fernández-Armesto, *The Spanish Armada: The Experience of War in 1588* (New York: Oxford University Press, 1988).

22. John Smith, *Advertisements for the Inexperienced Planters of New England, or Anywhere or The Pathway to Experience to Erect a Plantation* (London: Haviland, 1631), 16.

23. George Percy, "A True Relation of the Proceedings and Occurrents of Moment Which Have Hap'ned in Virginia," quoted in *Jamestown Narratives: Eyewitness Accounts of the Virginia Colony, the First Decade, 1607–1617*, ed. Edward Wright Haile (Champlain, VA: Round House, 1998), 505.

24. Eric A. Powell, "Chilling Discovery at Jamestown," *Archaeology* (June 10, 2013). http://www.archaeology.org/issues/96-1307/trenches/973-jamestown -starving-time-cannibalism.

25. Dennis Montgomery, *1607: Jamestown and the New World* (Williamsburg, VA: Colonial Williamsburg Foundation, 2007), 126.

26. Rebecca Goetz, *The Baptism of Early Virginia: How Christianity Created Race* (Baltimore: Johns Hopkins University Press, 2012), 57.

27. Daniel K. Richter, *Facing East from Indian Country: A Native History of Early America* (Cambridge, MA: Harvard University Press, 2009), 75.

28. Winthrop Jordan, *White over Black: American Attitudes Toward the Negro, 1550–12* (Chapel Hill: University of North Carolina Press, 1968), 7.

29. Ibid., 16.

30. T. H. Breen and Stephen Innes, *"Myne Owne Ground": Race and Freedom on Virginia's Eastern Shore, 1640–1676* (New York: Oxford University Press, 2005).

31. John Winthrop, *A Modell of Christian Charity* (1830), first published in *Collections of the Massachusetts Historical Society* (Boston, 1838), 3rd series, no. 7: 31–48. http://history.hanover.edu/texts/winthmod.html.

32. Alan Taylor, *American Colonies: The Settling of North America* (New York: Penguin, 2002), 170.

33. Virginia DeJohn Anderson, *New England's Generation: The Great Migration and the Formation of Society and Culture in the Seventeenth Century* (New York: Cambridge University Press, 1991), 90–91.

34. Increase Mather, *A Testimony Against Several Prophane and Superstitious Customs, Now Practised by Some in New-England* (London: s.n., 1687).

35. Samuel Sewall, *Diary of Samuel Sewall: 1674–1729*, Vol. 3 (Boston: Massachusetts Historical Society, 1882), 389.

36. *Diary of Cotton Mather, 1709–1724* (Boston: Massachusetts Historical Society, 1912), 146.

RECOMMENDED READING

Armitage, David, and Michael J. Braddick, eds. *The British Atlantic World, 1500–1800*. New York: Palgrave Macmillan, 2002.

Barr, Juliana. *Peace Came in the Form of a Woman: Indians and Spaniards in the Texas Borderlands*. Chapel Hill: University of North Carolina Press, 2009.

Blackburn, Robin. *The Making of New World Slavery: From the Baroque to the Modern, 1492–1800*. London: Verso, 1997.

Calloway, Colin G. *New Worlds for All: Indians, Europeans, and the Remaking of Early America*. Baltimore: Johns Hopkins University Press, 1997.

Cañizares-Esguerra, Jorge. *Puritan Conquistadors. Iberianizing the Atlantic, 1550–1700*. Stanford, CA: Stanford University Press, 2006.

Cronon, William. *Changes in the Land: Indians, Colonists, and the Ecology of New England*. New York: Hill and Wang, 1983.

Daniels, Christine, and Michael V. Kennedy, eds. *Negotiated Empires: Centers and Peripheries in the Americas, 1500–1820*. New York: Routledge, 2002.

Dubcovsky, Alejandra. *Informed Power: Communication in the Early American South*. Cambridge, MA: Harvard University Press, 2016.

Elliott, John H. *Empires of the Atlantic World: Britain and Spain in America, 1492–1830*. New Haven, CT: Yale University Press, 2006.

Fuentes, Marisa J. *Dispossessed Lives: Enslaved Women, Violence, and the Archive*. Philadelphia: University of Pennsylvania Press, 2016.

Goetz, Rebecca Anne. *The Baptism of Early Virginia: How Christianity Created Race*. Baltimore: Johns Hopkins University Press, 2012.

Gould, Eliga H. "Entangled Histories, Entangled Worlds: The English-Speaking Atlantic as a Spanish Periphery." *American Historical Review* 112, no. 3 (June 2007): 764–786.

Grandjean, Katherine. *American Passage: The Communications Frontier in Early New England*. Cambridge, MA: Harvard University Press, 2015.

Mancall, Peter C. *Hakluyt's Promise: An Elizabethan's Obsession for an English America*. New Haven, CT: Yale University Press, 2007.

Morgan, Edmund S. *American Slavery, American Freedom: The Ordeal of Colonial Virginia*. New York: Norton, 1975.

Morgan, Jennifer. *Laboring Women: Reproduction and Gender in New World Slavery*. Philadelphia: University of Pennsylvania Press, 2004.

Reséndez, Andrés. *The Other Slavery: The Uncovered Story of Indian Enslavement in America*. New York: Houghton Mifflin Harcourt, 2017.

Seed, Patricia. *Ceremonies of Possession in Europe's Conquest of the New World, 1492–1640*. New York: Cambridge University Press, 1995.

Snyder, Christina. *Slavery in Indian Country: The Changing Face of Captivity in Early America*. Cambridge, MA: Harvard University Press, 2010.

Socolow, Susan Migden. *The Women of Colonial Latin America*. New York: Cambridge University Press, 2000.

Stoler, Ann Laura. "Tense and Tender Ties: The Politics of Comparison in North American History and (Post) Colonial Studies." *Journal of American History* 88, no. 3 (December 2001): 829–897.

Thornton, John. *Africa and Africans in the Making of the Atlantic World, 1400–1800*. New York: Cambridge University Press, 1992.

Warren, Wendy. *New England Bound: Slavery and Colonization in Early America*. New York: Norton, 2016.

Weimer, Adrian. *Martyrs' Mirror: Persecution and Holiness in Early New England*. New York: Oxford University Press, 2011.

White, Richard. *The Middle Ground: Indians, Empires, and Republics in the Great Lakes Region, 1650–1815*. New York: Cambridge University Press, 1991.

3

British North America

I. Introduction

Whether they came as servants, enslaved laborers, free farmers, religious refugees, or powerful planters, the men and women of the American colonies created new worlds. Native Americans saw fledgling settlements grow into unstoppable beachheads of vast new populations that increasingly monopolized resources and remade the land into something else entirely. Meanwhile, as colonial societies developed in the seventeenth and eighteenth centuries, fluid labor arrangements and racial categories solidified into the race-based, chattel slavery that increasingly defined the economy of the British Empire. The North American mainland originally occupied a small and marginal place in that broad empire, as even the output of its most prosperous colonies paled before the tremendous wealth of Caribbean sugar islands. And yet the colonial backwaters on the North American mainland, ignored by many imperial officials, were nevertheless deeply tied into these larger Atlantic networks. A new and increasingly complex Atlantic World connected the continents of Europe, Africa, and the Americas.

Unidentified artist, *The Old Plantation*, c. 1790–1800, Abby Aldrich Rockefeller Folk Art Museum. Wikimedia.

Events across the ocean continued to influence the lives of American colonists. Civil war, religious conflict, and nation building transformed seventeenth-century Britain and remade societies on both sides of the ocean. At the same time, colonial settlements grew and matured, developing into powerful societies capable of warring against Native Americans and subduing internal upheaval. Patterns and systems established during the colonial era would continue to shape American society for centuries. And none, perhaps, would be as brutal and destructive as the institution of slavery.

II. Slavery and the Making of Race

After his arrival as a missionary in Charles Town, Carolina, in 1706, Reverend Francis Le Jau quickly grew disillusioned by the horrors of American slavery. He met enslaved Africans ravaged by the Middle Passage, Native Americans traveling south to enslave enemy villages, and colonists terrified of invasions from French Louisiana and Spanish Florida. Slavery and death surrounded him.

Le Jau's strongest complaints were reserved for his own countrymen, the English. English traders encouraged wars with Native Americans in order to purchase and enslave captives, and planters justified the use of an enslaved workforce by claiming white servants were "good for nothing at all." Although the minister thought otherwise and baptized and educated a substantial number of enslaved people, he was unable to overcome enslavers, fears that Christian baptism would lead to slave emancipation.[1]

The 1660s marked a turning point for Black men and women in English colonies like Virginia in North America and Barbados in the West Indies. New laws gave legal sanction to the enslavement of people of African descent for life. The permanent deprivation of freedom and the separate legal status of enslaved Africans facilitated the maintenance of strict racial barriers. Skin color became more than a superficial difference; it became the marker of a transcendent, all-encompassing division between two distinct peoples, two races, white and black.[2]

All seventeenth-century racial thought did not point directly toward modern classifications of racial hierarchy. Captain Thomas Phillips, master of a slave ship in 1694, did not justify his work with any such creed: "I can't think there is any intrinsic value in one color more than another, nor that white is better than black, only we think it so because we are so."[3] For Phillips, the profitability of slavery was the only justification he needed.

Wars offered the most common means for colonists to acquire enslaved Native Americans. Seventeenth-century European legal thought held that enslaving prisoners of war was not only legal but more merciful than killing the captives outright. After the Pequot War (1636–1637), Massachusetts Bay colonists sold hundreds of Native Americans into slavery in the West Indies. A few years later, Dutch colonists in New Netherland (New York and New Jersey) enslaved Algonquians during both Governor Kieft's War (1641–1645) and the two Esopus Wars (1659–1663). The Dutch sent these war captives to English-settled Bermuda as well as Curaçao, a Dutch plantation colony in the southern Caribbean. An even larger number of enslaved Native Americans were captured during King Philip's War (1675–1676), an uprising against the encroachments of the New England colonies. Hundreds of Native Americans were bound and shipped into slavery. The New England colonists also tried to send enslaved Native Americans to Barbados, but the Barbados Assembly refused to import them for fear they would encourage rebellion.

In the eighteenth century, wars in Florida, South Carolina, and the Mississippi Valley produced even more enslaved Native Americans. Some wars emerged from contests between Native Americans and colonists for land, while others were manufactured as pretenses for acquiring captives. Some were not wars at all but merely illegal raids performed by slave traders. Historians estimate that between 24,000 and 51,000 Native Americans were forced into slavery throughout the southern colonies between 1670 and 1715.[4] While some of the enslaved Native Americans remained in the region, many were exported through Charles Town, South Carolina, to other ports in the British Atlantic—most likely to Barbados, Jamaica, and Bermuda. Many of the English colonists who wished to claim land in frontier territories were threatened by the violence inherent in the Native American slave trade. By the eighteenth century, colonial governments often discouraged the practice, although it never ceased entirely as long as slavery was, in general, a legal institution.

Enslaved Native Americans died quickly, mostly from disease, but others were murdered or died from starvation. The demands of growing plantation economies required a more reliable labor force, and the transatlantic slave trade provided such a workforce. European slavers transported millions of Africans across the ocean in a terrifying journey known as the Middle Passage. Writing at the end of the eighteenth century, Olaudah Equiano recalled the fearsomeness of the crew, the filth and gloom of the hold, the inadequate provisions allotted for the captives, and the desperation that drove some enslaved people to suicide. (Equiano claimed to have been born in Igboland in modern-day Nigeria, but he may have been born in colonial South Carolina, where he collected memories of the Middle Passage from African-born enslaved people.) In the same time period, Alexander Falconbridge, a slave ship surgeon, described the sufferings of enslaved Africans from shipboard infections and close quarters in the hold. Dysentery, known as "the bloody flux," left captives lying in pools of excrement. Chained in small spaces in the hold, enslaved people could lose so much skin and flesh from chafing against metal and timber that their bones protruded. Other sources detailed rapes, whippings, and diseases like smallpox and conjunctivitis aboard slave ships.[5]

"Middle" had various meanings in the Atlantic slave trade. For the captains and crews of slave ships, the Middle Passage was one leg in the maritime trade in sugar and other semifinished American goods, manufactured European commodities, and enslaved Africans. For the enslaved Africans, the Middle Passage was the middle leg of three distinct journeys from Africa to the Americas. First was an overland journey in Africa to a coastal slave-trading factory, often a trek of hundreds of miles. Second—and middle—was an oceanic trip lasting from one to six months in a

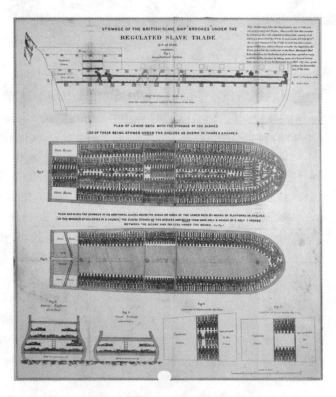

Slave ships transported 11–12 million Africans to destinations in North and South America, but it was not until the end of the 18th century that any regulation was introduced. The Brookes print dates to after the Regulated Slave Trade Act of 1788, but still shows enslaved Africans chained in rows using iron leg shackles. The slave ship Brookes was allowed to carry up to 454 enslaved people, allotting 6 feet (1.8 m) by 1 foot 4 inches (0.41 m) to each man; 5 feet 10 inches (1.78 m) by 1 foot 4 inches (0.41 m) to each woman, and 5 feet (1.5 m) by 1 foot 2 inches (0.36 m) to each child, but one slave trader alleged that before 1788, the ship carried as many as 609 enslaved Africans. *Stowage of the British slave ship* Brookes *under the regulated slave trade act of 1788*, 1789. Wikimedia.

slaver. Third was acculturation (known as "seasoning") and transportation to the American mine, plantation, or other location where new enslaved people were forced to labor.

The impact of the Middle Passage on the cultures of the Americas remains evident today. Many foods associated with Africans, such as cassava, were originally imported to West Africa as part of the slave trade and were then adopted by African cooks before being brought to the Americas, where they are still consumed. West African rhythms and melodies live in new forms today in music as varied as religious spirituals and synthesized drumbeats. African influences appear in the basket making and language of the Gullah people on the Carolina coastal islands.

Recent estimates count between eleven and twelve million Africans forced across the Atlantic between the sixteenth and nineteenth centuries, with about two million deaths at sea as well as an additional several million dying in the trade's overland African leg or during seasoning.[6] Conditions in all three legs of the slave trade were horrible, but the first abolitionists focused especially on the abuses of the Middle Passage.

Southern European trading empires like the Catalans and Aragonese were brought into contact with a Levantine commerce in sugar and enslaved laborers in the fourteenth and fifteenth centuries. Europeans made the first steps toward an Atlantic slave trade in the 1440s when Portuguese sailors landed in West Africa in search of gold, spices, and allies against the Muslims who dominated Mediterranean trade. Beginning in the 1440s, ship captains carried enslaved Africans to Portugal. These Africans were valued primarily as domestic servants, as peasants provided the primary agricultural labor force in Western Europe.[7] European expansion into the Americas introduced both settlers and European authorities to a new situation—an abundance of land and a scarcity of labor. Portuguese, Dutch, and English ships became the conduits for Africans forced to America. The western coast of Africa, the Gulf of Guinea, and the west-central coast were the sources of African captives. Wars of expansion and raiding parties produced captives who could be sold in coastal factories. African slave traders bartered for European finished goods such as beads, cloth, rum, firearms, and metal wares.

Slavers often landed in the British West Indies, where enslaved laborers were seasoned in places like Barbados. Charleston, South Carolina, became the leading entry point for the slave trade on the mainland. The founding of Charleston ("Charles Town" until the 1780s) in 1670 was viewed as a serious threat by the Spanish in neighboring Florida, who began construc-

The first trading post built on the Gulf of Guinea and the oldest European building southern of the Sahara, Elmina Castle was established as a trade settlement by the Portuguese in the fifteenth century. The fort became one of the largest and most important markets for enslaved Africans along the Atlantic slave trade. "View of the castle of Elmina on the north-west side, seen from the river. Located on the gold coast in Guinea," in *Atlas Blaeu van der Hem*, c. 1665–1668. Wikimedia.

tion of Castillo de San Marcos in St. Augustine as a response. In 1693 the Spanish king issued the Decree of Sanctuary, which granted freedom to enslaved people fleeing the English colonies if they converted to Catholicism and swore an oath of loyalty to Spain.[8] The presence of Africans who bore arms and served in the Spanish militia testifies to the different conceptions of race among the English and Spanish in America.

About 450,000 Africans landed in British North America, a relatively small portion of the eleven to twelve million victims of the trade.[9] As a proportion of the enslaved population, there were more enslaved women in North America than in other colonial enslaved populations. Enslaved African women also bore more children than their counterparts in the Caribbean or South America, facilitating the natural reproduction of enslaved people on the North American continent.[10] A 1662 Virginia law stated that an enslaved woman's children inherited the "condition" of their mother; other colonies soon passed similar statutes.[11] This economic strategy on the part of planters created a legal system in which all children born to enslaved women would be enslaved for life, whether the father was white or Black, enslaved or free.

Most fundamentally, the emergence of modern notions of race was closely related to the colonization of the Americas and the slave trade. African slave traders lacked a firm category of race that might have led them to think that they were selling their own people, in much the same way that Native Americans did not view other Indigenous groups as part of the same "race." Similarly, most English citizens felt no racial identification with the Irish or the even the Welsh. The modern idea of race as an inherited physical difference (most often skin color) that is used to support systems of oppression was new in the early modern Atlantic world.

In the early years of slavery, especially in the South, the distinction between indentured servants and enslaved people was initially unclear. In 1643, however, a law was passed in Virginia that made African women "tithable."[12] This, in effect, associated African women's work with difficult agricultural labor. There was no similar tax levied on white women; the law was an attempt to distinguish white women from African women. The English ideal was to have enough hired hands and servants working on a farm so that wives and daughters did not have to partake in manual labor. Instead, white women were expected to labor in dairy sheds, small gardens, and kitchens. Of course, because of the labor shortage in early America, white women did participate in field labor. But this idealized gendered division of labor contributed to the English conceiving of themselves as better than other groups who did not divide labor in this fashion, including the West Africans arriving in slave ships to the colonies. For many white colonists, the association of a gendered division of labor with Englishness provided a further justification for the enslavement and subordination of Africans.

Ideas about the rule of the household were informed by legal and customary understandings of marriage and the home in England. A man was expected to hold "paternal dominion" over his household, which included his wife, children, servants, and enslaved laborers. In contrast, enslaved people were not legally masters of a household and were therefore subject to the authority of the white enslaver. Marriages between enslaved people were not recognized in colonial law. Some enslaved men and women married "abroad"; that is, they married individuals who were not owned by the same enslaver and did not live on the same plantation. These husbands and wives had to travel miles at a time, typically only once a week on Sundays, to visit their spouses. Legal or religious authority did not protect these marriages, and enslavers could refuse to let their enslaved laborers visit a spouse, or even sell an enslaved person to a new enslaver hundreds of miles away from their spouse and children. Within the patriarchal and exploitative colonial environment, enslaved men and women struggled to establish families and communities.

III. Turmoil in Britain

Religious conflict plagued sixteenth-century England. While Spain plundered the New World and built an empire, Catholic and Protestant English monarchs vied for supremacy and attacked their opponents as heretics. Queen Elizabeth cemented Protestantism as the official religion of the realm, but questions endured as to what kind of Protestantism would hold sway. Many radical Protestants (often called "Puritans" by their critics) looked to the New World as an opportunity to create a beacon of Calvinist Christianity, while others continued the struggle in England. By the 1640s, political and economic conflicts between Parliament and the Crown merged with long-simmering religious tensions, made worse by a king who seemed sympathetic to Catholicism. The result was a bloody civil war. Colonists reacted in a variety of ways as England waged war on itself, but all were affected by these decades of turmoil.

Between 1629 and 1640 the absolute rule of Charles I caused considerable friction between the English Parliament and the king. Conflict erupted in 1640 when a Parliament called by Charles refused to grant him subsidies to suppress a rebellion in Scotland. The Irish rebelled the following year, and by 1642 strained relations between Charles and Parliament led to civil war in England. In 1649 Parliament won, Charles I was executed, and England became a republic and protectorate under Oliver Cromwell. These changes redefined England's relationship with its American colonies, as the new government under Cromwell attempted to consolidate its hold over its overseas territories.

In 1642, no permanent British North American colony was more than thirty-five years old. The Crown and various proprietors controlled most of the colonies, but settlers from Barbados to Maine enjoyed a great deal of independence. This was especially true in Massachusetts Bay, where Puritan settlers governed themselves according to the colony's 1629 charter. Trade in tobacco and naval stores tied the colonies to England economically, as did religion and political culture, but in general the English government left the colonies to their own devices.

The English Revolution of the 1640s forced settlers in America to reconsider their place within the empire. Older colonies like Virginia and proprietary colonies like Maryland sympathized with the Crown. Newer colonies like Massachusetts Bay, populated by religious dissenters taking part in the Great Migration of the 1630s, tended to favor Parliament. Yet during the war the colonies remained neutral, fearing that support for either side could involve them in war. Even Massachusetts Bay, which nurtured ties to radical Protestants in Parliament, remained neutral.

Charles's execution in 1649 challenged American neutrality. Six colonies, including Virginia and Barbados, declared allegiance to the dead monarch's son, Charles II. Parliament responded with an act in 1650 that leveled an economic embargo on the rebelling colonies, forcing them to accept Parliament's authority. Parliament argued that America had been "planted at the Cost, and settled" by the English nation, and that it, as the embodiment of that commonwealth, possessed ultimate jurisdiction

King Charles I, pictured with the blue sash of the Order of the Garter, listens to his commanders detail the strategy for what would be the first pitched battle of the First English Civil War. As all previous constitutional compromises between King Charles and Parliament had broken down, both sides raised large armies in the hopes of forcing the other side to concede their position. The Battle of Edgehill ended with no clear winner, leading to a prolonged war of over four years and an even longer series of wars (known generally as the English Civil War) that eventually established the Commonwealth of England in 1649. Charles Landseer, *The Eve of the Battle of Edge Hill*, 1642, 1845. Wikimedia.

England found itself in crisis after the death of Oliver Cromwell in 1658, leading in time to the reestablishment of the monarchy. On his thirtieth birthday (May 29, 1660), Charles II sailed from the Netherlands to his restoration after nine years in exile. He was received in London to great acclaim, as depicted in this contemporary painting. Lieve Verschuler, *The Arrival of King Charles II of England in Rotterdam, 24 May 1660*. c. 1660–1665. Wikimedia.

over the colonies.[13] It followed up the embargo with the Navigation Act of 1651, which compelled merchants in every colony to ship goods directly to England in English ships. Parliament sought to bind the colonies more closely to England and prevent other European nations, especially the Dutch, from interfering with its American possessions.

The monarchy was restored with Charles II, but popular suspicions of the Crown's Catholic and French sympathies lingered. Charles II's suppression of the religious and press freedoms that flourished during the civil war years demonstrated the Crown's desire to reimpose order and royal rule. But it was the openly Catholic and pro-French policies of his successor, James II, that once again led to the overthrow of the monarchy in 1688. In that year a group of bishops and Parliamentarians offered the English throne to the Dutch Prince William of Holland and his English bride, Mary, the daughter of James II. This coup was called the Glorious Revolution and was accomplished with little bloodshed in England but considerable warfare in Ireland.

In the decades before the Glorious Revolution, English colonists experienced religious and political conflict that reflected transformations in Europe as well as distinctly colonial conditions. In the 1670s and early

1680s, King Charles II tightened English control over North America and the West Indies through the creation of new colonies, the imposition of new Navigation Acts, and the establishment of a new executive council called the Lords of Trade and Plantations.[14] As imperial officials attempted to curb colonists' autonomy, threats from Native Americans and New France on the continent led many colonists to believe that Native Americans and Catholics sought to destroy English America. In New England an uprising beginning in 1675 led by the Wampanoag leader Metacom, or King Philip as the English called him, seemed to confirm these fears. Conflicts with Native Americans helped trigger the revolt against royal authorities known as Bacon's Rebellion in Virginia the following year.

James II worked to place the colonies on firmer administrative and defensive footing by creating the Dominion of New England in 1686. The Dominion consolidated the New England colonies, New York, and New Jersey into one administrative unit to counter French Canada, but colonists strongly resented the loss of their individual provinces. The Dominion's governor, Sir Edmund Andros, did little to assuage fears of arbitrary power when he forced colonists into military service for a campaign against the Native Americans in Maine in early 1687. Impressment into military service was a long-standing grievance among English commoners that was transplanted to the colonies.

In England, James's push for religious toleration of Catholics and dissenters brought him into conflict with Parliament and the Anglican establishment in England. After the 1688 invasion by the Protestant William of Orange, James fled to France. When colonists learned imperial officials in Boston and New York City attempted to keep news of the Glorious Revolution secret, simmering hostilities toward provincial leaders burst into the open. In Massachusetts, New York, and Maryland, colonists overthrew colonial governments as local social antagonisms fused with popular animosity toward imperial rule. Colonists in America quickly declared allegiance to the new monarchs. They did so in part to maintain order in their respective colonies. As one Virginia official explained, if there was "no King in England, there was no Government here."[15] A declaration of allegiance was therefore a means toward stability.

More importantly, colonists declared for William and Mary because they believed that their ascension marked the rejection of absolutism and confirmed the centrality of Protestantism and liberty in English life. Settlers joined in the revolution by overthrowing the Dominion government, restoring the provinces to their previous status, and forcing out the Catholic-dominated Maryland government. They launched several assaults against French Canada as part of King William's War and rejoiced in Parliament's 1689 passage of a Bill of Rights, which curtailed the power of the monarchy and cemented Protestantism in England. For English colonists, it was indeed a "glorious" revolution as it united them in a Protestant empire that stood counter to Catholic tyranny, absolutism, and French power.

IV. New Colonies

Despite the turmoil in Britain, colonial settlement grew considerably throughout the seventeenth century, and several new settlements joined the two original colonies of Virginia and Massachusetts.

In 1632, Charles I set a tract of about 12 million acres of land at the northern tip of the Chesapeake Bay aside for a second colony in America. Named for the new monarch's queen, Maryland was granted to Charles's friend and political ally, Cecilius Calvert, the second Lord Baltimore. Calvert hoped to gain additional wealth from the colony, as well as to create a haven for fellow Catholics. In England, many of that faith found themselves harassed by the Protestant majority and more than a few considered migrating to America. Charles I, a Catholic sympathizer, was in favor of Lord Baltimore's plan to create a colony that would demonstrate that Catholics and Protestants could live together peacefully.

In late 1633, both Protestant and Catholic settlers left England for the Chesapeake, arriving in Maryland in March 1634. Men of middling means found greater opportunities in Maryland, which prospered as a tobacco colony without the growing pains suffered by Virginia.

Unfortunately, Lord Baltimore's hopes of a diverse Christian colony were thwarted. Most colonists were Protestants relocating from Virginia. Many of these Protestants were radical Quakers and Puritans who were frustrated with Virginia's efforts to force adherence to the Anglican Church, also known as the Church of England. In 1650, Puritans revolted, setting up a new government that prohibited both Catholicism and Anglicanism. Governor William Stone attempted to put down the revolt in 1655 but was not successful until 1658. Two years after the Glorious Revolution (1688–1689), the Calverts lost control of Maryland and the province became a royal colony.

Religion was a motivating factor in the creation of several other colonies as well, including the New England colonies of Connecticut and Rhode Island. The settlements that would eventually compose Connecticut grew out of settlements in Saybrook and New Haven. Thomas Hooker and his congregation left Massachusetts for Connecticut because the area around Boston was becoming increasingly crowded. The Connecticut River Valley was large enough for more cattle and agriculture. In June 1636, Hooker led one hundred people and a variety of livestock in settling an area they called Newtown (later Hartford).

New Haven Colony had a more directly religious origin, as the founders attempted a new experiment in Puritanism. In 1638, John Davenport, Theophilus Eaton, and other supporters of the Puritan faith settled in the Quinnipiac River Valley (New Haven) area of Connecticut. In 1643 New Haven Colony was officially organized, with Eaton named governor. In the early 1660s, three men who had signed the death warrant for Charles I were concealed in New Haven. This did not win the colony any favors, and it became increasingly poorer and weaker. In 1665, New Haven was absorbed into Connecticut, but its singular religious tradition endured with the creation of Yale College.

Religious radicals similarly founded Rhode Island. After his exile from Massachusetts, Roger Williams created a settlement called Providence in 1636. He negotiated for the land with the local Narragansett sachems Canonicus and Miantonomi. Williams and his fellow settlers agreed on an egalitarian constitution and established religious and political freedom in the colony. The following year, another Massachusetts exile, Anne Hutchinson, and her followers settled near Providence. Others soon arrived, and the colony was granted a charter by Parliament in 1644. Persistently independent and with republican sympathies, the settlers refused a governor and instead elected a president and council. These separate communities passed laws abolishing witchcraft trials, imprisonment for debt and, in 1652, chattel slavery. Because of the colony's policy of toleration, it became a haven for Quakers, Jews, and other persecuted religious groups. In 1663, Charles II granted the colony a royal charter establishing the colony of Rhode Island and Providence Plantations.

Until the middle of the seventeenth century, the English neglected the area between Virginia and New England despite obvious environmental advantages. The climate was healthier than the Chesapeake and more temperate than New England. The mid-Atlantic had three highly navigable rivers: the Susquehanna, the Delaware, and the Hudson. The Swedes and Dutch established their own colonies in the region: New Sweden in the Delaware Valley and New Netherland in the Hudson Valley.

Compared to other Dutch colonies around the globe, the settlements on the Hudson River were relatively minor. The Dutch West India Company realized that in order to secure its fur trade in the area, it needed to establish a greater presence in New Netherland. Toward this end, the company formed New Amsterdam on Manhattan Island in 1625.

Although the Dutch extended religious tolerance to those who settled in New Netherland, the population remained small. This left the colony vulnerable to English attack during the 1650s and 1660s, resulting in the handover of New Netherland to England in 1664. The new colony of New York was named for the proprietor, James, the Duke of York, brother to Charles II and funder of the expedition against the Dutch in 1664. New York was briefly reconquered by the Netherlands in 1667, and class and ethnic conflicts in New York City contributed to the rebellion against English authorities during the Glorious Revolution of 1688–1689. Colonists of Dutch ancestry resisted assimilation into English culture well into the eighteenth century, prompting New York Anglicans to note that the colony was "rather like a conquered foreign province."[16]

After the acquisition of New Netherland, Charles II and the Duke of York wished to strengthen English control over the Atlantic seaboard. In theory, this was to better tax the colonies; in practice, the awarding of the new proprietary colonies of New Jersey, Pennsylvania, and the Carolinas was a payoff of debts and political favors.

In 1664, the Duke of York granted the area between the Hudson and Delaware rivers to two English noblemen. These lands were split into two distinct colonies, East Jersey and West Jersey. One of West Jersey's proprietors included William Penn. The ambitious Penn wanted his own, larger colony, the lands for which would be granted by both Charles II and the Duke of York. Pennsylvania consisted of about forty-five thousand square miles west of the Delaware River and the former New Sweden. Penn was a member of the Society of Friends, otherwise known as Quakers, and he intended his colony to be a "colony of Heaven for the children of Light."[17] Like New England's aspirations to be a City Upon a Hill, Pennsylvania was to be an example of godliness. But Penn's dream was to create not a colony of unity but rather a colony of harmony. He noted in 1685 that "the people are a collection of diverse nations in Europe, as French, Dutch, Germans, Swedes, Danes, Finns, Scotch, and English; and of the last equal to all the rest."[18] Because Quakers in Pennsylvania extended to others in America the same rights they had demanded for themselves in England, the colony attracted a diverse collection of migrants. Slavery was particularly troublesome for some pacifist Quakers of Pennsylvania on the grounds that it required violence. In 1688, members of the Society of Friends in Germantown, outside Philadelphia, signed a petition protesting the institution of slavery among fellow Quakers.

The Pennsylvania soil did not lend itself to the slave-based agriculture of the Chesapeake, but other colonies depended heavily on slavery from their very foundations. The creation of the colony of Carolina, later divided into North and South Carolina and Georgia, was part of Charles II's scheme to strengthen the English hold on the Eastern Seaboard and pay off political and cash debts. The Lords Proprietor of Carolina—eight powerful favorites of the king—used the model of the colonization of Barbados to settle the area. In 1670, three ships of colonists from Barbados arrived at the mouth of the Ashley River, where they founded Charles Town. This defiance of Spanish claims to the area signified England's growing confidence as a colonial power.

To attract colonists, the Lords Proprietor offered alluring incentives: religious tolerance, political representation by assembly, exemption from fees, and large land grants. These incentives worked, and Carolina grew quickly, attracting not only middling farmers and artisans but also wealthy planters. Colonists who could pay their own way to Carolina were granted 150 acres per family member. The Lords Proprietor allowed for enslaved people to be counted as members of the family. This encouraged the creation of large rice and indigo plantations along the coast of Carolina; these were more stable commodities than deerskins and enslaved Native Americans. Because of the size of Carolina, the authority of the Lords Proprietor was especially weak in the northern reaches on Albemarle Sound. This region had been settled by Virginians in the 1650s and

Henry Popple, *A map of the British Empire in America with the French and Spanish settlements adjacent thereto*, 1733. Library of Congress.

was increasingly resistant to Carolina authority. As a result, the Lords Proprietor founded the separate province of North Carolina in 1691.[19]

V. Riot, Rebellion, and Revolt

The seventeenth century saw the establishment and solidification of the British North American colonies, but this process did not occur peacefully. English settlements on the continent were rocked by explosions of violence, including the Pequot War, the Mystic massacre, King Philip's War, the Susquehannock War, Bacon's Rebellion, and the Pueblo Revolt.

In May 1637, an armed contingent of English Puritans from Massachusetts Bay, Plymouth, and Connecticut colonies trekked into Native American territory that was claimed by New England. Referring to themselves as the "Sword of the Lord," this military force intended to attack "that insolent and barbarous Nation, called the Pequots." In the resulting violence, Puritans put the Mystic community to the torch, beginning with the north and south ends of the town. As Pequot men, women, and children tried to escape the blaze, other soldiers waited with swords and guns. One commander estimated that of the "four hundred souls in this Fort . . . not above five of them escaped out of our hands," although another counted near "six or seven hundred" dead. In a span of less than two months, the English Puritans boasted that the Pequot "were drove out of their country, and slain by the sword, to the number of fifteen hundred."[20]

The foundations of the war lay within the rivalry between the Pequot, the Narragansett, and the Mohegan, who battled for control of the fur and wampum trades in the northeast. This rivalry eventually forced the English and Dutch to choose sides. The war remained a conflict of Native interests and initiative, especially as the Mohegan hedged their bets on the English and reaped the rewards that came with displacing the Pequot.

Victory over the Pequot not only provided security and stability for the English colonies but also propelled the Mohegan to new heights of political and economic influence as the primary power in New England. Ironically, history seemingly repeated itself later in the century as the Mohegan, desperate for a remedy to their diminishing strength, joined the Wampanoag war against the Puritans. This produced a more violent conflict in 1675 known as King Philip's War, bringing a decisive end to Native American power in New England.

In the winter of 1675, the body of John Sassamon, a Christian, Harvard-educated Wampanoag, was found under the ice of a nearby pond. A fellow Christian Native American informed English authorities that three warriors under the local sachem named Metacom, known to the English as King Philip, had killed Sassamon, who had previously accused Metacom of planning an offensive against the English. The three alleged killers appeared before the Plymouth court in June 1675. They were found guilty of murder and executed. Several weeks later, a group of Wampanoags killed nine English colonists in the town of Swansea.

Metacom—like most other New England sachems—had entered into covenants of "submission" to various colonies, viewing the arrangements as relationships of protection and reciprocity rather than subjugation. Native Americans and the English lived, traded, worshipped, and arbitrated disputes in close proximity before 1675, but the execution of three of Metacom's men at the hands of Plymouth Colony epitomized what many Native Americans viewed as the growing inequality of that relationship. The Wampanoags who attacked Swansea may have sought to restore balance, or to retaliate for the recent executions. Neither they nor anyone else sought to engulf all of New England in war, but that is precisely what happened. Authorities in Plymouth sprang into action, enlisting help from the neighboring colonies of Connecticut and Massachusetts.

Metacom and his followers eluded colonial forces in the summer of 1675, striking more Plymouth towns as they moved northwest. Some groups joined his forces, while others remained neutral or supported the English. The war badly divided some Indigenous communities. Metacom himself had little control over events as panic and violence spread throughout New England in the autumn of 1675. English mistrust of neutral Native Americans, sometimes accompanied by demands that they surrender their weapons, pushed many into open war. By the end of 1675, most of the Native Americans of present-day western and central Massachusetts had entered the war, laying waste to nearby English towns like Deerfield, Hadley, and Brookfield. Hapless colonial forces, spurning the military assistance of allies such as the Mohegans, proved unable to locate more mobile Native communities or intercept attacks.

The English compounded their problems by attacking the powerful and neutral Narragansett of Rhode Island in December 1675. In an action called the Great Swamp Fight, 1,000 Englishmen put the main Narragansett village to the torch, gunning down as many as 1,000 Narragansett men, women, and children as they fled the maelstrom. The surviving Narragansett joined those already fighting the English. Between

February and April 1676, Native forces devastated a succession of English towns closer and closer to Boston.

In the spring of 1676, the tide turned. The New England colonies took the advice of men like Benjamin Church, who urged the greater use of Native allies, including Pequot and Mohegan, to find and fight the mobile warriors. As the combatants were unable to plant crops and forced to live off the land, their will to continue the struggle waned as companies of English and Native allies pursued them. Growing numbers of fighters fled the region, switched sides, or surrendered in the spring and summer. The English sold many of the latter group into slavery. Colonial forces finally caught up with Metacom in August 1676, and the sachem was slain by a Christian Native American fighting with the English.

The war permanently altered the political and demographic landscape of New England. Between eight hundred and one thousand English and at least three thousand Native Americans perished in the fourteen-month conflict. Thousands of others fled the region or were sold into slavery. In 1670, Native Americans comprised roughly 25 percent of New England's population; a decade later, they made up perhaps 10 percent.[21] The war's brutality also encouraged a growing hatred of all Indigenous people among many New England colonists. Though the fighting ceased in 1676, the bitter legacy of King Philip's War lived on.

Sixteen years later, New England faced a new fear: the supernatural. Beginning in early 1692 and culminating in 1693, Salem Town, Salem Village, Ipswich, and Andover all tried women and men as witches. Paranoia swept through the region, and fourteen women and six men were executed. Five other individuals died in prison. The causes of the trials are numerous and include local rivalries, political turmoil, enduring trauma of war, faulty legal procedure where accusing others became a method of self-defense, or perhaps even low-level environmental contamination. Enduring tensions with Native people framed the events, however, and a Native American or African woman named Tituba enslaved by the local minister was at the center of the tragedy.[22]

Native American communities in Virginia had already been decimated by wars in 1622 and 1644. But a new clash arose in Virginia the same year that New Englanders crushed Metacom's forces. This conflict, known as Bacon's Rebellion, grew out of tensions between Native Americans and English settlers as well as tensions between wealthy English landowners and the poor settlers who continually pushed west into territory controlled by Native Americans.

Bacon's Rebellion began, appropriately enough, with an argument over a pig. In the summer of 1675, a group of Doeg people visited Thomas Mathew on his plantation in northern Virginia to collect a debt that he owed them. When Mathew refused to pay, they took some of his pigs to settle the debt. This "theft" sparked a series of raids and counter-raids. The Susquehannock people were caught in the crossfire when the militia mistook them for Doegs, leaving fourteen dead. A similar pattern of escalating violence then repeated: the Susquehannocks retaliated by killing colonists in Virginia and Maryland, and the English marshaled their forces and laid siege to the Susquehannock. The conflict became uglier after the militia executed a delegation of Susquehannock ambassadors under a flag of truce. A few parties of warriors intent on revenge launched raids along the frontier and killed dozens of English colonists.

The sudden and unpredictable violence of the Susquehannock War triggered a political crisis in Virginia. Panicked colonists fled en masse from the vulnerable frontiers, flooding into coastal communities and begging the government for help. But the cautious governor, Sir William Berkeley, did not send an army after the Susquehannock. He worried that a full-scale war would inevitably drag other Native Americans into the conflict, turning allies into deadly enemies. Berkeley therefore insisted on a defensive strategy centered on a string of new fortifications to protect the frontier and strict instructions not to antagonize friendly Native Americans. It was a sound military policy but a public relations disaster. Terrified colonists condemned Berkeley. Building contracts for the forts went to Berkeley's wealthy friends, who conveniently decided that their own plantations were the most strategically vital. Colonists denounced the government as a corrupt band of oligarchs more interested in lining their pockets than protecting the people.

By the spring of 1676, a small group of frontier colonists took matters into their own hands. Naming the charismatic young Nathaniel Bacon as their leader, these self-styled "volunteers" proclaimed that they took up arms in defense of their homes and families. They took pains to assure Berkeley that they intended no disloyalty, but Berkeley feared a coup and branded the volunteers as traitors. Berkeley finally mobilized an army— not to pursue Susquehannock, but to crush the colonists' rebellion. His drastic response catapulted a small band of vigilantes into full-fledged rebels whose survival necessitated bringing down the colonial government.

Bacon and the rebels stalked the Susquehannock as well as friendly Native Americans like the Pamunkeys and the Occaneechi. The rebels became convinced that there was a massive Native American conspiracy to destroy the English. Berkeley's stubborn persistence in defending friendly Natives and destroying the rebels led Bacon to accuse the governor of conspiring with a "powerful cabal" of elite planters and with "the protected and darling Indians" to slaughter his English enemies.[23]

In the early summer of 1676, Bacon's neighbors elected him their burgess and sent him to Jamestown to confront Berkeley. Though the House of Burgesses enacted pro-rebel reforms like prohibiting the sale of arms to Native Americans and restoring suffrage rights to landless freemen, Bacon's supporters remained unsatisfied. Berkeley soon had Bacon arrested and forced the rebel leader into the humiliating position of publicly begging forgiveness for his treason. Bacon swallowed this indignity but turned the tables by gathering an army of followers and surrounding the State House, demanding that Berkeley name him the general of Virginia and bless his universal war against Native Americans. Instead, the seventy-year-old governor stepped onto the field in front of the crowd of angry men, unafraid, and called Bacon a traitor to his face. Then he tore open his shirt and dared Bacon to shoot him in the heart, if he was so intent on overthrowing his government. "Here!" he shouted before the crowd, "shoot me, before God, it is a fair mark. Shoot!" When Bacon hesitated, Berkeley drew his sword and challenged the young man to a duel, knowing that Bacon could neither back down from a challenge without looking like a coward nor kill him without making himself into a villain. Instead, Bacon resorted to bluster and blasphemy. Threatening to slaughter the entire assembly if necessary, he cursed, "God damn my blood, I came for a commission, and a commission I will have before I go."[24] Berkeley stood defiant, but the cowed burgesses finally prevailed upon him to grant Bacon's request. Virginia had its general, and Bacon had his war.

After this dramatic showdown in Jamestown, Bacon's Rebellion quickly spiraled out of control. Berkeley slowly rebuilt his loyalist army, forcing Bacon to divert his attention to the coasts and away from the Native Americans. But most rebels were more interested in defending their homes and families than in fighting other Englishmen, and they deserted in droves at every rumor of Native activity. In many places, the "rebellion" was less an organized military campaign than a collection of local grievances and personal rivalries. Both rebels and loyalists smelled the opportunities for plunder, seizing their rivals' estates and confiscating their property.

For a small but vocal minority of rebels, however, the rebellion became an ideological revolution: Sarah Drummond, wife of rebel leader

William Drummond, advocated independence from England and the formation of a Virginian Republic, declaring "I fear the power of England no more than a broken straw." Others struggled for a different kind of independence: white servants and enslaved Black people fought side by side in both armies after promises of freedom for military service. Everyone accused everyone else of treason, rebels and loyalists switched sides depending on which side was winning, and the whole Chesapeake disintegrated into a confused melee of secret plots and grandiose crusades, sordid vendettas and desperate gambits, with Native Americans and English alike struggling for supremacy and survival. One Virginian summed up the rebellion as "our time of anarchy."[25]

The rebels steadily lost ground and ultimately suffered a crushing defeat. Bacon died of typhus in the autumn of 1676, and his successors surrendered to Berkeley in January 1677. Berkeley summarily tried and executed the rebel leadership in a succession of kangaroo courts-martial. Before long, however, the royal fleet arrived, bearing over one thousand red-coated troops and a royal commission of investigation charged with restoring order to the colony. The commissioners replaced the governor and dispatched Berkeley to London, where he died in disgrace.

But the conclusion of Bacon's Rebellion was uncertain, and the maintenance of order remained precarious for years afterward. The garrison of royal troops discouraged both incursion by Native Americans and insurrection by discontented colonists, allowing the king to continue profiting from tobacco revenues. The end of armed resistance did not mean a resolution to the underlying tensions destabilizing colonial society. Native Americans inside Virginia remained an embattled minority, and those outside Virginia remained a terrifying threat. Elite planters continued to grow rich by exploiting their indentured servants and marginalizing small farmers. Most Virginians continued to resent their exploitation with a simmering fury. Virginia legislators did recognize the extent of popular hostility toward colonial rule, however, and improved the social and political conditions of poor white Virginians in the years after the rebellion. During the same period, the increasing availability of enslaved workers through the Atlantic slave trade contributed to planters' large-scale adoption of slave labor in the Chesapeake.

Just a few years after Bacon's Rebellion, the Spanish experienced their own tumult in the area of contemporary New Mexico. The Spanish had been maintaining control partly by suppressing Native American beliefs. Friars aggressively enforced Catholic practice, burning native idols and masks and other sacred objects and banishing traditional spiritual

Built sometime between 1000 and 1450 CE, the Taos Pueblo located near modern-day Taos, New Mexico, functioned as a base for the leader Popé during the Pueblo Revolt. Luca Galuzzi (photographer), Taos Pueblo, 2007. Wikimedia. Creative Commons Attribution-Share Alike 2.5 Generic.

practices. In 1680, the Puebloan religious leader Popé, who had been arrested and whipped for "sorcery" five years earlier, led various Puebloan groups in rebellion. Several thousand Puebloan warriors razed the Spanish countryside and besieged Santa Fe. They killed four hundred, including twenty-one Franciscan priests, and allowed two thousand other Spaniards and Christian Puebloans to flee. It was perhaps the greatest act of Indigenous resistance in North American history.

In New Mexico, the Puebloans eradicated all traces of Spanish rule. They destroyed churches and threw themselves into rivers to wash away their Christian baptisms. "The God of the Christians is dead," Popé proclaimed, and the Puebloans resumed traditional spiritual practices.[26] The Spanish were exiled for twelve years. They returned in 1692, weakened, to reconquer New Mexico.

The late seventeenth century was a time of great violence and turmoil. Bacon's Rebellion turned white Virginians against one another, King Philip's War shattered Native American resistance in New England, and the Pueblo Revolt struck a major blow to Spanish power. It would take several more decades before similar patterns erupted in Carolina and Pennsylvania, but the constant advance of European settlements provoked conflict in these areas as well.

In 1715, the Yamasee, Carolina's closest allies and most lucrative trading partners, turned against the colony and nearly destroyed it entirely. Writing from Carolina to London, the settler George Rodd believed the Yamasee wanted nothing less than "the whole continent and to kill us or chase us all out."[27] The Yamasee would eventually advance within miles of Charles Town.

The Yamasee War's first victims were traders. The governor had dispatched two of the colony's most prominent men to visit and pacify a Yamasee council following rumors of native unrest. The Yamasee quickly proved the fears well founded by killing the emissaries and every English trader they could corral.

The Yamasee, like many other Native Americans, had come to depend on English courts as much as the flintlock rifles and ammunition that traders offered them for enslaved laborers and animal skins. Feuds between English agents had crippled the court of trade and shut down all diplomacy, provoking the violent Yamasee reprisal. Most villages in the southeast sent at least a few warriors to join what quickly became a cause against the colony that united various Native American peoples.

Yet Charles Town ultimately survived the onslaught by preserving one crucial alliance with the Cherokee. By 1717, the conflict had largely dried up, and the only remaining menace was roaming Yamasee bands operating from Spanish Florida. Most Native American villages returned to terms with Carolina and resumed trading. The lucrative trade in enslaved Native Americans, however, which had consumed fifty thousand souls in five decades, largely dwindled after the war. The danger was too high for traders, and the colonies discovered even greater profits by importing Africans to work new rice plantations. Herein lies the birth of the Old South, that expanse of plantations that created untold wealth and misery. Native Americans retained the strongest militaries in the region, but they never again threatened the survival of English colonies.

If a colony existed where peace with Indigenous people might continue, it would be Pennsylvania. At the colony's founding, William Penn created a Quaker religious imperative for the peaceful treatment of Native Americans. While Penn never doubted that the English would appropriate Native lands, he demanded that his colonists obtain these territories through purchase rather than violence. Though Pennsylvanians maintained relatively peaceful relations with Native Americans, increased immigration and booming land speculation increased the demand for land. Coercive and fraudulent methods of negotiation became increasingly prominent. The Walking Purchase of 1737 was emblematic of both colonists' desire for cheap land and the changing relationship between Pennsylvanians and their Native neighbors.

Through treaty negotiation in 1737, Native Delaware leaders agreed to sell Pennsylvania all of the land that a man could walk in a day and a half, a common measurement used by Delawares in evaluating distances. John and Thomas Penn, joined by the land speculator and longtime friend of the Penns James Logan, hired a team of skilled runners to complete the "walk" on a prepared trail. The runners traveled from Wrightstown to the present-day town of Jim Thorpe, and proprietary officials then drew the new boundary line perpendicular to the runners' route, extending northeast to the Delaware River. The colonial government thus measured out a tract much larger than the Delaware had originally intended to sell, roughly 1,200 square miles. As a result, Delaware-proprietary relations suffered. Many Delaware left the lands in question and migrated westward to join Shawnee and other Delaware already living in the Ohio Valley. There they established diplomatic and trade relationships with the French. Memories of the suspect purchase endured into the 1750s and became a chief point of contention between the Pennsylvanian government and the Delaware during the upcoming Seven Years' War.[28]

VI. Conclusion

The seventeenth century saw the creation and maturation of Britain's North American colonies. Colonists warred against unforgiving climates, imperial intrigue, and Native Americans. They did so largely through ruthless expressions of power. Colonists attacked Native Americans, provoked European rivals, and joined a highly lucrative transatlantic economy rooted in slavery. After surviving a century of desperation and war, British North American colonists fashioned increasingly complex societies with unique religious cultures, economic ties, and political traditions. These societies would come to shape not only North America but soon the entirety of the Atlantic World.

VII. Reference Material

This chapter was edited by Daniel Johnson, with content contributions by Gregory Ablavsky, James Ambuske, Carolyn Arena, L. D. Burnett, Lori Daggar, Daniel Johnson, Hendrick Isom, D. Andrew Johnson, Matthew Kruer, Joseph Locke,

Samantha Miller, Melissa Morris, Bryan Rindfleisch, Emily Romeo, John Saillant, Ian Saxine, Marie Stango, Luke Willert, and Ben Wright.

Recommended citation: Gregory Ablavsky et al., "British North America," Daniel Johnson, ed., in *The American Yawp*, eds. Joseph Locke and Ben Wright (Stanford, CA: Stanford University Press, 2019).

NOTES TO CHAPTER 3

1. Edgar Legare Pennington, "The Reverend Francis Le Jau's Work Among Indians and Negro Slaves," *Journal of Southern History*, 1, no. 4 (November 1935): 442–458.

2. William Waller Hening, *Statutes at Large; Being a Collection of all the Laws of Virginia*, Vol. 2 (Richmond, VA: Samuel Pleasants, 1809–1823), 170, 260, 266, 270.

3. Captain Thomas Phillips, "A Journal of a Voyage Made in the *Hannibal* of London, 16," in *Documents Illustrative of the Slave Trade to America: Volume 1, 1441–1700*, ed. Elizabeth Donnan (New York: Octagon Books, 1969), 403.

4. Alan Gallay, *The Indian Slave Trade: The Rise of the English Empire in the American South 1670–1717* (New Haven, CT: Yale University Press, 2002), 299.

5. Alexander Falconbridge, *An Account of the Slave Trade on the Coast of Africa* (London: J. Phillips, 1788).

6. Phillip Curtin estimated that 9 million Africans were carried across the Atlantic. Joseph E. Inikori's figure estimated 15 million, and Patrick Manning estimated 12 million transported with 10.5 million surviving the voyage. See Phillip D. Curtin, *The Atlantic Slave Trade: A Census* (Madison: University of Wisconsin Press, 1969); Joseph E. Inikori, "Measuring the Atlantic Slave Trade: An Assessment of Curtin and Anstey," *Journal of Africa* 17 (1976): 197–223; and Patrick Manning, "Historical Datasets on Africa and the African Atlantic," *Journal of Comparative Economics* 40, no. 4 (2012): 604–607.

7. Paul E. Lovejoy, *Transformations in Slavery: A History of Slavery in Africa* (Cambridge, UK: Cambridge University Press, 2000), 36.

8. Jane Landers, "Slavery in the Lower South," *OAH Magazine of History* 17, no. 3 (2003): 23–27.

9. Lynn Dumenil, ed., *The Oxford Encyclopedia of American Social History* (New York: Oxford University Press, 2012), 512.

10. "Facts about the Slave Trade and Slavery," Gilder Lehrman Institute of American History. https://www.gilderlehrman.org/history-by-era/slavery-and-anti -slavery/resources/facts-about-slave-trade-and-slavery, accessed April 23, 2018.

11. Willie Lee Nichols Rose, ed., *A Documentary History of Slavery in North America* (Athens: University of Georgia Press, 1999), 19.

12. Stephanie M. H. Camp, *Closer to Freedom: Enslaved Women and Everyday Resistance in the Plantation South* (Chapel Hill: University of North Carolina Press, 2004), 63–64.

13. John H. Elliott, *Empires of the Atlantic World: Britain and Spain in America, 1492–1830* (New Haven, CT: Yale University Press, 2006), 148–49.

14. Paul Kléber Monod, *Imperial Island: A History of Britain and Its Empire, 1660–1837* (Malden, MA: Wiley-Blackwell, 2009), 80.

15. Owen Stanwood, "Rumours and Rebellions in the English Atlantic World, 1688–9," in *The Final Crisis of the Stuart Monarchy: The Revolutions of 1688–91 in Their British, Atlantic and European Contexts*, eds. Tim Harris and Steven Taylor (Woodbridge, UK: Boydell Press, 2013), 214.

16. Joyce D. Goodfriend, *Before the Melting Pot: Society and Culture in Colonial New York City, 1664–1730* (Princeton, NJ: Princeton University Press, 1992), 54.

17. Quoted in David Hackett Fischer, *Albion's Seed: Four British Folkways in America* (New York: Oxford University Press, 1989), 459.

18. Albert Cook Myers, ed., *Narratives of Early Pennsylvania, West New Jersey, and Delaware, 1630–1707* (New York: Scribner, 1912), 260.

19. Noeleen McIlvenna, *A Very Mutinous People: The Struggle for North Carolina, 1660–1713* (Chapel Hill: University of North Carolina Press, 2009).

20. John Mason, *A Brief History of the Pequot War (1736)* (Boston: S. Kneeland and T. Green, 1736). http://digitalcommons.unl.edu/cgi/viewcontent.cgi?article=1042&context=etas.

21. James David Drake, *King Philip's War: Civil War in New England, 1675–1676* (Amherst: University of Massachusetts Press, 1999), 169.

22. Paul Boyer and Stephen Nissenbaum, *Salem Possessed: The Social Origins of Witchcraft* (Cambridge, MA: Harvard University Press, 1993). For more on Tituba, see Elaine G. Breslaw, *Tituba, Reluctant Witch of Salem: Devilish Indians and Puritan Fantasies* (New York: New York University Press, 1996).

23. Nathaniel Bacon, "Manifesto (1676)," in *The English Literatures of America: 1500–1800*, ed. Myra Jehlen and Michael Warner (New York: Routledge, 1996), 226.

24. Mary Newton Stanard, *The Story of Bacon's Rebellion* (New York: Neale, 1907), 77–78.

25. Quoted in April Lee Hatfield, *Atlantic Virginia: Intercolonial Relations in the Seventeenth Century* (Philadelphia: University of Pennsylvania Press, 2004), 286 n. 27.

26. Robert Silverberg, *The Pueblo Revolt* (Lincoln: University of Nebraska Press, 1994), 131.

27. *Calendar of State Papers, Colonial Series, America and West Indies, August 1714–December 1715* (London: Kraus Reprint, 1928), 168–169.

28. Steven Craig Harper, *Promised Land: Penn's Holy Experiment, The Walking Purchase, and the Dispossession of Delawares, 1600–1763* (Bethlehem, PA: Lehigh University Press, 2006).

RECOMMENDED READING

Blackburn, Robin. *The Making of New World Slavery: From the Baroque to the Modern, 1492–1800*. London: Verso, 1997.

Braddick, Michael. *God's Fury, England's Fire: A New History of the English Civil Wars*. New York: Penguin, 2008.

Brown, Kathleen M. *Good Wives, Nasty Wenches, Anxious Patriarchs: Gender,*

Race, and Power in Colonial Virginia. Williamsburg, VA: University of North Carolina Press, 1996.

Chaplin, Joyce. *Subject Matter: Technology, the Body, and Science on the Anglo-American Frontier, 1500–1676*. Cambridge, MA: Harvard University Press, 2001.

Donoghue, John. *Fire Under the Ashes: An Atlantic History of the English Revolution*. Chicago: University of Chicago Press, 2013.

Gallay, Alan. *The Indian Slave Trade: The Rise of the English Empire in the American South, 1670–1717*. New Haven, CT: Yale University Press, 2003.

Goodfriend, Joyce D. *Before the Melting Pot: Society and Culture in Colonial New York City, 1664–1730*. Princeton, NJ: Princeton University Press, 1992.

Heywood, Linda M., and John K. Thornton. *Central Africans, Atlantic Creoles, and the Foundation of the Americas, 1585–1660*. New York: Cambridge University Press, 2007.

Landsman, Ned C. *Crossroads of Empire: The Middle Colonies in British North America*. Baltimore: Johns Hopkins University Press, 2010.

Lepore, Jill. *The Name of War: King Philip's War and the Origins of American Identity*. New York: Knopf Doubleday, 2009.

Little, Ann M. *Many Captivities of Esther Wheelright*. New Haven, CT: Yale University Press, 2016.

Merrell, James H. *Into the American Woods: Negotiations on the Pennsylvania Frontier*. New York: Norton, 2000.

Mustakeem, Sowande' M. *Slavery at Sea: Terror, Sex, and Sickness in the Middle Passage*. Urbana: University of Illinois Press, 2016.

O'Malley, Gregory E. *Final Passages: The Intercolonial Slave Trade of British America, 1619–1807*. Williamsburg, VA: University of North Carolina Press, 2014.

Parent, Anthony S. *Foul Means: The Formation of a Slave Society in Virginia, 1660–1740*. Williamsburg, VA: University of North Carolina Press, 2003.

Parrish, Susan Scott. *American Curiosity: Cultures of Natural History in the Colonial British Atlantic World*. Chapel Hill: University of North Carolina Press, 2006.

Pestana, Carla Gardina. *The English Atlantic in an Age of Revolution, 1640–1661*. Cambridge, MA: Harvard University Press, 2004.

Pulsipher, Jenny Hale. *Subjects unto the Same King: Indians, English, and the Contest for Authority in Colonial New England*. Philadelphia: University of Pennsylvania Press, 2005.

Ramsey, William L. *The Yamasee War: A Study of Culture, Economy, and Conflict in the Colonial South*. Lincoln: University of Nebraska Press, 2008.

Rice, James D. *Tales from a Revolution: Bacon's Rebellion and the Transformation of Early America*. New York: Oxford University Press, 2012.

Roney, Jessica Choppin. *Governed by a Spirit of Opposition: The Origins of American Political Practice in Colonial Philadelphia*. Baltimore: Johns Hopkins University Press, 2014.

Smallwood, Stephanie E. *Saltwater Slavery: A Middle Passage from Africa to American Diaspora*. Cambridge, MA: Harvard University Press, 2008.

Stanwood, Owen. *The Empire Reformed: English America in the Age of the Glorious Revolution*. Philadelphia: University of Pennsylvania Press, 2011.

Taylor, Alan. *American Colonies: The Settling of North America*. New York: Penguin, 2002.

Wood, Peter H. *Black Majority: Negroes in Colonial South Carolina from 1670 through the Stono Rebellion*. New York: Norton, 1975.

4

Colonial Society

I. Introduction

Eighteenth-century American culture moved in competing directions. Commercial, military, and cultural ties between Great Britain and the North American colonies tightened while a new distinctly American culture began to form and bind together colonists from New Hampshire to Georgia. Immigrants from other European nations meanwhile combined with Native Americans and enslaved Africans to create an increasingly diverse colonial population. All—men and women, European, Native American, and African—led distinct lives and wrought new distinct societies. While life in the thirteen colonies was shaped in part by English practices and participation in the larger Atlantic World, emerging cultural patterns increasingly transformed North America into something wholly different.

Charles Willson Peale, *The Peale Family*, c. 1771–1773. Collection of the New-York Historical Society, object #1867.298.

II. Consumption and Trade in the British Atlantic

Transatlantic trade greatly enriched Britain, but it also created high standards of living for many North American colonists. This two-way relationship reinforced the colonial feeling of commonality with British culture. It was not until trade relations, disturbed by political changes and the demands of warfare, became strained in the 1760s that colonists began to question these ties.

During the seventeenth and eighteenth centuries, improvements in manufacturing, transportation, and the availability of credit increased the opportunity for colonists to purchase consumer goods. Instead of making their own tools, clothes, and utensils, colonists increasingly purchased luxury items made by specialized artisans and manufacturers. As the incomes of Americans rose and the prices of these commodities fell, these items shifted from luxuries to common goods. The average person's ability to spend money on consumer goods became a sign of their respectability. Historians have called this process the "consumer revolution."[1]

Britain relied on the colonies as a source of raw materials, such as lumber and tobacco. Americans engaged with new forms of trade and financing that increased their ability to buy British-made goods. But the

Joseph Highmore, *The Harlowe Family, from Samuel Richardson's "Clarissa,"* 1745–1747. Wikimedia.

ways in which colonists paid for these goods varied sharply from those in Britain. When settlers first arrived in North America, they typically carried very little hard or metallic British money with them. Discovering no precious metals (and lacking the Crown's authority to mint coins), colonists relied on barter and nontraditional forms of exchange, including everything from nails to the wampum used by Native American groups in the Northeast. To deal with the lack of currency, many colonies resorted to "commodity money," which varied from place to place. In Virginia, for example, the colonial legislature stipulated a rate of exchange for tobacco, standardizing it as a form of money in the colony. Commodities could be cumbersome and difficult to transport, so a system of notes developed. These notes allowed individuals to deposit a certain amount of tobacco in a warehouse and receive a note bearing the value of the deposit that could be traded as money. In 1690, colonial Massachusetts became the first place in the Western world to issue paper bills to be used as money.[2] These notes, called bills of credit, were issued for finite periods of time on the colony's credit and varied in denomination.

While these notes provided colonists with a much-needed medium for exchange, it was not without its problems. Currency that worked in Virginia might be worthless in Pennsylvania. Colonists and officials in Britain debated whether it was right or desirable to use mere paper, as opposed to gold or silver, as a medium of exchange. Paper money tended to lose value quicker than coins and was often counterfeited. These problems, as well as British merchants' reluctance to accept depreciated paper notes, caused the Board of Trade to restrict the uses of paper money in the Currency Acts of 1751 and 1763. Paper money was not the only medium of exchange, however. Colonists also used metal coins. Barter and the extension of credit—which could take the form of bills of exchange, akin to modern-day personal checks—remained important forces throughout the colonial period. Still, trade between colonies was greatly hampered by the lack of standardized money.

Businesses on both sides of the Atlantic advertised both their goods and promises of obtaining credit. The consistent availability of credit allowed families of modest means to buy consumer items previously available only to elites. Cheap consumption allowed middle-class Americans to match many of the trends in clothing, food, and household décor that traditionally marked the wealthiest, aristocratic classes. Provincial Americans, often seen by their London peers as less cultivated or "backwater," could present themselves as lords and ladies of their own communities by purchasing and displaying British-made goods. Visiting the home of a successful businessman in Boston, John Adams described "the Furniture, which alone cost a thousand Pounds sterling. A seat it is for a noble Man, a Prince. The Turkey Carpets, the painted Hangings, the Marble Table, the rich Beds with crimson Damask Curtains and Counterpins, the beautiful Chimney Clock, the Spacious Garden, are the most magnificent of any thing I have seen."[3] But many Americans worried about the consequences of rising consumerism. A writer for the *Boston Evening Post* remarked on this new practice of purchasing status: "For 'tis well known how Credit is a mighty inducement with many People to purchase this and the other Thing which they may well enough do without."[4] Americans became more likely to find themselves in debt, whether to their local shopkeeper or a prominent London merchant, creating new feelings of dependence.

Of course, the thirteen continental colonies were not the only British colonies in the Western Hemisphere. In fact, they were considerably less important to the Crown than the sugar-producing islands of the Caribbean, including Jamaica, Barbados, the Leeward Islands, Grenada, St. Vincent, and Dominica. These British colonies were also inextricably connected to the continental colonies. Caribbean plantations dedicated nearly all of their land to the wildly profitable crop of sugarcane, so North American colonies sold surplus food and raw materials to these wealthy island colonies. Lumber was in high demand, especially in Barbados, where planters nearly deforested the island to make room for sugar plantations. To compensate for a lack of lumber, Barbadian colonists ordered house frames from New England. These prefabricated frames were sent via ships from which planters transported them to their plantations. Caribbean colonists also relied on the continental colonies for livestock, purchasing cattle and horses. The most lucrative exchange was the slave trade.

Connections between the Caribbean and North America benefited both sides. Those living on the continent relied on the Caribbean colonists to satisfy their craving for sugar and other goods like mahogany. British colonists in the Caribbean began cultivating sugar in the 1640s, and sugar took the Atlantic World by storm. In fact, by 1680, sugar exports from the tiny island of Barbados valued more than the total exports of all the continental colonies.[5] Jamaica, acquired by the Crown in 1655, surpassed Barbados in sugar production toward the end of the seventeenth century. North American colonists, like Britons around

A Representation of the SUGAR-CANE and the Art of Making Sugar.

John Hinton, *A representation of the sugar cane and the art of making sugar*, 1749. Library of Congress.

the world, craved sugar to sweeten their tea and food. Colonial elites also sought to decorate their parlors and dining rooms with the silky, polished surfaces of rare mahogany as opposed to local wood. While the bulk of this in-demand material went to Britain and Europe, New England merchants imported the wood from the Caribbean, where it was then transformed into exquisite furniture for those who could afford it.

These systems of trade all existed with the purpose of enriching Great Britain. To ensure that profits ended up in Britain, Parliament issued taxes on trade under the Navigation Acts. These taxes intertwined consumption with politics. Prior to 1763, Britain found that enforcing the regulatory laws they passed was difficult and often cost them more than the duty revenue they would bring in. As a result, colonists found it relatively easy to violate the law and trade with foreign nations, pirates, or smugglers. Customs officials were easily bribed and it was not uncommon to see Dutch, French, or West Indies ships laden with prohibited goods in American ports. When smugglers were caught, their American peers often acquitted them. British officials estimated that nearly £700,000 worth of illicit goods was brought into the American colonies annually.[6] Pirates also helped to perpetuate the illegal trading activities by providing a buffer between merchants and foreign ships.

Beginning with the Sugar Act in 1764, and continuing with the Stamp Act and the Townshend Acts, Parliament levied taxes on sugar, paper, lead, glass, and tea, all products that contributed to colonists' sense of gentility. In response, patriots organized nonimportation agreements and reverted to domestic products. Homespun cloth became a political statement. A writer in the *Essex Gazette* in 1769 proclaimed, "I presume there never was a Time when, or a Place where, the Spinning Wheel could more influence the Affairs of Men, than at present."[7]

The consumer revolution fueled the growth of colonial cities. Cities in colonial America were crossroads for the movement of people and goods. One in twenty colonists lived in cities by 1775.[8] Some cities grew organically over time, while others were planned from the start. New York's and Boston's seventeenth-century street plans reflected the haphazard arrangement of medieval cities in Europe. In other cities like Philadelphia and Charleston, civic leaders laid out urban plans according to calculated systems of regular blocks and squares. Planners in Annapolis and Williamsburg also imposed regularity and order over their city streets through the placement of government, civic, and educational buildings.

By 1775, Boston, Newport, New York, Philadelphia, and Charleston were the five largest cities in British North America. Philadelphia, New York, Boston, and Charleston had populations of approximately 40,000, 25,000, 16,000, and 12,000 people, respectively.[9] Urban society was highly stratified. At the base of the social ladder were the laboring classes, which included both enslaved and free people ranging from apprentices to master craftsmen. Next came the middling sort: shopkeepers, artisans, and skilled mariners. Above them stood the merchant elites, who tended to be actively involved in the city's social and political affairs, as well as in the buying, selling, and trading of goods. Enslaved men and women had a visible presence in both northern and southern cities.

The bulk of the enslaved population lived in rural areas and performed agricultural labor. In port cities, enslaved laborers often worked as domestic servants and in skilled trades: distilleries, shipyards, lumberyards, and ropewalks. Between 1725 and 1775, slavery became increasingly significant in the northern colonies as urban residents sought greater participation in the maritime economy. Massachusetts was the first slaveholding colony in New England. New York traced its connections to slavery and the slave trade back to the Dutch settlers of New Netherland in the seventeenth century. Philadelphia also became an active site of the Atlantic enslaved people trade, and enslaved people accounted for nearly 8 percent of the city's population in 1770.[10] In southern cities, including Charleston, urban slavery played an important role in the market economy. Enslaved people, both rural and urban, made up the majority of the laboring population on the eve of the American Revolution.

III. Slavery, Antislavery, and Atlantic Exchange

Slavery was a transatlantic institution, but it developed distinct characteristics in British North America. By 1750, slavery was legal in every North American colony, but local economic imperatives, demographic trends, and cultural practices all contributed to distinct colonial variants of slavery.

Virginia, the oldest of the English mainland colonies, imported its first enslaved laborers in 1619. Virginia planters built larger and larger estates and guaranteed that these estates would remain intact through the use of primogeniture (in which a family's estate would descend to the eldest male heir) and the entail (a legal procedure that prevented the breakup and sale of estates). This distribution of property, which kept wealth and property consolidated, guaranteed that the great planters would dominate social and economic life in the Chesapeake. This system also fostered an economy dominated by tobacco. By 1750, there were approximately one hundred thousand enslaved Africans in Virginia, at least 40 percent of the colony's total population.[11] Most of these enslaved people worked on large estates under the gang system of labor, working from dawn to dusk in groups with close supervision by a white overseer or enslaved "driver" who could use physical force to compel labor.

Virginians used the law to protect the interests of enslavers. In 1705 the House of Burgesses passed its first comprehensive slave code. Earlier laws had already guaranteed that the children of enslaved women would be born enslaved, conversion to Christianity would not lead to freedom, and owners could not free their slaves unless they transported them out of the colony. Enslavers could not be convicted of murder for killing an enslaved person; conversely, any Black Virginian who struck a white colonist would be severely whipped. Virginia planters used the law to maximize the profitability of their enslaved laborers and closely regulate every aspect of their daily lives.

In South Carolina and Georgia, slavery was also central to colonial life, but specific local conditions created a very different system. Georgia was founded by a philanthropic group that included James Oglethorpe. The trustees banned slavery from the colony. But by 1750, slavery was legal throughout the region. South Carolina had been a slave colony from its founding and, by 1750, was the only mainland colony with a majority enslaved African population. The Fundamental Constitutions of Carolina, coauthored by the philosopher John Locke in 1669, explicitly legalized slavery from the very beginning. Many early settlers in Carolina were enslavers from British Caribbean sugar islands, and they brought their brutal slave codes with them. Defiant enslaved people could legally be beaten, branded, mutilated, even castrated. In 1740 a new law stated that killing a rebellious enslaved person was not a crime and even the murder of an enslaved person was treated as a minor misdemeanor. South Carolina also banned the freeing of enslaved laborers unless the freed slave left the colony.[12]

Despite this brutal regime, a number of factors combined to give enslaved people in South Carolina more independence in their daily lives. Rice, the staple crop underpinning the early Carolina economy, was widely cultivated in West Africa, and planters commonly requested that merchants sell them enslaved laborers skilled in the complex process of rice cultivation. Enslaved people from Senegambia were particularly prized.[13] The expertise of these enslaved people contributed to one of the most lucrative economies in the colonies. The swampy conditions of rice plantations, however, fostered dangerous diseases. Malaria and other tropical diseases spread and caused many enslavers to live away from their plantations. These elites, who commonly owned a number of plantations, typically lived in Charleston town houses to avoid the diseases of the rice fields. West Africans, however, were far more likely to have a level of immunity to malaria (due to a genetic trait that also contributes to higher levels of sickle cell anemia), reinforcing planters' racial belief that Africans were particularly suited to labor in tropical environments.

With plantation owners often far from home, Carolina enslaved laborers had less direct oversight than those in the Chesapeake. Furthermore, many Carolina rice plantations used the task system to organize enslaved laborers. Under this system, enslaved laborers were given a number of specific tasks to complete in a day. Once those tasks were complete, enslaved people often had time to grow their own crops on garden plots allotted by their enslavers. Thriving underground markets allowed enslaved people here a degree of economic autonomy. Enslaved people in Carolina also had an unparalleled degree of cultural autonomy.

This autonomy coupled with the frequent arrival of new Africans enabled a culture that retained many African practices.[14] Syncretic languages like Gullah and Geechee contained many borrowed African terms, and traditional African basket weaving (often combined with Native American techniques) survives in the region to this day.

This unique Lowcountry culture contributed to the Stono Rebellion in September 1739. On a Sunday morning while planters attended church, a group of about eighty enslaved people set out for Spanish Florida under a banner that read "Liberty!," burning plantations and killing at least twenty white settlers as they marched. They were headed for Fort Mose, a free Black settlement on the Georgia-Florida border, emboldened by the Spanish Empire's offer of freedom to anyone enslaved by the English. The local militia defeated the rebels in battle, captured and executed many of the enslaved people, and sold others to the sugar plantations of the West Indies. Though the rebellion was ultimately unsuccessful, it was a violent reminder that enslaved people would fight for freedom.

Slavery was also an important institution in the mid-Atlantic colonies. While New York, New Jersey, and Pennsylvania never developed plantation economies, enslaved laborers were often employed on larger farms growing cereal grains. Enslaved Africans worked alongside European tenant farmers on New York's Hudson Valley "patroonships," huge tracts of land granted to a few early Dutch families. As previously mentioned, enslaved people were also a common sight in Philadelphia, New York City, and other ports where they worked in the maritime trades and domestic service. New York City's economy was so reliant on slavery that over 40 percent of its population was enslaved by 1700, while 15 to 20 percent of Pennsylvania's colonial population was enslaved by 1750.[15] In New York, the high density of enslaved people and a particularly diverse European population increased the threat of rebellion. A 1712 slave rebellion in New York City resulted in the deaths of nine white colonists. In retribution, twenty-one enslaved people were executed and six others died by suicide before they could be burned alive. In 1741, authorities uncovered another planned rebellion by enslaved Africans and poor Black and white men. Panic unleashed a witch hunt that only stopped after thirty-two Black men, both enslaved and free, were executed alongside five poor white men. Another seventy enslaved laborers were deported, likely to the sugarcane fields of the West Indies.[16]

Increasingly uneasy about the growth of slavery in the region, Quakers were the first group to turn against slavery. Quaker beliefs in radical nonviolence and the fundamental equality of all human souls made slavery hard to justify. Most commentators argued that slavery originated in war, where captives were enslaved rather than executed. To pacifist Quakers, then, the very foundation of slavery was illegitimate. Furthermore, Quaker belief in the equality of souls challenged the racial basis of slavery. By 1758, Quakers in Pennsylvania disowned members who engaged in the slave trade, and by 1772 slave-owning Quakers could be expelled from their meetings. These local activities in Pennsylvania had broad implications as the decision to ban slavery and slave trading was debated in Quaker meetings throughout the English-speaking world. The free Black population in Philadelphia and other northern cities also continually agitated against slavery.

Slavery as a system of labor never took off in Massachusetts, Connecticut, or New Hampshire, though it was legal throughout the region. The absence of cash crops like tobacco or rice minimized the economic use of slavery. In Massachusetts, only about 2 percent of the population was enslaved as late as the 1760s. The few enslaved people in the colony were concentrated in Boston along with a sizable free Black community that made up about 10 percent of the city's population.[17] While slavery itself never really took root in New England, the slave trade was a central element of the region's economy. Every major port in the region participated to some extent in the transatlantic trade—Newport, Rhode Island, alone had at least 150 ships active in the trade by 1740—and New England also provided foodstuffs and manufactured goods to West Indian plantations.[18]

IV. Pursuing Political, Religious, and Individual Freedom

Consumption, trade, and slavery drew the colonies closer to Great Britain, but politics and government split them further apart. Democracy in Europe more closely resembled oligarchies rather than republics, with only elite members of society eligible to serve in elected positions. Most European states did not hold regular elections, with Britain and the Dutch Republic being the two major exceptions. However, even in these countries, only a tiny portion of males could vote. In the North American colonies, by contrast, white male suffrage was far more widespread. In addition to having greater popular involvement, colonial government also had more power in a variety of areas. Assemblies and legislatures regulated businesses, imposed new taxes, cared for the poor in their communities, built roads and bridges, and made most decisions concerning education. Colonial Americans sued often, which in turn led to more power for local judges and more prestige in jury service. Thus, lawyers became extremely important in American society and in turn played a greater role in American politics.

American society was less tightly controlled than European society. This led to the rise of various interest groups, each at odds with the other. These various interest groups arose based on commonalities in various areas. Some commonalities arose over class-based distinctions, while others were due to ethnic or religious ties. One of the major differences between modern politics and colonial political culture was the lack of distinct, stable political parties. The most common disagreement in colonial politics was between the elected assemblies and the royal governor. Generally, the various colonial legislatures were divided into factions who either supported or opposed the current governor's political ideology.

Political structures in the colonies fell under one of three main categories: provincial (New Hampshire, New York, Virginia, North Carolina, South Carolina, and Georgia), proprietary (Pennsylvania, Delaware, New Jersey, and Maryland), and charter (Massachusetts, Rhode Island, and Connecticut). Provincial colonies were the most tightly controlled by the Crown. The British king appointed all provincial governors and these Crown governors could veto any decision made by their colony's legislative assemblies. Proprietary colonies had a similar structure, with one important difference: governors were appointed by a lord proprietor, an individual who had purchased or received the rights to the colony from the Crown. Proprietary colonies therefore often had more freedoms and liberties than other North American colonies. Charter colonies had the most complex system of government: they were formed by political corporations or interest groups that drew up a charter clearly delineating powers between the executive, legislative, and judiciary branches of government. Rather than having appointed governors, charter colonies elected their own from among property-owning men in the colony.

After the governor, colonial government was broken down into two main divisions: the council and the assembly. The council was essentially the governor's cabinet, often composed of prominent individuals within the colony, such as the head of the militia or the attorney general. The governor appointed these men, although the appointments were often subject to approval from Parliament. The assembly was composed of elected, property-owning men whose official goal was to ensure that colonial law conformed to English law. The colonial assemblies approved

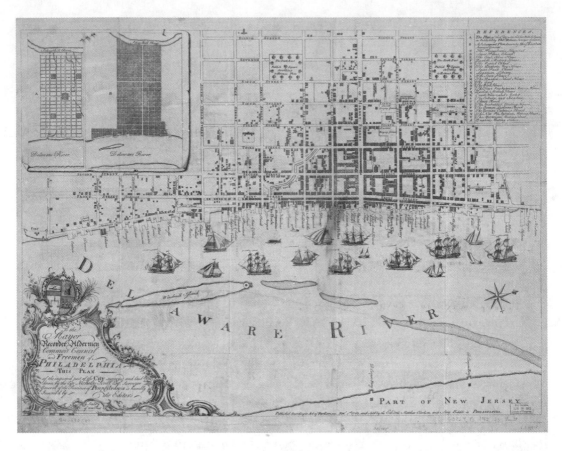

Nicholas Scull, *To the mayor, recorder, aldermen, common council, and freemen of Philadelphia this plan of the improved part of the city surveyed and laid down by the late Nicholas Scull,* Philadelphia, 1762. Library of Congress.

new taxes and the colonial budgets. However, many of these assemblies saw it as their duty to check the power of the governor and ensure that he did not take too much power within colonial government. Unlike Parliament, most of the men who were elected to an assembly came from local districts, with their constituency able to hold their elected officials accountable to promises made.

An elected assembly was an offshoot of the idea of civic duty, the notion that men had a responsibility to support and uphold the government through voting, paying taxes, and service in the militia. Americans firmly accepted the idea of a social contract, the idea that government was put in place by the people. Philosophers such as Thomas Hobbes and John Locke pioneered this idea, and there is evidence to suggest that these writers influenced the colonists. While in practice elites controlled colonial politics, in theory many colonists believed in the notion of equality before the law and opposed special treatment for any members of colonial society.

Whether African Americans, Native Americans, and women would be included in this notion of equality before the law was far less clear. Women's role in the family became particularly complicated. Many historians view this period as a significant time of transition.[19] Anglo-American families during the colonial period differed from their European counterparts. Widely available land and plentiful natural resources allowed for greater fertility and thus encouraged more people to marry earlier in life. Yet while young marriages and large families were common throughout the colonial period, family sizes started to shrink by the end of the 1700s as wives asserted more control over their own bodies.

New ideas governing romantic love helped change the nature of husband-wife relationships. Deriving from sentimentalism, a contemporary literary movement, many Americans began to view marriage as an emotionally fulfilling relationship rather than a strictly economic partnership. Referring to one another as "Beloved of my Soul" or "My More Than Friend," newspaper editor John Fenno and his wife Mary Curtis Fenno illustrate what some historians refer to as the "companionate ideal."[20] While away from his wife, John felt a "vacuum in my existence," a sentiment returned by Mary's "Doting Heart."[21] Indeed, after independence, wives began to not only provide emotional sustenance to their husbands but inculcate the principles of republican citizenship as "republican wives."[22]

Marriage opened up new emotional realms for some but remained oppressive for others. For the millions of Americans bound in chattel slavery, marriage remained an informal arrangement rather than a codified legal relationship. For white women, the legal practice of coverture meant that women lost all their political and economic rights to their husband. Divorce rates rose throughout the 1790s, as did less formal cases of abandonment. Newspapers published advertisements by deserted men and women denouncing their partners. Known as "elopement notices," they cataloged the misbehaviors of deviant spouses, such as wives' "indecent manner," a way of implying sexual impropriety. As violence and inequality continued in many American marriages, wives in return highlighted their husbands' "drunken fits" and violent rages. One woman noted that her partner "presented his gun at my breast . . . and swore he would kill me."[23]

That couples would turn to newspapers as a source of expression illustrates the importance of what historians call print culture.[24] Print culture includes the wide range of factors contributing to how books and other printed objects are made, including the relationship between the author and the publisher, the technical constraints of the printer, and the tastes of readers. In colonial America, regional differences in daily life impacted the way colonists made and used printed matter. However, all the colonies dealt with threats of censorship and control from imperial supervision. In particular, political content stirred the most controversy.

From the establishment of Virginia in 1607, printing was either regarded as unnecessary given such harsh living conditions or actively discouraged. The governor of Virginia, Sir William Berkeley, summed up the attitude of the ruling class in 1671: "I thank God there are no free schools nor printing . . . for learning has brought disobedience, and heresy . . . and printing has divulged them."[25] Ironically, the circulation of handwritten tracts contributed to Berkeley's undoing. The popularity of Nathaniel Bacon's uprising was in part due to widely circulated tracts questioning Berkeley's competence. Berkeley's harsh repression of Bacon's Rebellion was equally well documented. It was only after Berkeley's death in 1677 that the idea of printing in the southern colonies was revived. William Nuthead, an experienced English printer, set up shop in 1682, although the next governor of the colony, Thomas Culpeper, forbade Nuthead from completing a single project. It wasn't until William Parks set up his printing shop in Annapolis in 1726 that the Chesapeake had a stable local trade in printing and books.

Print culture was very different in New England. Puritans had a respect for print from the beginning. Unfortunately, New England's authors were content to publish in London, making the foundations of Stephen Daye's first print shop in 1639 very shaky. Typically, printers made their money from printing sheets, not books to be bound. The case was similar in Massachusetts, where the first printed work was a *Freeman's Oath*.[26] The first book was not issued until 1640, the *Bay Psalm Book*, of which eleven known copies survive. Daye's contemporaries recognized the significance of his printing, and he was awarded 140 acres of land. The next large project, the first Bible to be printed in America, was undertaken by Samuel Green and Marmaduke Johnson and published in 1660. That same year, the Eliot Bible, named for its translator John Eliot, was printed in the Natick dialect of the local Algonquin tribes.

Massachusetts remained the center of colonial printing for a hundred years, until Philadelphia overtook Boston in 1770. Philadelphia's rise as the printing capital of the colonies began with two important features: first, the arrival of Benjamin Franklin, a scholar and businessman, in 1723, and second, waves of German immigrants who created a demand for a German-language press. From the mid-1730s, Christopher Sauer, and later his son, met the demand for German-language newspapers and

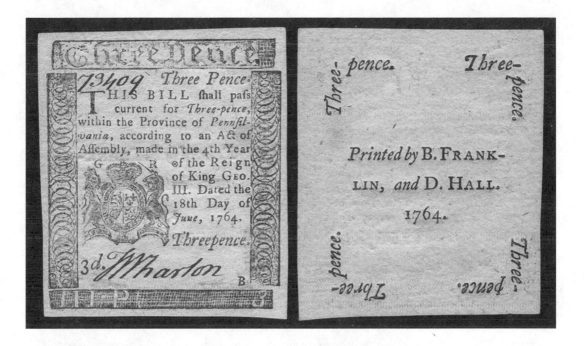

Benjamin Franklin and David Hall, printers, Pennsylvania Currency, 1764. Wikimedia.

religious texts. Nevertheless, Franklin was a one-man culture of print, revolutionizing the book trade in addition to creating public learning initiatives such as the Library Company and the Academy of Philadelphia. His *Autobiography* offers one of the most detailed glimpses of life in a eighteenth-century print shop. Franklin's Philadelphia enjoyed a flurry of newspapers, pamphlets, and books for sale. The flurry would only grow in 1776, when the Philadelphia printer Robert Bell issued hundreds of thousands of copies of Thomas Paine's revolutionary *Common Sense*.

Debates on religious expression continued throughout the eighteenth century. In 1711, a group of New England ministers published a collection of sermons titled *Early Piety*. The most famous minister, Increase Mather, wrote the preface. In it he asked the question, "What did our forefathers come into this wilderness for?"[27] His answer was simple: to test their faith against the challenges of America and win. The grandchildren of the first settlers had been born into the comfort of well-established colonies and worried that their faith had suffered. This sense of inferiority sent colonists looking for a reinvigorated religious experience. The result came to be known as the Great Awakening.

Only with hindsight does the Great Awakening look like a unified movement. The first revivals began unexpectedly in the Congregational churches of New England in the 1730s and then spread through the 1740s and 1750s to Presbyterians, Baptists, and Methodists in the rest of the thirteen colonies. Different places at different times experienced revivals of different intensities. Yet in all of these communities, colonists discussed the same need to strip their lives of worldly concerns and return to a more pious lifestyle. The form it took was something of a contradiction. Preachers became key figures in encouraging individuals to find a personal relationship with God.

The first signs of religious revival appeared in Jonathan Edwards' congregation in Northampton, Massachusetts. Edwards was a theologian who shared the faith of the early Puritan settlers. In particular, he believed in the idea of predestination, in which God had long ago decided who was damned and who was saved. However, Edwards worried that his congregation had stopped searching their souls and were merely doing good works to prove they were saved. With a missionary zeal, Edwards preached against worldly sins and called for his congregation to look inward for signs of God's saving grace. His most famous sermon was "Sinners in the Hands of an Angry God." Suddenly, in the winter of 1734, these sermons sent his congregation into violent convulsions. The spasms first appeared among known sinners in the community. Over the next six months the physical symptoms spread to half of the six hundred-person congregation. Edwards shared the work of his revival in a widely circulated pamphlet.

Over the next decade itinerant preachers were more successful in spreading the spirit of revival around America. These preachers had the same spiritual goal as Edwards but brought with them a new religious experience. They abandoned traditional sermons in favor of outside meetings where they could whip the congregation into an emotional frenzy to reveal evidence of saving grace. Many religious leaders were suspicious of the enthusiasm and message of these revivals, but colonists flocked to the spectacle.

The most famous itinerant preacher was George Whitefield. According to Whitefield, the only type of faith that pleased God was heartfelt. The established churches too often only encouraged apathy. "The Christian World is dead asleep," Whitefield explained. "Nothing but a loud voice can awaken them out of it."[28] He would be that voice. Whitefield was a former actor with a dramatic style of preaching and a simple message. Thundering against sin and for Jesus Christ, Whitefield invited everyone to be born again. It worked. Through the 1730s he traveled from New York to South Carolina converting ordinary men, women, and children. "I have seen upwards of a thousand people hang on his words with

George Whitefield is shown supported by two women, "Hypocrisy" and "Defeat." The image also includes other visual indications of the engraver's disapproval of Whitefield, including a monkey and jester's staff in the right-hand corner. C. Corbett, publisher, *Enthusiasm display'd: or, the Moor Fields congregation*, 1739. Library of Congress.

breathless silence," wrote a socialite in Philadelphia, "broken only by an occasional half suppressed sob."[29] A farmer recorded the powerful impact this rhetoric could have: "And my hearing him preach gave me a heart wound; by God's blessing my old foundation was broken up, and I saw that my righteousness would not save me."[30] The number of people trying to hear Whitefield's message was so large that he preached in the meadows at the edges of cities. Contemporaries regularly testified to crowds of thousands and in one case over twenty thousand in Philadelphia. Whitefield and the other itinerant preachers had achieved what Edwards could not: making the revivals popular.

Ultimately the religious revivals became a victim of the preachers' success. As itinerant preachers became more experimental, they alienated as many people as they converted. In 1742, one preacher from Connecticut, James Davenport, persuaded his congregation that he had special knowledge from God. To be saved they had to dance naked in circles at night while screaming and laughing. Or they could burn the books he disapproved of. Either way, such extremism demonstrated for many that revivalism had gone wrong.[31] A divide appeared by the 1740s and 1750s between "New Lights," who still believed in a revived faith, and "Old Lights," who thought it was deluded nonsense.

By the 1760s, the religious revivals had petered out; however, they left a profound impact on America. Leaders like Edwards and Whitefield encouraged individuals to question the world around them. This idea reformed religion in America and created a language of individualism that promised to change everything else. If you challenged the Church, what other authority figures might you question? The Great Awakening provided a language of individualism, reinforced in print culture, which reappeared in the call for independence. While prerevolutionary America had profoundly oligarchical qualities, the groundwork was laid for a more republican society. However, society did not transform easily overnight. It would take intense, often physical, conflict to change colonial life.

V. Seven Years' War

Of the eighty-seven years between the Glorious Revolution (1688) and the American Revolution (1775), Britain was at war with France and French-allied Native Americans for thirty-seven of them. These were not wars in which European soldiers fought other European soldiers. American militiamen fought for the British against French Catholics and their Native American allies in all of these engagements. Warfare took a physical and spiritual toll on British colonists. British towns located on the border between New England and New France experienced intermittent raiding by French-allied Native Americans. Raiding parties destroyed

Christ Church, Virginia. Library of Congress.

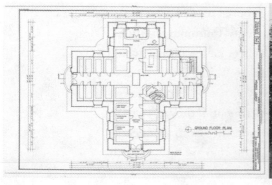

houses and burned crops, but they also took captives. They brought these captives to French Quebec, where some were ransomed back to their families in New England and others converted to Catholicism and remained in New France. In this sense, Catholicism threatened to capture Protestant lands and souls.

France and Britain feuded over the boundaries of their respective North American empires. The feud turned bloody in 1754 when a force of British colonists and Native American allies, led by young George Washington, killed a French diplomat. This incident led to a war, which would become known as the Seven Years' War or the French and Indian War. In North America, the French achieved victory in the early portion of this war. They attacked and burned multiple British outposts, such as Fort William Henry in 1757. In addition, the French seemed to easily defeat British attacks, such as General Braddock's attack on Fort Duquesne, and General Abercrombie's attack on Fort Carillon (Ticonderoga) in 1758. These victories were often the result of alliances with Native Americans.

In Europe, the war did not fully begin until 1756, when British-allied Frederick II of Prussia invaded the neutral state of Saxony. As a result of this invasion, a massive coalition of France, Austria, Russia, and Sweden attacked Prussia and the few German states allied with Prussia. The ruler of Austria, Maria Theresa, hoped to conquer the province of Silesia, which had been lost to Prussia in a previous war. In the European war, the British monetarily supported the Prussians, as well as the minor western German states of Hesse-Kassel and Braunschweig-Wolfenbüttel. These subsidy payments enabled the smaller German states to fight France and allowed the excellent Prussian army to fight against the large enemy alliance.

However, as in North America, the early part of the war went against the British. The French defeated Britain's German allies and forced them to surrender after the Battle of Hastenbeck in 1757. That same year, the Austrians defeated the Prussians in the Battle of Kolín and Frederick of Prussia defeated the French at the Battle of Rossbach. The latter battle allowed the British to rejoin the war in Europe. Just a month later, in December 1757, Frederick's army defeated the Austrians at the Battle of Leuthen, reclaiming the vital province of Silesia. In India and throughout the world's oceans, the British and their fleet consistently defeated the French. In June, for instance, Robert Clive and his Indian allies had defeated the French at the Battle of Plassey. With the sea firmly in their control, the British could send additional troops to North America.

These newly arrived soldiers allowed the British to launch new offensives. The large French port and fortress of Louisbourg, in present-day Nova Scotia, fell to the British in 1758. In 1759, British general James Wolfe defeated French general Louis-Joseph de Montcalm in the Battle of the Plains of Abraham, outside Quebec City. In Europe, 1759 saw the British defeat the French at the Battle of Minden and destroy large portions of the French fleet. The British referred to 1759 as the *annus mirabilis* or the year of miracles. These victories brought about the fall of French Canada, and war in North America ended in 1760 with the British capture of Montreal. The British continued to fight against the Spanish, who entered the war in 1762. In this war, the Spanish successfully defended Nicaragua against British attacks but were unable to prevent the conquest of Cuba and the Philippines.

Albert Bobbett, engraver, *Montcalm trying to stop the massacre*, c. 1870–1880. Library of Congress.

The Seven Years' War ended with the peace treaties of Paris and Hubertusburg in 1763. The British received much of Canada and North America from the French, while the Prussians retained the important

MONTCALM TRYING TO STOP THE MASSACRE.

province of Silesia. This gave the British a larger empire than they could control, which contributed to tensions that would lead to revolution. In particular, it exposed divisions within the newly expanded empire, including language, national affiliation, and religious views. When the British captured Quebec in 1760, a newspaper distributed in the colonies to celebrate the event boasted: "The time will come, when Pope and Friar/ Shall both be roasted in the fire/When the proud Antichristian whore/will sink, and never rise more."[32]

American colonists rejoiced over the defeat of Catholic France and felt secure that the Catholics in Quebec could no longer threaten them. Of course, some American colonies had been a haven for religious minorities since the seventeenth century. Catholic Maryland, for example, evidenced early religious pluralism. But practical toleration of Catholics existed alongside virulent anti-Catholicism in public and political arenas. It was a powerful and enduring rhetorical tool borne out of warfare and competition between Britain and France.

In part because of constant conflict with Catholic France, Britons on either side of the Atlantic rallied around Protestantism. British ministers in England called for a coalition to fight French and Catholic empires. Missionary organizations such as the Society for Promoting Christian Knowledge and the Society for the Propagation of the Gospel were founded at the turn of the eighteenth century to evangelize Native Americans and limit Jesuit conversions. The Protestant revivals of the so-called Great Awakening crisscrossed the Atlantic and founded a participatory religious movement during the 1730s and 1740s that united British Protestant churches. Preachers and merchants alike urged greater Atlantic trade to bind the Anglophone Protestant Atlantic through commerce and religion.

VI. Pontiac's War

Relationships between colonists and Native Americans were complex and often violent. In 1761, Neolin, a prophet, received a vision from his religion's main deity, known as the Master of Life. The Master of Life told Neolin that the only way to enter heaven would be to cast off the corrupting influence of Europeans by expelling the British: "This land where ye dwell I have made for you and not for others. Whence comes it that ye permit the Whites upon your lands. . . . Drive them out, make war upon them."[33] Neolin preached the avoidance of alcohol, a return to traditional rituals, and unity among Indigenous people to his disciples, including Pontiac, an Ottawa leader.

Pontiac took Neolin's words to heart and sparked the beginning of what would become known as Pontiac's War. At its height, the uprising included Native peoples from the territory between the Great Lakes, the Appalachians, and the Mississippi River. Though Pontiac did not command all of those participating in the war, his actions were influential in its development. Pontiac and three hundred warriors sought to take Fort Detroit by surprise in May 1763, but the plan was foiled, resulting in a six-month siege of the British fort. News of the siege quickly spread and inspired more attacks on British forts and settlers. In May, Native Americans captured Forts Sandusky, St. Joseph, and Miami. In June, a coalition of Ottawas and Ojibwes captured Fort Michilimackinac by staging a game of stickball (lacrosse) outside the fort. They chased the ball into the fort, gathered arms that had been smuggled in by a group of Native American women, and killed almost half of the fort's British soldiers.

Though these Native Americans were indeed responding to Neolin's religious message, there were many other practical reasons for waging war on the British. After the Seven Years' War, Britain gained control of formerly French territory as a result of the Treaty of Paris. Whereas the French had maintained a peaceful and relatively equal relationship with their Native American allies through trade, the British hoped to profit from and impose "order." For example, the French often engaged in the Indigenous practice of diplomatic gift giving. However, British general Jeffrey Amherst discouraged this practice and regulated the trade or sale of firearms and ammunition to Indigenous people. Most Native Americans, including Pontiac, saw this not as frugal imperial policy but preparation for war.

Pontiac's War lasted until 1766. Native American warriors attacked British forts and frontier settlements, killing as many as four hundred soldiers and two thousand settlers.[34] Disease and a shortage of supplies ultimately undermined the war effort, and in July 1766 Pontiac met with British official and diplomat William Johnson at Fort Ontario and settled for peace. Though they did not win Pontiac's War, the Native Americans succeeded in fundamentally altering the British government's policy. The war made British officials recognize that peace in the West would require royal protection of Native American lands and heavy-handed regulation of Anglo-American trade activity in territory controlled by Native Americans. During the war, the British Crown issued the Royal Proclamation of 1763, which created the proclamation line marking the Appalachian Mountains as the boundary between the British colonies and land controlled by Native Americans.

The effects of Pontiac's War were substantial and widespread. The war proved that coercion was not an effective strategy for imperial control, though the British government would continue to employ this strategy to consolidate their power in North America, most notably through the various acts imposed on their colonies. Additionally, the prohibition of Anglo-American settlement in Native American territory, especially the Ohio River Valley, sparked discontent. The French immigrant Michel-Guillaume-Saint-Jean de Crèvecoeur articulated this discontent most clearly in his 1782 *Letters from an American Farmer* when he asked, "What then is the American, this new man?" In other words, why did colonists start thinking of themselves as Americans, not Britons? Crèvecoeur suggested that America was a melting pot of self-reliant individual landholders, fiercely independent in pursuit of their own interests, and free from the burdens of European class systems. It was an answer many wanted to hear and fit with self-conceptions of the new nation, albeit one that imagined itself as white, male, and generally Protestant.[35] The Seven Years' War pushed the thirteen American colonies closer together politically and culturally than ever before. In 1754, at the Albany Congress, Benjamin Franklin suggested a plan of union to coordinate defenses across the continent. Tens of thousands of colonials fought during the war. At the French surrender in 1760, 11,000 British soldiers joined 6,500 militia members drawn from every colony north of Pennsylvania.[36] At home, many heard or read sermons that portrayed the war as a struggle between civilizations with liberty-loving Britons arrayed against tyrannical Frenchmen and savage Indigenous people. American colonists rejoiced in their collective victory as a moment of newfound peace and prosperity. After nearly seven decades of warfare they looked to the newly acquired lands west of the Appalachian Mountains as their reward.

The Seven Years' War was tremendously expensive and precipitated imperial reforms on taxation, commerce, and politics. Britain spent over £140 million, an astronomical figure for the day, and the expenses kept coming as new territory required new security obligations. Britain wanted to recoup some of its expenses and looked to the colonies to share the costs of their own security. To do this, Parliament started legislating over all the colonies in a way rarely done before. As a result, the colonies

JOIN, or DIE.

Benjamin Franklin, *Join or Die*, May 9, 1754. Library of Congress.

began seeing themselves as a collective group, rather than just distinct entities. Different taxation schemes implemented across the colonies between 1763 and 1774 placed duties on items like tea, paper, molasses, and stamps for almost every kind of document. Consumption and trade, an important bond between Britain and the colonies, was being threatened. To enforce these unpopular measures, Britain implemented increasingly restrictive policies that eroded civil liberties like protection from unlawful searches and jury trials. The rise of an antislavery movement made many colonists worry that slavery would soon be attacked. The moratorium on new settlements in the West after Pontiac's War was yet another disappointment.

VII. Conclusion

By 1763, Americans had never been more united. They fought and they celebrated together. But they also recognized that they were not considered full British subjects, that they were considered something else. Americans across the colonies viewed imperial reforms as threats to the British liberties they saw as their birthright. The Stamp Act Congress of 1765 brought colonial leaders together in an unprecedented show of cooperation against taxes imposed by Parliament, and popular boycotts of British goods created a common narrative of sacrifice, resistance, and shared political identity. A rebellion loomed.

VIII. Reference Material

This chapter was edited by Nora Slonimsky, with content contributions by Emily Arendt, Ethan R. Bennett, John Blanton, Alexander Burns, Mary Draper, Jamie Goodall, Jane Fiegen Green, Hendrick Isom, Kathryn Lasdow, Allison Madar, Brooke Palmieri, Katherine Smoak, Christopher Sparshott, Ben Wright, and Garrett Wright.

Recommended citation: Emily Arendt et al., "Colonial Society," Nora Slonimsky, ed., in *The American Yawp*, eds. Joseph Locke and Ben Wright (Stanford, CA: Stanford University Press, 2019).

NOTES TO CHAPTER 4

1. T. H. Breen, *The Marketplace of Revolution: How Consumer Politics Shaped American Independence* (New York: Oxford University Press, 2004).

2. Alvin Rabushka, *Taxation in Colonial America* (Princeton, NJ: Princeton University Press, 2008), 360.

3. T. H. Breen, "'Baubles of Britain': The American and Consumer Revolutions of the Eighteenth Century," *Past and Present*, 119, no. 1 (May 1988): 79.

4. "To the Publisher of the Boston Evening Post," *Boston Evening Post*, no. 150 (June 6, 1738): 1.

5. Richard B. Sheridan, *Sugar and Slavery: An Economic History of the British West Indies, 1623–1775* (Baltimore: Johns Hopkins University Press, 1974), 144.

6. Archibald Paton Thornton, *The Habit of Authority: Paternalism in British History* (Toronto: University of Toronto Press, 1966), 123.

7. Cited in Laurel Thatcher Ulrich, *The Age of Homespun: Objects and Stories in the Creation of an American Myth* (New York: Knopf, 2001), 37.

8. Gary B. Nash, *The Urban Crucible: The Northern Seaports and the Origins of the American Revolution, Abridged Edition* (Cambridge, MA: Harvard University Press, 2009), ix.

9. Kenneth T. Jackson and Stanley K. Schultz, *Cities in American History* (New York: Knopf, 1972), 45.

10. Gary B. Nash, "Slaves and Slave Owners in Colonial Philadelphia," in *African Americans in Pennsylvania: Shifting Historical Perspectives*, ed. Joe Trotter and Eric Ledell Smith (University Park: Pennsylvania State University Press, 1997), 49–50.

11. Donald Matthews, *Religion in the Old South* (Chicago: University of Chicago Press, 1977), 6.

12. Robert Olwell, *Masters, Slaves, & Subjects: The Culture of Power in the South Carolina Lowcountry* (Ithaca, NY: Cornell University Press, 1998), 67.

13. Daniel C. Littlefield, *Rice and Slaves: Ethnicity and the Slave Trade in Colonial South Carolina* (Urbana: University of Illinois Press, 1991), 8.

14. Sylvia R. Frey and Betty Wood, *Come Shouting to Zion: African American Protestantism in the American South and British Caribbean to 1830* (Chapel Hill: University of North Carolina Press, 1998).

15. See Appendix D of Dorothy Schneider and Carl J. Schneider, *Slavery in America* (New York: Infobase, 2007).

16. Thomas Joseph Davis, *A Rumor of Revolt: The "Great Negro Plot" in Colonial New York* (New York: Free Press, 1985).

17. U.S. Census Bureau, "Colonial and Pre-Federal Statistics," http://www2 .census.gov/prod2/statcomp/documents/CT1970p2-13.pdf, accessed April 24, 2018; James Oliver Horton, and Lois E. Horton, *Black Bostonians: Family Life and Community Struggle in the Antebellum North* (New York: Holmes and Meier, 1999), xiv.

18. Elaine F. Crane, "'The First Wheel of Commerce': Newport, Rhode Island and the Slave Trade, 1760–1776," *Slavery and Abolition* 1, no. 2 (1980): 178–198.

19. Rosemarie Zagarri, *Revolutionary Backlash: Women and Politics in the Early American Republic* (Philadelphia: University of Pennsylvania Press, 2007).

20. Lucia McMahon, *Mere Equals: The Paradox of Educated Women in the Early American Republic* (Ithaca, NY: Cornell University Press, 2012).

21. Fenno-Hoffman Family Papers, Clements Library, University of Michigan, Ann Arbor; Anya Jabour, *Marriage in the Early Republic: Elizabeth and William Wirt and the Companionate Ideal* (Baltimore: Johns Hopkins University Press, 1998).

22. Jan Lewis, "The Republican Wife: Virtue and Seduction in the Early Republic," *William and Mary Quarterly* 44, no. 4 (1987): 689–721.

23. *New York Packet*, January 9, 1790; *New-Jersey Journal*, January 20, 1790; Mary Beth Sievens, *Stray Wives: Marital Conflict in Early National New England* (New York: New York University Press, 2005).

24. Trish Loughran, *The Republic in Print: Print Culture in the Age of U.S. Nation-Building, 1770–1870* (New York: Columbia University Press, 2007).

25. Cited in David D. Hall, *Cultures in Print: Essays in the History of the Book* (Amherst: University of Massachusetts Press, 1996), 99.

26. Hugh Amory and David D. Hall, *A History of the Book in America: Volume 1, The Colonial Book in the Atlantic World* (New York: Cambridge University Press, 2000): 111.

27. John Gillies, *Historical Collections Relating to the Remarkable Success of the Gospel and Eminent Instruments Employed in Promoting It, Volume II* (Glasgow: Foulis, 1754), 19.

28. George Whitefield, *The Works of the Reverend George Whitefield, Vol. I* (London: Dilly, 1771), 73.

29. William G. McLoughlin, *Revivals, Awakenings, and Reform* (Chicago: University of Chicago Press, 1978), 62.

30. Thomas S. Kidd, *George Whitefield: America's Spiritual Founding Father* (New Haven, CT: Yale University Press, 2014), 131.

31. Leigh Eric Schmidt, "'A Second and Glorious Reformation': The New Light Extremism of Andrew Croswell," *William and Mary Quarterly* 43, no. 2 (April 1986): 214–244.

32. "Canada Subjected: A New Song" ([n.p., 1760?]), quoted in Thomas Kidd, *God of Liberty: A Religious History of the American Revolution* (New York: Basic Books, 2010), 29.

33. Daniel K. Richter, *Before the Revolution: America's Ancient Pasts* (Cambridge, MA: Harvard University Press, 2011), 403.

34. Gregory Evans Dowd, *War Under Heaven: Pontiac, the Indian Nations, and British Empire* (Baltimore: Johns Hopkins University Press, 2004).

35. Read de Crèvecoeur's *Letters from an American Farmer* online at http://xroads.virginia.edu/~hyper/crev/home.html.

36. Fred Anderson, *Crucible of War: The Seven Years' War and the Fate of Empire in British North America, 1754–1766* (New York: Knopf Doubleday, 2007), 410.

RECOMMENDED READING

Anishanslin, Zara. *Portrait of a Woman in Silk: Hidden Histories of the British Atlantic World*. New Haven, CT: Yale University Press, 2016.

Breen, T. H. *The Marketplace of Revolution: How Consumer Politics Shaped American Independence*. New York: Oxford University Press, 2004.

Bushman, Richard L. *The Refinement of America: Persons, Houses, Cities*. New York: Vintage Books, 1992.

Butler, Jon. *Becoming America: The Revolution Before 1776*. Cambridge, MA: Harvard University Press, 2001.

Carp, Benjamin L. *Rebels Rising: Cities and the American Revolution*. New York: Oxford University Press, 2007.

Carté-Engel, Katherine. *Religion and Profit: Moravians in Early America*. Philadelphia: University of Pennsylvania Press, 2009.

Demos, John P. *The Unredeemed Captive: A Family Story from Early America*. New York: Vintage Books, 1994.

Dowd, Gregory Evans. *War Under Heaven: Pontiac, the Indian Nations, and British Empire*. Baltimore: Johns Hopkins University Press, 2004.

Frey, Sylvia R., and Betty Wood. *Come Shouting to Zion: African American Protestantism in the American South and British Caribbean to 1830*. Chapel Hill: University of North Carolina Press, 1998.

Hackel, Heidi Brayman, and Catherine E. Kelly, eds. *Reading Women: Literacy, Authorship, and Culture in the Atlantic World, 1500–1800*. Philadelphia: University of Pennsylvania Press, 2009.

Hancock, David. *Citizens of the World: London Merchants and the Integration of the British Atlantic Community, 1735–1785*. New York: Cambridge University Press, 1997.

Heyrman, Christine. *Southern Cross: The Beginnings of the Bible Belt*. New York: Knopf, 1997.

Holton, Woody. *Forced Founders: Indians, Debtors, Slaves, and the Making of the American Revolution in Virginia.* Chapel Hill: University of North Carolina Press, 1999.

Klepp, Susan E. *Revolutionary Conceptions: Women, Fertility, and Family Limitation in America, 1760–1820.* Chapel Hill: University of North Carolina Press, 2009.

Lepore, Jill. *New York Burning: Liberty, Slavery, and Conspiracy in Eighteenth-Century Manhattan.* New York: Vintage Books, 2005.

McConville, Brendan. *The King's Three Faces: The Rise and Fall of Royal America, 1688–1776.* Chapel Hill: University of North Carolina Press, 2007.

Merritt, Jane T. *At the Crossroads: Indians and Empires on a Mid–Atlantic Frontier, 1700–1763.* Chapel Hill: University of North Carolina Press, 2003.

Podruchny, Carolyn. *Making the Voyageur World: Travelers and Traders in the North American Fur Trade.* Lincoln: University of Nebraska Press, 2006.

Richter, Daniel K. *Facing East from Indian Country: A Native History of Early America.* Cambridge, MA: Harvard University Press, 2003.

Sensbach, Jon F. *Rebecca's Revival: Creating Black Christianity in the Atlantic World.* Cambridge, MA: Harvard University Press, 2006.

Sheridan, Richard B. *Sugar and Slavery: An Economic History of the British West Indies, 1623–1775.* Baltimore: Johns Hopkins University Press, 1974.

Taylor, Alan. *The Divided Ground: Indians, Settlers, and the Northern Borderland of the American Revolution.* New York: Vintage Books, 2006.

Ulrich, Laurel Thatcher. *The Age of Homespun: Objects and Stories in the Creation of an American Myth.* New York: Knopf, 2001.

———. *A Midwife's Tale: The Life of Martha Ballard, Based on Her Diary, 1785–1812.* New York: Knopf, 1990.

Zabin, Serena R. *Dangerous Economies: Status and Commerce in Imperial New York.* Philadelphia: University of Pennsylvania Press, 2011.

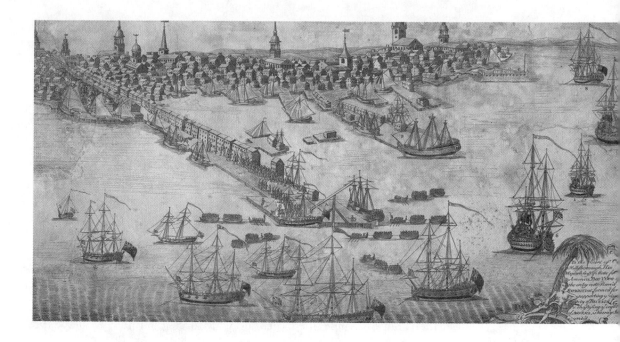

5

The American Revolution

I. Introduction

In the 1760s, Benjamin Rush, a native of Philadelphia, recounted a visit to Parliament. Upon seeing the king's throne in the House of Lords, Rush said he "felt as if he walked on sacred ground" with "emotions that I cannot describe."[1] Throughout the eighteenth century, colonists had developed significant emotional ties with both the British monarchy and the British constitution. The British North American colonists had just helped to win a world war and most, like Rush, had never been more proud to be British. And yet, in a little over a decade, those same colonists would declare their independence and break away from the British Empire. Seen from 1763, nothing would have seemed as improbable as the American Revolution.

The Revolution built institutions and codified the language and ideas that still define Americans' image of themselves. Moreover, revolutionar-

Paul Revere, *Landing of the Troops*, c. 1770. Courtesy American Antiquarian Society. Attribution-NonCommercial-ShareAlike 4.0 International (CC BY-NC-SA 4.0).

ies justified their new nation with radical new ideals that changed the course of history and sparked a global "age of revolution." But the Revolution was as paradoxical as it was unpredictable. A revolution fought in the name of liberty allowed slavery to persist. Resistance to centralized authority tied disparate colonies ever closer together under new governments. The revolution created politicians eager to foster republican selflessness and protect the public good but also encouraged individual self-interest and personal gain. The "founding fathers" instigated and fought a revolution to secure independence from Britain, but they did not fight that revolution to create a "democracy." To successfully rebel against Britain, however, required more than a few dozen "founding fathers." Common colonists joined the fight, unleashing popular forces that shaped the Revolution itself, often in ways not welcomed by elite leaders. But once unleashed, these popular forces continued to shape the new nation and indeed the rest of American history.

II. The Origins of the American Revolution

The American Revolution had both long-term origins and short-term causes. In this section, we will look broadly at some of the long-term political, intellectual, cultural, and economic developments in the eighteenth century that set the context for the crisis of the 1760s and 1770s.

Between the Glorious Revolution of 1688 and the middle of the eighteenth century, Britain had largely failed to define the colonies' relationship to the empire and institute a coherent program of imperial reform. Two factors contributed to these failures. First, Britain was at war from the War of the Spanish Succession at the start of the century through the Seven Years' War in 1763. Constant war was politically consuming and economically expensive. Second, competing visions of empire divided British officials. Old Whigs and their Tory supporters envisioned an authoritarian empire, based on conquering territory and extracting resources. They sought to eliminate Britain's growing national debt by raising taxes and cutting spending on the colonies. The radical (or patriot) Whigs based their imperial vision on trade and manufacturing instead of land and resources. They argued that economic growth, not raising taxes, would solve the national debt. Instead of an authoritarian empire, "patriot Whigs" argued that the colonies should have equal status with the mother country. There were occasional attempts to reform the administration of the colonies, but debate between the two sides prevented coherent reform.[2]

Colonists developed their own understanding of how they fit into the empire. They saw themselves as British subjects "entitled to all the natural, essential, inherent, and inseparable rights of our fellow subjects in Great-Britain." The eighteenth century brought significant economic and demographic growth in the colonies. This success, they believed, resulted partly from Britain's hands-off approach to the colonies, an approach that has been called salutary neglect. By midcentury, colonists believed that they held a special place in the empire, which justified Britain's hands-off policy. In 1764, James Otis Jr. wrote, "The colonists are entitled to as *ample* rights, liberties, and privileges as the subjects of the mother country are, and in some respects *to more*."[3]

In this same period, the colonies developed their own local political institutions. Samuel Adams, in the *Boston Gazette*, described the colonies as each being a "separate body politic" from Britain. Almost immediately upon each colony's settlement, they created a colonial assembly. These assemblies assumed many of the same duties as the Commons exercised in Britain, including taxing residents, managing the spending of the colonies' revenue, and granting salaries to royal officials. In the early 1700s, colonial leaders unsuccessfully lobbied the British government to define their assemblies' legal prerogatives, but Britain was too occupied with European wars. In the first half of the eighteenth century, royal governors tasked by the Board of Trade attempted to limit the power of the assemblies, but the assemblies' power only grew. Many colonists came to see their assemblies as having the same jurisdiction over them that Parliament exercised over those in England. They interpreted British inaction as justifying their tradition of local governance. The Crown and Parliament, however, disagreed.[4]

Political culture in the colonies also developed differently than that of the mother country. In both Britain and the colonies, land was the key to political participation, but because land was more easily obtained in the colonies, a higher proportion of male colonists participated in politics. Colonial political culture drew inspiration from the "country" party in Britain. These ideas—generally referred to as the ideology of republicanism—stressed the corrupting nature of power and the need for those involved in self-governing to be virtuous (i.e., putting the "public good" over their own self-interest). Patriots would need to be ever vigilant against the rise of conspiracies, centralized control, and tyranny. Only a small fringe in Britain held these ideas, but in the colonies, they were widely accepted.[5]

In the 1740s, two seemingly conflicting bodies of thought—the Enlightenment and the Great Awakening—began to combine in the colonies
and challenge older ideas about authority. Perhaps no single philosopher
had a greater impact on colonial thinking than John Locke. In his *Essay
Concerning Human Understanding*, Locke argued that the mind was
originally a *tabula rasa* (or blank slate) and that individuals were formed
primarily by their environment. The aristocracy then were wealthy or
successful because they had greater access to wealth, education, and patronage and not because they were innately superior. Locke followed this
essay with *Some Thoughts Concerning Education*, which introduced
radical new ideas about the importance of education. Education would
produce rational human beings capable of thinking for themselves and
questioning authority rather than tacitly accepting tradition. These ideas
slowly came to have far-reaching effects in the colonies and, later, the
new nation.

At the same time that Locke's ideas about knowledge and education
spread in North America, the colonies also experienced an unprecedented
wave of evangelical Protestant revivalism. Between 1739 and 1740, the
Rev. George Whitefield, an enigmatic, itinerant preacher, traveled the colonies preaching Calvinist sermons to huge crowds. Unlike the rationalism
of Locke, his sermons were designed to appeal to his listeners' emotions.
Whitefield told his listeners that salvation could only be found by taking
personal responsibility for one's own unmediated relationship with God,
a process that came to be known as a "conversion" experience. He also
argued that the current Church hierarchies populated by "unconverted"
ministers only stood as a barrier between the individual and God. In his
wake, new traveling preachers picked up his message and many congregations split. Both Locke and Whitefield had empowered individuals to
question authority and to take their lives into their own hands.

In other ways, eighteenth-century colonists were becoming more culturally similar to Britons, a process often referred to as Anglicization.
As colonial economies grew, they quickly became an important market
for British manufacturing exports. Colonists with disposable income
and access to British markets attempted to mimic British culture. By the
middle of the eighteenth century, middling-class colonists could also afford items previously thought of as luxuries like British fashions, dining
wares, and more. The desire to purchase British goods meshed with the
desire to enjoy British liberties.[6] These political, intellectual, cultural, and
economic developments built tensions that rose to the surface when, after

the Seven Years' War, Britain finally began to implement a program of imperial reform that conflicted with colonists' understanding of the empire and their place in it.

III. The Causes of the American Revolution

Most immediately, the American Revolution resulted directly from attempts to reform the British Empire after the Seven Years' War. The Seven Years' War culminated nearly a half century of war between Europe's imperial powers. It was truly a world war, fought between multiple empires on multiple continents. At its conclusion, the British Empire had never been larger. Britain now controlled the North American continent east of the Mississippi River, including French Canada. It had also consolidated its control over India. But the realities and responsibilities of the postwar empire were daunting. War (let alone victory) on such a scale was costly. Britain doubled the national debt to 13.5 times its annual revenue. Britain faced significant new costs required to secure and defend its far-flung empire, especially the western frontiers of the North American colonies. These factors led Britain in the 1760s to attempt to consolidate control over its North American colonies, which, in turn, led to resistance.

King George III took the crown in 1760 and brought Tories into his government after three decades of Whig rule. They represented an authoritarian vision of empire in which colonies would be subordinate. The Royal Proclamation of 1763 was Britain's first major postwar imperial action targeting North America. The king forbade settlement west of the Appalachian Mountains in an attempt to limit costly wars with Native Americans. Colonists, however, protested and demanded access to the territory for which they had fought alongside the British.

In 1764, Parliament passed two more reforms. The Sugar Act sought to combat widespread smuggling of molasses in New England by cutting the duty in half but increasing enforcement. Also, smugglers would be tried by vice-admiralty courts and not juries. Parliament also passed the Currency Act, which restricted colonies from producing paper money. Hard money, such as gold and silver coins, was scarce in the colonies. The lack of currency impeded the colonies' increasingly sophisticated transatlantic economies, but it was especially damaging in 1764 because a postwar recession had already begun. Between the restrictions of the Proclamation of 1763, the Currency Act, and the Sugar Act's canceling of trials-by-jury for smugglers, some colonists began to fear a pattern of increased taxation and restricted liberties.

In March 1765, Parliament passed the Stamp Act. The act required that many documents be printed on paper that had been stamped to show the duty had been paid, including newspapers, pamphlets, diplomas, legal documents, and even playing cards. The Sugar Act of 1764 was an attempt to get merchants to pay an already existing duty, but the Stamp Act created a new, direct (or "internal") tax. Parliament had never before directly taxed the colonists. Instead, colonies contributed to the empire through the payment of indirect, "external" taxes, such as customs duties. In 1765, Daniel Dulany of Maryland wrote, "A right to impose an internal tax on the colonies, without their consent for the single purpose of revenue, is denied, a right to regulate their trade without their consent is, admitted."[7] Also, unlike the Sugar Act, which primarily affected merchants, the Stamp Act directly affected numerous groups throughout colonial society, including printers, lawyers, college graduates, and even sailors who played cards. This led, in part, to broader, more popular resistance.

Resistance to the Stamp Act took three forms, distinguished largely by class: legislative resistance by elites, economic resistance by merchants, and popular protest by common colonists. Colonial elites responded by passing resolutions in their assemblies. The most famous of the anti-Stamp Act resolutions were the Virginia Resolves, passed by the House of Burgesses on May 30, 1765, which declared that the colonists were entitled to "all the liberties, privileges, franchises, and immunities . . . possessed by the people of Great Britain." When the Virginia Resolves were printed throughout the colonies, however, they often included a few extra, far more radical resolutions not passed by the Virginia House of Burgesses, the last of which asserted that only "the general assembly of this colony have any right or power to impose or lay any taxation" and that anyone who argued differently "shall be deemed an enemy to this his majesty's colony."[8] These additional items spread throughout the colonies and helped radicalize subsequent responses in other colonial assemblies. These responses eventually led to the calling of the Stamp Act Congress in New York City in October 1765. Nine colonies sent delegates, who included Benjamin Franklin, John Dickinson, Thomas Hutchinson, Philip Livingston, and James Otis.[9]

The Stamp Act Congress issued a "Declaration of Rights and Grievances," which, like the Virginia Resolves, declared allegiance to the king

Men and women politicized the domestic sphere by buying and displaying items that conspicuously revealed their position for or against parliamentary actions. This witty teapot, which celebrates the end of taxation on goods like tea itself, makes clear the owner's perspective on the egregious taxation. *Teapot, Stamp Act Repeal'd*, 1786. In Peabody Essex Museum, Salem State University.

and "all due subordination" to Parliament but also reasserted the idea that colonists were entitled to the same rights as Britons. Those rights included trial by jury, which had been abridged by the Sugar Act, and the right to be taxed only by their own elected representatives. As Daniel Dulany wrote in 1765, "It is an essential principle of the English constitution, that the subject shall not be taxed without his consent."[10] Benjamin Franklin called it the "prime Maxim of all free Government."[11] Because the colonies did not elect members to Parliament, they believed that they were not represented and could not be taxed by that body. In response, Parliament and the Crown argued that the colonists were "virtually represented," just like the residents of those boroughs or counties in England that did not elect members to Parliament. However, the colonists rejected the notion of virtual representation, with one pamphleteer calling it a "monstrous idea."[12]

The second type of resistance to the Stamp Act was economic. While the Stamp Act Congress deliberated, merchants in major port cities were preparing nonimportation agreements, hoping that their refusal to import British goods would lead British merchants to lobby for the repeal of the Stamp Act. In New York City, "upwards of two hundred principal merchants" agreed not to import, sell, or buy "any goods, wares, or merchandises" from Great Britain.[13] In Philadelphia, merchants gathered at "a general meeting" to agree that "they would not Import any Goods from Great-Britain until the Stamp-Act was Repealed."[14] The plan worked. By January 1766, London merchants sent a letter to Parliament arguing that they had been "reduced to the necessity of pending ruin" by the Stamp Act and the subsequent boycotts.[15]

The third, and perhaps, most crucial type of resistance was popular protest. Riots broke out in Boston. Crowds burned the appointed stamp distributor for Massachusetts, Andrew Oliver, in effigy and pulled a building he owned "down to the Ground in five minutes."[16] Oliver resigned the position the next day. The following week, a crowd also set upon the home of his brother-in-law, Lieutenant Governor Thomas Hutchinson, who had publicly argued for submission to the stamp tax. Before the evening was over, much of Hutchinson's home and belongings had been destroyed.[17]

Popular violence and intimidation spread quickly throughout the colonies. In New York City, posted notices read:

PRO PATRIA,
The first Man that either
distributes or makes use of Stampt
Paper, let him take care of
his House, Person, & Effects.
Vox Populi;
We dare."[18]

By November 16, all of the original twelve stamp distributors had resigned, and by 1766, groups calling themselves the Sons of Liberty were formed in most colonies to direct and organize further resistance. These tactics had the dual effect of sending a message to Parliament and discouraging colonists from accepting appointments as stamp collectors. With no one to distribute the stamps, the act became unenforceable.

Pressure on Parliament grew until, in February 1766, it repealed the Stamp Act. But to save face and to try to avoid this kind of problem in the future, Parliament also passed the Declaratory Act, asserting that Parliament had the "full power and authority to make laws . . . to bind the colonies and people of America . . . in all cases whatsoever." However, colonists were too busy celebrating the repeal of the Stamp Act to take much notice of the Declaratory Act. In New York City, the inhabitants raised a huge lead statue of King George III in honor of the Stamp Act's repeal. It could be argued that there was no moment at which colonists

Violent protest by groups like the Sons of Liberty created quite a stir in the colonies and in England. While extreme acts like the tarring and feathering of Boston's commissioner of customs in 1774 propagated more protest against symbols of Parliament's tyranny throughout the colonies, violent demonstrations were regarded as acts of terrorism by British officials. This print of the 1774 event was from the British perspective, picturing the Sons as brutal instigators with almost demonic smiles on their faces as they enacted this excruciating punishment on the customs commissioner. Philip Dawe (attributed), *The Bostonians Paying the Excise-man, or Tarring and Feathering.* Wikimedia.

felt more proud to be members of the free British Empire than 1766. But Britain still needed revenue from the colonies.[19]

The colonies had resisted the implementation of direct taxes, but the Declaratory Act reserved Parliament's right to impose them. And, in the colonists' dispatches to Parliament and in numerous pamphlets, they had explicitly acknowledged the right of Parliament to regulate colonial trade. So Britain's next attempt to draw revenues from the colonies, the Townshend Acts, were passed in June 1767, creating new customs duties on common items, like lead, glass, paint, and tea, instead of direct taxes. The acts also created and strengthened formal mechanisms to enforce compliance, including a new American Board of Customs Commissioners and more vice-admiralty courts to try smugglers. Revenues from customs seizures would be used to pay customs officers and other royal officials, including the governors, thereby incentivizing them to convict offenders. These acts increased the presence of the British government in the colonies and circumscribed the authority of the colonial assemblies, since paying the governor's salary had long given the assemblies significant power over them. Unsurprisingly, colonists, once again, resisted.

Even though these were duties, many colonial resistance authors still referred to them as "taxes," because they were designed primarily to extract revenues from the colonies not to regulate trade. John Dickinson, in his "Letters from a Farmer in Pennsylvania," wrote, "That we may legally be bound to pay any general duties on these commodities, relative to the regulation of trade, is granted; but we being obliged by her laws to take them from Great Britain, any special duties imposed on their exportation to us only, with intention to raise a revenue from us only, are as much taxes upon us, as those imposed by the Stamp Act." Hence, many authors asked: once the colonists assented to a tax *in any form*, what would stop the British from imposing ever more and greater taxes on the colonists?[20]

New forms of resistance emerged in which elite, middling, and working-class colonists participated together. Merchants reinstituted nonimportation agreements, and common colonists agreed not to consume these same products. Lists were circulated with signatories promising not to buy any British goods. These lists were often published in newspapers, bestowing recognition on those who had signed and led to pressure on those who had not.

Women, too, became involved to an unprecedented degree in resistance to the Townshend Acts. They circulated subscription lists and gathered signatures. The first political commentaries in newspapers written by women appeared.[21] Also, without new imports of British clothes, colonists took to wearing simple, homespun clothing. Spinning clubs were formed, in which local women would gather at one of their homes and spin cloth for homespun clothing for their families and even for the community.[22]

Homespun clothing quickly became a marker of one's virtue and patriotism, and women were an important part of this cultural shift. At the same time, British goods and luxuries previously desired now became symbols of tyranny. Nonimportation and, especially, nonconsumption agreements changed colonists' cultural relationship with the mother country. Committees of Inspection monitored merchants and residents to make sure that no one broke the agreements. Offenders could expect to be shamed by having their names and offenses published in the newspaper and in broadsides.

Nonimportation and nonconsumption helped forge colonial unity. Colonies formed Committees of Correspondence to keep each other informed of the resistance efforts throughout the colonies. Newspapers reprinted exploits of resistance, giving colonists a sense that they were part of a broader political community. The best example of this new "continental conversation" came in the wake of the Boston Massacre. Britain sent regiments to Boston in 1768 to help enforce the new acts and quell the resistance. On the evening of March 5, 1770, a crowd gathered outside the Custom House and began hurling insults, snowballs, and perhaps more at the young sentry. When a small number of soldiers came to the sentry's aid, the crowd grew increasingly hostile until the soldiers fired. After the smoke cleared, five Bostonians were dead, including one of the ringleaders, Crispus Attucks, a formerly enslaved man turned free dockworker. The soldiers were tried in Boston and won acquittal, thanks, in part, to their defense attorney, John Adams. News of the Boston Massacre spread quickly through the new resistance communication networks, aided by a famous engraving initially circulated by Paul Revere, which depicted bloodthirsty British soldiers with grins on their faces firing into a peaceful crowd. The engraving was quickly circulated and reprinted throughout the colonies, generating sympathy for Boston and anger with Britain.

Resistance again led to repeal. In March 1770, Parliament repealed all of the new duties except the one on tea, which, like the Declaratory

This iconic image of the Boston Massacre by Paul Revere sparked fury in both Americans and the British by portraying the redcoats as brutal slaughterers and the onlookers as helpless victims. The events of March 5, 1770, did not actually play out as Revere pictured them, yet his intention was not simply to recount the affair. Revere created an effective propaganda piece that lent credence to those demanding that the British authoritarian rule be stopped. Paul Revere (engraver), *The bloody massacre perpetrated in King Street Boston on March 5th 1770 by a party of the 29th Regt.*, 1770. Library of Congress.

Act, was left, in part, to save face and assert that Parliament still retained the right to tax the colonies. The character of colonial resistance had changed between 1765 and 1770. During the Stamp Act resistance, elites wrote resolves and held congresses while violent, popular mobs burned effigies and tore down houses, with minimal coordination between colonies. But methods of resistance against the Townshend Acts became more inclusive and more coordinated. Colonists previously excluded from meaningful political participation now gathered signatures, and colonists of all ranks participated in the resistance by not buying British goods and monitoring and enforcing the boycotts.

Britain's failed attempts at imperial reform in the 1760s created an increasingly vigilant and resistant colonial population and, most importantly, an enlarged political sphere—both on the colonial and continental levels—far beyond anything anyone could have imagined a few years earlier. A new sense of shared grievances began to join the colonists in a shared American political identity.

IV. Independence

Tensions between the colonies and England eased for a time after the Boston Massacre. The colonial economy improved as the postwar recession receded. The Sons of Liberty in some colonies sought to continue nonimportation even after the repeal of the Townshend Acts. But in New York, a door-to-door poll of the population revealed that the majority wanted to end nonimportation.[23] Yet Britain's desire and need to reform imperial administration remained.

In April 1773, Parliament passed two acts to aid the failing East India Company, which had fallen behind in the annual payments it owed Britain. But the company was not only drowning in debt; it was also drowning in tea, with almost fifteen million pounds of it in stored in warehouses from India to England. In 1773, Parliament passed the Regulating Act, which effectively put the troubled company under government control. It then passed the Tea Act, which would allow the company to sell its tea in the colonies directly and without the company having to pay the export tax in London. Even though this would greatly lower the cost of tea for colonists, they resisted.

Merchants resisted the Tea Act because they resented the East India Company's monopoly. But like the Sugar Act, the Tea Act affected only a small, specific group of people. The widespread support for resisting the Tea Act had more to do with principles. By buying tea, even though it was cheaper, colonists would be paying the duty and thereby implicitly acknowledging Parliament's right to tax them. According to the *Pennsylvania Chronicle*, Prime Minister Lord North was a "great schemer" who sought "to out wit us, and to effectually establish that Act, which will forever after be pleaded as a precedent for every imposition the Parliament of Great-Britain shall think proper to saddle us with."[24]

The Tea Act stipulated that the duty had to be paid when the ship unloaded. Newspaper essays and letters throughout the summer of 1773 in the major port cities debated what to do upon the ships' arrival. In November, the Boston Sons of Liberty, led by Samuel Adams and John Hancock, resolved to "prevent the landing and sale of the [tea], and the payment of any duty thereon" and to do so "at the risk of their lives and property."[25] The meeting appointed men to guard the wharfs and make sure the tea remained on the ships until they returned to London. This worked and the tea did not reach the shore, but by December 16, the ships were still there. Hence, another town meeting was held at the Old South Meeting House, at the end of which dozens of men disguised as Mohawks made their way to the wharf. The *Boston Gazette* reported what happened next:

> But, behold what followed! A number of brave & resolute men, determined to do all in their power to save their country from the ruin which their enemies had plotted, in less than four hours, emptied every chest of tea on board the three ships . . . amounting to 342 chests, into the sea ! ! without the least damage done to the ships or any other property.[26]

As word spread throughout the colonies, patriots were emboldened to do the same to the tea sitting in their harbors. Tea was either dumped or seized in Charleston, Philadelphia, and New York, with numerous other smaller "tea parties" taking place throughout 1774.

Popular protest spread across the continent and down through all levels of colonial society. Fifty-one women in Edenton, North Carolina, for example, signed an agreement—published in numerous newspapers—in which they promised "to do every Thing as far as lies in our Power" to support the boycotts.[27] The ladies of Edenton were not alone in their desire to support the war effort by what means they could. Women across the thirteen colonies could most readily express their political sentiments as consumers and producers. Because women often made decisions regarding household purchases, their participation in consumer boycotts held particular weight.[28] Some women also took to the streets as part of more unruly mob actions, participating in grain riots, raids on the offices of royal officials, and demonstrations against the impressment of men into naval service. The agitation of so many helped elicit responses from both Britain and the colonial elites.

Britain's response was swift. The following spring, Parliament passed four acts known collectively, by the British, as the Coercive Acts. Colonists, however, referred to them as the Intolerable Acts. First, the Boston Port Act shut down the harbor and cut off all trade to and from the city. The Massachusetts Government Act put the colonial government entirely under British control, dissolving the assembly and restricting town meetings. The Administration of Justice Act allowed any royal official accused of a crime to be tried in Britain rather than by Massachusetts courts and juries. Finally, the Quartering Act, passed for all colonies, allowed the British army to quarter newly arrived soldiers in colonists' homes. Boston had been deemed in open rebellion, and the king, his advisors, and Parliament acted decisively to end the rebellion.

The Crown, however, did not anticipate the other colonies coming to the aid of Massachusetts. Colonists collected food to send to Boston. Virginia's House of Burgesses called for a day of prayer and fasting to show their support. Rather than isolating Massachusetts, the Coercive Acts fostered the sense of shared identity created over the previous decade. After all, if the Crown and Parliament could dissolve Massachusetts's government, nothing could stop them from doing the same to any of her sister colonies. In Massachusetts, patriots created the Provincial Congress, and, throughout 1774, they seized control of local and county governments and courts.[29] In New York, citizens elected committees to direct the colonies' response to the Coercive Acts, including a Mechanics' Committee of middling colonists. By early 1774, Committees of Correspondence and/or extralegal assemblies were established in all of the colonies except Georgia. And throughout the year, they followed Massachusetts's example by seizing the powers of the royal governments.

Committees of Correspondence agreed to send delegates to a Continental Congress to coordinate an intercolonial response. The First Continental Congress convened on September 5, 1774. Over the next six weeks, elite delegates from every colony but Georgia issued a number of documents, including a "Declaration of Rights and Grievances." This document repeated the arguments that colonists had been making since 1765: colonists retained all the rights of native Britons, including the right to be taxed only by their own elected representatives as well as the right to a trial by jury.

Most importantly, the Congress issued a document known as the "Continental Association." The Association declared that "the present unhappy situation of our affairs is occasioned by a ruinous system of colony administration adopted by the British Ministry about the year 1763, evidently calculated for enslaving these Colonies, and, with them, the British Empire." The Association recommended "that a committee be chosen in every county, city, and town . . . whose business it shall be attentively to observe the conduct of all persons touching this association." These Committees of Inspection would consist largely of common colonists. They were effectively deputized to police their communities and instructed to publish the names of anyone who violated the Association so they "may be publicly known, and universally condemned as the enemies of American liberty." The delegates also agreed to a continental nonimportation, nonconsumption, and nonexportation agreement and to "wholly discontinue the slave trade." In all, the Continental Association was perhaps the most radical document of the period. It sought to unite and direct twelve revolutionary governments, establish economic and moral policies, and empower common colonists by giving them an important and unprecedented degree of on-the-ground political power.[30]

But not all colonists were patriots. Indeed, many remained faithful to the king and Parliament, while a good number took a neutral stance. As the situation intensified throughout 1774 and early 1775, factions emerged within the resistance movements in many colonies. Elite merchants who traded primarily with Britain, Anglican clergy, and colonists holding royal offices depended on and received privileges directly from their relationship with Britain. Initially, they sought to exert a moderating influence on the resistance committees, but, following the Association, a number of these colonists began to worry that the resistance was too radical and aimed at independence. They, like most colonists in this period, still expected a peaceful conciliation with Britain and grew increasingly suspicious of the resistance movement.

However, by the time the Continental Congress met again in May 1775, war had already broken out in Massachusetts. On April 19, 1775, British regiments set out to seize local militias' arms and powder stores in Lexington and Concord. The town militia met them at the Lexington Green. The British ordered the militia to disperse when someone fired, setting off a volley from the British. The battle continued all the way to the next town, Concord. News of the events at Lexington spread rapidly throughout the countryside. Militia members, known as minutemen, responded quickly and inflicted significant casualties on the British regiments as they chased them back to Boston. Approximately twenty thousand colonial militiamen laid siege to Boston, effectively trapping the British. In June, the militia set up fortifications on Breed's Hill overlooking the city. In the misnamed "Battle of Bunker Hill," the British attempted to dislodge them from the position with a frontal assault, and, despite eventually taking the hill, they suffered severe casualties at the hands of the colonists.

While men in Boston fought and died, the Continental Congress struggled to organize a response. The radical Massachusetts delegates—including John Adams, Samuel Adams, and John Hancock—implored the Congress to support the Massachusetts militia, who without supplies were laying siege to Boston. Meanwhile, many delegates from the Middle Colonies—including New York, New Jersey, and Philadelphia—took a more moderate position, calling for renewed attempts at reconciliation. In the South, the Virginia delegation contained radicals such as Richard Henry Lee and Thomas Jefferson, while South Carolina's delegation included moderates like John and Edward Rutledge. The moderates worried that supporting the Massachusetts militia would be akin to declaring war.

The Congress struck a compromise, agreeing to adopt the Massachusetts militia and form a Continental Army, naming Virginia delegate

The Battle of Lexington, published by John H. Daniels & Son, c. 1903. Library of Congress.

George Washington commander in chief. They also issued a "Declaration of the Causes of Necessity of Taking Up Arms" to justify the decision. At the same time, the moderates drafted an "Olive Branch Petition," which assured the king that the colonists "most ardently desire[d] the former Harmony between [the mother country] and these Colonies." Many understood that the opportunities for reconciliation were running out. After Congress had approved the document, Benjamin Franklin wrote to a friend saying, "The Congress will send one more Petition to the King which I suppose will be treated as the former was, and therefore will probably be the last."[31] Congress was in the strange position of attempting reconciliation while publicly raising an army.

The petition arrived in England on August 13, 1775, but before it was delivered, the king issued his own "Proclamation for Suppressing Rebellion and Sedition." He believed his subjects in North America were being "misled by dangerous and ill-designing men," who were "traitorously preparing, ordering, and levying war against us." In an October speech to Parliament, he dismissed the colonists' petition. The king had no doubt that the resistance was "manifestly carried on for the purpose of establishing an independent empire."[32] By the start of 1776, talk of independence was growing while the prospect of reconciliation dimmed.

In the opening months of 1776, independence, for the first time, became part of the popular debate. Town meetings approved resolutions in support of independence. Yet, with moderates still hanging on, it would take another seven months before the Continental Congress officially passed the independence resolution. A small forty-six-page pamphlet published in Philadelphia and written by a recent immigrant from England captured the American conversation. Thomas Paine's *Common Sense* argued for independence by denouncing monarchy and challenging the logic behind the British Empire, saying, "There is something absurd, in supposing a continent to be perpetually governed by an island."[33] His combination of easy language, biblical references, and fiery rhetoric proved potent, and the pamphlet was quickly published and dispersed. Arguments over political philosophy and rumors of battlefield developments filled taverns throughout the colonies.

George Washington had taken control of the army and after laying siege to Boston forced the British to retreat to Halifax. In Virginia, the royal governor, Lord Dunmore, issued a proclamation declaring martial law and offering freedom to "all indentured servants, Negros, and others" if they would leave their enslavers and join the British. Though only about five hundred to a thousand enslaved people joined Lord Dunmore's

"Ethiopian regiment," thousands more flocked to the British later in the war, risking capture and punishment for a chance at freedom. Formerly enslaved people occasionally fought, but primarily served in companies called Black Pioneers as laborers, skilled workers, and spies. British motives for offering freedom were practical rather than humanitarian, but the proclamation was the first mass emancipation of enslaved people in American history. Enslaved people could now choose to run and risk their lives for possible freedom with the British army or hope that the United States would live up to its ideals of liberty.[34]

Dunmore's proclamation unnerved white southerners already suspicious of rising antislavery sentiments in the mother country. Four years earlier, English courts dealt a serious blow to slavery in the empire. In *Somerset v Stewart*, James Somerset sued for his freedom, and the court not only granted it but also undercut the very legality of slavery on the British mainland. Somerset and now Dunmore began to convince some enslavers that a new independent nation might offer a surer protection for slavery. Indeed, the proclamation laid the groundwork for the very unrest that loyal southerners had hoped to avoid. Consequently, enslavers often used violence to prevent their enslaved laborers from joining the British or rising against them. Virginia enacted regulations to prevent freedom seeking, threatening to ship rebellious enslaved people to the West Indies or execute them. Many enslavers transported their enslaved people inland, away from the coastal temptation to join the British armies, sometimes separating families in the process.

On May 10, 1776, nearly two months before the Declaration of Independence, the Congress voted on a resolution calling on all colonies that had not already established revolutionary governments to do so and to wrest control from royal officials.[35] The Congress also recommended that the colonies should begin preparing new written constitutions. In many ways, this was the Congress's first declaration of independence. A few weeks later, on June 7, Richard Henry Lee offered the following resolution:

> Resolved, That these United Colonies are, and of right ought to be, Free and Independent States, that they are absolved from all allegiance to the British Crown, and that all political connexion between them and the state of Great Britain is, and ought to be, totally dissolved.[36]

Delegates went scurrying back to their assemblies for new instructions and nearly a month later, on July 2, the resolution finally came to a vote. It passed 12–0, with New York, under imminent threat of British invasion, abstaining.

The passage of Lee's resolution was the official legal declaration of independence, but, between the proposal and vote, a committee had been named to draft a public declaration in case the resolution passed. Virginian Thomas Jefferson drafted the document, with edits being made by his fellow committee members John Adams and Benjamin Franklin, and then again by the Congress as a whole. The famous preamble went beyond the arguments about the rights of British subjects under the British Constitution, instead referring to "natural law":

> We hold these truths to be self-evident, that all men are created equal, that they are endowed by their Creator with certain unalienable Rights, that among these are Life, Liberty and the pursuit of Happiness. That to secure these rights, Governments are instituted among Men, deriving their just powers from the consent of the governed, That whenever any Form of Government becomes destructive of these ends, it is the Right of the People to alter or to abolish it, and to institute new Government.[37]

The majority of the document outlined a list of specific grievances that the colonists had with British attempts to reform imperial administration during the 1760s and 1770s. An early draft blamed the British for the transatlantic slave trade and even for discouraging attempts by the colonists to promote abolition. Delegates from South Carolina and

The Declaration of Independence. National Archives and Records Administration.

Georgia as well as those from northern states who profited from the trade all opposed this language, and it was removed.[38]

Neither the grievances nor the rhetoric of the preamble were new. Instead, they were the culmination of both a decade of popular resistance to imperial reform and decades more of long-term developments that saw both sides develop incompatible understandings of the British Empire and the colonies' place within it. The Congress approved the document on July 4, 1776. However, it was one thing to declare independence; it was quite another to win it on the battlefield.

V. The War for Independence

The war began at Lexington and Concord, more than a year before Congress declared independence. In 1775, the British believed that the mere threat of war and a few minor incursions to seize supplies would be enough to cow the colonial rebellion. Those minor incursions, however, turned into a full-out military conflict. Despite an early American victory at Boston, the new states faced the daunting task of taking on the world's largest military.

In the summer of 1776, the British forces that had abandoned Boston arrived at New York. The largest expeditionary force in British history, including tens of thousands of German mercenaries known as Hessians, followed soon after. New York was the perfect location to launch expeditions aimed at seizing control of the Hudson River and isolating New England from the rest of the continent. Also, New York contained many loyalists, particularly among its merchant and Anglican communities. In October, the British finally launched an attack on Brooklyn and Manhattan. The Continental Army took severe losses before retreating through New Jersey.[39] With the onset of winter, Washington needed something to lift morale and encourage reenlistment. Therefore, he launched a successful surprise attack on the Hessian camp at Trenton on Christmas Day by ferrying the few thousand men he had left across the Delaware River under the cover of night. The victory won the Continental Army much-needed supplies and a morale boost following the disaster at New York.[40]

An even greater success followed in upstate New York. In 1777, British general John Burgoyne led an army from Canada to secure the Hudson River. In upstate New York, he was to meet up with a detachment of General William Howe's forces marching north from Manhattan. However, Howe abandoned the plan without telling Burgoyne and instead sailed to Philadelphia to capture the new nation's capital. The Continental Army defeated Burgoyne's men at Saratoga, New York.[41] This victory proved a major turning point in the war. Benjamin Franklin had been in Paris trying to secure a treaty of alliance with the French. However, the French were reluctant to back what seemed like an unlikely cause. News of the victory at Saratoga convinced the French that the cause might not have been as unlikely as they had thought. A Treaty of Amity and Commerce was signed on February 6, 1778. The treaty effectively turned a colonial rebellion into a global war as fighting between the British and French soon broke out in Europe and India.[42]

Howe had taken Philadelphia in 1777 but returned to New York once winter ended. He slowly realized that European military tactics would not work in North America. In Europe, armies fought head-on battles in attempt to seize major cities. However, in 1777, the British had held Philadelphia and New York and yet still weakened their position. Meanwhile, Washington realized after New York that the largely untrained Continental Army could not win head-on battles with the professional British army. So he developed his own logic of warfare that involved smaller, more frequent skirmishes and avoided major engagements that would risk his entire army. As long as he kept the army intact, the war would continue, no matter how many cities the British captured.

In 1778, the British shifted their attentions to the South, where they believed they enjoyed more popular support. Campaigns from Virginia to South Carolina and Georgia captured major cities, but the British simply did not have the manpower to retain military control. And upon their departures, severe fighting ensued between local patriots and loyalists,

In this 1782 cartoon, the British lion faces a spaniel (Spain), a rooster (France), a rattlesnake (America), and a pug dog (Netherlands). Though the caption predicts Britain's success, it illustrates that Britain faced challenges—and therefore drains on their military and treasury—from more than just the American rebels. J. Barrow, *The British Lion Engaging Four Powers*, 1782. National Maritime Museum, Greenwich, London.

often pitting family members against one another. The War in the South was truly a civil war.[43]

By 1781, the British were also fighting France, Spain, and Holland. The British public's support for the costly war in North America was quickly waning. The Americans took advantage of the British southern strategy with significant aid from the French army and navy. In October, Washington marched his troops from New York to Virginia in an effort to trap the British southern army under the command of General Charles Cornwallis. Cornwallis had dug his men in at Yorktown awaiting supplies and reinforcements from New York. However, the Continental and French armies arrived first, quickly followed by a French navy contingent, encircling Cornwallis's forces and, after laying siege to the city, forcing his surrender. The capture of another army left the British without a new strategy and without public support to continue the war. Peace negotiations took place in France, and the war came to an official end on September 3, 1783.[44]

Americans celebrated their victory, but it came at great cost. Soldiers suffered through brutal winters with inadequate resources. During the

Lord Cornwallis's surrender signaled the victory of the American revolutionaries over what they considered to be the despotic rule of Britain. This moment would live on in American memory as a pivotal one in the nation's origin story, prompting the United States government to commission artist John Trumbull to create this painting of the event in 1817. John Trumbull, *Surrender of Lord Cornwallis*, 1820. Wikimedia.

single winter at Valley Forge in 1777–1778, over 2,500 Americans died from disease and exposure. Life was not easy on the home front either. Women on both sides of the conflict were frequently left alone to care for their households. In addition to their existing duties, women took on roles usually assigned to men on farms and in shops and taverns. Abigail Adams addressed the difficulties she encountered while "minding family affairs" on their farm in Braintree, Massachusetts. Abigail managed the planting and harvesting of crops, in the midst of severe labor shortages and inflation, while dealing with several tenants on the Adams property, raising her children, and making clothing and other household goods. In order to support the family economically during John's frequent absences and the uncertainties of war, Abigail also invested in several speculative schemes and sold imported goods.[45]

While Abigail remained safely out of the fray, other women were not so fortunate. The Revolution was not only fought on distant battle-fields. It was fought on women's very doorsteps, in the fields next to their homes. There was no way for women to avoid the conflict or the disruptions and devastations it caused. As the leader of the state militia during the Revolution, Mary Silliman's husband, Gold, was absent from their home for much of the conflict. On the morning of July 7, 1779, when a British fleet attacked nearby Fairfield, Connecticut, it was Mary who calmly evacuated her household, including her children and servants, to North Stratford. When Gold was captured by loyalists and held prisoner,

American soldiers came from a variety of backgrounds and had numerous reasons for fighting with the American army. Jean-Baptiste-Antoine DeVerger, a French sublieutenant at the Battle of Yorktown, painted this watercolor soon after that battle and chose to depict four men in military dress: an African American soldier from the 2nd Rhode Island Regiment, a man in the homespun of the militia, another wearing the common "hunting shirt" of the frontier, and the French soldier on the end. Jean-Baptiste-Antoine DeVerger, *American Soldiers at the Siege of Yorktown*, 1781. Wikimedia.

Mary, six months pregnant with their second child, wrote letters to try to secure his release. When such appeals were ineffectual, Mary spearheaded an effort, along with Connecticut Governor, John Trumbull, to capture a prominent Tory leader to exchange for her husband's freedom.[46]

Black Americans, enslaved and free, also impacted (and were impacted by) the Revolution. The British were the first to recruit Black (or "Ethiopian") regiments, as early as Dunmore's Proclamation of 1775 in Virginia, which promised freedom to any enslaved people who would escape their enslavers and join the British cause. At first, Washington, an enslaver himself, resisted allowing Black men to join the Continental Army, but he eventually relented. In 1775, Peter Salem's enslaver freed him to fight with the militia. Salem faced British Regulars in the battles at Lexington and Bunker Hill, where he fought valiantly with around three dozen other Black Americans. Salem not only contributed to the cause, he earned the ability to determine his own life after his enlistment ended. Salem was not alone, but many more enslaved people seized on the tu-

Another John Trumbull piece commissioned for the Capitol in 1817, this painting depicts what would be remembered as the moment the new United States became a republic. On December 23, 1783, George Washington, widely considered the hero of the Revolution, resigned his position as the most powerful man in the former thirteen colonies. Giving up his role as commander-in-chief of the army ensured that civilian rule would define the new nation, and that a republic would be set in place rather than a dictatorship. John Trumbull, *General George Washington Resigning His Commission*, c. 1817–1824. From the Architect of the Capitol.

mult of war to run away and secure their own freedom directly. Historians estimate that between thirty thousand and one hundred thousand enslaved people deserted their masters during the war.[47]

Men and women together struggled through years of war and hardship. For patriots (and those who remained neutral), victory brought new political, social, and economic opportunities, but it also brought new uncertainties. The war decimated entire communities, particularly in the South. Thousands of women throughout the nation had been widowed. The American economy, weighed down by war debt and depreciated currencies, would have to be rebuilt following the war. State constitutions had created governments, but now men would have to figure out how to govern. The opportunities created by the Revolution had come at great cost, in both lives and fortune, and it was left to the survivors to seize those opportunities and help forge and define the new nation-state.

VI. The Consequences of the American Revolution

Like the earlier distinction between "origins" and "causes," the Revolution also had short- and long-term consequences. Perhaps the most important immediate consequence of declaring independence was the creation of state constitutions in 1776 and 1777. The Revolution also unleashed powerful political, social, and economic forces that would transform the new nation's politics and society, including increased participation in politics and governance, the legal institutionalization of religious toleration, and the growth and diffusion of the population, particularly westward. The Revolution affected Native Americans by opening up western settlement and creating governments hostile to their territorial claims. Even more broadly, the Revolution ended the mercantilist economy, opening new opportunities in trade and manufacturing.

The new states drafted written constitutions, which, at the time, was an important innovation from the traditionally unwritten British Constitution. These new state constitutions were based on the idea of "popular sovereignty," that is, that the power and authority of the government derived from the people.[48] Most created weak governors and strong legislatures with more regular elections and moderately increased the size of the electorate. A number of states followed the example of Virginia and included a declaration or "bill" of rights in their constitution designed to protect the rights of individuals and circumscribe the prerogative of the government. Pennsylvania's first state constitution was the most radical and democratic. They created a unicameral legislature and an Executive Council but no genuine executive. All free men could vote, including those who did not own property. Massachusetts's constitution, passed in 1780, was less democratic in structure but underwent a more popular process of ratification. In the fall of 1779, each town sent delegates—312 in all—to a constitutional convention in Cambridge. Town meetings debated the constitution draft and offered suggestions. Anticipating the later federal constitution, Massachusetts established a three-branch government based on checks and balances between the branches. Independence came in 1776, and so did an unprecedented period of constitution making and state building.

The Continental Congress ratified the Articles of Confederation in 1781. The articles allowed each state one vote in the Continental Congress. But the articles are perhaps most notable for what they did not allow. Congress was given no power to levy or collect taxes, regulate foreign or interstate commerce, or establish a federal judiciary. These shortcomings rendered the postwar Congress weak and largely ineffectual.

Political and social life changed drastically after independence. Political participation grew as more people gained the right to vote, leading to greater importance being placed on representation within government.[49] In addition, more common citizens (or "new men") played increasingly important roles in local and state governance. Hierarchy within the states underwent significant changes. Society became less deferential and more egalitarian, less aristocratic and more meritocratic.

The Revolution's most important long-term economic consequence was the end of mercantilism. The British Empire had imposed various restrictions on the colonial economies including limiting trade, settlement, and manufacturing. The Revolution opened new markets and new trade relationships. The Americans' victory also opened the western territories for invasion and settlement, which created new domestic markets. Americans began to create their own manufactures, no longer content to rely on those in Britain.

Despite these important changes, the American Revolution had its limits. Following their unprecedented expansion into political affairs during the imperial resistance, women also served the patriot cause during the war. However, the Revolution did not result in civic equality for women. Instead, during the immediate postwar period, women became incorporated into the polity to some degree as "republican mothers." Republican societies required virtuous citizens, and it became mothers' responsibility to raise and educate future citizens. This opened opportunity for women regarding education, but they still remained largely on the peripheries of the new American polity.

A SOCIETY of PATRIOTIC LADIES,
AT
EDENTON in NORTH CAROLINA.
Plate V.

In the thirteen colonies, boycotting women were seen as patriots. In British prints such as this, they were mocked as as immoral harlots sticking their noses in the business of men. Philip Dawe, *A Society of Patriotic Ladies at Edenton in North Carolina*, March 1775. Metropolitan Museum of Art.

Approximately sixty thousand loyalists ended up leaving America because of the Revolution. Loyalists came from all ranks of American society, and many lived the rest of their lives in exile from their homeland. A clause in the Treaty of Paris was supposed to protect their property and require the Americans to compensate Loyalists who had lost property during the war because of their allegiance. The Americans, however, reneged on this promise and, throughout the 1780s, states continued seizing property held by Loyalists. Some colonists went to England, where they were strangers and outsiders in what they had thought of as their mother country. Many more, however, settled on the peripheries of the British Empire throughout the world, especially Nova Scotia, New Brunswick, and Quebec. The Loyalists had come out on the losing side of a Revolution, and many lost everything they had and were forced to create new lives far from the land of their birth.[50]

In 1783, thousands of formerly enslaved Loyalists fled with the British army. They hoped that the British government would uphold the promise of freedom and help them establish new homes elsewhere in the Empire. The Treaty of Paris, which ended the war, demanded that British troops leave formerly enslaved people behind, but the British military commanders

Joseph Brandt as painted by George Romney.
Brandt was a Mohawk leader who led Mohawk
and British forces in western New York. Wikimedia.

upheld earlier promises and evacuated thousands of freedmen, transporting
them to Canada, the Caribbean, or Great Britain. They would eventually
play a role in settling Nova Scotia, and through the subsequent efforts of
David George, a Black loyalist and Baptist preacher, some settled in Sierra
Leone in Africa. Black loyalists, however, continued to face social and economic marginalization, including restrictions on land ownership within the
British Empire.[51]

The fight for liberty led some Americans to manumit their enslaved
laborers, and most of the new northern states soon passed gradual emancipation laws. Some manumissions also occurred in the Upper South, but
in the Lower South, some enslavers revoked their offers of freedom for
service, and other freedmen were forced back into bondage. The Revolution's rhetoric of equality created a "revolutionary generation" of enslaved people and free Black Americans that would eventually encourage

the antislavery movement. Slave revolts began to incorporate claims for freedom based on revolutionary ideals. In the long term, the Revolution failed to reconcile slavery with these new egalitarian republican societies, a tension that eventually boiled over in the 1830s and 1840s and effectively tore the nation in two in the 1850s and 1860s.[52]

Native Americans, too, participated in and were affected by the Revolution. Many Native American groups, such as the Shawnee, Creek, Cherokee, and Iroquois, had sided with the British. They had hoped for a British victory that would continue to restrain the land-hungry colonial settlers from moving west beyond the Appalachian Mountains. Unfortunately, the Americans' victory and Native Americans' support for the British created a pretense for justifying rapid and often brutal expansion into the western territories. Native American peoples would continue to be displaced and pushed farther west throughout the nineteenth century. Ultimately, American independence marked the beginning of the end of what had remained of Native American independence.

VII. Conclusion

The American Revolution freed colonists from British rule and offered the first blow in what historians have called "the age of democratic revolutions." The American Revolution was a global event.[53] Revolutions followed in France, then Haiti, and then South America. The American Revolution meanwhile wrought significant changes to the British Empire. Many British historians even use the Revolution as a dividing point between a "first British Empire" and a "second British Empire." At home, however, the Revolution created a new nation-state, the United States of America. By September 1783, independence had been won. What the new nation would look like, however, was still very much up for grabs. In the 1780s, Americans would shape and then reshape that nation-state, first with the Articles of Confederation, ratified in 1781, and then with the Constitution in 1787 and 1788.

Historians have long argued over the causes and character of the American Revolution. Was the Revolution caused by British imperial policy or by internal tensions within the colonies? Were colonists primarily motivated by constitutional principles, ideals of equality, or economic self-interest? Was the Revolution radical or conservative? But such questions are hardly limited to historians. From Abraham Lincoln's use of the Declaration of Independence in the Gettysburg Address to twenty-first-century Tea Party members wearing knee breeches, the Revolution has remained at the center of American political culture. Indeed, how one understands the Revolution often dictates how one defines what it means to be American.

The Revolution was not won by a few founding fathers. Men and women of all ranks contributed to the colonies' most improbable victory, from the commoners who protested the Stamp Act to the women who helped organize boycotts against the Townshend duties; from the men, Black and white, who fought in the army to the women who contributed to its support. The Revolution, however, did not aim to end all social and civic inequalities in the new nation, and, in the case of Native Americans, it created new inequalities. But over time, the Revolution's rhetoric of equality, as encapsulated in the Declaration of Independence, helped highlight some of those inequalities and became a shared aspiration for future social and political movements, including, among others, the abolitionist and women's rights movements of the nineteenth century, the suffragist and civil rights movements of the twentieth century, and the gay rights movement of the twenty-first century.

VIII. Reference Material

This chapter was edited by Michael Hattem, with content contributions by James Ambuske, Alexander Burns, Joshua Beatty, Christina Carrick, Christopher Consolino, Michael Hattem, Timothy C. Hemmis, Joseph Moore, Emily Romeo, and Christopher Sparshott.

Recommended citation: James Ambuske et al., "The American Revolution," Michael Hattem, ed., in *The American Yawp*, eds. Joseph Locke and Ben Wright (Stanford, CA: Stanford University Press, 2019).

NOTES TO CHAPTER 5

1. Benjamin Rush to Ebenezer Hazard, October 22, 1768, in L. H. Butterfield, ed., *Letters of Benjamin Rush*, 2 vols. (Princeton, NJ: Princeton University Press, 1951), vol. 1, 68.

2. Jack P. Greene, *The Constitutional Origins of the American Revolution* (Cambridge, UK: New York: Cambridge University Press, 2010).

3. James Otis, *The Rights of the Colonies Asserted and Proved* (Boston: Edes and Gill, 1764), 52, 38.

4. Greene, *Constitutional Origins of the American Revolution*, 118.

5. Bernard Bailyn, *The Ideological Origins of the American Revolution* (Cambridge, MA: Belknap Press, 1967).

6. Jack P. Greene, *Pursuits of Happiness: The Social Development of Early Modern British Colonies and the Formation of American Culture* (Chapel Hill: University of North Carolina Press, 1988), 170–171. Also see John Murrin,

"Anglicizing an American Colony: The Transformation of Provincial Massachusetts," PhD diss., Yale University, 1966.

7. Daniel Dulany, *Considerations on the Propriety of Imposing Taxes in the British Colonies, for the Purpose of Raising a Revenue, by Act of Parliament. The Second Edition* (Annapolis, MD: Jonas Green, 1765), 34. For a 1766 London reprint, see https://archive.org/details/cihm_20394, accessed April 24, 2018.

8. *Newport Mercury*, June 24, 1765. This version was also reprinted in newspapers in New York, Boston, Philadelphia, and Maryland.

9. *Proceedings of the Congress at New-York* (Annapolis, MD: Jonas Green, 1766).

10. Dulany, *Considerations on the Propriety of Imposing Taxes in the British Colonies*, 8.

11. "The Colonist's Advocate: III, 11 January 1770," Founders Online, National Archives. http://founders.archives.gov/documents/Franklin/01-17-02-0009, last modified June 29, 2017.

12. George Canning, *A Letter to the Right Honourable Wills Earl of Hillsborough, on the Connection Between Great Britain and Her American Colonies* (London: T. Becket, 1768), 9.

13. "New York, October 31, 1765," *New-York Gazette, or Weekly Mercury*, November 7, 1765.

14. "Resolution of Non-Importation made by the Citizens of Philadelphia," October 25, 1765, mss., Historical Society of Pennsylvania. http://digitalhistory
.hsp.org/pafrm/doc/resolution-non-importation-made-citizens-philadelphia
-october-25-1765. For the published notice of the resolution, see "Philadelphia, November 7, 1765," broadside, "Pennsylvania Stamp Act and Non-Importation Resolutions Collection," American Philosophical Society, Philadelphia, PA.

15. "The Petition of the London Merchants to the House of Commons," in *Prologue to Revolution: Sources and Documents on the Stamp Act Crisis, 1764–1766*, ed. Edmund S. Morgan (Chapel Hill: University of North Carolina Press, 1959), 130–131.

16. Governor Francis Bernard to Lord Halifax, August 15, 1765, in ibid., 107.

17. For Hutchinson's own account of the events, see Thomas Hutchinson to Richard Jackson, August 30, 1765, in *The Correspondence of Thomas Hutchinson, Volume 1: 1740–1766*, ed. John W. Tyler (Boston: Colonial Society of Massachusetts, 2014), 291–294.

18. *Documents Relative to the Colonial History of the State of New-York, procured in Holland, England, and France*, 13 vols., ed. Edmund O'Callaghan (Albany, NY: Weed, Parsons, 1856), vol. 7, 770. https://pbs.twimg.com/media
/Btm5M84IMAA4MCY.png:large, accessed April 24, 2018.

19. "The Declaratory Act," The Avalon Project: Documents in Law, History, and Diplomacy. http://avalon.law.yale.edu/18th_century/declaratory_act_1766
.asp, accessed April 24, 2018.

20. "Letters from a Farmer in Pennsylvania, to the Inhabitants of the British Colonies. Letter II," *Pennsylvania Gazette*, December 10, 1767.

21. "Address to the Ladies," *Boston Post-Boy*, November 16, 1767; *Boston Evening-Post*, February 12, 1770. Many female contributions to political commentary took the form of poems and drama, as in the poetry of Hannah Griffitts and satirical plays by Mercy Otis Warren.

22. Carol Berkin, *Revolutionary Mothers: Women in the Struggle for America's Independence* (New York: Knopf, 2005), 17–18.

23. *New York Gazette, or Weekly Post-Boy*, June 18, July 9, 16, 1770.

24. *Pennsylvania Chronicle*, September 27, 1773. For an example of how fast news and propaganda was spreading throughout the colonies, this piece was reprinted in *Massachusetts Gazette*, October 4, 1773; *New-Hampshire Gazette, and Historical Chronicle*, October 15, 1773; and *Virginia Gazette*, October 21, 1773.

25. *Massachusetts Gazette, and Boston Post-Boy*, November 29, 1773.

26. *Boston Gazette*, December 20, 1773.

27. *Virginia Gazette*, November 3, 1774; Cynthia A. Kierner, "The Edenton Ladies: Women, Tea, and Politics in Revolutionary North Carolina," in *North Carolina Women: Their Lives and Times*, ed. Michele Gillespie and Sally G. McMillen (Athens: University of Georgia Press, 2014), 12–33.

28. Ellen Hartigan-O'Connor, *The Ties That Buy: Women and Commerce in Revolutionary America* (Philadelphia: University of Pennsylvania Press, 2009), 178–184.

29. Ray Raphael, *The First American Revolution: Before Lexington and Concord* (New York: New Press, 2002), 59–168.

30. *American Archives: Fourth Series Containing a Documentary History of the English Colonies in North America*, ed. Peter Force (Washington, D.C.: Clarke and Force, 1837), vol. 1, 913–916. https://archive.org/stream/AmericanArchives-FourthSeriesVolume1-ContainingADocumentaryHistory/AaSeries4VolumeI#page/n455/mode/2up, accessed April 24, 2018.

31. "From Benjamin Franklin to Jonathan Shipley, 7 July 1775," Founders Online, National Archives. http://founders.archives.gov/documents/Franklin/01-22-02-0057, last modified June 29, 2017.

32. Gt. Brit. Soveriengs, Etc., "His Majesty's Most Gracious Speech to Both Houses of Parliament, on Friday, October 27, 1775 . . . New York? 1775]." https://www.loc.gov/item/rbpe.10803800/, accessed April 24, 2018.

33. Thomas Paine, *Common Sense* (Philadelphia: W. T. and Bradford, 1776). https://www.gutenberg.org/files/147/147-h/147-h.htm, accessed April 24, 2018.

34. *Pennsylvania Evening Post*, September 21, 1776.

35. *Journals of the Continental Congress, 1774–1789*, 34 vols. (Washington, DC: U.S. Government Printing Office, 1904–1937), vol. 4, 342. http://memory.loc.gov/cgi-bin/query/r?ammem/hlaw:@field(DOCID+@lit(jc004109.

36. "Report & the Resolution for Independancy Agreed to July 2d. 1776," Papers of the Continental Congress, No. 23, folio 17, National Archives, Washington, DC. http://www.archives.gov/exhibits/american_originals/declarat.html.

37. *Journals of the Continental Congress* 5: 510–516.

38. For more on the process of writing the Declaration of Independence, see Pauline Maier, *American Scripture: Making the Declaration of Independence* (New York: Knopf, 1997).

39. Barnet Schecter, *The Battle for New York: The City at the Heart of the American Revolution* (New York: Walker, 2002).

40. David Hackett Fischer, *Washington's Crossing* (New York: Oxford University Press, 2004).

41. Richard M. Ketchum, *Saratoga: Turning Point of America's Revolutionary War* (New York: Holt, 1997).

42. For more on Franklin's diplomacy in France, see Stacy Schiff, *A Great Improvisation: Franklin, France, and the Birth of America* (New York: Thorndike Press, 2005).

43. David K. Wilson, *The Southern Strategy: Britain's Conquest of South Carolina and Georgia, 1775–1780* (Columbia: University of South Carolina Press, 2005).

44. Richard M. Ketchum, *Victory at Yorktown: The Campaign That Won the Revolution* (New York: Holt, 2004).

45. Woody Holton, *Abigail Adams* (New York: Free Press, 2009), 208–217.

46. Joy Day Buel and Richard Buel, *The Way of Duty: A Woman and Her Family in Revolutionary America* (New York: Norton, 1995), 145–170.

47. For discussion of these numerical estimates, see Gary Nash's introduction to Benjamin Quarles, *The Negro in the American Revolution* (Chapel Hill: University of North Carolina, Press, 1996), xxiii.

48. Willi Paul Adams, *The First American Constitutions: Republican Ideology and the Making of the State Constitutions in the Revolutionary Era* (Lanham, MD: Rowman and Littlefield, 2001), 126–146.

49. Gordon S. Wood, *The Creation of the American Republic, 1776–1787* (Chapel Hill: University of North Carolina Press, 1969).

50. Maya Jasanoff, *Liberty's Exiles: American Loyalists in the Revolutionary World* (New York: Knopf, 2011).

51. Alan Gilbert, *Black Patriots and Loyalists: Fighting for Emancipation in the War of Independence* (Chicago: University of Chicago Press, 2012).

52. Ira Berlin, *Many Thousands Gone: The First Two Centuries of Slavery in North America* (Cambridge, MA: Harvard University Press, 1998), 217–289.

53. For a summary of the global aspects of the Revolution, see Ted Brackemyre, "The American Revolution: A Very European Ordeal," *U.S. History Scene*, http://ushistoryscene.com/article/am-rev-european-ordeal, accessed April 24, 2018.

RECOMMENDED READING

Bailyn, Bernard. *The Ideological Origins of the American Revolution*. Cambridge, MA: Belknap Press, 1967.

Berkin, Carol. *Revolutionary Mothers: Women in the Struggle for America's Independence*. New York: Knopf, 2005.

Breen, T. H. *The Marketplace of Revolution: How Consumer Politics Shaped American Independence*. New York: Oxford University Press, 2004.

Carp, Benjamin L. *Rebels Rising: Cities and the American Revolution*. New York: Oxford University Press, 2007.

Duvall, Kathleen. *Independence Lost: Lives on the Edge of the American Revolution*. New York: Random House, 2015.

Egerton, Douglas R. *Death or Liberty: African Americans and Revolutionary America.* New York: Oxford University Press, 2008.

Eustace, Nicole. *Passion Is the Gale: Emotion, Power, and the Coming of the American Revolution.* Chapel Hill: University of North Carolina Press, 2008.

Fliegelman, Jay. *Prodigals and Pilgrims: The American Revolution Against Patriarchal Authority 1750–1800.* New York: Cambridge University Press, 1985.

Gould, Eliga. *Among the Powers of the Earth: The American Revolution and the Making of a New World Empire.* Cambridge, MA: Harvard University Press, 2012.

Greene, Jack P. *The Constitutional Origins of the American Revolution.* New York: Cambridge University Press, 2010.

Holton, Woody. *Forced Founders: Indians, Debtors, Slaves, and the Making of the American Revolution in Virginia.* Chapel Hill: University of North Carolina Press, 1999.

Jasanoff, Maya. *Liberty's Exiles: American Loyalists in the Revolutionary World.* New York: Knopf, 2011.

Kamensky, Jane. *A Revolution in Color: The World of John Singleton Copley.* New York: Norton, 2016.

Kerber, Linda K. *Women of the Republic: Intellect and Ideology in Revolutionary America.* Chapel Hill: University of North Carolina Press, 1980.

Knott, Sarah. *Sensibility and the American Revolution.* Chapel Hill: University of North Carolina Press, 2009.

Landers, Jane G. *Atlantic Creoles in the Age of Revolutions.* Cambridge, MA: Harvard University Press, 2010.

Maier, Pauline. *American Scripture: Making the Declaration of Independence.* New York: Knopf, 1997.

———. *From Resistance to Revolution: Colonial Radicals and the Development of American Opposition to Britain, 1765–1776.* New York: Vintage Books, 1974.

Nash, Gary B. *The Unknown American Revolution: The Unruly Birth of Democracy and the Struggle to Create America.* New York: Viking, 2005.

Norton, Mary Beth. *Liberty's Daughters: The Revolutionary Experience of American Women, 1750–1800.* Ithaca, NY: Cornell University Press, 1980.

O'Shaughnessy, Andrew Jackson. *The Men Who Lost America: British Leadership, the American Revolution, and the Fate of the Empire.* New Haven, CT: Yale University Press, 2013.

Schiff, Stacy. *A Great Improvisation: Franklin, France, and the Birth of America.* New York: Thorndike Press, 2005.

Waldstreicher, David. *Slavery's Constitution: From Revolution to Ratification.* New York: Hill and Wang, 2009.

Wood, Gordon S. *The Radicalism of the American Revolution.* New York: Vintage Books, 1992.

Young, Alfred F., and Gregory Nobles. *Whose American Revolution Was It? Historians Interpret the Founding.* New York: New York University Press, 2011.

REDEUNT SATURNIA REGNA.

On the erection of the Eleventh PILLAR of the great Na-tional DOME, we beg leave most sincerely to felicitate " OUR DEAR COUNT-

Rise it will.

The foundation good—it may ye be SAVED.

The FEDERAL EDIFICE.
ELEVEN STARS. in quick succession rise—

6

A New Nation

I. Introduction

On July 4, 1788, Philadelphians turned out for a "grand federal procession" in honor of the new national constitution. Workers in various trades and professions demonstrated. Blacksmiths carted around a working forge, on which they symbolically beat swords into farm tools. Potters proudly carried a sign paraphrasing from the Bible, "The potter hath power over his clay," linking God's power with an artisan's work and a citizen's control over the country. Christian clergymen meanwhile marched arm-in-arm with Jewish rabbis. The grand procession represented what many Americans hoped the United States would become: a diverse but cohesive, prosperous nation.[1]

Over the next few years, Americans would celebrate more of these patriotic holidays. In April 1789, for example, thousands gathered in New York to see George Washington take the presidential oath of office. That November, Washington called his fellow citizens to celebrate with a day of thanksgiving, particularly for "the peaceable and rational manner" in which the government had been established.[2]

"The Federal Pillars," from the *Massachusetts Centinel,* August 2, 1789. Library of Congress.

But the new nation was never as cohesive as its champions had hoped. Although the officials of the new federal government—and the people who supported it—placed great emphasis on unity and cooperation, the country was often anything but unified. The Constitution itself had been a controversial document adopted to strengthen the government so that it could withstand internal conflicts. Whatever the later celebrations, the new nation had looked to the future with uncertainty. Less than two years before the national celebrations of 1788 and 1789, the United States had faced the threat of collapse.

II. Shays's Rebellion

In 1786 and 1787, a few years after the Revolution ended, thousands of farmers in western Massachusetts were struggling under a heavy burden of debt. Their problems were made worse by weak local and national economies. Many political leaders saw both the debt and the struggling economy as a consequence of the Articles of Confederation, which provided the federal government with no way to raise revenue and did little

Daniel Shays became a divisive figure, to some a violent rebel seeking to upend the new American government, to others an upholder of the true revolutionary virtues Shays and others fought for. This contemporary depiction of Shays and his accomplice Job Shattuck portrays them in the latter light as rising "illustrious from the Jail." Unidentified artist, *Daniel Shays and Job Shattuck*, 1787. Wikimedia.

to create a cohesive nation out of the various states. The farmers wanted the Massachusetts government to protect them from their creditors, but the state supported the lenders instead. As creditors threatened to foreclose on their property, many of these farmers, including Revolutionary War veterans, took up arms.

Led by a fellow veteran named Daniel Shays, these armed men, the "Shaysites," resorted to tactics like the patriots had used before the Revolution, forming blockades around courthouses to keep judges from issuing foreclosure orders. These protesters saw their cause and their methods as an extension of the "Spirit of 1776"; they were protecting their rights and demanding redress for the people's grievances.

Governor James Bowdoin, however, saw the Shaysites as rebels who wanted to rule the government through mob violence. He called up thousands of militiamen to disperse them. A former Revolutionary general, Benjamin Lincoln, led the state force, insisting that Massachusetts must prevent "a state of anarchy, confusion and slavery."[3] In January 1787, Lincoln's militia arrested more than one thousand Shaysites and reopened the courts.

Daniel Shays and other leaders were indicted for treason, and several were sentenced to death, but eventually Shays and most of his followers received pardons. Their protest, which became known as Shays's Rebellion, generated intense national debate. While some Americans, like Thomas Jefferson, thought "a little rebellion now and then" helped keep the country free, others feared the nation was sliding toward anarchy and complained that the states could not maintain control. For nationalists like James Madison of Virginia, Shays's Rebellion was a prime example of why the country needed a strong central government. "Liberty," Madison warned, "may be endangered by the abuses of liberty as well as the abuses of power."[4]

III. The Constitutional Convention

The uprising in Massachusetts convinced leaders around the country to act. After years of goading by James Madison and other nationalists, delegates from twelve of the thirteen states met at the Pennsylvania state house in Philadelphia in the summer of 1787. Only Rhode Island declined to send a representative. The delegates arrived at the convention with instructions to revise the Articles of Confederation.

The biggest problem the convention needed to solve was the federal government's inability to levy taxes. That weakness meant that the burden of paying back debt from the Revolutionary War fell on the states.

The states, in turn, found themselves beholden to the lenders who had bought up their war bonds. That was part of why Massachusetts had chosen to side with its wealthy bondholders over poor western farmers.[5]

James Madison, however, had no intention of simply revising the Articles of Confederation. He intended to produce a completely new national constitution. In the preceding year, he had completed two extensive research projects—one on the history of government in the United States, the other on the history of republics around the world. He used this research as the basis for a proposal he brought with him to Philadelphia. It came to be called the Virginia Plan, named after Madison's home state.[6]

The Virginia Plan was daring. Classical learning said that a republican form of government required a small and homogenous state: the Roman republic, or a small country like Denmark, for example. Citizens who were too far apart or too different could not govern themselves successfully. Conventional wisdom said the United States needed to have a very weak central government, which should simply represent the states on certain matters they had in common. Otherwise, power should stay at the state or local level. But Madison's research had led him in a different direction. He believed it was possible to create "an extended republic" encompassing a diversity of people, climates, and customs.

The Virginia Plan, therefore, proposed that the United States should have a strong federal government. It was to have three branches—legislative, executive, and judicial—with power to act on any issues of na-

James Madison was a central figure in the reconfiguration of the national government. Madison's Virginia Plan was a guiding document in the formation of a new government under the Constitution. John Vanderlyn, *Portrait of James Madison*, 1816. Wikimedia.

tional concern. The legislature, or Congress, would have two houses, in which every state would be represented according to its population size or tax base. The national legislature would have veto power over state laws.[7]

Other delegates to the convention generally agreed with Madison that the Articles of Confederation had failed. But they did not agree on what kind of government should replace them. In particular, they disagreed about the best method of representation in the new Congress. Representation was an important issue that influenced a host of other decisions, including deciding how the national executive branch should work, what specific powers the federal government should have, and even what to do about the divisive issue of slavery.

For more than a decade, each state had enjoyed a single vote in the Continental Congress. William Patterson's New Jersey Plan proposed to keep things that way. The Connecticut delegate Roger Sherman, furthermore, argued that members of Congress should be appointed by the state legislatures. Ordinary voters, Sherman said, lacked information, were "constantly liable to be misled" and "should have as little to do as may be" about most national decisions.[8] Large states, however, preferred the Virginia Plan, which would give their citizens far more power over the legislative branch. James Wilson of Pennsylvania argued that since the Virginia Plan would vastly increase the powers of the national government, representation should be drawn as directly as possible from the public. No government, he warned, "could long subsist without the confidence of the people."[9]

Ultimately, Roger Sherman suggested a compromise. Congress would have a lower house, the House of Representatives, in which members were assigned according to each state's population, and an upper house, which became the Senate, in which each state would have one vote. This proposal, after months of debate, was adopted in a slightly altered form as the Great Compromise: each state would have two senators, who could vote independently. In addition to establishing both types of representation, this compromise also counted three-fifths of a state's enslaved population for representation and tax purposes.

The delegates took even longer to decide on the form of the national executive branch. Should executive power be in the hands of a committee or a single person? How should its officeholders be chosen? On June 1, James Wilson moved that the national executive power reside in a single person. Coming only four years after the American Revolution, that proposal was extremely contentious; it conjured up images of an elected monarchy.[10] The delegates also worried about how to protect the executive branch from corruption or undue control. They endlessly debated these questions, and not until early September did they decide the president would be elected by a special electoral college.

In the end, the Constitutional Convention proposed a government unlike any other, combining elements copied from ancient republics and English political tradition but making some limited democratic innovations—all while trying to maintain a delicate balance between national and state sovereignty. It was a complicated and highly controversial scheme.

IV. Ratifying the Constitution

The convention voted to send its proposed Constitution to Congress, which was then sitting in New York, with a cover letter from George Washington. The plan for adopting the new Constitution, however, required approval from special state ratification conventions, not just Congress. During the ratification process, critics of the Constitution organized to persuade voters in the different states to oppose it.

Importantly, the Constitutional Convention had voted down a proposal from Virginia's George Mason, the author of Virginia's state Declaration of Rights, for a national bill of rights. This omission became a

Delegates to the Constitutional Convention assembled, argued, and finally agreed in this room, styled in the same manner as during the Convention. Photograph of the Assembly Room, Independence Hall, Philadelphia, Pennsylvania. Wikimedia. Creative Commons Attribution-Share Alike 3.0 Unported.

rallying point for opponents of the document. Many of these Anti-Federalists argued that without such a guarantee of specific rights, American citizens risked losing their personal liberty to the powerful federal government. The pro-ratification Federalists, on the other hand, argued that including a bill of rights was not only redundant but dangerous; it could limit future citizens from adding new rights.[11]

Citizens debated the merits of the Constitution in newspaper articles, letters, sermons, and coffeehouse quarrels across America. Some of the most famous, and most important, arguments came from Alexander Hamilton, John Jay, and James Madison in the *Federalist Papers*, which were published in various New York newspapers in 1787 and 1788.[12] The first crucial vote came at the beginning of 1788 in Massachusetts. At first, the Anti-Federalists at the Massachusetts ratifying convention probably had the upper hand, but after weeks of debate, enough delegates changed their votes to narrowly approve the Constitution. But they also approved a number of proposed amendments, which were to be submitted to the first Congress. This pattern—ratifying the Constitution but attaching proposed amendments—was followed by other state conventions.

The most high-profile convention was held in Richmond, Virginia, in June 1788, when Federalists like James Madison, Edmund Randolph, and John Marshall squared off against equally influential Anti-Federalists like Patrick Henry and George Mason. Virginia was America's most populous state, it had produced some of the country's highest-profile leaders, and the success of the new government rested upon its cooperation. After nearly a month of debate, Virginia voted 89 to 79 in favor of ratification.[13]

On July 2, 1788, Congress announced that a majority of states had ratified the Constitution and that the document was now in effect. Yet this did not mean the debates were over. North Carolina, New York, and Rhode Island had not completed their ratification conventions, and Anti-Federalists still argued that the Constitution would lead to tyranny. The New York convention would ratify the Constitution by just three votes, and finally Rhode Island would ratify it by two votes—a full year after George Washington was inaugurated as president.

V. Rights and Compromises

Although debates continued, Washington's election as president cemented the Constitution's authority. By 1793, the term *Anti-Federalist* would be essentially meaningless. Yet the debates produced a piece of the Constitution that seems irreplaceable today. Ten amendments were added in 1791. Together, they constitute the Bill of Rights. James Madison, against his original wishes, supported these amendments as an act of political compromise and necessity. He had won election to the House of Representatives only by promising his Virginia constituents such a list of rights.

There was much the Bill of Rights did not cover. Women found no special protections or guarantee of a voice in government. Many states continued to restrict voting only to men who owned significant amounts of property. And slavery not only continued to exist; it was condoned and protected by the Constitution.

Of all the compromises that formed the Constitution, perhaps none would be more important than the compromise over the slave trade. Americans generally perceived the transatlantic slave trade as more violent and immoral than slavery itself. Many northerners opposed it on moral grounds. But they also understood that letting southern states import more Africans would increase their political power. The Constitution counted each Black individual as three-fifths of a person for purposes of representation, so in districts with many enslaved people, the white voters had extra influence. On the other hand, the states of the Upper South also welcomed a ban on the Atlantic trade because they already had a surplus of enslaved laborers. Banning importation meant enslavers in Virginia and Maryland could get higher prices when they sold their enslaved laborers to states like South Carolina and Georgia that were dependent on a continued slave trade.

New England and the Deep South agreed to what was called a "dirty compromise" at the Constitutional Convention in 1787. New Englanders agreed to include a constitutional provision that protected the foreign slave trade for twenty years; in exchange, South Carolina and Georgia delegates had agreed to support a constitutional clause that made it easier for Congress to pass commercial legislation. As a result, the Atlantic slave trade resumed until 1808 when it was outlawed for three reasons. First, Britain was also in the process of outlawing the slave trade in 1807, and the United States did not want to concede any moral high ground to its rival. Second, the Haitian Revolution (1791–1804), a successful slave revolt against French colonial rule in the West Indies, had changed the stakes in the debate. The image of thousands of armed Black revolutionaries terrified white Americans. Third, the Haitian Revolution had ended France's plans to expand its presence in the Americas, so in 1803, the United States had purchased the Louisiana Territory from the French at a fire-sale price. This massive new territory, which had doubled the size of the United States, had put the question of slavery's expansion at the top of the national agenda. Many white Americans, including President Thomas Jefferson, thought that ending the external slave trade and dispersing the domestic slave population would keep the United States a white man's republic and perhaps even lead to the disappearance of slavery.

The ban on the slave trade, however, lacked effective enforcement measures and funding. Moreover, instead of freeing illegally imported Africans, the act left their fate to the individual states, and many of those states simply sold intercepted enslaved people at auction. Thus, the ban preserved the logic of property ownership in human beings. The new federal government protected slavery as much as it expanded democratic rights and privileges for white men.[14]

VI. Hamilton's Financial System

President George Washington's cabinet choices reflected continuing political tensions over the size and power of the federal government. The vice president was John Adams, and Washington chose Alexander Hamilton to be his secretary of the treasury. Both men wanted an active government that would promote prosperity by supporting American industry.

Alexander Hamilton saw America's future as a metropolitan, commercial, industrial society, in contrast to Thomas Jefferson's nation of small farmers. While both men had the ear of President Washington, Hamilton's vision proved most appealing and enduring. John Trumbull, *Portrait of Alexander Hamilton*, 1806. Wikimedia.

However, Washington chose Thomas Jefferson to be his secretary of state, and Jefferson was committed to restricting federal power and preserving an economy based on agriculture. Almost from the beginning, Washington struggled to reconcile the Federalist and Republican (or Democratic-Republican) factions within his own administration.[15]

Alexander Hamilton believed that self-interest was the "most powerful incentive of human actions." Self-interest drove humans to accumulate property, and that effort created commerce and industry. According to Hamilton, government had important roles to play in this process. First, the state should protect private property from theft. Second, according to Hamilton, the state should use human "passions" and "make them subservient to the public good."[16] In other words, a wise government would harness its citizens' desire for property so that both private individuals and the state would benefit.

Hamilton, like many of his contemporary statesmen, did not believe the state should ensure an equal distribution of property. Inequality was understood as "the great & fundamental distinction in Society," and Hamilton saw no reason why this should change. Instead, Hamilton wanted to tie the economic interests of wealthy Americans, or "monied men," to the federal government's financial health. If the rich needed the government, then they would direct their energies to making sure it remained solvent.[17]

Hamilton, therefore, believed that the federal government must be "a Repository of the Rights of the wealthy."[18] As the nation's first secretary of the treasury, he proposed an ambitious financial plan to achieve just that.

The first part of Hamilton's plan involved federal "assumption" of state debts, which were mostly left over from the Revolutionary War. The federal government would assume responsibility for the states' unpaid debts, which totaled about $25 million. Second, Hamilton wanted Congress to create a bank—a Bank of the United States.

The goal of these proposals was to link federal power and the country's economic vitality. Under the assumption proposal, the states' creditors (people who owned state bonds or promissory notes) would turn their old notes in to the treasury and receive new federal notes of the same face value. Hamilton foresaw that these bonds would circulate like money, acting as "an engine of business, and instrument of industry and commerce."[19] This part of his plan, however, was controversial for two reasons.

First, many taxpayers objected to paying the full face value on old notes, which had fallen in market value. Often the current holders had purchased them from the original creditors for pennies on the dollar. To pay them at full face value, therefore, would mean rewarding speculators at taxpayer expense. Hamilton countered that government debts must be honored in full, or else citizens would lose all trust in the government. Second, many southerners objected that they had already paid their outstanding state debts, so federal assumption would mean forcing them to pay again for the debts of New Englanders. Nevertheless, President Washington and Congress both accepted Hamilton's argument. By the end of 1794, 98 percent of the country's domestic debt had been converted into new federal bonds.[20]

Hamilton's plan for a Bank of the United States, similarly, won congressional approval despite strong opposition. Thomas Jefferson and other Republicans argued that the plan was unconstitutional; the Constitution did not authorize Congress to create a bank. Hamilton, however, argued that the bank was not only constitutional but also important for the country's prosperity. The Bank of the United States would fulfill several needs. It would act as a convenient depository for federal funds. It would print paper banknotes backed by specie (gold or silver). Its agents would also help control inflation by periodically taking state bank notes to their banks of origin and demanding specie in exchange, limiting the amount of notes the state banks printed. Furthermore, it would give wealthy people a vested interest in the federal government's finances. The government would control just 20 percent of the bank's stock; the other eighty percent would be owned by private investors. Thus, an "intimate connexion" between the government and wealthy men would benefit both, and this connection would promote American commerce.

In 1791, therefore, Congress approved a twenty-year charter for the Bank of the United States. The bank's stocks, together with federal bonds, created over $70 million in new financial instruments. These spurred the formation of securities markets, which allowed the federal government to borrow more money and underwrote the rapid spread of state-chartered banks and other private business corporations in the 1790s. For Federalists, this was one of the major purposes of the federal government. For opponents who wanted a more limited role for industry, however, or who lived on the frontier and lacked access to capital, Hamilton's system seemed to reinforce class boundaries and give the rich inordinate power over the federal government.

Hamilton's plan, furthermore, had another highly controversial element. In order to pay what it owed on the new bonds, the federal government needed reliable sources of tax revenue. In 1791, Hamilton proposed a federal excise tax on the production, sale, and consumption of a number of goods, including whiskey.

VII. The Whiskey Rebellion and Jay's Treaty

Grain was the most valuable cash crop for many American farmers. In the West, selling grain to a local distillery for alcohol production was typically more profitable than shipping it over the Appalachians to eastern markets. Hamilton's whiskey tax thus placed a special burden on western farmers. It seemed to divide the young republic in half—geographically between the East and West, economically between merchants and farmers, and culturally between cities and the countryside.

In the fall of 1791, sixteen men in western Pennsylvania, disguised in women's clothes, assaulted a tax collector named Robert Johnson. They tarred and feathered him, and the local deputy marshals seeking justice met similar fates. They were robbed and beaten, whipped and flogged, tarred and feathered, and tied up and left for dead. The rebel farmers also adopted other protest methods from the Revolution and Shays's Rebellion, writing local petitions and erecting liberty poles. For the next two years, tax collections in the region dwindled.

Then, in July 1794, groups of armed farmers attacked federal marshals and tax collectors, burning down at least two tax collectors' homes. At the end of the month, an armed force of about seven thousand, led by the radical attorney David Bradford, robbed the U.S. mail and gathered about eight miles east of Pittsburgh. President Washington responded quickly.

First, Washington dispatched a committee of three distinguished Pennsylvanians to meet with the rebels and try to bring about a peaceful resolution. Meanwhile, he gathered an army of thirteen thousand militiamen in Carlisle, Pennsylvania. On September 19, Washington became the only sitting president to lead troops in the field, though he quickly turned over the army to the command of Henry Lee, a Revolutionary hero and the current governor of Virginia.

As the federal army moved westward, the farmers scattered. Hoping to make a dramatic display of federal authority, Alexander Hamilton oversaw the arrest and trial of a number of rebels. Many were released because of a lack of evidence, and most of those who remained, including two men sentenced to death for treason, were soon pardoned by the president. The Whiskey Rebellion had shown that the federal government was capable of quelling internal unrest. But it also demonstrated that some citizens, especially poor westerners, viewed it as their enemy.[21]

Around the same time, another national issue also aroused fierce protest. Along with his vision of a strong financial system, Hamilton also had a vision of a nation busily engaged in foreign trade. In his mind, that meant pursuing a friendly relationship with one nation in particular: Great Britain.

America's relationship with Britain since the end of the Revolution had been tense, partly because of warfare between the British and French. Their naval war threatened American shipping, and the impressment of men into Britain's navy terrorized American sailors. American trade could be risky and expensive, and impressment threatened seafaring families. Nevertheless, President Washington was conscious of American weakness and was determined not to take sides. In April 1793, he officially declared that the United States would remain neutral.[22] With his blessing, Hamilton's political ally John Jay, who was currently serving as chief justice of the Supreme Court, sailed to London to negotiate a treaty that would satisfy both Britain and the United States.

Jefferson and Madison strongly opposed these negotiations. They mistrusted Britain and saw the treaty as the American state favoring Britain over France. The French had recently overthrown their own monarchy, and Republicans thought the United States should be glad to have the friendship of a new revolutionary state. They also suspected that a treaty with Britain would favor northern merchants and manufacturers over the agricultural South.

In November 1794, despite their misgivings, John Jay signed a "treaty of amity, commerce, and navigation" with the British. Jay's Treaty, as it was commonly called, required Britain to abandon its military positions in the Northwest Territory (especially Fort Detroit, Fort Mackinac, and Fort Niagara) by 1796. Britain also agreed to compensate American merchants for their losses. The United States, in return, agreed to treat Britain as its most prized trade partner, which meant tacitly supporting Britain in its current conflict with France. Unfortunately, Jay had failed to secure an end to impressment.[23]

For Federalists, this treaty was a significant accomplishment. Jay's Treaty gave the United States, a relatively weak power, the ability to stay officially neutral in European wars, and it preserved American prosperity by protecting trade. For Jefferson's Republicans, however, the treaty was proof of Federalist treachery. The Federalists had sided with a monarchy against a republic, and they had submitted to British influence in American affairs without even ending impressment. In Congress, debate over the treaty transformed the Federalists and Republicans from temporary factions into two distinct (though still loosely organized) political parties.

VIII. The French Revolution and the Limits of Liberty

In part, the Federalists were turning toward Britain because they feared the most radical forms of democratic thought. In the wake of Shays's Rebellion, the Whiskey Rebellion, and other internal protests, Federalists sought to preserve social stability. The course of the French Revolution seemed to justify their concerns.

In 1789, news had arrived in America that the French had revolted against their king. Most Americans imagined that liberty was spreading

The mounting body count of the French Revolution included that of the queen and king, who were beheaded in a public ceremony in early 1793, as depicted in the engraving. While Americans disdained the concept of monarchy, the execution of King Louis XVI was regarded by many Americans as an abomination, an indication of the chaos and savagery reigning in France at the time. Charles Monnet (artist), Antoine-Jean Duclos and Isidore-Stanislas Helman (engravers), *Day of 21 January 1793 the death of Louis Capet on the Place de la Révolution*, 1794. Wikimedia.

from America to Europe, carried there by the returning French heroes who had taken part in the American Revolution.

Initially, nearly all Americans had praised the French Revolution. Towns all over the country hosted speeches and parades on July 14 to commemorate the day it began. Women had worn neoclassical dress to honor republican principles, and men had pinned revolutionary cockades to their hats. John Randolph, a Virginia planter, named two of his favorite horses Jacobin and Sans-Culotte after French revolutionary factions.[24]

In April 1793, a new French ambassador, "Citizen" Edmond-Charles Genêt, arrived in the United States. During his tour of several cities, Americans greeted him with wild enthusiasm. Citizen Genêt encouraged Americans to act against Spain, a British ally, by attacking its colonies of Florida and Louisiana. When President Washington refused, Genêt threatened to appeal to the American people directly. In response, Washington demanded that France recall its diplomat. In the meantime, however, Genêt's faction had fallen from power in France. Knowing that a return home might cost him his head, he decided to remain in America.

Genêt's intuition was correct. A radical coalition of revolutionaries had seized power in France. They initiated a bloody purge of their enemies, the Reign of Terror. As Americans learned about Genêt's impropriety and the mounting body count in France, many began to have second thoughts about the French Revolution.

Americans who feared that the French Revolution was spiraling out of control tended to become Federalists. Those who remained hopeful about the revolution tended to become Republicans. Not deterred by the violence, Thomas Jefferson declared that he would rather see "half the earth desolated" than see the French Revolution fail. "Were there but an Adam and an Eve left in every country, and left free," he wrote, "it would be better than as it now is."[25] Meanwhile, the Federalists sought closer ties with Britain.

Despite the political rancor, in late 1796 there came one sign of hope: the United States peacefully elected a new president. For now, as Washington stepped down and executive power changed hands, the country did not descend into the anarchy that many leaders feared.

The new president was John Adams, Washington's vice president. Adams was less beloved than the old general, and he governed a deeply divided nation. The foreign crisis also presented him with a major test.

In response to Jay's Treaty, the French government authorized its vessels to attack American shipping. To resolve this, President Adams sent envoys to France in 1797. The French insulted these diplomats. Some officials, whom the Americans code-named X, Y, and Z in their correspondence, hinted that negotiations could begin only after the Americans offered a bribe. When the story became public, this XYZ Affair infuriated American citizens. Dozens of towns wrote addresses to President Adams, pledging him their support against France. Many people seemed eager for war. "Millions for defense," toasted South Carolina representative Robert Goodloe Harper, "but not one cent for tribute."[26]

By 1798, the people of Charleston watched the ocean's horizon apprehensively because they feared the arrival of the French navy at any moment. Many people now worried that the same ships that had aided Americans during the Revolutionary War might discharge an invasion force on their shores. Some southerners were sure that this force would consist of Black troops from France's Caribbean colonies, who would attack the southern states and cause their enslaved laborers to revolt. Many Americans also worried that France had covert agents in the country. In the streets of Charleston, armed bands of young men searched for French disorganizers. Even the little children prepared for the looming conflict by fighting with sticks.[27]

Meanwhile, during the crisis, New Englanders were some of the most outspoken opponents of France. In 1798, they found a new reason for Francophobia. An influential Massachusetts minister, Jedidiah Morse, announced to his congregation that the French Revolution had been hatched in a conspiracy led by a mysterious anti-Christian organization called the Illuminati. The story was a hoax, but rumors of Illuminati infiltration spread throughout New England like wildfire, adding a new dimension to the foreign threat.[28]

Against this backdrop of fear, the French Quasi-War, as it would come to be known, was fought on the Atlantic, mostly between French naval vessels and American merchant ships. During this crisis, however, anxiety about foreign agents ran high, and members of Congress took action to prevent internal subversion. The most controversial of these steps were the Alien and Sedition Acts. These two laws, passed in 1798, were intended to prevent French agents and sympathizers from compromising America's resistance, but they also attacked Americans who criticized the president and the Federalist Party.

The Alien Act allowed the federal government to deport foreign nationals, or "aliens," who seemed to pose a national security threat. Even more dramatically, the Sedition Act allowed the government to prosecute anyone found to be speaking or publishing "false, scandalous, and malicious writing" against the government.[29]

These laws were not simply brought on by war hysteria. They reflected common assumptions about the nature of the American Revolution and the limits of liberty. In fact, most of the advocates for the Constitution and the First Amendment accepted that free speech simply meant a lack of prior censorship or restraint, not a guarantee against punishment. According to this logic, "licentious" or unruly speech made society less free, not more. James Wilson, one of the principal architects of the Constitution, argued that "every author is responsible when he attacks the security or welfare of the government."[30]

In 1798, most Federalists were inclined to agree. Under the terms of the Sedition Act, they indicted and prosecuted several Republican printers—and even a Republican congressman who had criticized President Adams. Meanwhile, although the Adams administration never enforced the Alien Act, its passage was enough to convince some foreign nationals to leave the country. For the president and most other Federalists, the Alien and Sedition Acts represented a continuation of a conservative rather than radical American Revolution.

However, the Alien and Sedition Acts caused a backlash in two ways. First, shocked opponents articulated a new and expansive vision for liberty. The New York lawyer Tunis Wortman, for example, demanded an "absolute independence" of the press.[31] Likewise, the Virginia judge George Hay called for "any publication whatever criminal" to be exempt from legal punishment.[32] Many Americans began to argue that free speech meant the ability to say virtually anything without fear of prosecution.

Second, James Madison and Thomas Jefferson helped organize opposition from state governments. Ironically, both of them had expressed support for the principle behind the Sedition Act in previous years. Jefferson, for example, had written to Madison in 1789 that the nation should punish citizens for speaking "false facts" that injured the country.[33] Nevertheless, both men now opposed the Alien and Sedition Acts on constitutional grounds. In 1798, Jefferson made this point in a resolution adopted by the Kentucky state legislature. A short time later, the Virginia legislature adopted a similar document written by Madison.

The Kentucky and Virginia Resolutions argued that the national government's authority was limited to the powers expressly granted by the U.S. Constitution. More importantly, they asserted that the states could declare federal laws unconstitutional. For the time being, these resolutions were simply gestures of defiance. Their bold claim, however, would have important effects in later decades.

In just a few years, many Americans' feelings toward France had changed dramatically. Far from rejoicing in the "light of freedom," many Americans now feared the "contagion" of French-style liberty. Debates over the French Revolution in the 1790s gave Americans some of their earliest opportunities to articulate what it meant to be American. Did American national character rest on a radical and universal vision of human liberty? Or was America supposed to be essentially pious and traditional, an outgrowth of Great Britain? They couldn't agree. It was on this cracked foundation that many conflicts of the nineteenth century would rest.

IX. Religious Freedom

One reason the debates over the French Revolution became so heated was that Americans were unsure about their own religious future. The Illuminati scare of 1798 was just one manifestation of this fear. Across the United States, a slow but profound shift in attitudes toward religion and government began.

In 1776, none of the American state governments observed the separation of church and state. On the contrary, all thirteen states either had established, official, and tax-supported state churches, or at least required their officeholders to profess a certain faith. Most officials believed this was necessary to protect morality and social order. Over the next six decades, however, that changed. In 1833, the final state, Massachusetts, stopped supporting an official religious denomination. Historians call that gradual process *disestablishment*.

In many states, the process of disestablishment had started before the creation of the Constitution. South Carolina, for example, had been nominally Anglican before the Revolution, but it had dropped denominational restrictions in its 1778 constitution. Instead, it now allowed any church consisting of at least fifteen adult males to become "incorporated," or recognized for tax purposes as a state-supported church. Churches needed only to agree to a set of basic Christian theological tenets, which were vague enough that most denominations could support them.[34]

South Carolina tried to balance religious freedom with the religious practice that was supposed to be necessary for social order. Officeholders were still expected to be Christians; their oaths were witnessed by

God, they were compelled by their religious beliefs to tell the truth, and they were called to live according to the Bible. This list of minimal requirements came to define acceptable Christianity in many states. As new Christian denominations proliferated between 1780 and 1840, however, more and more Christians fell outside this definition.

South Carolina continued its general establishment law until 1790, when a constitutional revision removed the establishment clause and religious restrictions on officeholders. Many other states, though, continued to support an established church well into the nineteenth century. The federal Constitution did not prevent this. The religious freedom clause in the Bill of Rights, during these decades, limited the federal government but not state governments. It was not until 1833 that a state supreme court decision ended Massachusetts's support for the Congregational Church.

Many political leaders, including Thomas Jefferson and James Madison, favored disestablishment because they saw the relationship between church and state as a tool of oppression. Jefferson proposed a Statute for Religious Freedom in the Virginia state assembly in 1779, but his bill failed in the overwhelmingly Anglican legislature. Madison proposed it again in 1785, and it defeated a rival bill that would have given equal revenue to all Protestant churches. Instead Virginia would not use public money to support religion. "The Religion then of every man," Jefferson wrote, "must be left to the conviction and conscience of every man; and it is the right of every man to exercise it as these may dictate."[35]

At the federal level, the delegates to the Constitutional Convention of 1787 easily agreed that the national government should not have an official religion. This principle was upheld in 1791 when the First Amendment was ratified, with its guarantee of religious liberty. The limits of federal disestablishment, however, required discussion. The federal government, for example, supported Native American missionaries and congressional chaplains. Well into the nineteenth century, debate raged over whether the postal service should operate on Sundays, and whether non-Christians could act as witnesses in federal courts. Americans continued to struggle to understand what it meant for Congress not to "establish" a religion.

X. The Election of 1800

Meanwhile, the Sedition and Alien Acts expired in 1800 and 1801. They had been relatively ineffective at suppressing dissent. On the contrary,

The year 1800 brought about a host of changes in government, in particular the first successful and peaceful transfer of power from one political party to another. But the year was important for another reason: the U.S. Capitol in Washington, D.C. (pictured here in 1800) was finally opened to be occupied by Congress, the Supreme Court, the Library of Congress, and the courts of the District of Columbia. William Russell Birch, *A view of the Capitol of Washington before it was burnt down by the British*, c. 1800. Wikimedia.

they were much more important for the loud reactions they had inspired. They had helped many Americans decide what they *didn't* want from their national government.

By 1800, therefore, President Adams had lost the confidence of many Americans. They had let him know it. In 1798, for instance, he had issued a national thanksgiving proclamation. Instead of enjoying a day of celebration and thankfulness, Adams and his family had been forced by rioters to flee the capital city of Philadelphia until the day was over. Conversely, his prickly independence had also put him at odds with Alexander Hamilton, the leader of his own party, who offered him little support. After four years in office, Adams found himself widely reviled.

In the election of 1800, therefore, the Republicans defeated Adams in a bitter and complicated presidential race. During the election, one Federalist newspaper article predicted that a Republican victory would fill America with "murder, robbery, rape, adultery, and incest."[36] A Republican newspaper, on the other hand, flung sexual slurs against President Adams, saying he had "neither the force and firmness of a man, nor the gentleness and sensibility of a woman." Both sides predicted disaster and possibly war if the other should win.[37]

In the end, the contest came down to a tie between two Republicans, Thomas Jefferson of Virginia and Aaron Burr of New York, who each had seventy-three electoral votes. (Adams had sixty-five.) Burr was supposed to be a candidate for vice president, not president, but under the Constitution's original rules, a tie-breaking vote had to take place in the House of Representatives. It was controlled by Federalists bitter at Jefferson. House members voted dozens of times without breaking the tie. On the thirty-sixth ballot, Thomas Jefferson emerged victorious.

Republicans believed they had saved the United States from grave danger. An assembly of Republicans in New York City called the election a "bloodless revolution." They thought of their victory as a revolution in part because the Constitution (and eighteenth-century political theory)

This image attacks Jefferson's support of the French Revolution and religious freedom. The letter, "To Mazzei," refers to a 1796 correspondence that criticized the Federalists and, by association, President Washington. *Providential Detection*, 1797. Courtesy American Antiquarian Society. Attribution-NonCommercial-ShareAlike 4.0 International (CC BY-NC-SA 4.0).

made no provision for political parties. The Republicans thought they were fighting to rescue the country from an aristocratic takeover, not just taking part in a normal constitutional process.

In his first inaugural address, however, Thomas Jefferson offered an olive branch to the Federalists. He pledged to follow the will of the American majority, whom he believed were Republicans, but to respect the rights of the Federalist minority. His election set an important precedent. Adams accepted his electoral defeat and left the White House peacefully. "The revolution of 1800," Jefferson wrote years later, did for American principles what the Revolution of 1776 had done for its structure. But this time, the revolution was accomplished not "by the sword" but "by the rational and peaceable instrument of reform, the suffrage of the people."[38] Four years later, when the Twelfth Amendment changed the rules for presidential elections to prevent future deadlocks, it was designed to accommodate the way political parties worked.

Despite Adams's and Jefferson's attempts to tame party politics, though, the tension between federal power and the liberties of states and individuals would exist long into the nineteenth century. And while Jefferson's administration attempted to decrease federal influence, Chief Justice John Marshall, an Adams appointee, worked to increase the authority of the Supreme Court. These competing agendas clashed most famously in the 1803 case of *Marbury v. Madison*, which Marshall used to establish a major precedent.

The *Marbury* case seemed insignificant at first. The night before leaving office in early 1801, Adams had appointed several men to serve as justices of the peace in Washington, D.C. By making these "midnight appointments," Adams had sought to put Federalists into vacant positions at the last minute. On taking office, however, Jefferson and his secretary of state, James Madison, had refused to deliver the federal commissions to the men Adams had appointed. Several of the appointees, including William Marbury, sued the government, and the case was argued before the Supreme Court.

Marshall used Marbury's case to make a clever ruling. On the issue of the commissions, the Supreme Court ruled in favor of the Jefferson administration. But Chief Justice Marshall went further in his decision, ruling that the Supreme Court reserved the right to decide whether an act of Congress violated the Constitution. In other words, the court assumed the power of judicial review. This was a major (and lasting) blow to the Republican agenda, especially after 1810, when the Supreme Court extended judicial review to state laws. Jefferson was particularly frustrated by the decision, arguing that the power of judicial review "would make the Judiciary a despotic branch."[39]

XI. Conclusion

A grand debate over political power engulfed the young United States. The Constitution ensured that there would be a strong federal government capable of taxing, waging war, and making law, but it could never resolve the young nation's many conflicting constituencies. The Whiskey Rebellion proved that the nation could stifle internal dissent but exposed a new threat to liberty. Hamilton's banking system provided the nation with credit but also constrained frontier farmers. The Constitution's guarantee of religious liberty conflicted with many popular prerogatives. Dissension only deepened, and as the 1790s progressed, Americans became bitterly divided over political parties and foreign war.

During the ratification debates, Alexander Hamilton had written of the wonders of the Constitution. "A nation, without a national government," he wrote, would be "an awful spectacle." But, he added, "the establishment of a Constitution, in time of profound peace, by the voluntary consent of a whole people, is a prodigy," a miracle that should be witnessed "with trembling anxiety."[40] Anti-Federalists had grave concerns about the Constitution, but even they could celebrate the idea of national unity. By 1795, even the staunchest critics would have grudgingly agreed with Hamilton's convictions about the Constitution. Yet these same individuals could also take the cautions in Washington's 1796 farewell address to heart. "There is an opinion," Washington wrote, "that parties in free countries are useful checks upon the administration of the government and serve to keep alive the spirit of liberty." This, he conceded, was probably true, but in a republic, he said, the danger was not too little partisanship, but too much. "A fire not to be quenched," Washington warned, "it demands a uniform vigilance to prevent its bursting into a flame, lest, instead of warming, it should consume."[41]

For every parade, thanksgiving proclamation, or grand procession honoring the unity of the nation, there was also some political controversy reminding American citizens of how fragile their union was. And as party differences and regional quarrels tested the federal government, the new nation increasingly explored the limits of its democracy.

XII. Reference Material

This chapter was edited by Tara Strauch, with content contributions by Marco Basile, Nathaniel C. Green, Brenden Kennedy, Spencer McBride, Andrea Nero, Cara Rogers, Tara Strauch, Michael Harrison Taylor, Jordan Taylor, Kevin Wisniewski, and Ben Wright.

Recommended citation: Marco Basile et al., "A New Nation," Tara Strauch, ed., in *The American Yawp*, eds. Joseph Locke and Ben Wright (Stanford, CA: Stanford University Press, 2019).

NOTES TO CHAPTER 6

1. Francis Hopkinson, *An Account of the Grand Federal Procession, Philadelphia, July 4, 1788* (Philadelphia: Carey, 1788).

2. George Washington, *Thanksgiving Proclamation*, October, 3, 1789; Fed. Reg., Presidential Proclamations, 1791–1991.

3. *Hampshire Gazette* (CT), September 13, 1786.

4. James Madison, *The Federalist Papers*, (New York: Signet Classics, 2003), no. 63.

5. Woody Holton, *Unruly Americans and the Origins of the Constitution* (New York: Hill and Wang, 2007), 8–9.

6. Madison took an active role during the convention. He also did more than anyone else to shape historians' understandings of the convention by taking meticulous notes. Many of the quotes included here come from Madison's notes. To learn more about this important document, read Mary Sarah Bilder, *Madison's Hand: Revising the Constitutional Convention* (Cambridge, MA: Harvard University Press, 2015).

7. Virginia (Randolph) Plan as Amended (National Archives Microfilm Publication M866, 1 roll); The Official Records of the Constitutional Convention; Records of the Continental and Confederation Congresses and the Constitutional Convention, 1774–1789, Record Group 360; National Archives.

8. Richard Beeman, *Plain, Honest Men: The Making of the American Constitution* (New York: Random House, 2009), 114.

9. Herbert J. Storing, *What the Anti-Federalists Were For: The Political Thought of the Opponents of the Constitution* (Chicago: University of Chicago Press, 1981), 16.

10. Ray Raphael, *Mr. President: How and Why the Founders Created a Chief Executive* (New York: Knopf, 2012), 50. See also Kathleen Bartoloni-Tuazon, *For Fear of an Elected King: George Washington and the Presidential Title Controversy of 1789* (Ithaca, NY: Cornell University Press, 2014).

11. David J. Siemers, *Ratifying the Republic: Antifederalists and Federalists in Constitutional Time* (Stanford, CA: Stanford University Press, 2002).

12. Alexander Hamilton, James Madison, and John Jay, *The Federalist Papers*, ed. Ian Shapiro (New Haven, CT: Yale University Press, 2009).

13. Pauline Maier, *Ratification: The People Debate the Constitution, 1787–1788* (New York: Simon and Schuster, 2010), 225–237.

14. David Waldstreicher, *Slavery's Constitution: From Revolution to Ratification* (New York: Hill and Wang, 2009).

15. Carson Holloway, *Hamilton Versus Jefferson in the Washington Administration: Completing the Founding or Betraying the Founding?* (New York: Cambridge University Press, 2015).

16. Alexander Hamilton, *The Works of Alexander Hamilton, Volume 1*, ed. Henry Cabot Lodge, ed. (New York: Putnam, 1904), 70, 408.

17. Alexander Hamilton, *Report on Manufactures* (New York: Childs and Swaine, 1791).

18. James H. Hutson, ed., *Supplement to Max Farrand's the Records of the Federal Convention of 1787* (New Haven, CT: Yale University Press, 1987), 119.

19. Hamilton, *Report on Manufactures*.

20. Richard Sylla, "National Foundations: Public Credit, the National Bank, and Securities Markets," in *Founding Choices: American Economic Policy in the 1790s*, ed. Douglas A. Irwin and Richard Sylla (Chicago: University of Chicago Press, 2011), 68.

21. Thomas P. Slaughter, *The Whiskey Rebellion: Frontier Epilogue to the American Revolution* (New York: Oxford University Press, 1986).

22. "Proclamation of Neutrality, 1793," in *A Compilation of the Messages and Papers of the Presidents Prepared Under the Direction of the Joint Committee on printing, of the House and Senate Pursuant to an Act of the Fifty-Second Congress of the United States* (New York: Bureau of National Literature, 1897).

23. United States, *Treaty of Amity, Commerce, and Navigation, signed at London November 19, 1794*, Submitted to the Senate June 8, Resolution of Advice and Consent, on condition, June 24, 1795. Ratified by the United States August 14, 1795. Ratified by Great Britain October 28, 1795. Ratifications exchanged at London October 28, 1795. Proclaimed February 29, 1796.

24. Elizabeth Fox-Genovese and Eugene D. Genovese, *The Mind of the Master Class: History and Faith in the Southern Slaveholders Worldview* (New York: Cambridge University Press, 2005), 18.

25. "From Thomas Jefferson to William Short, 3 January 1793," Founders Online, National Archives. http://founders.archives.gov/documents/Jefferson/01-25-02-0016, last modified June 29, 2015; *The Papers of Thomas Jefferson*, vol. 25, *1 January–10 May 1793*, ed. John Catanzariti (Princeton, NJ: Princeton University Press, 1992), 14–17.

26. Robert Goodloe Harper, June 18, 1798, quoted in *American Daily Advertiser* (Philadelphia), June 20, 1798.

27. Robert J. Alderson Jr., *This Bright Era of Happy Revolutions: French Consul Michel-Ange-Bernard Mangourit and International Republicanism in Charleston, 1792–1794* (Columbia: University of South Carolina Press, 2008).

28. Rachel Hope Cleves, *The Reign of Terror in America: Visions of Violence from Anti-Jacobinism to Antislavery* (New York: Cambridge University Press, 2012), 47.

29. Alien Act, July 6, 1798, and An Act in Addition to the Act, Entitled "An Act for the Punishment of Certain Crimes Against the United States," July 14,

1798; Fifth Congress; Enrolled Acts and Resolutions; General Records of the United States Government; Record Group 11; National Archives.

30. James Wilson, Congressional Debate, December 1, 1787, in Jonathan Elliot, ed., *The Debates in the Several State Conventions on the Adoption of the Federal Constitution as Recommended by the General Convention at Philadelphia in 1787*, Vol. 2 (New York: s.n., 1888) 448–450.

31. Tunis Wortman, *A Treatise Concerning Political Enquiry, and the Liberty of the Press* (New York: Forman, 1800), 181.

32. George Hay, *An Essay on the Liberty of the Press* (Philadelphia: s.n., 1799), 43.

33. Thomas Jefferson to James Madison, August 28, 1789, from *The Works of Thomas Jefferson in Twelve Volumes*, Federal Edition, ed. Paul Leicester Ford. http://www.loc.gov/resource/mtj1.011_0853_0861.

34. Francis Newton Thorpe, ed., *The Federal and State Constitutions, Colonial Charters, and Other Organic Laws of the States, Territories, and Colonies Now or Heretofore Forming the United States of America Compiled and Edited Under the Act of Congress of June 30, 1906* (Washington, DC: U.S. Government Printing Office, 1909).

35. Thomas Jefferson, *An Act for Establishing Religious Freedom*, 16 January 1786, Manuscript, Records of the General Assembly, Enrolled Bills, Record Group 78, Library of Virginia.

36. Catherine Allgor, *Parlor Politics: In Which the Ladies of Washington Help Build a City and a Government* (Charlottesville: University of Virginia Press, 2000), 14.

37. James T. Callender, *The Prospect Before Us* (Richmond: s.n., 1800).

38. Letter from Thomas Jefferson to Spencer Roane, September 6, 1819, in *The Writings of Thomas Jefferson*, 20 vols., ed. Albert Ellery Bergh (Washington, DC: Thomas Jefferson Memorial Association of the United States, 1903), 142.

39. Harold H. Bruff, *Untrodden Ground: How Presidents Interpret the Constitution* (Chicago: University of Chicago Press, 2015), 65.

40. Alexander Hamilton, *The Federalist Papers* (New York: Signet Classics, 2003), no. 85.

41. George Washington, Farewell Address, *Annals of Congress*, 4th Congress, 2869–2870.

RECOMMENDED READING

Allgor, Catherine. *Parlor Politics: In Which the Ladies of Washington Help Build a City and a Government*. Charlottesville: University of Virginia Press, 2000.

Appleby, Joyce. *Inheriting the Revolution: The First Generation of Americans*. Cambridge, MA: Belknap Press, 2001.

Bartolini-Tuazon, Kathleen. *For Fear of an Elective King: George Washington and the Presidential Title Controversy of 1789*. Ithaca, NY: Cornell University Press, 2014.

Beeman, Richard, Stephen Botein, and Edward C. Carter II, eds. *Beyond Confederation: Origins of the Constitution and American National Identity*. Chapel Hill: University of North Carolina Press, 1987.

Bilder, Mary Sarah. *Madison's Hand: Revising the Constitutional Convention*. Cambridge, MA: Harvard University Press, 2015.

Bouton, Terry. "A Road Closed: Rural Insurgency in Post-Independence Pennsylvania." *Journal of American History* 87, no. 3 (December 2000): 855–887.

Cunningham, Noble E. *The Jeffersonian Republicans: The Formation of Party Organization, 1789–1801*. Chapel Hill: University of North Carolina Press, 1967.

Dunn, Susan. *Jefferson's Second Revolution: The Election of 1800 and the Triumph of Republicanism*. Boston: Houghton Mifflin, 2004.

Edling, Max. *A Revolution in Favor of Government: Origins of the U.S. Constitution and the Making of the American State*. New York: Oxford University Press, 2003

Gordon-Reed, Annette. *The Hemingses of Monticello: An American Family*. New York: W. W. Norton, 2008.

Halperin, Terri Diane. *The Alien and Sedition Acts of 1798: Testing the Constitution*. Baltimore: Johns Hopkins University Press, 2016.

Holton, Woody. *Unruly Americans and the Origins of the Constitution*. 1st edition. New York: Hill and Wang, 2007.

Kierner, Cynthia A. *Martha Jefferson Randolph, Daughter of Monticello: Her Life and Times*. Chapel Hill: University of North Carolina Press, 2012.

Maier, Pauline. *Ratification: The People Debate the Constitution, 1787–1788*. New York: Simon and Schuster, 2010.

Papenfuse, Eric Robert. "Unleashing the 'Wildness': The Mobilization of Grassroots Antifederalism in Maryland." *Journal of the Early Republic* 16, no. 1 (Spring 1996): 73–106.

Pasley, Jeffrey L. *The First Presidential Contest: 1796 and the Founding of American Democracy*. Lawrence: University of Kansas Press, 2013.

Rakove, Jack N. *Original Meanings: Politics and Ideas in the Making of the Constitution*. New York: Vintage Books, 1996.

Salmon, Marylynn. *Women and the Law of Property in Early America*. Chapel Hill: University of North Carolina Press, 1989.

Sharp, James Roger. *American Politics in the Early Republic: The New Nation in Crisis*. New Haven, CT: Yale University Press, 1993.

Slaughter, Thomas P. *The Whiskey Rebellion: Frontier Epilogue to the American Revolution*. New York: Oxford University Press, 1986.

Smith-Rosenberg, Carroll. "Dis-Covering the Subject of the 'Great Constitutional Discussion,' 1786–1789." *Journal of American History* 79, no. 3 (December 1992): 841–873.

Taylor, Alan. *William Cooper's Town: Power and Persuasion on the Frontier of the Early American Republic*. New York: Vintage, 1996.

Waldstreicher, David. *In the Midst of Perpetual Fetes : The Making of American Nationalism, 1776–1820*. Chapel Hill: University of North Carolina Press, 1997.

Wood, Gordon. *Empire of Liberty: A History of the Early Republic, 1789–1815*. Oxford, UK: Oxford University Press, 2011.

Zagarri, Rosemarie. *Revolutionary Backlash: Women and Politics in the Early American Republic*. Philadelphia: University of Pennsylvania Press, 2007.

7

The Early Republic

I. Introduction

Thomas Jefferson's electoral victory over John Adams—and the larger victory of the Democratic-Republicans over the Federalists—was but one of many changes in the early republic. Some, like Jefferson's victory, were accomplished peacefully, and others violently. The wealthy and the powerful, middling and poor whites, Native Americans, free and enslaved African Americans, influential and poor women: all demanded a voice in the new nation that Thomas Paine called an "asylum" for liberty.[1] All would, in their own way, lay claim to the freedom and equality promised, if not fully realized, by the Revolution.

America guided by wisdom An allegorical representation of the United States depicting their independence and prosperity, 1815. Library of Congress.

II. Free and Enslaved Black Americans and the Challenge to Slavery

Led by the enslaved man Gabriel, close to one thousand enslaved men planned to end slavery in Virginia by attacking Richmond in late August 1800. Some of the conspirators would set diversionary fires in the city's warehouse district. Others would attack Richmond's white residents, seize weapons, and capture Virginia governor James Monroe. On August 30, two enslaved men revealed the plot to their enslaver, who notified authorities. Faced with bad weather, Gabriel and other leaders postponed the attack until the next night, giving Governor Monroe and the militia time to capture the conspirators. After briefly escaping, Gabriel was seized, tried, and hanged along with twenty-five others. Their executions sent the message that others would be punished if they challenged slavery. Subsequently, the Virginia government increased restrictions on free people of color.

Gabriel's Rebellion, as the plot came to be known, taught Virginia's white residents several lessons. First, it suggested that enslaved Black Virginians were capable of preparing and carrying out a sophisticated and violent revolution—undermining white supremacist assumptions about the inherent intellectual inferiority of Black people. Furthermore, it demonstrated that white efforts to suppress news of other slave revolts—especially the 1791 slave rebellion in Haiti—had failed. Not only did some literate enslaved people read accounts of the successful attack in Virginia's newspapers, but others also heard about the rebellion firsthand when slaveholding refugees from Haiti arrived in Virginia with their enslaved laborers after July 1793.

The Haitian Revolution (1791–1804) inspired free and enslaved Black Americans, and terrified white Americans. Port cities in the United States were flooded with news and refugees. Free people of color embraced the revolution, understanding it as a call for full abolition and the rights of citizenship denied in the United States. Over the next several decades, Black Americans continually looked to Haiti as an inspiration in their struggle for freedom. For example, in 1829 David Walker, a Black abolitionist in Boston, wrote an *Appeal* that called for resistance to slavery and racism. Walker called Haiti the "glory of the blacks and terror of the tyrants" and said that Haitians, "according to their word, are bound to protect and comfort us." Haiti also proved that, given equal opportunities, people of color could achieve as much as white people.[2] In 1826 the third college graduate of color in the United States, John Russwurm, gave a commencement address at Bowdoin College, noting that, "Haytiens have adopted the republican form of government . . . [and] in no country are the rights and privileges of citizens and foreigners more respected, and crimes less frequent."[3] In 1838 the *Colored American*, an early Black newspaper, professed that "no one who reads, with an unprejudiced mind, the history of Hayti . . . can doubt the capacity of colored men, nor the propriety of removing all their disabilities."[4] Haiti, and the activism it inspired, sent the message that enslaved and free Black people could not be omitted from conversations about the meaning of liberty and equality. Their words and actions—on plantations, streets, and the printed page—left an indelible mark on early national political culture.

The Black activism inspired by Haiti's revolution was so powerful that anxious white leaders scrambled to use the violence of the Haitian revolt to reinforce white supremacy and pro-slavery views by limiting the social and political lives of people of color. White publications mocked Black Americans as buffoons, ridiculing calls for abolition and equal rights. The most (in)famous of these, the "Bobalition" broadsides, published in Boston in the 1810s, crudely caricatured African Americans. Widely distributed materials like these became the basis for racist ideas that thrived in the nineteenth century. But such ridicule also implied that Black Americans' presence in the political conversation was significant enough to require it. The need to reinforce such an obvious difference between whiteness and blackness implied that the differences might not be so obvious after all.

Henry Moss, an enslaved man in Virginia, became arguably the most famous Black man of the day when white spots appeared on his body in 1792, turning him visibly white within three years. As his skin changed, Moss marketed himself as "a great curiosity" in Philadelphia and soon earned enough money to buy his freedom. He met the great scientists of the era—including Samuel Stanhope Smith and Dr. Benjamin Rush—who joyously deemed Moss to be living proof of their theory that "the Black Color (as it is called) of the Negroes is derived from the leprosy."[5] Something, somehow, was "curing" Moss of his blackness. In the whitening body of slave-turned-patriot-turned-curiosity, many Americans fostered ideas of race that would cause major problems in the years ahead.

The first decades of the new American republic coincided with a radical shift in understandings of race. Politically and culturally, Enlightenment thinking fostered beliefs in common humanity, the possibil-

The idea and image of Black Haitian revolutionaries sent shock waves throughout white America. That Black people, enslaved and free, might turn violent against white people, so obvious in this image where a Black soldier holds up the head of a white soldier, remained a serious fear in the hearts and minds of white Southerners throughout the antebellum period. January Suchodolski, *Battle at San Domingo*, 1845. Wikimedia.

ity of societal progress, the remaking of oneself, and the importance of one's social and ecological environment—a four-pronged revolt against the hierarchies of the Old World. Yet a tension arose due to Enlightenment thinkers' desire to classify and order the natural world. Carolus Linnaeus, Comte de Buffon, Johann Friedrich Blumenbach, and others created connections between race and place as they divided the racial "types" of the world according to skin color, cranial measurements, and hair. They claimed that years under the hot sun and tropical climate of Africa darkened the skin and reconfigured the skulls of the African race, whereas the cold northern latitudes of Europe molded and sustained the "Caucasian" race. The environments endowed both races with respective characteristics, which accounted for differences in humankind tracing back to a common ancestry. A universal human nature, therefore, housed not fundamental differences but rather the "civilized" and the "primitive"—two poles on a scale of social progress.

Informed by European anthropology and republican optimism, Americans confronted their own uniquely problematic racial landscape. In 1787, Samuel Stanhope Smith published his treatise *Essay on the Causes of the Variety of Complexion and Figure in the Human Species*, which further articulated the theory of racial change and suggested that improving the social environment would tap into the innate equality of humankind and dramatically uplift nonwhite races. The proper society, he and others believed, could gradually "whiten" men the way nature spontaneously chose to whiten Henry Moss. Thomas Jefferson disagreed. While Jefferson thought Native Americans could improve and become "civilized," he declared in his *Notes on the State of Virginia* (1784) that Black people were incapable of mental improvement and that they might even have a separate ancestry—a theory known as polygenesis, or multiple creations. His belief in polygenesis was less to justify slavery— enslavers universally rejected the theory as antibiblical and thus a threat to their primary instrument of justification, the Bible—and more to justify schemes for a white America, such as the plan to gradually send freed Black people to Africa. Many Americans believed nature had made the white and Black races too different to peacefully coexist, and they viewed African colonization as the solution to America's racial problem.

Jefferson's *Notes on the State of Virginia* sparked considerable backlash from antislavery and Black communities. The celebrated Black surveyor Benjamin Banneker, for example, immediately wrote to Jefferson and demanded he "eradicate that train of absurd and false ideas" and instead embrace the belief that we are "all of one flesh" and with "all the same sensations and endowed . . . with the same faculties."[6] Many years later, in his *Appeal to the Colored Citizens of the World* (1829), David Walker channeled decades of Black protest, simultaneously denouncing the moral rot of slavery and racism while praising the inner strength of the race.

Jefferson had his defenders. White men such as Charles Caldwell and Samuel George Morton hardened Jefferson's skepticism, offering a "biological" case for Black and white people not only having separate creations but actually being different species, a position increasingly articulated throughout the antebellum period. Few Americans subscribed wholesale to such theories, but many shared beliefs in white supremacy. As the decades passed, white Americans were forced to acknowledge that if the Black population was indeed whitening, it resulted from sexual violence and not the environment. The sense of inspiration and wonder that followed Henry Moss in the 1790s would have been impossible just a generation later.

III. Jeffersonian Republicanism

Free and enslaved Black Americans were not alone in pushing against political hierarchies. Jefferson's election to the presidency in 1800 represented a victory for non-elite white Americans in their bid to assume more direct control over the government. Elites had made no secret of their hostility toward the direct control of government by the people. In both private correspondence and published works, many of the nation's founders argued that pure democracy would lead to anarchy. Massachusetts Federalist Fisher Ames spoke for many of his colleagues when he lamented the dangers that democracy posed because it depended on public opinion, which "shifts with every current of caprice." Jefferson's election, for Federalists like Ames, heralded a slide "down into the mire of a democracy."[7]

Indeed, many political leaders and non-elite citizens believed Jefferson embraced the politics of the masses. "In a government like ours it is the duty of the Chief-magistrate . . . to unite in himself the confidence of the whole people," Jefferson wrote in 1810.[8] Nine years later, looking back on his monumental election, Jefferson again linked his triumph to the political engagement of ordinary citizens: "The revolution of 1800 . . . was as real a revolution in the principles of our government as that of 76 was in it's form," he wrote, "not effected indeed by the sword . . . but by the rational and peaceable instrument of reform, the suffrage [voting] of the people."[9] Jefferson desired to convince Americans, and the world, that a government that answered directly to the people would lead to lasting national union, not anarchic division. He wanted to prove that free people could govern themselves democratically.

Jefferson set out to differentiate his administration from the Federalists. He defined American union by the voluntary bonds of fellow citizens toward one another and toward the government. In contrast, the Federalists supposedly imagined a union defined by expansive state power and public submission to the rule of aristocratic elites. For Jefferson, the American nation drew its "energy" and its strength from the "confidence" of a "reasonable" and "rational" people.

Democratic-Republican celebrations often credited Jefferson with saving the nation's republican principles. In a move that enraged Federalists, they used the image of George Washington, who had passed away in 1799, linking the republican virtue Washington epitomized to the democratic liberty Jefferson championed. Leaving behind the military pomp of power-obsessed Federalists, Democratic-Republicans had peacefully elected the scribe of national independence, the philosopher-patriot who had battled tyranny with his pen, not with a sword or a gun.

The celebrations of Jefferson's presidency and the defeat of the Federalists expressed many citizens' willingness to assert greater direct control over the government as citizens. The definition of citizenship was changing. Early American national identity was coded masculine, just as it was coded white and wealthy; yet, since the Revolution, women had repeatedly called for a place in the conversation. Mercy Otis Warren was one of the most noteworthy female contributors to the public ratification debate over the Constitution of 1787 and 1788, but women all over the country were urged to participate in the discussion over the Constitution. "It is the duty of the American ladies, in a particular manner, to interest themselves in the success of the measures that are now pursuing by the Federal Convention for the happiness of America," a Philadelphia essayist announced. "They can retain their rank as rational beings only in a free government. In a monarchy . . . they will be considered as valuable members of a society, only in proportion as they are capable of being mothers for soldiers, who are the pillars of crowned heads."[10] American women were more than mothers to soldiers; they were mothers to liberty.

Historians have used the term *Republican Motherhood* to describe the early American belief that women were essential in nurturing the principles of liberty in the citizenry. Women would pass along important values of independence and virtue to their children, ensuring that each generation cherished the same values of the American Revolution. Because of these ideas, women's actions became politicized. Some even described women's choice of sexual partner as crucial to the health and well-being of both the party and the nation. "The fair Daughters of America" should "never disgrace themselves by giving their hands in marriage to any but real republicans," a group of New Jersey Democratic-Republicans asserted. A Philadelphia paper toasted "The fair Daughters of Columbia. May their smiles be the reward of Republicans only."[11] Though unmistakably steeped in the gendered assumptions about female sexuality and domesticity that denied women an equal share of the political rights men

enjoyed, these statements also conceded the pivotal role women played as active participants in partisan politics.[12]

IV. Jefferson as President

Buttressed by robust public support, Jefferson sought to implement policies that reflected his own political ideology. He worked to reduce taxes and cut the government's budget, believing that this would expand the economic opportunities of free Americans. His cuts included national defense, and Jefferson restricted the regular army to three thousand men. England may have needed taxes and debt to support its military empire, but Jefferson was determined to live in peace—and that belief led him to reduce America's national debt while getting rid of all internal taxes during his first term. In a move that became the crowning achievement of his presidency, Jefferson authorized the acquisition of Louisiana from France in 1803 in what is considered the largest real estate deal in American history. France had ceded Louisiana to Spain in exchange for West Florida after the Seven Years' War decades earlier. Jefferson was concerned about American access to New Orleans, which served as an important port for western farmers. His worries multiplied when the French secretly reacquired Louisiana in 1800. Spain remained in Louisiana for two more years while the U.S. minister to France, Robert R. Livingston, tried to

The artist James Peale painted this portrait of his wife, Mary, and five of their eventual six children. Peale and others represented women as responsible for the health of the republic through their roles as wives as mothers. Historians call this view of women *Republican Motherhood*. Wikimedia.

Thomas Jefferson's victory over John Adams in the election of 1800 was celebrated through everyday Americans' material culture, including this victory banner. Smithsonian Institution, National Museum of American History.

strike a compromise. Fortunately for the United States, the pressures of war in Europe and the slave insurrection in Haiti forced Napoleon to rethink his vast North American holdings. Rebellious enslaved people coupled with a yellow fever outbreak in Haiti defeated French forces, stripping Napoleon of his ability to control Haiti (the home of profitable sugar plantations). Deciding to cut his losses, Napoleon offered to sell the entire Louisiana Territory for $15 million—roughly equivalent to $250 million today. Negotiations between Livingston and Napoleon's foreign minister, Talleyrand, succeeded more spectacularly than either Jefferson or Livingston could have imagined.

Jefferson made an inquiry to his cabinet regarding the constitutionality of the Louisiana Purchase, but he believed he was obliged to operate outside the strict limitations of the Constitution if the good of the nation was at stake, as his ultimate responsibility was to the American people. Jefferson felt he should be able to "throw himself on the justice of his country" when he facilitated the interests of the very people he served.[13]

Jefferson's foreign policy, particularly the Embargo Act of 1807, elicited the most outrage from his Federalist critics. As Napoleon Bonaparte's armies moved across Europe, Jefferson wrote to a European friend that he was glad that God had "divided the dry lands of your hemisphere from the dry lands of ours, and said 'here, at least, be there peace.'"[14] Unfortunately, the Atlantic Ocean soon became the site of Jefferson's greatest foreign policy test, as England, France, and Spain refused to respect American ships' neutrality. The greatest offenses came from the British, who resumed the policy of impressment, seizing thousands of American sailors and forcing them to fight for the British navy.

Many Americans called for war when the British attacked the USS *Chesapeake* in 1807. The president, however, decided on a policy of "peaceable coercion" and Congress agreed. Under the Embargo Act of 1807, American ports were closed to all foreign trade in hopes of avoiding war. Jefferson hoped that an embargo would force European nations to respect American neutrality. Historians disagree over the wisdom of peaceable coercion. At first, withholding commerce rather than declaring war appeared to be the ultimate means of nonviolent conflict resolution. In practice, the embargo hurt the U.S. economy. Even Jefferson's personal finances suffered. When Americans resorted to smuggling their goods out of the country, Jefferson expanded governmental powers to try to enforce their compliance, leading some to label him a "tyrant."

Criticism of Jefferson's policies reflected the same rhetoric his supporters had used earlier against Adams and the Federalists. Federalists attacked the

The attack of the *Chesapeake* caused such furor in the hearts of Americans that even eighty years after the incident, an artist sketched this drawing of the event. Fred S. Cozzens, *The incident between HMS "Leopard" and USS "Chesapeake" that sparked the Chesapeake-Leopard Affair*, 1897. Wikimedia.

American Philosophical Society and the study of natural history, believing both to be too saturated with Democratic Republicans. Some Federalists lamented the alleged decline of educational standards for children. Moreover, James Callender published accusations (that were later proven credible by DNA evidence) that Jefferson was involved in a sexual relationship with Sally Hemings, one of his enslaved laborers.[15] Callender referred to Jefferson as "our little mulatto president," suggesting that sex with an enslaved person had somehow compromised Jefferson's racial integrity.[16] Callender's accusation joined previous Federalist attacks on Jefferson's racial politics, including a scathing pamphlet written by South Carolinian William Loughton Smith in 1796 that described the principles of Jeffersonian democracy as the beginning of a slippery slope to dangerous racial equality.[17]

Arguments lamenting the democratization of America were far less effective than those that borrowed from democratic language and alleged that Jefferson's actions undermined the sovereignty of the people. When Federalists attacked Jefferson, they often accused him of acting against the interests of the very public he claimed to serve. This tactic represented a pivotal development. As the Federalists scrambled to stay politically relevant, it became apparent that their ideology—rooted in eighteenth-century notions of virtue, paternalistic rule by wealthy elite, and the deference of ordinary citizens to an aristocracy of merit—was no longer tenable. The Federalists' adoption of republican political rhetoric signaled a new political landscape in which both parties embraced the direct involvement of the citizenry. The Democratic-Republican Party rose to power on the promise to expand voting and promote a more direct link between political leaders and the electorate. The American populace continued to demand more direct access to political power. Jefferson, James Madison, and James Monroe sought to expand voting through policies that made it easier for Americans to purchase land. Under their leadership, seven new states entered the Union. By 1824, only three states still had rules about how much property someone had to own before he could vote. Never again would the Federalists regain dominance over either Congress or the presidency; the last Federalist to run for president, Rufus King, lost to Monroe in 1816.

V. Native American Power and the United States

The Jeffersonian rhetoric of equality contrasted harshly with the reality of a nation stratified along the lines of gender, class, race, and ethnicity. Diplomatic relations between Native Americans and local, state, and national governments offer a dramatic example of the dangers of those inequalities. Prior to the Revolution, many Native American nations had balanced a delicate diplomacy between European empires, which scholars have called the Play-off System.[18] Moreover, in many parts of North America, Indigenous peoples dominated social relations.

Americans pushed for more land in all their interactions with Native diplomats and leaders. But boundaries were only one source of tension. Trade, criminal jurisdiction, roads, the sale of liquor, and alliances were also key negotiating points. Despite their role in fighting on both sides, Native American negotiators were not included in the diplomatic negotiations that ended the Revolutionary War. Unsurprisingly, the final document omitted concessions for Native allies. Even as Native peoples proved vital trading partners, scouts, and allies against hostile nations, they were often condemned by white settlers and government officials as "savages." White ridicule of Indigenous practices and disregard for Indigenous nations' property rights and sovereignty prompted some Indigenous peoples to turn away from white practices.

In the wake of the American Revolution, Native American diplomats developed relationships with the United States, maintained or ceased relations with the British Empire (or with Spain in the South), and negotiated their relationship with other Native nations. Formal diplomatic negotiations included Native rituals to reestablish relationships and open communication. Treaty conferences took place in Native towns, at neutral sites in borderlands, and in state and federal capitals. While chiefs were politically important, skilled orators, such as Red Jacket, as well as intermediaries, and interpreters also played key roles in negotiations. Native American orators were known for metaphorical language, command of an audience, and compelling voice and gestures.

Throughout the early republic, diplomacy was preferred to war. Violence and warfare carried enormous costs for all parties—in lives, money, trade disruptions, and reputation. Diplomacy allowed parties to air their grievances, negotiate their relationships, and minimize violence. Violent conflicts arose when diplomacy failed.

Native diplomacy testified to the complexity of Indigenous cultures and their role in shaping the politics and policy of American communities, states, and the federal government. Yet white attitudes, words, and policies frequently relegated Native peoples to the literal and figurative margins as "ignorant savages." Poor treatment like this inspired hostility

RED JACKET.

Shown in this portrait as a refined gentle-man, Red Jacket proved to be one of the most effective middlemen between Native Americans and U.S. officials. The medal worn around his neck, apparently given to him by George Washington, reflects his position as an intermediary. Campbell & Burns, *Red Jacket. Seneca war chief*, Philadelphia: C. Hullmandel, 1838. Library of Congress.

and calls for alliances from leaders of distinct Native nations, including the Shawnee leader Tecumseh.

Tecumseh and his brother, Tenskwatawa, the Prophet, helped envision an alliance of North America's Indigenous populations to halt the encroachments of the United States. They created towns in present-day Indiana, first at Greenville, then at Prophetstown, in defiance of the Treaty of Greenville (1795). Tecumseh traveled to many diverse Native nations from Canada to Georgia, calling for unification, resistance, and the restoration of sacred power.

Tecumseh and Tenskwatawa's confederacy was the culmination of many movements that swept through Indigenous North America during the eighteenth century. An earlier coalition fought in Pontiac's War. Neolin, the Delaware prophet, influenced Pontiac, an Ottawa (Odawa) war chief, with his vision of Native independence, cultural renewal, and religious revitalization. Through Neolin, the Master of Life—the Great Spirit—urged Native peoples to shrug off their dependency on European goods and technologies, reassert their faith in Native spirituality and rituals, and cooperate with one another against the "White people's ways and nature."[19] Additionally, Neolin advocated violence against British encroachments on Native American lands, which escalated after the Seven Years' War. His message was particularly effective in the Ohio and Upper Susquehanna Valleys, where polyglot communities of Indigenous refugees and migrants from across eastern North America lived together. When combined with the militant leadership of Pontiac, who took up Neolin's message, the many Native peoples of the region united in attacks against British forts and people. From 1763 until 1765, the Great Lakes, Ohio Valley, and Upper Susquehanna Valley areas were embroiled in a war between Pontiac's confederacy and the British Empire, a war that ultimately forced the English to restructure how they managed Native-British relations and trade.

In the interim between 1765 and 1811, other Native prophets kept Neolin's message alive while encouraging Indigenous peoples to resist Euro-American encroachments. These individuals included the Ottawa leader "the Trout," also called Maya-Ga-Wy; Joseph Brant of the Iroquois (Haudenosaunee); the Creek headman Mad Dog; Painted Pole of the Shawnee; a Mohawk woman named Coocoochee; Main Poc of the Potawatomi; and the Seneca prophet Handsome Lake. Once again, the epicenter of this resistance and revitalization originated in the Ohio Valley and Great Lakes regions, where from 1791 to 1795 a joint force of Shawnee, Delaware, Miami, Iroquois, Ojibwe, Ottawa, Huron, Potawatomi, Mingo, Chickamauga, and other Indigenous peoples waged war against the American republic. Although this "Western Confederacy" ultimately suffered defeat at the Battle of Fallen Timbers in 1794, this Native coalition achieved a number of military victories against the republic, including the destruction of two American armies, forcing President Washington to reformulate federal policy. Tecumseh's experiences as a warrior against the American military in this conflict probably influenced his later efforts to generate solidarity among North American Indigenous communities.

Tecumseh and Tenskwatawa articulated ideas and beliefs similar to their eighteenth-century predecessors. In particular, Tenskwatawa pronounced that the Master of Life entrusted him and Tecumseh with the responsibility for returning Native peoples to the one true path and to rid Native communities of the dangerous and corrupting influences of Euro-American trade and culture. Tenskwatawa stressed the need for cultural and religious renewal, which coincided with his blending of the tenets, traditions, and rituals of Indigenous religions and Christianity. In

Tenskwatawa
as painted by
George Catlin,
in 1831. Catlin
acknowledged the
prophet's spiri-
tual power and
painted him with
a medicine stick.
Wikimedia.

particular, Tenskwatawa emphasized apocalyptic visions that he and his
followers would usher in a new world and restore Native power to the
continent. For Native peoples who gravitated to the Shawnee brothers,
this emphasis on cultural and religious revitalization was empowering
and spiritually liberating, especially given the continuous American assaults on Native land and power in the early nineteenth century.

Tecumseh's confederacy drew heavily from Indigenous communities
in the Old Northwest and the festering hatred for land-hungry Americans. Tecumseh attracted a wealth of allies in his adamant refusal to concede any more land. Tecumseh proclaimed that the Master of Life tasked
him with the responsibility of returning Native lands to their rightful
owners. In his efforts to promote unity among Native peoples, Tecumseh
also offered these communities a distinctly Native American identity that
brought disparate Native peoples together under the banner of a common spirituality, together resisting an oppressive force. In short, spirituality tied together the resistance movement. Tecumseh and Tenskwatawa
were not above using this unifying rhetoric to legitimate their own authority within Indigenous communities at the expense of other Native
leaders. This manifested most visibly during Tenskwatawa's witch hunts
of the 1800s. Those who opposed Tenskwatawa or sought to accommodate Americans were labeled witches.

While Tecumseh attracted Native peoples from around the Northwest, the Red Stick Creeks brought these ideas to the Southeast. Led by
the Creek prophet Hillis Hadjo, who accompanied Tecumseh when he
toured throughout the Southeast in 1811, the Red Sticks integrated certain religious tenets from the north and invented new religious practices
specific to the Creeks, all the while communicating and coordinating with
Tecumseh after he left Creek Country. In doing so, the Red Sticks joined
Tecumseh in his resistance movement while seeking to purge Creek society of its Euro-American dependencies. Creek leaders who maintained
relationships with the United States, in contrast, believed that accommodation and diplomacy might stave off American encroachments better
than violence.

Additionally, the Red Sticks discovered that most southeastern Indigenous leaders cared little for Tecumseh's confederacy. This lack of allies
hindered the spread of a movement in the southeast, and the Red Sticks
soon found themselves in a civil war against other Creeks. Tecumseh thus
found little support in the Southeast beyond the Red Sticks, who by 1813
were cut off from the North by Andrew Jackson. Shortly thereafter, Jackson's forces were joined by Lower Creek and Cherokee forces that helped
defeat the Red Sticks, culminating in Jackson's victory at the Battle of
Horseshoe Bend. Following their defeat, the Red Sticks were forced to
cede an unprecedented fourteen million acres of land in the Treaty of Fort
Jackson. As historian Adam Rothman argues, the defeat of the Red Sticks
allowed the United States to expand west of the Mississippi, guaranteeing
the continued existence and profitability of slavery.[20]

Many Native leaders refused to join Tecumseh and instead maintained their loyalties to the American republic. After the failures of Native
American unity and loss at the Battle of Tippecanoe in 1811, Tecumseh's
confederation floundered. The War of 1812 between the United States
and Britain offered new opportunities for Tecumseh and his followers.[21]
With the United States distracted, Tecumseh and his confederated army
seized several American forts on their own initiative. Eventually Tecumseh solicited British aid after sustaining heavy losses from American fighters at Fort Wayne and Fort Harrison. Even then, the confederacy faced an
uphill battle, particularly after American naval forces secured control of
the Great Lakes in September 1813, forcing British ships and reinforcements to retreat. Yet Tecumseh and his Native allies fought on despite
being surrounded by American forces. Tecumseh told the British commander Henry Proctor, "Our lives are in the hands of the Great Spirit.
We are determined to defend our lands, and if it is his will, we wish

to leave our bones upon them."[22] Soon thereafter, Tecumseh fell on the battlefields of Moraviantown, Ontario, in October 1813. His death dealt a severe blow to Native American resistance against the United States. Men like Tecumseh and Pontiac, however, left behind a legacy of Native American unity that was not soon forgotten.

VI. The War of 1812

Soon after Jefferson retired from the presidency in 1808, Congress ended the embargo and the British relaxed their policies toward American ships. Despite the embargo's unpopularity, Jefferson still believed that more time would have proven that peaceable coercion worked. Yet war with Britain loomed—a war that would galvanize the young American nation.

The War of 1812 stemmed from American entanglement in two distinct sets of international issues. The first had to do with the nation's desire to maintain its position as a neutral trading nation during the series of Anglo-French wars, which began in the aftermath of the French Revolution in 1793. The second had older roots in the colonial and Revolutionary era. In both cases, American interests conflicted with those of the British Empire. British leaders showed little interest in accommodating the Americans.

Impressments, the practice of forcing American sailors to join the British Navy, was among the most important sources of conflict between the two nations. Driven in part by trade with Europe, the American economy grew quickly during the first decade of the nineteenth century, creating a labor shortage in the American shipping industry. In response, pay rates for sailors increased and American captains recruited heavily from the ranks of British sailors. As a result, around 30 percent of sailors employed on American merchant ships were British. As a republic, the Americans advanced the notion that people could become citizens by renouncing their allegiance to their home nation. To the British, a person born in the British Empire was a subject of that empire for life, a status they could not change. The British Navy was embroiled in a difficult war and was unwilling to lose any of its labor force. In order to regain lost crewmen, the British often boarded American ships to reclaim their sailors. Of course, many American sailors found themselves caught up in these sweeps and "impressed" into the service of the British Navy. Between 1803 and 1812, some six thousand Americans suffered this fate. The British would release Americans who could prove their identity, but this process could take years while the sailor endured harsh conditions and the dangers of the Royal Navy.

In 1806, responding to a French declaration of a complete naval blockade of Great Britain, the British demanded that neutral ships first carry their goods to Britain to pay a transit duty before they could proceed to France. Despite loopholes in these policies between 1807 and 1812, Britain, France, and their allies seized about nine hundred American ships, prompting a swift and angry American response. Jefferson's embargo sent the nation into a deep depression and drove exports down from $108 million in 1807 to $22 million in 1808, all while having little effect on Europeans.[23] Within fifteen months Congress repealed the Embargo Act, replacing it with smaller restrictions on trade with Britain and France. Although efforts to stand against Great Britain had failed, resentment of British trade policy remained widespread.

Far from the Atlantic Ocean on the American frontier, Americans were also at odds with the British Empire. From their position in Canada, the British maintained relations with Native Americans in the Old Northwest, supplying them with goods and weapons in attempts to maintain ties in case of another war with the United States. The threat of a Native uprising increased after 1805 when Tenskwatawa and Tecumseh built their alliance. The territorial governor of Indiana, William Henry Harrison, eventually convinced the Madison administration to allow for military action against the Native Americans in the Ohio Valley. The resulting Battle of Tippecanoe drove the followers of the Prophet from their gathering place but did little to change the dynamics of the region. British efforts to arm and supply Native Americans, however, angered Americans and strengthened anti-British sentiments.

Democratic-Republicans began to talk of war as a solution to these problems, arguing that it was necessary to complete the War for Independence by preventing British efforts to keep America subjugated at sea and on land. The war would also represent another battle against the Loyalists, some thirty-eight thousand of whom had populated Upper Canada after the Revolution and sought to establish a counter to the radical experiment of the United States.[24]

In 1812, the Democratic-Republicans held 75 percent of the seats in the House and 82 percent of the Senate, giving them a free hand to set national policy. Among them were the "War Hawks," whom one historian describes as "too young to remember the horrors of the American Revolution" and thus "willing to risk another British war to vindicate the nation's rights and independence."[25] This group included men who would remain influential long after the War of 1812, such as Henry Clay of Kentucky and John C. Calhoun of South Carolina.

Convinced by the War Hawks in his party, Madison drafted a statement of the nation's disputes with the British and asked Congress for a war declaration on June 1, 1812. The Democratic-Republicans hoped that an invasion of Canada might remove the British from their backyard and force the empire to change their naval policies. After much negotiation in Congress over the details of the bill, Madison signed a declaration of war on June 18, 1812. For the second time, the United States was at war with Great Britain.

While the War of 1812 contained two key players—the United States and Great Britain—it also drew in other groups, such as Tecumseh and his Confederacy. The war can be organized into three stages or theaters. The first, the Atlantic Theater, lasted until the spring of 1813. During this time, Great Britain was chiefly occupied in Europe against Napoleon, and the United States invaded Canada and sent their fledgling navy against British ships. During the second stage, from early 1813 to 1814, the United States launched their second offensive against Canada and the Great Lakes. In this period, the Americans won their first successes. The third stage, the Southern Theater, concluded with Andrew Jackson's January 1815 victory outside New Orleans, Louisiana.

During the war, the Americans were greatly interested in Canada and the Great Lakes borderlands. In July 1812, the United States launched their first offensive against Canada. By August, however, the British and their allies rebuffed the Americans, costing the United States control over Detroit and parts of the Michigan Territory. By the close of 1813, the Americans recaptured Detroit, shattered the Confederacy, killed Tecumseh, and eliminated the British threat in that theater. Despite these accomplishments, the American land forces proved outmatched by their adversaries.

After the land campaign of 1812 failed to secure America's war aims, Americans turned to the infant navy in 1813. Privateers and the U.S. Navy rallied behind the slogan "Free Trade and Sailors' Rights!" Although the British possessed the most powerful navy in the world, surprisingly the young American navy extracted early victories with larger, more heavily armed ships. By 1814, however, the major naval battles had been fought with little effect on the war's outcome.

With Britain's main naval fleet fighting in the Napoleonic Wars, smaller ships and armaments stationed in North America were generally

As pictured in this 1812 political cartoon published in Philadelphia, Americans lambasted the British and their native allies for what they considered "savage" offenses during war, though Americans too were engaging in such heinous acts. William Charles, *A scene on the frontiers as practiced by the "humane" British and their "worthy" allies*, Philadelphia, 1812. Library of Congress.

no match for their American counterparts. Early on, Americans humiliated the British in single ship battles. In retaliation, Captain Philip Broke of the HMS *Shannon* attacked the USS *Chesapeake*, captained by James Lawrence, on June 1, 1813. Within six minutes, the *Chesapeake* was destroyed and Lawrence mortally wounded. Yet the Americans did not give up. Lawrence commanded them, "Tell the men to fire faster! Don't give up the ship!"[26] Lawrence died of his wounds three days later, and although the *Shannon* defeated the *Chesapeake*, Lawrence's words became a rallying cry for the Americans.

Two and a half months later the USS *Constitution* squared off with the HMS *Guerriere*. As the *Guerriere* tried to outmaneuver the Americans, the *Constitution* pulled along broadside and began hammering the British frigate. The *Guerriere* returned fire, but as one sailor observed, the cannonballs simply bounced off the *Constitution*'s thick hull. "Huzzah! Her sides are made of iron!" shouted the sailor, and henceforth, the *Constitution* became known as "Old Ironsides." In less than thirty-five minutes, the *Guerriere* was so badly damaged that it was set aflame rather than taken as a prize.

In 1814, Americans gained naval victories on Lake Champlain near Plattsburgh, preventing a British land invasion of the United States and on the Chesapeake Bay at Fort McHenry in Baltimore. Fort McHenry repelled the nineteen-ship British fleet, enduring twenty-seven hours of bombardment virtually unscathed. Watching from aboard a British ship, American poet Francis Scott Key penned the stanzas of the poem that would later become the national anthem, "The Star Spangled Banner."

Impressive though these accomplishments were, they belied what was actually a poorly executed military campaign against the British. The U.S. Navy won their most significant victories in the Atlantic Ocean in 1813. Napoleon's defeat in early 1814, however, allowed the British to focus on North America and blockade American ports. Thanks to the blockade, the British were able to burn Washington, D.C., on August 24, 1814 and open a new theater of operations in the South. The British sailed for New Orleans, where they achieved a naval victory at Lake Borgne before losing the land invasion to Major General Andrew Jackson's troops in January 1815. This American victory actually came after the United States and the United Kingdom signed the Treaty of Ghent on

The artist shows Washington, D.C., engulfed in flames as the British troops set fire to the city in 1814. *Capture of the City of Washington*, August 1814. Wikimedia.

December 24, 1814, but the Battle of New Orleans proved to be a psychological victory that boosted American morale and affected how the war has been remembered.

But not all Americans supported the war. In 1814, New England Federalists met in Hartford, Connecticut, to try to end the war and curb the power of the Democratic-Republican Party. They produced a document that proposed abolishing the three-fifths rule that afforded southern enslavers disproportionate representation in Congress, limiting the president to a single term in office, and most importantly, demanding a two-thirds congressional majority, rather than a simple majority, for legislation that declared war, admitted new states into the Union, or regulated commerce. With the two-thirds majority, New England's Federalist politicians believed they could limit the power of their political foes.

These proposals were sent to Washington, but unfortunately for the Federalists, the victory at New Orleans buoyed popular support for the Madison administration. With little evidence, newspapers accused the Hartford Convention's delegates of plotting secession. The episode demonstrated the waning power of Federalism and the need for the region's politicians to shed their aristocratic and Anglophile image. The next New England politician to assume the presidency, John Quincy

Contemplating the possibility of secession over the War of 1812 (fueled in large part by the economic interests of New England merchants), the Hartford Convention posed the possibility of disaster for the still-young United States. England, represented by the figure John Bull on the right side, is shown in this political cartoon with arms open to accept New England back into its empire. William Charles Jr., *The Hartford Convention or Leap No Leap*. Wikimedia.

The Hartford Convention or *LEAP NO LEAP.*

Adams, would, in 1824, emerge not from within the Federalist fold but having served as secretary of state under President James Monroe, the leader of the Virginia Democratic-Republicans.

The Treaty of Ghent essentially returned relations between the United States and Britain to their prewar status. The war, however, mattered politically and strengthened American nationalism. During the war, Americans read patriotic newspaper stories, sang patriotic songs, and bought consumer goods decorated with national emblems. They also heard stories about how the British and their Native allies threatened to bring violence into American homes. For examples, rumors spread that British officers promised rewards of "beauty and booty" for their soldiers when they attacked New Orleans.[27] In the Great Lakes borderlands, wartime propaganda fueled Americans' fear of Britain's Native American allies, whom they believed would slaughter men, women, and children indiscriminately. Terror and love worked together to make American citizens feel a stronger bond with their country. Because the war mostly cut off America's trade with Europe, it also encouraged Americans to see themselves as different and separate; it fostered a sense that the country had been reborn.

Former treasury secretary Albert Gallatin claimed that the War of 1812 revived "national feelings" that had dwindled after the Revolution. "The people," he wrote, were now "more American; they feel and act more like a nation."[28] Politicians proposed measures to reinforce the fragile Union through capitalism and built on these sentiments of nationalism. The United States continued to expand into Native American territories with westward settlement in far-flung new states like Tennessee, Ohio, Mississippi, and Illinois. Between 1810 and 1830, the country added more than six thousand new post offices.

In 1817, South Carolina congressman John C. Calhoun called for building projects to "bind the republic together with a perfect system of roads and canals."[29] He joined with other politicians, such as Kentucky's powerful Henry Clay, to promote what came to be called an American System. They aimed to make America economically independent and encouraged commerce between the states over trade with Europe and the West Indies. The American System would include a new Bank of the United States to provide capital; a high protective tariff, which would raise the prices of imported goods and help American-made products compete; and a network of "internal improvements," roads and canals to let people take American goods to market.

These projects were controversial. Many people believed that they were unconstitutional or would increase the federal government's power at the expense of the states. Even Calhoun later changed his mind and joined the opposition. The War of 1812, however, had reinforced Americans' sense of the nation's importance in their political and economic life. Even when the federal government did not act, states created banks, roads, and canals of their own.

What may have been the boldest declaration of America's postwar pride came in 1823. President James Monroe issued an ultimatum to the empires of Europe in order to support several wars of independence in Latin America. The Monroe Doctrine declared that the United States considered its entire hemisphere, both North and South America, off-limits to new European colonization. Although Monroe was a Jeffersonian, some of his principles echoed Federalist policies. Whereas Jefferson cut the size of the military and ended all internal taxes in his first term, Monroe advocated the need for a strong military and an aggressive foreign policy. Since Americans were spreading out over the continent, Monroe authorized the federal government to invest in canals and roads, which he said would "shorten distances and, by making each part more accessible to and dependent on the other . . . shall bind the Union more closely together."[30] As Federalists had attempted two decades earlier, Democratic-Republican leaders after the War of 1812 advocated strengthening the government to strengthen the nation.

VII. Conclusion

Monroe's election after the conclusion of the War of 1812 signaled the death knell of the Federalists. Some predicted an "era of good feelings" and an end to party divisions. The War had cultivated a profound sense of union among a diverse and divided people. Yet that "era of good feelings" would never really come. Political division continued. Though the dying Federalists would fade from political relevance, a schism within the Democratic-Republican Party would give rise to Jacksonian Democrats. Political limits continued along class, gender, and racial and ethnic lines. At the same time, industrialization and the development of American capitalism required new justifications of inequality. Social change and increased immigration prompted nativist reactions that would divide "true" Americans from dangerous or undeserving "others." Still, a cacophony of voices clamored to be heard and struggled to realize a social order compatible with the ideals of equality and individual liberty. As always, the meaning of democracy was in flux.

VIII. Reference Material

This chapter was edited by Nathaniel C. Green, with content contributions by Justin Clark, Adam Costanzo, Stephanie Gamble, Dale Kretz, Julie Richter, Bryan Rindfleisch, Angela Riotto, James Risk, Cara Rogers, Jonathan Wilfred Wilson, and Charlton Yingling.

Recommended citation: Justin Clark et al., "The Early Republic," Nathaniel C. Green, ed., in *The American Yawp*, eds. Joseph Locke and Ben Wright (Stanford, CA: Stanford University Press, 2019).

NOTES TO CHAPTER 7

1. Thomas Paine, *Common Sense* (1776), in Eric Foner, ed., *Thomas Paine: Collected Writings* (New York: Library of America, 1995), 23.

2. David Walker, *Appeal to the Coloured Citizens of the World, But in Particular, and Very Expressly, to Those of The United States of America* (New York: Hill and Wang, 1995), 21, 56.

3. John Russwurm, "The Condition and Prospects of Hayti," in *African Americans and the Haitian Revolution: Selected Essays and Historical Documents*, ed. Maurice Jackson and Jacqueline Bacon (New York: Routledge, 2013), 168.

4. "Republic of Hayti," *Colored American*, March 15, 1838, 2.

5. Benjamin Rush, "Observations Intended to Favour a Supposition That the Black Color (As It Is Called) of the Negroes is Derived from the Leprosy," *Transactions of the American Philosophical Society* 4 (1799): 289–297.

6. Banneker to Jefferson, August 19, 1791, Founders Online, National Archives, http://founders.archives.gov/documents/Jefferson/01-22-02-0049.

7. Fisher Ames, "The Mire of a Democracy," in *Works of Fisher Ames*, 2 vols., ed. W. B. Allen (Indianapolis, IN: Liberty Fund, 1984), Vol. 1: 6, 7.

8. Jefferson to John Garland Jefferson, January 25, 1810, in *The Papers of Thomas Jefferson, Retirement Series*, ed. Julian P. Boyd et al., 40 vols. to date (Princeton, NJ: Princeton University Press, 1950–), Vol. 2: 183. Hereafter cited as *PTJ, RS*.

9. Thomas Jefferson to Spencer Roane, September 6, 1819, http://www.loc.gov/exhibits/jefferson/137.html.

10. *Philadelphia Independent Gazetteer*, June 5, 1787, in Merrill Jensen, John P. Kaminski, Gaspare J. Saladino, et al., eds., *The Documentary History of the Ratification of the Constitution*, 22 vols. to date (Madison: State Historical Society of Wisconsin, 1976–), Vol. 13: 126–127. The digital edition of the first twenty volumes is available through the University of Virginia Press Rotunda project, edited by John P. Kaminski, Gaspare J. Saladino, et al., http://rotunda.upress.virginia.edu/founders/RNCN.html. Hereafter cited as *DHRC*.

11. *Alexandria Times, and District of Columbia Daily Advertiser* (Alexandria, VA), July 2, 1800; *Constitutional Telegraphe* (Boston, MA), February 15 and December 6, 1800; *Carlisle Gazette* (Carlisle, PA), November 6, 1799.

12. See Linda K. Kerber, *Women of the Republic: Intellect and Ideology in Revolutionary America* (Chapel Hill: University of North Carolina Press, 1997); and Mary Kelley, *Learning to Stand and Speak: Women, Education, and Public Life in America's Republic* (Chapel Hill: University of North Carolina Press, 2006).

13. Jefferson to John B. Colvin, September 20, 1810, in *PTJ, RS* 3: 99, 100, 101.

14. Jefferson to the Earl of Buchan Washington, July 10, 1803, in *Papers of Thomas Jefferson, Volume 40* (Princeton, NJ: Princeton University Press, 2013), 708–709.

15. For the Hemings controversy and the DNA evidence, see Annette Gordon-Reed, *Thomas Jefferson and Sally Hemings: An American Controversy* (Charlottesville: University of Virginia Press, 1997).

16. *Recorder* (Richmond, VA), November 3, 1802.

17. *The Pretensions of Thomas Jefferson to the Presidency Examined; and the Charges Against John Adams Refuted. Addressed to the Citizens of America in General; and Particularly to the Electors of the President*, 2 vols. (Philadelphia: s.n., 1796).

18. See, for example, Anthony F. C. Wallace, *The Death and Rebirth of the Seneca* (New York: Random House, 1969), 111.

19. Gregory Dowd, *A Spirited Resistance: The North American Indian Struggle for Unity, 1745–1815* (Baltimore: Johns Hopkins University Press, 1992), 33.

20. Adam Rothman, *Slave Country: American Expansion and the Origins of the Deep South* (Cambridge, MA: Harvard University Press, 2009).

21. Nicole Eustace, *1812: War and the Passions of Patriotism* (Philadelphia: University of Pennsylvania Press, 2012), 149–153.

22. Quoted in Edward Eggleston and Elizabeth Eggleston Seelye, *Tecumseh and the Shawnee Prophet* (New York: Dodd, Mead, 1878), 309.

23. Amanda Porterfield, *Conceived in Doubt: Religion and Politics in the New American Nation* (Chicago: University of Chicago Press, 2012), 187.

24. Alan Taylor, *The Civil War of 1812: American Citizens, British Subjects, Irish Rebels, and Indian Allies* (New York: Random House, 2010), 5.

25. Donald R. Hickey, *Glorious Victory: Andrew Jackson and the Battle of New Orleans* (Baltimore: Johns Hopkins University Press, 2015), 8.

26. Martin Bibbings, "The Battle," in *Broke of the Shannon: And the War of 1812*, ed. Tim Voelcker (London: Seaworth Publishing, 2013), 138.

27. Ronald L. Drez, *The War of 1812: Conflict and Deception* (Baton Rouge: LSU Press, 2014), 154.

28. Morton Keller, *America's Three Regimes: A New Political History: A New Political History* (New York: Oxford University Press, 2007), 69.

29. Brian Balogh, *A Government Out of Sight: The Mystery of National Authority in Nineteenth-Century America* (New York: Cambridge University Press, 2009), 130.

30. "Inaugural Address, March 4, 1817," in *The Writings of James Monroe*, ed. Stanislaus Murray Hamilton (New York: Putnam, 1902), Vol. 6: 11.

RECOMMENDED READING

Appleby, Joyce. *Liberalism and Republicanism in the Historical Imagination.* Cambridge, MA: Belknap Press, 1992.

Bailey, Jeremy D. *Thomas Jefferson and Executive Power.* Cambridge, UK: Cambridge University Press, 2010.

Blackhawk, Ned. *Violence over the Land: Indians and Empires in the Early American West.* Cambridge, MA: Harvard University Press, 2008.

Bradburn, Douglas. *The Citizenship Revolution: Politics and the Creation of the American Union, 1774–1804.* Charlottesville: University of Virginia Press, 2009.

Cleves, Rachel Hope. *The Reign of Terror in America: Visions of Violence from Anti-Jacobinism to Antislavery.* New York: Cambridge University Press, 2009.

Dubois, Laurent. *Avengers of the New World: The Story of the Haitian Revolution.* Cambridge, MA: Harvard University Press, 2005.

Edmunds, R. David. *The Shawnee Prophet.* Lincoln: University of Nebraska Press, 1983.

Eustace, Nicole. *1812: War and the Passions of Patriotism.* Philadelphia: University of Pennsylvania Press, 2012.

Fabian, Ann. *The Skull Collectors: Race, Science, and America's Unburied Dead.* Chicago: University of Chicago Press, 2010.

Freeman, Joanne B. *Affairs of Honor: National Politics in the New Republic.* New Haven, CT: Yale University Press, 2001.

Furstenberg, François. *In the Name of the Father: Washington's Legacy, Slavery, and the Making of a Nation.* New York: Penguin, 2006.

Kastor, Peter J. *The Nation's Crucible: The Louisiana Purchase and the Creation of America.* New Haven, CT: Yale University Press, 2004.

Kelley, Mary. *Learning to Stand and Speak: Women, Education, and Public Life in America's Republic.* Chapel Hill: University of North Carolina Press, 2006.

Kerber, Linda. *Federalists in Dissent: Imagery and Ideology in Jeffersonian America.* Ithaca, NY: Cornell University Press, 1970.

————. *Women of the Republic: Intellect and Ideology in Revolutionary America.* Chapel Hill: University of North Carolina Press, 1997.

Lewis, Jan. *The Pursuit of Happiness: Family and Values in Jefferson's Virginia.* New York: Cambridge University Press, 1985.

Manion, Jen. *Liberty's Prisoners: Carceral Culture in Early America.* Philadelphia: University of Pennsylvania Press, 2015.

Onuf, Peter. *Jefferson's Empire: The Language of American Nationhood.* Charlottesville: University of Virginia Press, 2000.

Porterfield, Amanda. *Conceived in Doubt: Religion and Politics in the New American Nation* (Chicago: University of Chicago Press, 2012.

Rothman, Adam. *Slave Country: American Expansion and the Origins of the Deep South.* Cambridge, MA: Harvard University Press, 2009.

Rothman, Joshua D. *Notorious in the Neighborhood: Sex and Families Across the Color Line in Virginia, 1787–1861.* Chapel Hill: University of North Carolina Press, 2003.

Sidbury, James. *Ploughshares into Swords: Race, Rebellion, and Identity in Gabriel's Virginia, 1730–1810.* Cambridge, UK: Cambridge University Press, 1997.

Smith-Rosenberg, Carroll. *This Violent Empire: The Birth of an American National Identity.* Chapel Hill: University of North Carolina Press, 2012.

Taylor, Alan. *The Civil War of 1812: American Citizens, British Subjects, Irish Rebels, and Indian Allies.* New York: Random House, 2010.

Waldstreicher, David. *In the Midst of Perpetual Fetes: The Making of American Nationalism 1776–1820.* Chapel Hill: University of North Carolina Press, 1997.

8

The Market Revolution

I. Introduction

In the early years of the nineteenth century, Americans' endless commercial ambition—what one Baltimore paper in 1815 called an "almost *universal ambition to get forward*"—remade the nation.[1] Between the Revolution and the Civil War, an old subsistence world died and a new more-commercial nation was born. Americans integrated the technologies of the Industrial Revolution into a new commercial economy. Steam power, the technology that moved steamboats and railroads, fueled the rise of American industry by powering mills and sparking new national transportation networks. A "market revolution" remade the nation.

The revolution reverberated across the country. More and more farmers grew crops for profit, not self-sufficiency. Vast factories and cities arose in the North. Enormous fortunes materialized. A new middle class ballooned. And as more men and women worked in the cash

William James Bennett, *View of South Street, from Maiden Lane, New York City*, c. 1827. Metropolitan Museum of New York.

economy, they were freed from the bound dependence of servitude. But there were costs to this revolution. As northern textile factories boomed, the demand for southern cotton swelled, and American slavery accelerated. Northern subsistence farmers became laborers bound to the whims of markets and bosses. The market revolution sparked explosive economic growth and new personal wealth, but it also created a growing lower class of property-less workers and a series of devastating depressions, called "panics." Many Americans labored for low wages and became trapped in endless cycles of poverty. Some workers, often immigrant women, worked thirteen hours a day, six days a week. Others labored in slavery. Massive northern textile mills turned southern cotton into cheap cloth. And although northern states washed their hands of slavery, their factories fueled the demand for slave-grown southern cotton and their banks provided the financing that ensured the profitability and continued existence of the American slave system. And so, as the economy advanced, the market revolution wrenched the United States in new directions as it became a nation of free labor and slavery, of wealth and inequality, and of endless promise and untold perils.

II. Early Republic Economic Development

The growth of the American economy reshaped American life in the decades before the Civil War. Americans increasingly produced goods for sale, not for consumption. Improved transportation enabled a larger exchange network. Labor-saving technology improved efficiency and enabled the separation of the public and domestic spheres. The market revolution fulfilled the revolutionary generation's expectations of progress but introduced troubling new trends. Class conflict, child labor, accelerated immigration, and the expansion of slavery followed. These strains required new family arrangements and transformed American cities.

American commerce had proceeded haltingly during the eighteenth century. American farmers increasingly exported foodstuffs to Europe as the French Revolutionary Wars devastated the continent between 1793 and 1815. America's exports rose in value from $20.2 million in 1790 to $108.3 million by 1807.[2] But while exports rose, exorbitant internal transportation costs hindered substantial economic development within the United States. In 1816, for instance, $9 could move one ton of goods across the Atlantic Ocean, but only thirty miles across land. An 1816

Senate Committee Report lamented that "the price of land carriage is too great" to allow the profitable production of American manufactures. But in the wake of the War of 1812, Americans rushed to build a new national infrastructure, new networks of roads, canals, and railroads. In his 1815 annual message to Congress, President James Madison stressed "the great importance of establishing throughout our country the roads and canals which can best be executed under national authority."[3] State governments continued to sponsor the greatest improvements in American transportation, but the federal government's annual expenditures on internal improvements climbed to a yearly average of $1,323,000 by Andrew Jackson's presidency.[4]

State legislatures meanwhile pumped capital into the economy by chartering banks. The number of state-chartered banks skyrocketed from 1 in 1783, 266 in 1820, and 702 in 1840 to 1,371 in 1860.[5] European capital also helped build American infrastructure. By 1844, one British traveler declared that "the prosperity of America, her railroads, canals, steam navigation, and banks, are the fruit of English capital."[6]

Economic growth, however, proceeded unevenly. Depressions devastated the economy in 1819, 1837, and 1857. Each followed rampant speculation in various commodities: land in 1819, land and enslaved la-

Clyde Osmer DeLand, *The First Locomotive. Aug. 8th, 1829. Trial Trip of the "Stourbridge Lion,"* 1916. Library of Congress.

borers in 1837, and railroad bonds in 1857. Eventually the bubbles all burst. The spread of paper currency untethered the economy from the physical signifiers of wealth familiar to the colonial generation, namely land. Counterfeit bills were endemic during this early period of banking. With so many fake bills circulating, Americans were constantly on the lookout for the "confidence man" and other deceptive characters in the urban landscape. Con men and women could look like regular honest Americans. Advice literature offered young men and women strategies for avoiding hypocrisy in an attempt to restore the social fiber. Intimacy in the domestic sphere became more important as duplicity proliferated in the public sphere. Fear of the confidence man, counterfeit bills, and a pending bust created anxiety in the new capitalist economy. But Americans refused to blame the logic of their new commercial system for these depressions. Instead, they kept pushing *"to get forward."*

The so-called Transportation Revolution opened the vast lands west of the Appalachian Mountains. In 1810, before the rapid explosion of American infrastructure, Margaret Dwight left New Haven, Connecticut, in a wagon headed for Ohio Territory. Her trip was less than five hundred miles but took six weeks to complete. The journey was a terrible ordeal, she said. The roads were "so rocky & so gullied as to be almost impassable."[7] Ten days into the journey, at Bethlehem, Pennsylvania, Dwight said "it appeared to me that we had come to the end of the habitable part of the globe." She finally concluded that "the reason so few are willing to return from the Western country, is not that the country is so good, but because the journey is so bad."[8] Nineteen years later, in 1829, English traveler Frances Trollope made the reverse journey across the Allegheny Mountains from Cincinnati to the East Coast. At Wheeling, Virginia, her coach encountered the National Road, the first federally funded interstate infrastructure project. The road was smooth and her journey across the Alleghenies was a scenic delight. "I really can hardly conceive a higher enjoyment than a botanical tour among the Alleghany Mountains," she declared. The ninety miles of the National Road was to her "a garden."[9]

If the two decades between Margaret Dwight's and Frances Trollope's journeys transformed the young nation, the pace of change only accelerated in the following years. If a transportation revolution began with improved road networks, it soon incorporated even greater improvements in the ways people and goods moved across the landscape.

New York State completed the Erie Canal in 1825. The 350-mile-long human-made waterway linked the Great Lakes with the Hudson River

Engraving based
on W. H. Bartlett,
*Lockport, Erie
Canal*, 1839.
Wikimedia.

and the Atlantic Ocean. Soon crops grown in the Great Lakes region
were carried by water to eastern cities, and goods from emerging eastern
factories made the reverse journey to midwestern farmers. The success of
New York's "artificial river" launched a canal-building boom. By 1840
Ohio created two navigable, all-water links from Lake Erie to the Ohio
River.

Robert Fulton established the first commercial steamboat service
up and down the Hudson River in New York in 1807. Soon thereafter
steamboats filled the waters of the Mississippi and Ohio Rivers. Down-
stream-only routes became watery two-way highways. By 1830, more
than two hundred steamboats moved up and down western rivers.

The United States' first long-distance rail line launched from Maryland in 1827. Baltimore's city government and the state government of
Maryland provided half the start-up funds for the new Baltimore & Ohio
(B&O) Rail Road Company. The B&O's founders imagined the line as a
means to funnel the agricultural products of the trans-Appalachian West
to an outlet on the Chesapeake Bay. Similar motivations led citizens in
Philadelphia, Boston, New York City, and Charleston, South Carolina
to launch their own rail lines. State and local governments provided the
means for the bulk of this initial wave of railroad construction, but eco-

nomic collapse following the Panic of 1837 made governments wary of such investments. Government supports continued throughout the century, but decades later the public origins of railroads were all but forgotten, and the railroad corporation became the most visible embodiment of corporate capitalism.

By 1860 Americans had laid more than thirty thousand miles of railroads.[10] The ensuing web of rail, roads, and canals meant that few farmers in the Northeast or Midwest had trouble getting goods to urban markets. Railroad development was slower in the South, but there a combination of rail lines and navigable rivers meant that few cotton planters struggled to transport their products to textile mills in the Northeast and in England.

Such internal improvements not only spread goods, they spread information. The transportation revolution was followed by a communications revolution. The telegraph redefined the limits of human communication. By 1843 Samuel Morse had persuaded Congress to fund a forty-mile telegraph line stretching from Washington, D.C., to Baltimore. Within a few short years, during the Mexican-American War, telegraph lines carried news of battlefield events to eastern newspapers within days. This contrasts starkly with the War of 1812, when the Battle of New Orleans took place nearly two full weeks after Britain and the United States had signed a peace treaty.

The consequences of the transportation and communication revolutions reshaped the lives of Americans. Farmers who previously produced crops mostly for their own family now turned to the market. They earned cash for what they had previously consumed; they purchased the goods they had previously made or gone without. Market-based farmers soon accessed credit through eastern banks, which provided them with the opportunity to expand their enterprise but left also them prone before the risk of catastrophic failure wrought by distant market forces. In the Northeast and Midwest, where farm labor was ever in short supply, ambitious farmers invested in new technologies that promised to increase the productivity of the limited labor supply. The years between 1815 and 1850 witnessed an explosion of patents on agricultural technologies. The most famous of these, perhaps, was Cyrus McCormick's horse-drawn mechanical reaper, which partially mechanized wheat harvesting, and John Deere's steel-bladed plow, which more easily allowed for the conversion of unbroken ground into fertile farmland.

Most visibly, the market revolution encouraged the growth of cities and reshaped the lives of urban workers. In 1820, only New York had

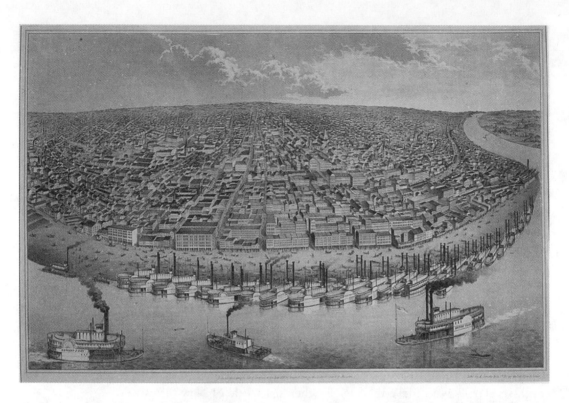

A. Janicke &
Co., *Our City,
(St. Louis, Mo.)*,
1859. Library of
Congress.

over one hundred thousand inhabitants. By 1850, six American cities met that threshold, including Chicago, which had been founded fewer than two decades earlier.[11] New technology and infrastructure paved the way for such growth. The Erie Canal captured the bulk of the trade emerging from the Great Lakes region, securing New York City's position as the nation's largest and most economically important city. The steamboat turned St. Louis and Cincinnati into centers of trade, and Chicago rose as it became the railroad hub of the western Great Lakes and Great Plains regions. The geographic center of the nation shifted westward. The development of steam power and the exploitation of Pennsylvania coalfields shifted the locus of American manufacturing. By the 1830s, for instance, New England was losing its competitive advantage to the West.

Meanwhile, the cash economy eclipsed the old, local, informal systems of barter and trade. Income became the measure of economic worth. Productivity and efficiencies paled before the measure of income. Cash facilitated new impersonal economic relationships and formalized new means of production. Young workers might simply earn wages, for instance, rather than receiving room and board and training as part of apprenticeships. Moreover, a new form of economic organization appeared: the business corporation.

States offered the privileges of incorporation to protect the fortunes and liabilities of entrepreneurs who invested in early industrial endeavors. A corporate charter allowed investors and directors to avoid personal liability for company debts. The legal status of incorporation had been designed to confer privileges to organizations embarking on expensive projects explicitly designed for the public good, such as universities, municipalities, and major public works projects. The business corporation was something new. Many Americans distrusted these new, impersonal business organizations whose officers lacked personal responsibility while nevertheless carrying legal rights. Many wanted limits. Thomas Jefferson himself wrote in 1816 that "I hope we shall crush in its birth the aristocracy of our monied corporations which dare already to challenge our government to a trial of strength, and bid defiance to the laws of our country."[12] But in *Dartmouth v. Woodward* (1819) the Supreme Court upheld the rights of private corporations when it denied the attempt of the government of New Hampshire to reorganize Dartmouth College on behalf of the common good. Still, suspicions remained. A group of journeymen cordwainers in New Jersey publically declared in 1835 that they "entirely disapprov[ed] of the incorporation of Companies, for carrying on manual mechanical business, inasmuch as we believe their tendency is to eventuate and produce monopolies, thereby crippling the energies of individual enterprise."[13]

III. The Decline of Northern Slavery and the Rise of the Cotton Kingdom

Slave labor helped fuel the market revolution. By 1832, textile companies made up 88 out of 106 American corporations valued at over $100,000.[14] These textile mills, worked by free labor, nevertheless depended on southern cotton, and the vast new market economy spurred the expansion of the plantation South.

By the early nineteenth century, states north of the Mason-Dixon Line had taken steps to abolish slavery. Vermont included abolition as a provision of its 1777 state constitution. Pennsylvania's emancipation act of 1780 stipulated that freed children must serve an indenture term of twenty-eight years. Gradualism brought emancipation while also defending the interests of northern enslavers and controlling still another generation of Black Americans. In 1804 New Jersey became the last of the northern states to adopt gradual emancipation plans. There was no immediate moment of jubilee, as many northern states only promised to

liberate future children born to enslaved mothers. Such laws also stipulated that such children remain in indentured servitude to their mother's
enslaver in order to compensate the enslaver's loss. James Mars, a young
man indentured under this system in Connecticut, risked being thrown
in jail when he protested the arrangement that kept him bound to his
mother's enslaver until age twenty-five.[15]

Quicker routes to freedom included escape or direct emancipation by
enslavers. But escape was dangerous and voluntary manumission rare.
Congress, for instance, made the harboring of a freedom-seeking enslaved
person a federal crime as early as 1793. Hopes for manumission were
even slimmer, as few northern enslavers emancipated their own enslaved
laborers. Roughly one fifth of the white families in New York City owned
enslaved laborers, and fewer than eighty enslavers in the city voluntarily
manumitted slaves between 1783 and 1800. By 1830, census data suggests that at least 3,500 people were still enslaved in the North. Elderly
enslaved people in Connecticut remained in bondage as late as 1848, and
in New Jersey slavery endured until after the Civil War.[16]

Emancipation proceeded slowly, but proceeded nonetheless. A free
Black population of fewer than 60,000 in 1790 increased to more than
186,000 by 1810. Growing free Black communities fought for their civil
rights. In a number of New England locales, free African Americans
could vote and send their children to public schools. Most northern states
granted Black citizens property rights and trial by jury. African Americans owned land and businesses, founded mutual aid societies, established churches, promoted education, developed print culture, and voted.

Nationally, however, the enslaved population continued to grow,
from less than 700,000 in 1790 to more than 1.5 million by 1820.[17] The
growth of abolition in the North and the acceleration of slavery in the
South created growing divisions. Cotton drove the process more than
any other crop. Eli Whitney's cotton gin, a simple hand-cranked device
designed to mechanically remove sticky green seeds from short staple cotton, allowed southern planters to dramatically expand cotton production
for the national and international markets. Water-powered textile factories in England and the American Northeast rapidly turned raw cotton
into cloth. Technology increased both the supply of and demand for cotton. White southerners responded by expanding cultivation farther west,
to the Mississippi River and beyond. Slavery had been growing less profitable in tobacco-planting regions like Virginia, but the growth of cotton
farther south and west increased the demand for human bondage. Eager
cotton planters invested their new profits in more enslaved laborers.

LOWELL Cº MILLS.

The cotton boom fueled speculation in slavery. Many enslavers lever-aged potential profits into loans used to purchase ever increasing num-bers of enslaved laborers. For example, one 1840 *Louisiana Courier* ad warned, "it is very difficult now to find persons willing to buy slaves from Mississippi or Alabama on account of the fears entertained that such prop-erty may be already mortgaged to the banks of the above named states."[18]

New national and international markets fueled the plantation boom. American cotton exports rose from 150,000 bales in 1815 to 4,541,000 bales in 1859. The Census Bureau's 1860 Census of Manufactures stated that "the manufacture of cotton constitutes the most striking feature of the industrial history of the last fifty years."[19] Enslavers shipped their cot-ton north to textile manufacturers and to northern financers for overseas shipments. Northern insurance brokers and exporters in the Northeast profited greatly.

While the United States ended its legal participation in the global slave trade in 1808, slave traders moved one million enslaved people from the tobacco-producing Upper South to cotton fields in the Lower South be-tween 1790 and 1860.[20] This harrowing trade in human flesh supported middle-class occupations in the North and South: bankers, doctors, law-yers, insurance brokers, and shipping agents all profited. And of course it facilitated the expansion of northeastern textile mills.

Sidney & Neff, de-tail from *Plan of the City of Low-ell, Massachusetts,* 1850. Wikimedia Commons.

IV. Changes in Labor Organization

While industrialization bypassed most of the American South, south-ern cotton production nevertheless nurtured industrialization in the Northeast and Midwest. The drive to produce cloth transformed the

American system of labor. In the early republic, laborers in manufacturing might typically have been expected to work at every stage of production. But a new system, piecework, divided much of production into discrete steps performed by different workers. In this new system, merchants or investors sent or "put out" materials to individuals and families to complete at home. These independent laborers then turned over the partially finished goods to the owner to be given to another laborer to finish.

As early as the 1790s, however, merchants in New England began experimenting with machines to replace the putting-out system. To effect this transition, merchants and factory owners relied on the theft of British technological knowledge to build the machines they needed. In 1789, for instance, a textile mill in Pawtucket, Rhode Island, contracted twenty-one-year-old British immigrant Samuel Slater to build a yarn-spinning machine and then a carding machine. Slater had apprenticed in an English mill and succeeded in mimicking the English machinery. The fruits of American industrial espionage peaked in 1813 when Francis Cabot Lowell and Paul Moody re-created the powered loom used in the mills of Manchester, England. Lowell had spent two years in Britain observing and touring mills in England. He committed the design of the powered loom to memory so that, no matter how many times British customs officials searched his luggage, he could smuggle England's industrial know-how into New England.

Lowell's contribution to American industrialism was not only technological, it was organizational. He helped reorganize and centralize the American manufacturing process. A new approach, the Waltham-Lowell System, created the textile mill that defined antebellum New England and American industrialism before the Civil War. The modern American textile mill was fully realized in the planned mill town of Lowell in 1821, four years after Lowell himself died. Powered by the Merrimack River in northern Massachusetts and operated by local farm girls, the mills of Lowell centralized the process of textile manufacturing under one roof. The modern American factory was born. Soon ten thousand workers labored in Lowell alone. Sarah Rice, who worked at the nearby Millbury factory, found it "a noisy place" that was "more confined than I like to be."[21] Working conditions were harsh for the many desperate "mill girls" who operated the factories relentlessly from sunup to sundown. One worker complained that "a large class of females are, and have been, destined to a state of servitude."[22] Female workers went on strike. They lobbied for better working hours. But the lure of wages was

NEW ENGLAND FACTORY LIFE—"BELL-TIME."—DRAWN BY WINSLOW HOMER.—[SEE PAGE 411.]

too much. As another worker noted, "very many Ladies . . . have given up millinery, dressmaking & school keeping for work in the mill."[23] With a large supply of eager workers, Lowell's vision brought a rush of capital and entrepreneurs into New England. The first American manufacturing boom was under way.

The market revolution shook other industries as well. Craftsmen began to understand that new markets increased the demand for their products. Some shoemakers, for instance, abandoned the traditional method of producing custom-built shoes at their home workshops and instead began producing larger quantities of shoes in ready-made sizes to be shipped to urban centers. Manufacturers wanting increased production abandoned the old personal approach of relying on a single live-in apprentice for labor and instead hired unskilled wage laborers who did not have to be trained in all aspects of making shoes but could simply be assigned a single repeatable aspect of the task. Factories slowly replaced shops. The old paternalistic apprentice system, which involved long-term obligations between apprentice and master, gave way to a more impersonal and more flexible labor system in which unskilled laborers could be hired and fired as the market dictated. A writer in the *New York*

Winslow Homer, "Bell-Time," *Harper's Weekly*, vol. 12 (July 1868): 472. Wikimedia.

Observer in 1826 complained, "The master no longer lives among his apprentices [and] watches over their moral as well as mechanical improvement."[24] Masters-turned-employers now not only had fewer obligations to their workers, they had a lesser attachment. They no longer shared the bonds of their trade but were subsumed under new class-based relationships: employers and employees, bosses and workers, capitalists and laborers. On the other hand, workers were freed from the long-term, paternalistic obligations of apprenticeship or the legal subjugation of indentured servitude. They could theoretically work when and where they wanted. When men or women made an agreement with an employer to work for wages, they were "left free to apportion among themselves their respective shares, untrammeled . . . by unwise laws," as Reverend Alonzo Potter rosily proclaimed in 1840.[25] But while the new labor system was celebrated throughout the northern United States as "free labor," it was simultaneously lamented by a growing powerless class of laborers.

As the northern United States rushed headlong toward commercialization and an early capitalist economy, many Americans grew uneasy with the growing gap between wealthy businessmen and impoverished wage laborers. Elites like Daniel Webster might defend their wealth and privilege by insisting that all workers could achieve "a career of usefulness and enterprise" if they were "industrious and sober," but labor activist Seth Luther countered that capitalism created "a cruel system of extraction on the bodies and minds of the producing classes . . . for no other object than to enable the 'rich' to 'take care of themselves' while the poor must work or starve."[26]

Americans embarked on their Industrial Revolution with the expectation that all men could start their careers as humble wage workers but later achieve positions of ownership and stability with hard work. Wage work had traditionally been looked down on as a state of dependence, suitable only as a temporary waypoint for young men without resources on their path toward the middle class and the economic success necessary to support a wife and children ensconced within the domestic sphere. Children's magazines—such as *Juvenile Miscellany* and *Parley's Magazine*—glorified the prospect of moving up the economic ladder. This "free labor ideology" provided many northerners with a keen sense of superiority over the slave economy of the southern states.[27]

But the commercial economy often failed in its promise of social mobility. Depressions and downturns might destroy businesses and reduce owners to wage work. Even in times of prosperity unskilled workers might perpetually lack good wages and economic security and therefore had to forever depend on supplemental income from their wives and young children.

Wage workers—a population disproportionately composed of immigrants and poorer Americans—faced low wages, long hours, and dangerous working conditions. Class conflict developed. Instead of the formal inequality of a master-servant contract, employer and employee entered a contract presumably as equals. But hierarchy was evident: employers had financial security and political power; employees faced uncertainty and powerlessness in the workplace. Dependent on the whims of their employers, some workers turned to strikes and unions to pool their resources. In 1825 a group of journeymen in Boston formed a Carpenters' Union to protest their inability "to maintain a family at the present time, with the wages which are now usually given."[28] Working men organized unions to assert themselves and win both the respect and the resources due to a breadwinner and a citizen.

For the middle-class managers and civic leaders caught between workers and owners, unions enflamed a dangerous antagonism between employers and employees. They countered any claims of inherent class conflict with the ideology of social mobility. Middle-class owners and managers justified their economic privilege as the natural product of superior character traits, including decision making and hard work. One group of master carpenters denounced their striking journeymen in 1825 with the claim that workers of "industrious and temperate habits, have, in their turn, become thriving and respectable Masters, and the great body of our Mechanics have been enabled to acquire property and respectability, with a just weight and influence in society."[29] In an 1856 speech in Kalamazoo, Michigan, Abraham Lincoln had to assure his audience that the country's commercial transformation had not reduced American laborers to slavery. Southerners, he said, "insist that their slaves are far better off than Northern freemen. What a mistaken view do these men have of Northern labourers! They think that men are always to remain labourers here— but there is no such class. The man who laboured for another last year, this year labours for himself. And next year he will hire others to labour for him."[30] This essential belief undergirded the northern commitment to "free labor" and won the market revolution much widespread acceptance.

V. Changes in Gender Roles and Family Life

In the first half of the nineteenth century, families in the northern United States increasingly participated in the cash economy created by the market revolution. The first stirrings of industrialization shifted work away from the home. These changes transformed Americans' notions of what constituted work and therefore shifted what it meant to be an American woman and an American man. As Americans encountered more goods in stores and produced fewer at home, the ability to remove women and children from work determined a family's class status. This ideal, of course, ignored the reality of women's work at home and was possible for only the wealthy. The market revolution therefore not only transformed the economy, it changed the nature of the American family. As the market revolution thrust workers into new systems of production, it redefined gender roles. The market integrated families into a new cash economy. As Americans purchased more goods in stores and produced fewer at home, the purity of the domestic sphere—the idealized realm of women and children—increasingly signified a family's class status.

Women and children worked to supplement the low wages of many male workers. Around age eleven or twelve, boys could take jobs as office runners or waiters, earning perhaps a dollar a week to support their parents' incomes. The ideal of an innocent and protected childhood was a privilege for middle- and upper-class families, who might look down upon poor families. Joseph Tuckerman, a Unitarian minister who served poor Bostonians, lamented the lack of discipline and regularity among poor children: "At one hour they are kept at work to procure fuel, or perform some other service; in the next are allowed to go where they will, and to do what they will."[31] Prevented from attending school, poor children served instead as economic assets for their destitute families.

Meanwhile, the education received by middle-class children provided a foundation for future economic privilege. As artisans lost control over their trades, young men had a greater incentive to invest time in education to find skilled positions later in life. Formal schooling was especially important for young men who desired apprenticeships in retail or commercial work. Enterprising instructors established schools to assist "young gentlemen preparing for mercantile and other pursuits, who may wish for an education superior to that usually obtained in the common schools, but different from a college education, and better adapted to their particular business," such as that organized in 1820 by Warren Colburn of Boston.[32] In response to this need, the Boston School Committee created the English High School (as opposed to the Latin School) that could "give a child an education that shall fit him for active life, and shall serve as a foundation for eminence in his profession, whether Mer-

THE SPHERE OF WOMAN.

"The Sphere of Woman," *Godey's Lady's Book*, vol. 40 (March 1850): 209. University of Virginia.

cantile or Mechanical" beyond that "which our public schools can now furnish."[33]

Education equipped young women with the tools to live sophisticated, genteel lives. After sixteen-year-old Elizabeth Davis left home in 1816 to attend school, her father explained that the experience would "lay a foundation for your future character & respectability."[34] After touring the United States in the 1830s, Alexis de Tocqueville praised the independence granted to the young American woman, who had "the great scene of the world . . . open to her" and whose education prepared her to exercise both reason and moral sense.[35] Middling young women also used their education to take positions as schoolteachers in the expanding common school system. Bristol Academy in Taunton, Massachusetts, for instance, advertised "instruction . . . in the art of teaching" for female pupils.[36] In 1825, Nancy Denison left Concord Academy with references indicating that she was "qualified to teach with success and profit" and "very cheerfully recommend[ed]" for "that very responsible employment."[37]

Middle-class youths found opportunities for respectable employment through formal education, but poor youths remained in marginalized positions. Their families' desperate financial state kept them from enjoying the fruits of education. When pauper children did receive teaching through institutions such the House of Refuge in New York City, they were often simultaneously indentured to successful families to serve as field hands or domestic laborers. The Society for the Reformation of Juvenile Delinquents in New York City sent its wards to places like Sylvester Lusk's farm in Enfield, Connecticut. Lusk took boys to learn "the trade and mystery of farming" and girls to learn "the trade and mystery of housewifery." In exchange for "sufficient Meat, Drink, Apparel, Lodging, and Washing, fitting for an Apprentice," and a rudimentary education, the apprentices promised obedience, morality, and loyalty.[38] Poor children also found work in factories such as Samuel Slater's textile mills in southern New England. Slater published a newspaper advertisement for "four or five active Lads, about 15 Years of Age to serve as Apprentices in the Cotton Factory."[39]

And so, during the early nineteenth century, opportunities for education and employment often depended on a given family's class. In colonial America, nearly all children worked within their parent's chosen profession, whether it be agricultural or artisanal. During the market revolution, however, more children were able to postpone employment. Americans aspired to provide a "Romantic Childhood"—a period in which boys and girls were sheltered within the home and nurtured through primary schooling.[40] This ideal was available to families that could survive without their children's labor. As these children matured, their early experiences often determined whether they entered respectable, well-paying positions or became dependent workers with little prospects for social mobility.

Just as children were expected to be sheltered from the adult world of work, American culture expected men and women to assume distinct gender roles as they prepared for marriage and family life. An ideology of "separate spheres" set the public realm—the world of economic production and political life—apart as a male domain, and the world of consumers and domestic life as a female one. (Even nonworking women labored by shopping for the household, producing food and clothing, cleaning, educating children, and performing similar activities. But these were considered "domestic" because they did not bring money into the household, although they too were essential to the household's economic viability.) While reality muddied the ideal, the divide between a private, female world of home and a public, male world of business defined American gender hierarchy.

The idea of separate spheres also displayed a distinct class bias. Middle and upper classes reinforced their status by shielding "their" women from the harsh realities of wage labor. Women were to be mothers and educators, not partners in production. But lower-class women continued to contribute directly to the household economy. The middle- and upper-class ideal was feasible only in households where women did not need to engage in paid labor. In poorer households, women engaged in wage labor as factory workers, pieceworkers producing items for market consumption, tavern- and innkeepers, and domestic servants. While many of the fundamental tasks women performed remained the same—producing clothing, cultivating vegetables, overseeing dairy production, and performing any number of other domestic labors—the key difference was whether and when they performed these tasks for cash in a market economy.

Domestic expectations constantly changed and the market revolution transformed many women's traditional domestic tasks. Cloth production, for instance, advanced throughout the market revolution as new mechanized production increased the volume and variety of fabrics available to ordinary people. This relieved many better-off women of a traditional labor obligation. As cloth production became commercialized, women's home-based cloth production became less important to household economies. Purchasing cloth and, later, ready-made clothes began to transform women from producers to consumers. One woman from Maine, Martha Ballard, regularly referenced spinning, weaving, and knitting in the diary she kept from 1785 to 1812.[41] Martha, her daughters, and her female neighbors spun and plied linen and woolen yarns and used them to produce a variety of fabrics to make clothing for her family. The production of cloth and clothing was a year-round, labor-intensive process, but it was for home consumption, not commercial markets.

In cities, where women could buy cheap imported cloth to turn into clothing, they became skilled consumers. They stewarded money earned by their husbands by comparing values and haggling over prices. In one typical experience, Mrs. Peter Simon, a captain's wife, inspected twenty-six yards of Holland cloth to ensure that it was worth the £130 price.[42] Even wealthy women shopped for high-value goods. While servants or enslaved people routinely made low-value purchases, the mistress of the household trusted her discriminating eye alone for expensive or specific purchases.

Women might also parlay their skills into businesses. In addition to working as seamstresses, milliners, or laundresses, women might undertake paid work for neighbors or acquaintances or combine clothing production with management of a boardinghouse. Even enslaved laborers

Thomas Horner, *Broadway, New York*, 1836. Smithsonian American Art Museum.

with particular skill at producing clothing could be hired out for a higher price or might even negotiate to work part-time for themselves. Most enslaved people, however, continued to produce domestic items, including simpler cloths and clothing, for home consumption.

Similar domestic expectations played out in the slave states. Enslaved women labored in the fields. Whites argued that African American women were less delicate and womanly than white women and therefore perfectly suited for agricultural labor. The southern ideal meanwhile established that white plantation mistresses were shielded from manual labor because of their very whiteness. Throughout the slave states, however, aside from the minority of plantations with dozens of enslaved laborers, most white women by necessity continued to assist with planting, harvesting, and processing agricultural projects despite the cultural stigma attached to it. White southerners continued to produce large portions of their food and clothing at home. Even when they were market-oriented producers of cash crops, white southerners still insisted that their adherence to plantation slavery and racial hierarchy made them morally superior to greedy northerners and their callous, cutthroat commerce. Southerners and northerners increasingly saw their ways of life as incompatible.

While the market revolution remade many women's economic roles, their legal status remained essentially unchanged. Upon marriage, women were rendered legally dead by the notion of coverture, the custom that counted married couples as a single unit represented by the husband. Without special precautions or interventions, women could not earn their own money, own their own property, sue, or be sued. Any money earned or spent belonged by law to their husbands. Women shopped on their husbands' credit and at any time husbands could terminate their wives' access to their credit. Although a handful of states made divorce available—divorce had before only been legal in Congregationalist states such as Massachusetts and Connecticut, where marriage was strictly a civil contract rather than a religious one—it remained extremely expensive, difficult, and rare. Marriage was typically a permanently binding legal contract.

Ideas of marriage, if not the legal realities, began to change. The late-eighteenth and early-nineteenth century marked the beginning of the shift from "institutional" to "companionate" marriage.[43] Institutional marriages were primarily labor arrangements that maximized the couple's and their children's chances of surviving and thriving. Men and women assessed each other's skills as they related to household production, although looks and personality certainly entered into the equation. But in the late eighteenth century, under the influence of Enlightenment thought, young people began to privilege character and compatibility in their potential partners. Money was still essential: marriages prompted the largest redistributions of property prior to the settling of estates at death. But the means of this redistribution was changing. Especially in the North, land became a less important foundation for matchmaking as wealthy young men became not only farmers and merchants but bankers, clerks, or professionals. The increased emphasis on affection and attraction that young people embraced was facilitated by an increasingly complex economy that offered new ways to store, move, and create wealth, which liberalized the criteria by which families evaluated potential in-laws.

To be considered a success in family life, a middle-class American man typically aspired to own a comfortable home and to marry a woman of strong morals and religious conviction who would take responsibility for raising virtuous, well-behaved children. The duties of the middle-class husband and wife would be clearly delineated into separate spheres. The husband alone was responsible for creating wealth and engaging in the commerce and politics—the public sphere. The wife was responsible for the private—keeping a good home, being careful with household expenses, and raising children, inculcating them with the middle-class virtues that would ensure their future success. But for poor families, sacrificing the potential economic contributions of wives and children was an impossibility.

VI. The Rise of Industrial Labor in Antebellum America

More than five million immigrants arrived in the United States between 1820 and 1860. Irish, German, and Jewish immigrants sought new lives and economic opportunities. By the Civil War, nearly one out of every eight Americans had been born outside the United States. A series of push and pull factors drew immigrants to the United States.

In England, an economic slump prompted Parliament to modernize British agriculture by revoking common land rights for Irish farmers. These policies generally targeted Catholics in the southern counties of Ireland and motivated many to seek greater opportunity elsewhere. The booming American economy pulled Irish immigrants toward ports along the eastern United States. Between 1820 and 1840, over 250,000 Irish immigrants arrived in the United States.[44] Without the capital and skills required to purchase and operate farms, Irish immigrants settled primarily in northeastern cities and towns and performed unskilled work. Irish men usually emigrated alone and, when possible, practiced what became known as chain migration. Chain migration allowed Irish men to send portions of their wages home, which would then be used either to support their families in Ireland or to purchase tickets for relatives to come to the United States. Irish immigration followed this pattern into the 1840s and 1850s, when the infamous Irish Famine sparked a massive exodus out of Ireland. Between 1840 and 1860, 1.7 million Irish fled starvation and the oppressive English policies that accompanied it.[45] As they entered manual, unskilled labor positions in urban America's dirtiest and most dangerous occupations, Irish workers in northern cities were compared to African Americans, and anti-immigrant newspapers portrayed them with apelike features. Despite hostility, Irish immigrants retained their social, cultural, and religious beliefs and left an indelible mark on American culture.

While the Irish settled mostly in coastal cities, most German immigrants used American ports and cities as temporary waypoints before settling in the rural countryside. Over 1.5 million immigrants from the various German states arrived in the United States during the antebellum era. Although some southern Germans fled declining agricultural conditions and repercussions of the failed revolutions of 1848, many Germans simply sought steadier economic opportunity. German immigrants tended to travel as families and carried with them skills and capital that enabled them to enter middle-class trades. Germans migrated to the Old

Northwest to farm in rural areas and practiced trades in growing communities such as St. Louis, Cincinnati, and Milwaukee, three cities that formed what came to be called the German Triangle.

Catholic and Jewish Germans transformed regions of the republic. Although records are sparse, New York's Jewish population rose from approximately five hundred in 1825 to forty thousand in 1860.[46] Similar gains were seen in other American cities. Jewish immigrants hailing from southwestern Germany and parts of occupied Poland moved to the United States through chain migration and as family units. Unlike other Germans, Jewish immigrants rarely settled in rural areas. Once established, Jewish immigrants found work in retail, commerce, and artisanal occupations such as tailoring. They quickly found their footing and established themselves as an intrinsic part of the American market economy. Just as Irish immigrants shaped the urban landscape through the construction of churches and Catholic schools, Jewish immigrants erected synagogues and made their mark on American culture.

The sudden influx of immigration triggered a backlash among many native-born Anglo-Protestant Americans. This nativist movement, especially fearful of the growing Catholic presence, sought to limit European immigration and prevent Catholics from establishing churches and other institutions. Popular in northern cities such as Boston, Chicago, Philadelphia, and other cities with large Catholic populations, nativism even spawned its own political party in the 1850s. The American Party, more commonly known as the Know-Nothing Party, found success in local and state elections throughout the North. The party even nominated candidates for president in 1852 and 1856. The rapid rise of the Know-Nothings, reflecting widespread anti-Catholic and anti-immigrant sentiment, slowed European immigration. Immigration declined precipitously after 1855 as nativism, the Crimean War, and improving economic conditions in Europe discouraged potential migrants from traveling to the United States. Only after the American Civil War would immigration levels match and eventually surpass the levels seen in the 1840s and 1850s.

In industrial northern cities, Irish immigrants swelled the ranks of the working class and quickly encountered the politics of industrial labor. Many workers formed trade unions during the early republic. Organizations such as Philadelphia's Federal Society of Journeymen Cordwainers or the Carpenters' Union of Boston operated within specific industries in major American cities. These unions worked to protect the economic power of their members by creating closed shops—workplaces wherein

THE PROPAGATION SOCIETY ___ MORE FREE THAN WELCOME.

This anti-Catholic print depicts Catholic priests arriving by boat and then threatening Uncle Sam and a young Protestant boy who holds out a Bible in resistance. An anti-Catholic cartoon, reflecting the nativist perception of the threat posed by the Roman Church's influence in the United States through Irish immigration and Catholic education. N. Currier, *The Propagation Society, More Free Than Welcome*, 1855. Library of Congress.

employers could only hire union members—and striking to improve working conditions. Political leaders denounced these organizations as unlawful combinations and conspiracies to promote the narrow self-interest of workers above the rights of property holders and the interests of the common good. Unions did not become legally acceptable until 1842 when the Massachusetts Supreme Judicial Court ruled in favor of a union organized among Boston bootmakers, arguing that the workers were capable of acting "in such a manner as best to subserve their own interests."[47] Even after the case, unions remained in a precarious legal position.

In the 1840s, labor activists organized to limit working hours and protect children in factories. The New England Association of Farmers, Mechanics and Other Workingmen (NEA) mobilized to establish a ten-hour workday across industries. They argued that the ten-hour day would improve the immediate conditions of laborers by allowing "time and opportunities for intellectual and moral improvement."[48] After a citywide strike in Boston in 1835, the Ten-Hour Movement quickly spread to other major cities such as Philadelphia. The campaign for leisure time was part of the male working-class effort to expose the hollowness of the paternalistic claims of employers and their rhetoric of moral superiority.[49]

Women, a dominant labor source for factories since the early 1800s, launched some of the earliest strikes for better conditions. Textile operatives in Lowell, Massachusetts, "turned out" (walked off) their jobs in 1834 and 1836. During the Ten-Hour Movement of the 1840s, female operatives provided crucial support. Under the leadership of Sarah Bagley, the Lowell Female Labor Reform Association organized petition drives that drew thousands of signatures from "mill girls." Like male activists, Bagley and her associates used the desire for mental improvement as a central argument for reform. An 1847 editorial in the *Voice of Industry*, a labor newspaper published by Bagley, asked, "who, after thirteen hours of steady application to monotonous work, can sit down and apply her mind to deep and long continued thought?"[50] Despite the widespread support for a ten-hour day, the movement achieved only partial success. President Martin Van Buren established a ten-hour-day policy for laborers on federal public works projects. New Hampshire passed a statewide law in 1847, and Pennsylvania followed a year later. Both states, however, allowed workers to voluntarily consent to work more than ten hours per day.

In 1842, child labor became a dominant issue in the American labor movement. The protection of child laborers gained more middle-class support than the protection of adult workers. A petition from parents in Fall River, a southern Massachusetts mill town that employed a high portion of child workers, asked the legislature for a law "prohibiting the employment of children in manufacturing establishments at an age and for a number of hours which must be permanently injurious to their health and inconsistent with the education which is essential to their welfare."[51] Massachusetts quickly passed a law prohibiting children under age twelve from working more than ten hours a day. By the midnineteenth century, every state in New England had followed Massachusetts's lead. Between the 1840s and 1860s, these statutes slowly extended the age of protection of labor and the assurance of schooling. Throughout the region, public officials agreed that young children (between ages nine and twelve) should be prevented from working in dangerous occupations, and older children (between ages twelve and fifteen) should balance their labor with education and time for leisure.[52]

Male workers sought to improve their income and working conditions to create a household that kept women and children protected within the domestic sphere. But labor gains were limited, and the movement remained moderate. Despite its challenge to industrial working conditions, labor activism in antebellum America remained largely wedded to the free labor ideal. The labor movement later supported the northern free soil movement, which challenged the spread of slavery in the 1840s, simultaneously promoting the superiority of the northern system of commerce over the southern institution of slavery while trying, much less successfully, to reform capitalism.

VII. Conclusion

During the early nineteenth century, southern agriculture produced by enslaved labor fueled northern industry produced by wage workers and managed by the new middle class. New transportation, new machinery, and new organizations of labor integrated the previously isolated pockets of the colonial economy into a national industrial operation. Industrialization and the cash economy tied diverse regions together at the same time that ideology drove Americans apart. By celebrating the freedom of contract that distinguished the wage worker from the indentured servant of previous generations or the enslaved laborer in the southern cotton field, political leaders claimed the American Revolution's legacy for the North. But the rise of industrial child labor, the demands of workers to unionize, the economic vulnerability of women, and the influx of non-Anglo immigrants left many Americans questioning the meaning of liberty after the market revolution.

VIII. Reference Material

This chapter was edited by Jane Fiegen Green, with content contributions by Kelly Arehart, Myles Beaurpre, Kristin Condotta, Jane Fiegen Green, Nathan Jeremie-Brink, Lindsay Keiter, Brenden Kennedy, William Kerrigan, Christopher Sawula, David Schley, and Evgenia Shayder Shoop.

Recommended citation: Kelly Arehart et al., "Market Revolution," Jane Fiegen Green, ed., in *The American Yawp*, eds. Joseph Locke and Ben Wright (Stanford, CA: Stanford University Press, 2019).

NOTES TO CHAPTER 8
1. *Niles' Weekly Register* (December 2, 1815), 238.
2. Douglass C. North, *Economic Growth in the United States, 1790–1860* (Englewood Cliffs, NJ: Prentice-Hall, 1961), 25.
3. James Madison, Annual Message to Congress, December 5, 1815.
4. William L. Garrison and David M. Levinson, *The Transportation Experience: Policy, Planning, and Deployment* (New York: Oxford University Press, 2014), 51.

5. Warren E. Weber, "Early State Banks in the United States: How Many Were There and When Did They Exist?" *Federal Reserve Bank of Minneapolis, Quarterly Review* 30, no. 1 (September 2006): 28–40.

6. John Robert Godley, *Letters from America* (London: Murray, 1844), 267.

7. Margaret Van Horn Dwight, *A Journey to Ohio in 1810*, ed. Max Farrand (New Haven, CT: Yale University Press, 1912), 13.

8. Ibid., 37.

9. Frances Trollope, *Domestic Manners of the Americans, Vol. 1* (London: Whittaker, Treacher, 1832), 274.

10. Cathy Matson and Wendy A. Woloson, *Risky Business: Winning and Losing in the Early American Economy, 1780–1850* (Philadelphia: Library Company of Philadelphia: 2003), 29.

11. Leonard P. Curry, *The Corporate City: The American City as a Political Entity, 1800–1850* (Westport, CT: Greenwood, 1997), 46.

12. Jefferson to George Logan, November 12, 1816, in *Works of Thomas Jefferson*, ed. Paul Leicester Ford, Federal Edition, Vol. 12 (New York: 1904), 12–43.

13. Quoted in Michael Zakim and Gary John Kornblith, eds., *Capitalism Takes Command: The Social Transformation of Nineteenth-Century America* (Chicago: University of Chicago Press, 2012), 158.

14. Philip Scranton, *Proprietary Capitalism: The Textile Manufacture at Philadelphia, 1800–1885* (New York: Cambridge University Press, 1983), 12.

15. Robert J. Cottrol, ed., *From African to Yankee: Narratives of Slavery and Freedom in Antebellum New England* (Armonk, NY: Sharpe, 1998), 62.

16. The 1830 census enumerates 3,568 enslaved people in the northern states (Connecticut, Illinois, Indiana, Massachusetts, Michigan, New Hampshire, New Jersey, New York, Ohio, Pennsylvania, Rhode Island, and Vermont). 1830 U.S. Census data taken from Minnesota Population Center, *National Historical Geographic Information System: Version 2.0* (Minneapolis: University of Minnesota, 2011), http://www.nhgis.org; David Menschel, "Abolition Without Deliverance: The Law of Connecticut Slavery 1784–1848," *Yale Law Journal* 111, no. 1 (October 2001): 191; James J. Gigantino II, *The Ragged Road to Abolition: Slavery and Freedom in New Jersey 1775–1865* (Philadelphia: University of Pennsylvania Press, 2015), 248.

17. Minnesota Population Center. *National Historical Geographic Information System: Version 2.0*.

18. *Louisiana Courier*, February 12, 1840.

19. U.S. Census Office 8th Census 1860 and James Madison Edmunds, *Manufactures of the United States in 1860: Compiled from the Original Returns of the Eighth Census, Under the Direction of the Secretary of the Interior* (Washington, DC: U.S. Government Printing Office, 1865).

20. Ira Berlin, *Generations of Captivity: A History of African-American Slaves* (Cambridge, MA: Belknap Press, 2003), 168–169.

21. Sarah "Sally" Rice to her father, February 23, 1845, published in *The New England Mill Village, 1790–1860* (Cambridge, MA: MIT Press, 1982), 390.

22. *Factory Tracts: Factory Life as It Is*, no. 1 (Lowell, MA: Female Labor Reform Association, 1845), 4.

23. Malenda M. Edwards to Sabrina Bennett, April 4, 1839, quoted in Thomas Dublin, ed., *Farm to Factory Women's Letters, 1830–1860* (New York: Columbia University Press, 1993), 74.

24. "Apprentices No. 2," *New York Observer*, October 14, 1826.

25. Reverend Alonzo Potter, *Political Economy: Its Objects, Uses, and Principles* (New York: Potter, 1840), 92.

26. Daniel Webster, "Lecture Before the Society for the Diffusion of Useful Knowledge," in *The Writings and Speeches of Daniel Webster: Writings and Speeches Hitherto Uncollected, vol. 1. Addresses on Various Occasions*, ed. Edward Everett (Boston: Little, Brown, 1903); Carl Siracusa, *A Mechanical People: Perceptions of the Industrial Order in Massachusetts, 1815–1880* (Middletown, CT: Wesleyan University Press, 1979), 157.

27. Eric Foner, *Free Soil, Free Labor, Free Men : The Ideology of the Republican Party Before the Civil War* (New York: Oxford University Press, 1970).

28. "Notice to House Carpenters in the Country," *Columbian Centinel*, April 23, 1825.

29. John R. Commons, ed., *A Documentary History of American Industrial Society* (New York: Russell and Russell, 1958), Vol. 6: 79.

30. Abraham Lincoln, Speech at Kalamazoo, Michigan, Aug. 27, 1856, in *Collected Works of Abraham Lincoln*, Vol. 2 (New Brunswick, NJ: Rutgers University Press, 1953), 364.

31. Joseph Tuckerman, *Mr. Tuckerman's Eight Semiannual Report in His Service as a Minister at Large in Boston* (Boston: Gray and Bowen, 1831), 21.

32. Warren Colburn, "Advertisement for Colburn's school for young gentlemen preparing for mercantile and other pursuits, 19 Sep 1820," Massachusetts Historical Society.

33. *Proceedings of the School Committee, of the Town of Boston, respecting an English Classical School* (Boston: The Committee, 1820).

34. William Davis to Elizabeth Davis, March 21, 1816; June 23, 1816; November 17, 1816; Davis Family Papers, Massachusetts Historical Society.

35. Alexis de Tocqueville, *Democracy in America*, Vol. II., ed. Phillips Bradley (New York: Knopf, 1945), 196.

36. *A Catalogue of the Officers, Teachers, and Pupils in Bristol Academy* (Tauton, MA: Bradford and Amsbury, 1837).

37. Nancy Denison recommendation, May 1825, Titus Orcott Brown Papers, Maine Historical Society.

38. Indentures and Other Documents Binding Minor Wards of the Society for the Reformation of Juvenile Delinquents of the City of New York as apprentices to Sylvester Lusk of Enfield, 1828–1838, Sylvester Lusk Papers, Connecticut Historical Society.

39. Advertisement in *Providence Gazette*, October 1794.

40. Steven Mintz, *Huck's Raft: A History of American Childhood* (Cambridge, MA: Belknap Press, 2004).

41. Laurel Thatcher Ulrich, *A Midwife's Tale: The Life of Martha Ballard, Based on Her Diary, 1785–1812* (New York: Knopf, 1990).

42. Ellen Hartigan-O'Connor, *The Ties That Buy: Women and Commerce in Revolutionary America* (Philadelphia: University of Pennsylvania Press, 2009), 138.

43. Anya Jabour, *Marriage in the Early Republic: Elizabeth and William Wirt and the Companionate Ideal* (Baltimore: Johns Hopkins University Press, 1998).

44. Bill Ong Hing, *Defining America Through Immigration Policy* (Philadelphia: Temple University Press, 2004), 278–284.

45. John Powell, *Encyclopedia of North American Immigration* (New York: Facts on File, 2005), 154.

46. H. B. Grinstein, *The Rise of the Jewish Community in New York, 1654–1860* (Philadelphia: Jewish Publication Society, 1945), 469.

47. *Commonwealth v. Hunt*, 45 Mass. 111 (1842).

48. *New England Artisan and Laboring Man's Repository* (Pawtucket, Providence, and Boston), March 8, 1832.

49. Teresa Anne Murphy, *Ten Hours' Labor: Religion, Reform, and Gender in Early New England* (Ithaca, NY: Cornell University Press, 1992).

50. [Sarah Bagley], "The Blindness of the Age," *Voice of Industry*, April 23, 1847.

51. Legislative Documents, 1842, House, No. 4, p. 3, in Elizabeth Dabney Langhorne Lewis Otey, *The Beginnings of Child Labor Legislation in Certain States: A Comparative Study* (New York: Arno Press, 1974), 78.

52. Miriam E. Loughran, "The Historical Development of Child-Labor Legislation in the United States," PhD diss., Catholic University of America, 1921, p. 67.

RECOMMENDED READING

Balleisen, Edward J. *Navigating Failure: Bankruptcy and Commercial Society in Antebellum America*. Chapel Hill: University of North Carolina Press, 2001.

Blewett, Mary H. *Men, Women, and Work: Class, Gender, and Protest in the New England Shoe Industry, 1780–1910*. Urbana: University of Illinois Press, 1988.

Boydston, Jeanne. *Home and Work: Housework, Wages, and the Ideology of Labor in the Early Republic*. New York: Oxford University Press, 1990.

Dublin, Thomas. *Transforming Women's Work: New England Lives in the Industrial Revolution*. Ithaca, NY: Cornell University Press, 1994.

Faler, Paul G. *Mechanics and Manufacturers in the Early Industrial Revolution: Lynn, Massachusetts, 1760–1860*. Albany: SUNY Press, 1981.

Foner, Eric. *Free Soil, Free Labor, Free Men: The Ideology of the Republican Party Before the Civil War*. New York: Oxford University Press, 1970.

Greenberg, Joshua R. *Advocating the Man: Masculinity, Organized Labor, and the Household in New York, 1800–1840*. New York: Columbia University Press, 2008.

Halttunen, Karen. *Confidence Men and Painted Women: A Study of Middle-Class Culture in America, 1830–1870*. Yale University Press, 1982.

Hartigan-O'Connor, Ellen. *The Ties That Buy: Women and Commerce in Revolutionary America*. Philadelphia: University of Pennsylvania Press, 2009.

Howe, Daniel Walker. *What Hath God Wrought: The Transformation of America, 1815–1848*. New York: Oxford University Press, 2007.

Innes, Stephen, ed. *Work and Labor in Early America*. Chapel Hill: University of North Carolina Press, 1988.

Jabour, Anya. *Marriage in the Early Republic: Elizabeth and William Wirt and the Companionate Ideal*. Baltimore: Johns Hopkins University Press, 1998.

Larson, John Lauritz. *The Market Revolution in America: Liberty, Ambition, and the Eclipse of the Common Good*. New York: Cambridge University Press, 2010.

Levy, Jonathan. *Freaks of Fortune: The Emerging World of Capitalism and Risk in America*. Cambridge, MA: Harvard University Press, 2012.

Luskey, Brian P. *On the Make: Clerks and the Quest for Capital in Nineteenth-Century America*. New York: New York University Press, 2010.

Matson, Cathy, and Wendy A. Woloson. *Risky Business: Winning and Losing in the Early American Economy, 1780–1850*. Philadelphia: Library Company of Philadelphia, 2003.

McNeur, Catherine. *Taming Manhattan: Environmental Battles in the Antebellum City*. Cambridge, MA: Harvard University Press, 2014.

Melish, Joanne Pope. *Disowning Slavery: Gradual Emancipation and "Race" in New England, 1780–1860*. Ithaca, NY: Cornell University Press, 1998.

Mihm, Stephen. *A Nation of Counterfeiters: Capitalists, Con Men, and the Making of the United States*. Cambridge, MA: Harvard University Press, 2009.

Murphy, Teresa Anne. *Ten Hours' Labor: Religion, Reform, and Gender in Early New England*. Ithaca, NY: Cornell University Press, 1992.

Rice, Stephen P. *Minding the Machine: Languages of Class in Early Industrial America*. Berkeley: University of California Press, 2004.

Rothenberg, Winifred Barr. *From Market-Places to a Market Economy: The Transformation of Rural Massachusetts, 1750–1850*. Chicago: University of Chicago Press, 1992.

Ryan, Mary P. *Cradle of the Middle Class: The Family in Oneida County, New York, 1790–1865*. New York: Cambridge University Press, 1981.

Sellers, Charles Grier. *The Market Revolution: Jacksonian America, 1815–1846*. New York: Oxford University Press, 1991.

Tucker, Barbara M. *Samuel Slater and the Origins of the American Textile Industry, 1790–1860*. Ithaca, NY: Cornell University Press, 1984.

9

Democracy in America

I. Introduction

On May 30, 1806, Andrew Jackson, a thirty-nine-year-old Tennessee lawyer, came within inches of death. A duelist's bullet struck him in the chest, just shy of his heart (the man who fired the gun was purportedly the best shot in Tennessee). But the wounded Jackson remained standing. Bleeding, he slowly steadied his aim and returned fire. The other man dropped to the ground, mortally wounded. Jackson—still carrying the bullet in his chest—later boasted, "I should have hit him, if he had shot me through the brain."[1]

The duel in Logan County, Kentucky, was one of many that Jackson fought during the course of his long and highly controversial career. The tenacity, toughness, and vengefulness that carried Jackson alive out of that duel, and the mythology and symbolism that would be attached to it, would also characterize many of his later dealings on the battlefield

George Caleb Bingham, *The County Election*, 1852. Reynolda House Museum of American Art.

and in politics. By the time of his death almost forty years later, Andrew Jackson would become an enduring and controversial symbol, a kind of cipher to gauge the ways that various Americans thought about their country.

II. Democracy in the Early Republic

Today, most Americans think democracy is a good thing. We tend to assume the nation's early political leaders believed the same. Wasn't the American Revolution a victory for democratic principles? For many of the founders, however, the answer was no.

A wide variety of people participated in early U.S. politics, especially at the local level. But ordinary citizens' growing direct influence on government frightened the founding elites. At the Constitutional Convention in 1787, Alexander Hamilton warned of the "vices of democracy" and said he considered the British government—with its powerful king and parliament—"the best in the world."[2] Another convention delegate, Elbridge Gerry of Massachusetts, who eventually refused to sign the finished Constitution, agreed. "The evils we experience flow from an excess of democracy," he proclaimed.[3]

Too much participation by the multitudes, the elite believed, would undermine good order. It would prevent the creation of a secure and united republican society. The Philadelphia physician and politician Benjamin Rush, for example, sensed that the Revolution had launched a wave of popular rebelliousness that could lead to a dangerous new type of despotism. "In our opposition to monarchy," he wrote, "we forgot that the temple of tyranny has two doors. We bolted one of them by proper restraints; but we left the other open, by neglecting to guard against the effects of our own ignorance and licentiousness."[4]

Such warnings did nothing to quell Americans' democratic impulses in the late eighteenth and early nineteenth centuries. Americans who were allowed to vote (and sometimes those who weren't) went to the polls in impressive numbers. Citizens also made public demonstrations. They delivered partisan speeches at patriotic holiday and anniversary celebrations. They petitioned Congress, openly criticized the president, and insisted that a free people should not defer even to elected leaders. In many people's eyes, the American republic was a *democratic* republic: the people were sovereign all the time, not only on election day.

The elite leaders of political parties could not afford to overlook "the cultivation of popular favour," as Alexander Hamilton put it.[5] Between the 1790s and 1830s, the elite of every state and party learned to listen—or pretend to listen—to the voices of the multitudes. And ironically, an American president, holding the office that most resembles a king's, would come to symbolize the democratizing spirit of American politics.

III. The Missouri Crisis

A more troubling pattern was also emerging in national politics and culture. During the first decades of the nineteenth century, American politics shifted toward "sectional" conflict among the states of the North, South, and West.

Since the ratification of the Constitution in 1789, the state of Virginia had wielded more influence on the federal government than any other state. Four of the first five presidents, for example, were from Virginia. Immigration caused by the market revolution, however, caused the country's population to grow fastest in northern states like New York. Northern political leaders were becoming wary of what they perceived to be a disproportionate influence in federal politics by Virginia and other southern states.

Furthermore, many northerners feared that the southern states' common interest in protecting slavery was creating a congressional voting bloc that would be difficult for "free states" to overcome. The North and South began to clash over federal policy as northern states gradually ended slavery but southern states came to depend even more on enslaved labor.

The most important instance of these rising tensions erupted in the Missouri Crisis. When white settlers in Missouri, a new territory carved out of the Louisiana Purchase, applied for statehood in 1819, the balance of political power between northern and southern states became the focus of public debate. Missouri already had more than ten thousand enslaved laborers and was poised to join the southern slave states in Congress.[6]

Accordingly, Congressman James Tallmadge of New York proposed an amendment to Missouri's application for statehood. Tallmadge claimed that the institution of slavery mocked the Declaration of Independence and the liberty it promised to "all men." He proposed that Congress should admit Missouri as a state only if bringing more enslaved people to Missouri were prohibited and children born to those enslaved there were freed at age twenty-five.

Congressmen like Tallmadge opposed slavery for moral reasons, but they also wanted to maintain a sectional balance of power. Unsurprisingly, the Tallmadge Amendment met with firm resistance from southern politicians. It passed in the House of Representatives because of the support of nearly all the northern congressmen, who had a majority there, but it was quickly defeated in the Senate.

When Congress reconvened in 1820, a senator from Illinois, another new western state, proposed a compromise. Jesse Thomas hoped his offer would not only end the Missouri Crisis but also prevent any future sectional disputes over slavery and statehood. Henry Clay of Kentucky joined in promoting the deal, earning himself the nickname "the Great Compromiser."

Their bargain, the Missouri Compromise of 1820, contained three parts.[7] First, Congress would admit Missouri as a slave state. Second, Congress would admit Maine (which until now had been a territory of Massachusetts) as a free state, maintaining the balance between the number of free and slave states. Third, the rest of the Louisiana Purchase territory would be divided along the 36°30' line of latitude—or in other words, along the southern border of Missouri. Slavery would be prohibited in other new states north of this line, but it would be permitted in new states to the south. The compromise passed both houses of Congress, and the Missouri Crisis ended peacefully.

Not everyone, however, felt relieved. The Missouri Crisis made the sectional nature of American politics impossible to ignore. The Missouri Crisis split the Democratic-Republican party entirely along sectional lines, suggesting trouble to come.

Worse, the Missouri Crisis demonstrated the volatility of the slavery debate. Many Americans, including seventy-seven-year-old Thomas Jefferson, were alarmed at how readily some Americans spoke of disunion and even civil war over the issue. "This momentous question, like a fire bell in the night, awakened and filled me with terror," Jefferson wrote. "I considered it at once as the [death] knell of the Union."[8]

For now, the Missouri Crisis did not result in disunion and civil war as Jefferson and others feared. But it also failed to settle the issue of slavery's expansion into new western territories. The issue would cause worse trouble in years ahead.

IV. The Rise of Andrew Jackson

The career of Andrew Jackson (1767–1845), the survivor of that backcountry Kentucky duel in 1806, exemplified both the opportunities and the dangers of political life in the early republic. A lawyer, enslaver, and general—and eventually the seventh president of the United States—he rose from humble frontier beginnings to become one of the most powerful Americans of the nineteenth century.

Andrew Jackson was born on March 15, 1767, on the border between North and South Carolina, to two immigrants from northern Ireland. He grew up during dangerous times. At age thirteen, he joined an American militia unit in the Revolutionary War. He was soon captured, and a British officer slashed at his head with a sword after he refused to shine the officer's shoes. Disease during the war had claimed the lives of his two brothers and his mother, leaving him an orphan. Their deaths and his wounds had left Jackson with a deep and abiding hatred of Great Britain.

After the war, Jackson moved west to frontier Tennessee, where despite his poor education, he prospered, working as a lawyer and acquiring land and enslaved laborers. (He would eventually come to keep 150 slaves at the Hermitage, his plantation near Nashville.) In 1796, Jackson was elected as a U.S. representative, and a year later he won a seat in the Senate, although he resigned within a year, citing financial difficulties.

Thanks to his political connections, Jackson obtained a general's commission at the outbreak of the War of 1812. Despite having no combat experience, General Jackson quickly impressed his troops, who nicknamed him "Old Hickory" after a particularly tough kind of tree.

Jackson led his militiamen into battle in the Southeast, first during the Creek War, a side conflict that started between different factions of Muskogee (Creek) fighters in present-day Alabama. In that war, he won a decisive victory at the Battle of Horseshoe Bend in 1814. A year later, he also defeated a large British invasion force at the Battle of New Orleans. There, Jackson's troops—including backwoods militiamen, free African Americans, Native Americans, and a company of slave-trading pirates—successfully defended the city and inflicted more than two thousand casualties against the British, sustaining barely three hundred casualties of their own.[9] The Battle of New Orleans was a thrilling victory for the United States, but it actually happened several days after a peace treaty was signed in Europe to end the war. News of the treaty had not yet reached New Orleans.

The end of the War of 1812 did not end Jackson's military career. In 1818, as commander of the U.S. southern military district, Jackson also launched an invasion of Spanish-owned Florida. He was acting on vague orders from the War Department to break the resistance of the region's Seminole people, who protected runaway enslaved people and attacked American settlers across the border. On Jackson's orders in 1816, U.S.

soldiers and their Creek allies had already destroyed the "Negro Fort," a British-built fortress on Spanish soil, killing 270 formerly enslaved people and executing some survivors.[10] In 1818, Jackson's troops crossed the border again. They occupied Pensacola, the main Spanish town in the region, and arrested two British subjects, whom Jackson executed for helping the Seminoles. The execution of these two Britons created an international diplomatic crisis.

Most officials in President James Monroe's administration called for Jackson's censure. But Secretary of State John Quincy Adams, the son of former president John Adams, found Jackson's behavior useful. He defended the impulsive general, arguing that he had been forced to act. Adams used Jackson's military successes in this First Seminole War to persuade Spain to accept the Adams-Onís Treaty of 1819, which gave Florida to the United States.

Any friendliness between John Quincy Adams and Andrew Jackson, however, did not survive long. In 1824, four nominees competed for the presidency in one of the closest elections in American history. Each

Images like this—showing a young Jackson defending his family from a British officer—established Jackson's legend. Currier & Ives, *The Brave Boy of the Waxhaws*, 1876. Wikimedia.

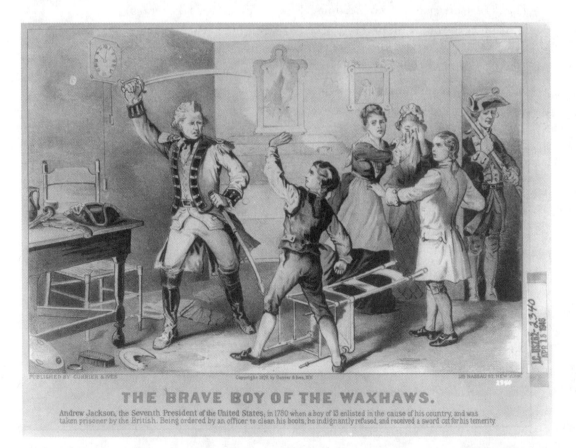

THE BRAVE BOY OF THE WAXHAWS.

Andrew Jackson, the Seventh President of the United States, in 1780 when a boy of 13 enlisted in the cause of his country, and was taken prisoner by the British. Being ordered by an officer to clean his boots, he indignantly refused, and received a sword cut for his temerity.

came from a different part of the country—Adams from Massachusetts, Jackson from Tennessee, William H. Crawford from Georgia, and Henry Clay from Kentucky. Jackson won more popular votes than anyone else. But with no majority winner in the Electoral College, the election was thrown into the House of Representatives. There, Adams used his political clout to claim the presidency, persuading Clay to support him. After his election, Adams named Henry Clay the Secretary of State, a position that had often been held by politicians before winning the presidency. Jackson would never forgive Adams, whom his supporters accused of engineering a "corrupt bargain" with Clay to circumvent the popular will.

Four years later, in 1828, Adams and Jackson squared off in one of the dirtiest presidential elections to date.[11] Pro-Jackson partisans accused Adams of elitism and claimed that while serving in Russia as a diplomat he had offered the Russian emperor an American prostitute. Adams's supporters, on the other hand, accused Jackson of murder and attacked the morality of his marriage, pointing out that Jackson had unwittingly married his wife Rachel before the divorce on her prior marriage was complete. This time, Andrew Jackson won the election easily, but Rachel Jackson died suddenly before his inauguration. Jackson would never forgive the people who attacked his wife's character during the campaign.

In 1828, Jackson's broad appeal as a military hero won him the presidency. He was "Old Hickory," the "Hero of New Orleans," a leader of plain frontier folk. His wartime accomplishments appealed to many voters' pride. Over the next eight years, he would claim to represent the interests of ordinary white Americans, especially from the South and West, against the country's wealthy and powerful elite. This attitude would lead him and his allies into a series of bitter political struggles.

V. The Nullification Crisis

Nearly every American had an opinion about President Jackson. To some, he epitomized democratic government and popular rule. To others, he represented the worst in a powerful and unaccountable executive, acting as president with the same arrogance he had shown as a general in Florida. One of the key issues dividing Americans during his presidency was a sectional dispute over national tax policy that would come to define Jackson's no-holds-barred approach to government.

Once Andrew Jackson moved into the White House, most southerners expected him to do away with the hated Tariff of 1828, the so-called

Tariff of Abominations. This import tax provided protection for northern manufacturing interests by raising the prices of European products in America. Southerners, however, blamed the tariff for a massive transfer of wealth. It forced them to purchase goods from the North's manufacturers at higher prices, and it provoked European countries to retaliate with high tariffs of their own, reducing foreign purchases of the South's raw materials.

Only in South Carolina, though, did the discomfort turn into organized action. The state was still trying to shrug off the economic problems of the Panic of 1819, but it had also recently endured the Denmark Vesey slave conspiracy, which convinced white South Carolinians that antislavery ideas put them in danger of a massive uprising.

Elite South Carolinians were especially worried that the tariff was merely an entering wedge for federal legislation that would limit slavery. Andrew Jackson's own vice president, John C. Calhoun, who was from South Carolina, asserted that the tariff was "the occasion, rather than the real cause of the present unhappy state of things." The real fear was that the federal government might attack "the peculiar domestick institution of the Southern States"—meaning slavery.[12] When Jackson failed to act against the tariff, Vice President Calhoun was caught in a tight position.

In 1828, Calhoun secretly drafted the "South Carolina Exposition and Protest," an essay and set of resolutions that laid out the doctrine of nullification.[13] Drawing from the Virginia and Kentucky Resolutions of 1798 and 1799, Calhoun argued that the United States was a compact among the states rather than among the whole American people. Since the states had created the Union, he reasoned, they were still sovereign, so a state could nullify a federal statute it considered unconstitutional. Other states would then have to concede the right of nullification or agree to amend the Constitution. If necessary, a nullifying state could leave the Union.

When Calhoun's authorship of the essay became public, Jackson was furious, interpreting it both as a personal betrayal and as a challenge to his authority as president. His most dramatic confrontation with Calhoun came in 1832 during a commemoration for Thomas Jefferson. At dinner, the president rose and toasted, "Our Federal Union: it must be preserved." Calhoun responded with a toast of his own: "The Union: next to our Liberty the most dear."[14] Their divorce was not pretty. Martin Van Buren, a New York political leader whose skill in making deals had earned him the nickname "the Little Magician," replaced Calhoun as vice president when Jackson ran for reelection in 1832.

Calhoun returned to South Carolina, where a special state convention nullified the federal tariffs of 1828 and 1832. It declared them unconstitutional and therefore "null, void, and no law" within South Carolina.[15] The convention ordered South Carolina customs officers not to collect tariff revenue and declared that any federal attempt to enforce the tariffs would cause the state to secede from the Union.

President Jackson responded dramatically. He denounced the ordinance of nullification and declared that "disunion, by armed force, is TREASON."[16] Vowing to hang Calhoun and any other nullifier who defied federal power, he persuaded Congress to pass a Force Bill that authorized him to send the military to enforce the tariffs. Faced with such threats, other southern states declined to join South Carolina. Privately, however, Jackson supported the idea of compromise and allowed his political enemy Henry Clay to broker a solution with Calhoun. Congress passed a compromise bill that slowly lowered federal tariff rates. South Carolina rescinded nullification for the tariffs but nullified the Force Bill.

The legacy of the Nullification Crisis is difficult to sort out. Jackson's decisive action seemed to have forced South Carolina to back down. But the crisis also united the ideas of secession and states' rights, two concepts that had not necessarily been linked before. Perhaps most clearly, nullification showed that the immense political power of enslavers was matched only by their immense anxiety about the future of slavery. During later debates in the 1840s and 1850s, they would raise the ideas of the Nullification Crisis again.

VI. The Eaton Affair and the Politics of Sexuality

Meanwhile, a more personal crisis during Jackson's first term also drove a wedge between him and Vice President Calhoun. The Eaton Affair, sometimes insultingly called the "Petticoat Affair," began as a disagreement among elite women in Washington, D.C., but it eventually led to the disbanding of Jackson's cabinet.

True to his backwoods reputation, when he took office in 1829, President Jackson chose mostly provincial politicians, not Washington veterans, to serve in his administration. One of them was his friend John Henry Eaton, a senator from Tennessee, whom Jackson nominated to be his secretary of war.

A few months earlier, Eaton had married Margaret O'Neale Timberlake, the recent widow of a navy officer. She was the daughter of Washing-

This photograph shows Eaton at a much older age. *Eaton, Mrs. Margaret (Peggy O'Neill), old lady*, c. 1870–1880. Library of Congress.

ton boardinghouse proprietors, and her humble origins and combination of beauty, outspokenness, and familiarity with so many men in the boardinghouse had led to gossip. During her first marriage, rumors had circulated that she and John Eaton were having an affair while her husband was at sea. When her first husband's death was originally (but incorrectly) labeled a suicide and she married Eaton just nine months later, the society women of Washington had been scandalized. One wrote that Margaret Eaton's reputation had been "totally destroyed."[17]

John Eaton was now secretary of war, but other cabinet members' wives refused have anything to do with his wife. No respectable lady who wanted to protect her own reputation could exchange visits with her, invite her to social events, or be seen chatting with her. Most importantly, the vice president's wife, Floride Calhoun, shunned Margaret Eaton, spending most of her time in South Carolina to avoid her. Even Jackson's own niece, Emily Donelson, visited Eaton once and then refused to have anything more to do with her.

Although women could not vote or hold office, they played an important role in politics as people who controlled influence.[18] They helped hold official Washington together. And according to one local society woman, "the ladies" had "as much rivalship and party spirit, desire of precedence and authority" as male politicians had.[19] These women upheld a strict code of femininity and sexual morality. They paid careful attention to the rules that governed personal interactions and official relationships.

Margaret Eaton's social exclusion thus greatly affected Jackson, his cabinet, and the rest of Washington society. At first, President Jackson blamed his rival Henry Clay for the attacks on the Eatons. But he soon perceived that Washington women and his new cabinet had initiated the gossip. Jackson scoffed, "I did not come here to make a cabinet for the ladies of this place," and claimed that he "had rather have live vermin on my back than the tongue of one of these Washington women on my reputation."[20] He began to blame the ambition of Vice President Calhoun for Floride Calhoun's actions, deciding "it was necessary to put him out of the cabinet and destroy him."[21]

Jackson was so indignant because he had recently been through a similar scandal with his late wife, Rachel. Her character, too, had been insulted by leading politicians' wives because of the circumstances of her marriage. Jackson believed that Rachel's death had been caused by those slanderous attacks. Furthermore, he saw the assaults on the Eatons as attacks on his authority.

In one of the most famous presidential meetings in American history, Jackson called together his cabinet members to discuss what they saw as the bedrock of society: women's position as protectors of the nation's values. There, the men of the cabinet debated Margaret Eaton's character. Jackson delivered a long defense, methodically presenting evidence against her attackers. But the men attending the meeting—and their wives—were not swayed. They continued to shun Margaret Eaton, and the scandal was resolved only with the resignation of four members of the cabinet, including Eaton's husband.

VII. The Bank War

Andrew Jackson's first term was full of controversy. For all of his reputation as a military and political warrior, however, the most characteristic struggle of his presidency was financial. As president, he waged a "war" against the Bank of the United States.

The charter of the controversial national bank that Congress established under Alexander Hamilton's financial plan had expired in 1811.

But five years later, Congress had given a new charter to the Second Bank of the United States. Headquartered in Philadelphia, the bank was designed to stabilize the growing American economy. By requiring other banks to pay their debts promptly in gold, it was supposed to prevent them from issuing too many paper banknotes that could drop suddenly in value. Of course, the Bank of the United States was also supposed to reap a healthy profit for its private stockholders, like the Philadelphia banker Stephen Girard and the New York merchant John Jacob Astor.

Though many Democratic-Republicans had supported the new bank, some never gave up their Jeffersonian suspicion that such a powerful institution was dangerous to the republic. Andrew Jackson was one of the skeptics. He and many of his supporters blamed the bank for the Panic of 1819, which had become a severe economic depression. The national bank had made that crisis worse, first by lending irresponsibly and then, when the panic hit, by hoarding gold currency to save itself at the expense of smaller banks and their customers. Jackson's supporters also believed the bank had corrupted many politicians by giving them financial favors.

In 1829, after a few months in office, Jackson set his sights on the bank and its director, Nicholas Biddle. Jackson became more and more insistent over the next three years as Biddle and the bank's supporters fought to save it. A visiting Frenchman observed that Jackson had "declared a war to the death against the Bank," attacking it "in the same cut-and-thrust style" with which he had once fought the Native Americans and the British. For Jackson, the struggle was a personal crisis. "The Bank is trying to kill me," he told Martin Van Buren, "but I will kill it!"[22]

The bank's charter was not due for renewal for several years, but in 1832, while Jackson was running for reelection, Congress held an early vote to reauthorize the Bank of the United States. The president vetoed the bill.

In his veto message, Jackson called the bank unconstitutional and "dangerous to the liberties of the people." The charter, he explained, didn't do enough to protect the bank from its British stockholders, who might not have Americans' interests at heart. In addition, Jackson wrote, the Bank of the United States was virtually a federal agency, but it had powers that were not granted anywhere in the Constitution. Worst of all, the bank was a way for well-connected people to get richer at everyone else's expense. "The rich and powerful," the president declared, "too often bend the acts of government to their selfish purposes."[23] Only a strictly limited government, Jackson believed, would treat people equally.

THE DOWNFALL OF MOTHER BANK.

"The bank," Andrew Jackson told Martin Van Buren, "is trying to kill me, but I will kill it!" That is just the unwavering force that Edward Clay depicted in this lithograph, which praised Jackson for terminating the Second Bank of the United States. Clay shows Nicholas Biddle as the Devil running away from Jackson as the bank collapses around him, his hirelings, and speculators. Edward W. Clay, c. 1832. Wikimedia.

Although its charter would not be renewed, the Bank of the United States could still operate for several more years. So in 1833, to diminish its power, Jackson also directed his cabinet to stop depositing federal funds in it. From now on, the government would do business with selected state banks instead. Critics called them Jackson's "pet banks."

Jackson's bank veto set off fierce controversy. Opponents in Philadelphia held a meeting and declared that the president's ideas were dangerous to private property. Jackson, they said, intended to "place the honest earnings of the industrious citizen at the disposal of the idle"—in other words, redistribute wealth to lazy people—and become a "dictator."[24] A newspaper editor said that Jackson was trying to set "the poor against the rich," perhaps in order to take over as a military tyrant.[25] But Jackson's supporters praised him. Pro-Jackson newspaper editors wrote that he had kept a "monied aristocracy" from conquering the people.[26]

By giving President Jackson a vivid way to defy the rich and powerful, or at least appear to do so, the Bank War gave his supporters a specific "democratic" idea to rally around. More than any other issue, opposition to the national bank came to define their beliefs. And by leading Jackson to exert executive power so dramatically against Congress, the Bank War also helped his political enemies organize.

Increasingly, supporters of Andrew Jackson referred to themselves as Democrats. Under the strategic leadership of Martin Van Buren, they built a highly organized national political party, the first modern party in the United States. Much more than earlier political parties, this Democratic Party had a centralized leadership structure and a consistent ideological program for all levels of government. Meanwhile, Jackson's enemies, mocking him as "King Andrew the First," named themselves after the patriots of the American Revolution, the Whigs.

VIII. The Panic of 1837

Unfortunately for Jackson's Democrats (and most other Americans), their victory over the Bank of the United States worsened rather than solved the country's economic problems.

Things looked good initially. Between 1834 and 1836, a combination of high cotton prices, freely available foreign and domestic credit, and an infusion of specie ("hard" currency in the form of gold and silver) from Europe spurred a sustained boom in the American economy. At the same time, sales of western land by the federal government promoted speculation and poorly regulated lending practices, creating a vast real estate bubble.

Meanwhile, the number of state-chartered banks grew from 329 in 1830 to 713 just six years later. As a result, the volume of paper banknotes per capita in circulation in the United States increased by 40 percent between 1834 and 1836. Low interest rates in Great Britain also encouraged British capitalists to make risky investments in America. British lending across the Atlantic surged, raising American foreign indebtedness from $110 million to $220 million over the same two years.[27]

As the boom accelerated, banks became more careless about the amount of hard currency they kept on hand to redeem their banknotes. And although Jackson had hoped his bank veto would reduce bankers' and speculators' power over the economy, it actually made the problems worse.

Two further federal actions late in the Jackson administration also worsened the situation. In June 1836, Congress decided to increase the number of banks receiving federal deposits. This plan undermined the banks that were already receiving federal money, since they saw their funds distributed to other banks. Next, seeking to reduce speculation on credit, the Treasury Department issued an order called the Specie Circular in July 1836, requiring payment in hard currency for all federal land purchases. As a result, land buyers drained eastern banks of even more gold and silver.

By late fall in 1836, America's economic bubbles began to burst. Federal land sales plummeted. The *New York Herald* reported that "lands in Illinois and Indiana that were cracked up to $10 an acre last year, are now to be got at $3, and even less." The newspaper warned darkly, "The reaction has begun, and nothing can stop it."[28]

Runs on banks began in New York on May 4, 1837, as panicked customers scrambled to exchange their banknotes for hard currency. By May 10, the New York banks, running out of gold and silver, stopped redeeming their notes. As news spread, banks around the nation did the same. By May 15, the largest crowd in Pennsylvania history had amassed

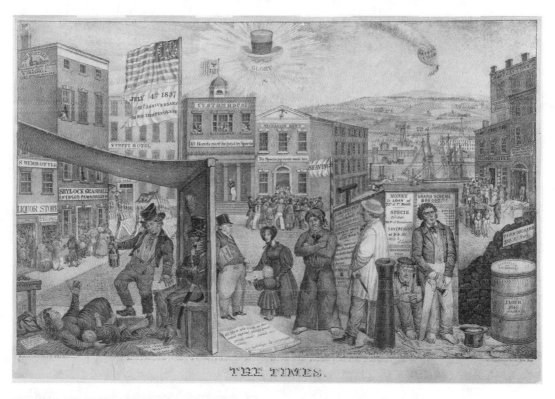

Many Americans blamed the Panic of 1837 on the economic policies of Andrew Jackson, who is sarcastically represented in the lithograph as the sun with top hat, spectacle, and a banner of "Glory" around him. The destitute people in the foreground (representing the common man) are suffering while a prosperous attorney rides in an elegant carriage in the background (right side of frame). Edward W. Clay, *The Times*, 1837. Wikimedia.

outside Independence Hall in Philadelphia, denouncing banking as a "system of fraud and oppression."[29]

The Panic of 1837 led to a general economic depression. Between 1839 and 1843, the total capital held by American banks dropped by 40 percent as prices fell and economic activity around the nation slowed to a crawl. The price of cotton in New Orleans, for instance, dropped 50 percent.[30]

Traveling through New Orleans in January 1842, a British diplomat reported that the country "presents a lamentable appearance of exhaustion and demoralization."[31] Over the previous decade, the American economy had soared to fantastic new heights and plunged to dramatic new depths.

Normal banking activity did not resume around the nation until late 1842. Meanwhile, two hundred banks closed, cash and credit became scarce, prices declined, and trade slowed. During this downturn, eight states and a territorial government defaulted on loans made by British banks to finance internal improvements.[32]

IX. Rise of the Whigs

The disaster of the Panic of 1837 created an opportunity for the Whig Party, which had grown partly out of the political coalition of John Quincy Adams and Henry Clay and opposed Andrew Jackson and the Democratic Party. The National Republicans, a loose alliance concentrated in the Northeast, had become the core of a new anti-Jackson movement. But Jackson's enemies were a varied group; they included pro-slavery southerners angry about Jackson's behavior during the Nullification Crisis as well as antislavery Yankees.

After they failed to prevent Andrew Jackson's reelection, this fragile coalition formally organized as a new party in 1834 "to rescue the Government and public liberty."[33] Henry Clay, who had run against Jackson for president and was now serving again as a senator from Kentucky, held private meetings to persuade anti-Jackson leaders from different backgrounds to unite. He also gave the new Whig Party its anti-monarchical name.

At first, the Whigs focused mainly on winning seats in Congress, opposing "King Andrew" from outside the presidency. They remained divided by regional and ideological differences. The Democratic presidential candidate, Vice President Martin Van Buren, easily won election

BORN TO COMMAND.

OF VETO MEMORY.

HAD I BEEN CONSULTED.

KING ANDREW THE FIRST.

Andrew Jackson portrayed himself as the defender of the common man, and in many ways he democratized American politics. His opponents, however, zeroed in on Jackson's willingness to utilize the powers of the executive office. Unwilling to defer to Congress and absolutely willing to use his veto power, Jackson came to be regarded by his adversaries as a tyrant (or, in this case, "King Andrew I.") Anonymous, c. 1832. Wikimedia.

as Jackson's successor in 1836. But the Whigs gained significant public support after the Panic of 1837, and they became increasingly well organized. In late 1839, they held their first national convention in Harrisburg, Pennsylvania.

To Henry Clay's disappointment, the convention voted to nominate not him but General William Henry Harrison of Ohio as the Whig candidate for president in 1840. Harrison was known primarily for defeating Shawnee warriors led by Tecumseh before and during the War of 1812, most famously at the Battle of Tippecanoe in present-day Indiana. Whig leaders viewed him as a candidate with broad patriotic appeal. They portrayed him as the "log cabin and hard cider" candidate, a plain man of the country, unlike the easterner Martin Van Buren. To balance the ticket with a southerner, the Whigs nominated a slave-owning Virginia senator, John Tyler, for vice president. Tyler had been a Jackson supporter but had broken with him over states' rights during the Nullification Crisis.

Although "Tippecanoe and Tyler Too" easily won the presidential election of 1840, this choice of ticket turned out to be disastrous for the Whigs. Harrison became ill (for unclear reasons, though tradition claims

The popular slogan "Tippe-canoe and Tyler Too" helped the Whigs and William Henry Harrison (with John Tyler) win the presidential election in 1840. Pictured here is a campaign banner with shortened "Tip and Ty," one of the many ways that Whigs waged the "log cabin campaign." Wikimedia.

he contracted pneumonia after delivering a nearly two-hour inaugural address without an overcoat or hat) and died after just thirty-one days in office. Harrison thus holds the ironic honor of having the longest inaugural address and the shortest term in office of any American president.[34] Vice President Tyler became president and soon adopted policies that looked far more like Andrew Jackson's than like a Whig's. After Tyler twice vetoed charters for another Bank of the United States, nearly his entire cabinet resigned, and the Whigs in Congress expelled "His Accidency" from the party.

The crisis of Tyler's administration was just one sign of the Whig Party's difficulty uniting around issues besides opposition to Democrats. The Whig Party succeeded in electing one more president but remained deeply divided. Its problems grew as the issue of slavery strained the Union in the 1850s. Unable to agree on a consistent national position on slavery, and unable to find another national issue to rally around, the Whigs broke apart by 1856.

X. Anti-Masons, Anti-Immigrants, and the Whig Coalition

The Whig coalition drew strength from several earlier political movements, including two that harnessed American political paranoia. The Anti-Masonic Party formed in the 1820s for the purpose of destroying the Free-masons. Later, anti-immigrant sentiment formed the American Party, also called the Know-Nothings. The American Party sought and won office across the country in the 1850s, but nativism had already been an influential force, particularly in the Whig Party, whose members could not fail to notice that urban Irish Catholics strongly tended to support Democrats.

Freemasonry, an international network of social clubs with arcane traditions and rituals, seems to have originated in medieval Europe as a trade organization for stonemasons. By the eighteenth century, however, it had outgrown its relationship with the masons' craft and had become a general secular fraternal order that proclaimed adherence to the ideals of the Enlightenment.

Freemasonry was an important part of the social life of men in the new republic's elite. George Washington, Benjamin Franklin, Andrew Jackson, and Henry Clay all claimed membership. Prince Hall, a free leather worker in Boston, founded a separate branch of the order for African American men. However, the Masonic brotherhood's secrecy, elitism, rituals, and secular ideals generated a deep suspicion of the organization among many Americans.

In 1820s upstate New York, which was fertile soil for new religious and social reform movements, anti-Masonic suspicion would emerge for the first time as an organized political force. The trigger for this was the strange disappearance and probable murder of William Morgan. Morgan announced plans to publish an exposé called *Illustrations of Masonry*.[35] This book purported to reveal the order's secret rites, and it outraged other local Freemasons. They launched a series of attempts to prevent the book from being published, including an attempt to burn the press and a conspiracy to have Morgan jailed for alleged debts. In September, Morgan disappeared. He was last seen being forced into a carriage by four men later identified as Masons. When a corpse washed up on the shore of Lake Ontario, Morgan's wife and friends claimed at first that it was his.

The Morgan story convinced many people that Masonry was a dangerous influence in the republic. The publicity surrounding the trials transformed local outrage into a political movement that, though small, had significant power in New York and parts of New England. This movement addressed Americans' widespread dissatisfaction about economic and political change by giving them a handy explanation: the republic was controlled by a secret society.

In 1827, local anti-Masonic committees began meeting across the state of New York, committing not to vote for any political candidate who belonged to the Freemasons. This boycott grew, and in 1828, a convention in the town of LeRoy produced an "Anti-Masonic Declaration of Independence," the basis for an Anti-Masonic Party. In 1828, Anti-Masonic politicians ran for state offices in New York, winning 12 percent of the vote for governor.[36]

In 1830, the Anti-Masons held a national convention in Philadelphia. But after a dismal showing in the 1832 presidential elections, the leaders of the Anti-Masonic Party folded their movement into the new Whig Party. The Anti-Masonic Party's absorption into the Whig coalition demonstrated the importance of conspiracy theories in American politics. Just as Andrew Jackson's followers detected a vast foreign plot in the form of the Bank of the United States, some of his enemies could detect it in the form of the Freemasons. Others, called nativists, blamed immigrants.

Nativists detected many foreign threats, but Catholicism may have been the most important. Nativists watched with horror as more and more Catholic immigrants (especially from Ireland and Germany) arrived in American cities. The immigrants professed different beliefs, often spoke unfamiliar languages, and participated in alien cultural traditions. Just as importantly, nativists remembered Europe's history of warfare between Catholics and Protestants. They feared that Catholics would bring religious violence with them to the United States.

In the summer of 1834, a mob of Protestants attacked a Catholic convent near Boston. The rioters had read newspaper rumors that a woman was being held against her will by the nuns. Angry men broke into the convent and burned it to the ground. Later, a young woman named Rebecca Reed, who had spent time in the convent, published a memoir describing abuses she claimed the nuns had directed toward novices and students.[37] The convent attack was among many eruptions of nativism, especially in New England and other parts of the Northeast, during the early nineteenth century.

Many Protestants saw the Catholic faith as a superstition that deprived individuals of the right to think for themselves and enslaved them to a dictator, the pope, in Rome. They accused Catholic priests of controlling their parishioners and preying sexually on young women. They feared that Catholicism would overrun and conquer the American political system, just as their ancestors had feared it would conquer England.

The painter and inventor Samuel F. B. Morse, for example, warned in 1834 that European tyrants were conspiring together to "carry Popery through all our borders" by sending Catholic immigrants to the

United States. If they succeeded, he predicted, Catholic dominance in America would mean "the *certain destruction of our free institutions.*"[38] Around the same time, the Protestant minister Lyman Beecher lectured in various cities, delivering a similar warning. "If the potentates of Europe have no design upon our liberties," Beecher demanded, then why were they sending over "such floods of pauper emigrants—the contents of the poorhouse and the sweepings of the streets—multiplying tumults and violence, filling our prisons, and crowding our poorhouses, and quadrupling our taxation"—not to mention voting in American elections?[39]

XI. Race and Jacksonian Democracy

More than anything else, however, it was racial inequality that exposed American democracy's limits. The most deadly racist policy of the era is discussed in Chapter 12—Jackson's seizure of Native American lands, culminating in the Trail of Tears. But other racist policies also attacked the purported ideas of American democracy, eroding freedom for Black Americans even as it expanded them for poor white people. Over several decades, state governments had lowered their property requirements so that poorer men could vote. But as northern states ended slavery, whites worried that free Black men could also go to the polls in large numbers. In response, they adopted new laws that made racial discrimination the basis of American democracy.

At the time of the Revolution, only two states explicitly limited Black voting rights. By 1839, almost all states did. (The four exceptions were all in New England, where the Democratic Party was weakest.) For example, New York's 1821 state constitution enfranchised nearly all white male taxpayers but only the richest Black men. In 1838, a similar constitution in Pennsylvania prohibited Black voting completely.

The new Pennsylvania constitution disenfranchised even one of the richest people in Philadelphia. James Forten, a free-born sailmaker who had served in the American Revolution, had become a wealthy merchant and landowner. He used his wealth and influence to promote the abolition of slavery, and after the 1838 constitution, he undertook a lawsuit to protect his right to vote. But he lost, and his voting rights were terminated. An English observer commented sarcastically that Forten wasn't "white enough" to vote, but "he has always been considered quite white enough to be *taxed.*"[40]

During the 1830s, furthermore, the social tensions that had promoted Andrew Jackson's rise also worsened race relations. Almost four hundred thousand free Black people lived in America by the end of the decade.[41] In the South and West, Native Americans stood in the way of white expansion. And the new Irish Catholic immigrants, along with native working-class whites, often despised nonwhites as competitors for scarce work, housing, and status.

Racial and ethnic resentment thus contributed to a wave of riots in American cities during the 1830s. In Philadelphia, thousands of white rioters torched an antislavery meeting house and attacked Black churches and homes. Near St. Louis, abolitionist newspaper editor Elijah Lovejoy was murdered as he defended his printing press. Contemplating the violence, another journalist wondered, "Does it not appear that the character of our people has suffered a considerable change for the worse?"[42]

Racial tensions also influenced popular culture. The white actor Thomas Dartmouth Rice appeared on stage in Blackface, singing and dancing as a clownish slave named "Jim Crow." Many other white entertainers copied him. Borrowing from the work of real Black performers but pandering to white audiences' prejudices, they turned cruel stereotypes into one of antebellum America's favorite forms of entertainment.

Some whites in the 1830s, however, joined free Black activists in protesting racial inequality. Usually, they lived in northern cities and came from the class of skilled laborers, or in other words, the lower middle class. Most of them were not rich, but they expected to rise in the world.

In Boston, for example, the Female Anti-Slavery Society included women whose husbands sold coal, mended clothes, and baked bread, as well as women from wealthy families. In the nearby village of Lynn, many abolitionists were shoemakers. They organized boycotts of consumer products like sugar that came from slave labor, and they sold their own handmade goods at antislavery fund-raising fairs. For many of them, the antislavery movement was a way to participate in "respectable" middle-class culture, a way for both men and women to have a say in American life.

Debates about slavery, therefore, reflected wider tensions in a changing society. The ultimate question was whether American democracy had room for people of different races as well as religions and classes. Some people said yes and struggled to make American society more welcoming. But the vast majority, whether Democrats or Whigs, said no.

XII. Reference Material

This chapter was edited by Jonathan Wilfred Wilson, with content contributions by Myles Beaupre, Christopher Childers, William Cossen, Adam Costanzo, Nathaniel C. Green, Robert Gudmestad, Spencer McBride, Kevin Waite, and Jonathan Wilfred Wilson.

Recommended citation: Myles Beupre et al., "Democracy in America," Jonathan Wilfred Wilson, ed., in *The American Yawp*, eds. Joseph Locke and Ben Wright (Stanford, CA: Stanford University Press, 2019).

NOTES TO CHAPTER 9

1. Quoted in James Parton, *Life of Andrew Jackson*, Vol. 1 (New York: Mason Brothers, 1860), 297.

2. Max Farrand, ed., *The Records of the Federal Convention of 1787*, Vol. 1 (New Haven, CT: Yale University Press, 1911), 288.

3. Ibid., 48.

4. Benjamin Rush, "Address to the People of the United States," in *Principles and Acts of the Revolution in America*, ed. Hezekiah Niles (Baltimore: William Ogden Niles, 1822), 402. http://catalog.hathitrust.org/Record/000315501.

5. Alexander Hamilton to James A. Bayard, April 1802, *Founders Online*, National Archives. http://founders.archives.gov/documents/Hamilton/01-25-02-0321. From *The Papers of Alexander Hamilton*, Vol. 25, July 1800–April 1802, ed. Harold C. Syrett (New York: Columbia University Press, 1977), 605–610.

6. *A Century of Population Growth: From the First Census of the United States to the Twelfth, 1790–1900* (Washington, DC: U.S. Government Printing Office, 1909), 133, table 60. http://www2.census.gov/prod2/decennial/documents/00165897ch14.pdf.

7. Conference committee report on the Missouri Compromise, March 1, 1820, Records of Joint Committees of Congress, 1789–1989, National Archives. http://www.ourdocuments.gov/doc.php?doc=22.

8. Thomas Jefferson to John Holmes, April 22, 1820, Founders Online, National Archives. http://founders.archives.gov/documents/Jefferson/98-01-02-1234.

9. Robert V. Remini, *The Battle of New Orleans: Andrew Jackson and America's First Military Victory* (New York: Penguin, 1999), 167–168.

10. Kenneth Wiggins Porter, "Negroes and the Seminole War, 1817–1818," *Journal of Negro History* 36, no. 3 (July 1951): 264.

11. See Lynn Hudson Parsons, *The Birth of Modern Politics: Andrew Jackson, John Quincy Adams, and the Election of 1828*. New York: Oxford University Press, 2009.

12. John C. Calhoun to Virgil Maxcy, September 11, 1830, quoted in William M. Meigs, *The Life of John Caldwell Calhoun*, Vol. 1 (New York: Stechert, 1917), 419.

13. John C. Calhoun, "Exposition and Protest," in *Union and Liberty: The Political Philosophy of John C. Calhoun*, ed. Ross M. Lence (Indianapolis, IN: Liberty Fund, 1992), 311–365. http://oll.libertyfund.org/titles/683.

14. Thomas Hart Benton, *Thirty Years' View: Or, a History of the Working of the American Government for Thirty Years, from 1820 to 1850*, Vol. 1 (New York: Appleton, 1854), 148. http://catalog.hathitrust.org/Record/000405607.

15. South Carolina ordinance of nullification, November 24, 1832, Avalon Project, Yale Law School. http://avalon.law.yale.edu/19th_century/ordnull.asp.

16. Andrew Jackson, proclamation regarding nullification, December 10, 1832, Avalon Project, Yale Law School. http://avalon.law.yale.edu/19th_century/jack01.asp.

17. Catherine Allgor, *Parlor Politics: In Which the Ladies of Washington Help Build a City and a Government* (Charlottesville: University Press of Virginia, 2000), 200.

18. Elizabeth R. Varon, *We Mean to Be Counted: White Women and Politics in Antebellum Virginia* (Chapel Hill: University of North Carolina Press, 1998).

19. Margaret Bayard Smith to Margaret Bayard Boyd, December 20 [?], 1828, Margaret Bayard Smith Papers, quoted in ibid., 215.

20. Andrew Jackson to John Christmas McLemore, April [26], 1829, in *The Papers of Andrew Jackson*, eds. Daniel Feller, Harold D. Moser, Laura-Eve Moss, and Thomas Coens, Vol. 7 (Knoxville: University of Tennessee Press, 2007), 184; John F. Marszalek, *The Petticoat Affair: Manners, Mutiny, and Sex in Andrew Jackson's White House* (Baton Rouge: LSU Press, 1997), 64.

21. Andrew Jackson to John McLemore, November 24, 1829, quoted in Richard E. Ellis, *The Union at Risk: Jacksonian Democracy, States' Rights and the Nullification Crisis* (New York: Oxford University Press, 1987), 61.

22. Michel Chevalier and Andrew Jackson, quoted in Andrew Burstein, *The Passions of Andrew Jackson* (New York: Knopf, 2003), 200.

23. Andrew Jackson, veto message regarding the Bank of the United States, July 10, 1832, Avalon Project, Yale Law School. http://avalon.law.yale.edu/19th_century/ajveto01.asp.

24. "The Philadelphia Meeting," *Niles' Weekly Register* (July 21, 1832), 375.

25. "The Bank Veto," *National Intelligencer*, August 9, 1832, in David A. Copeland, ed., *The Antebellum Era: Primary Documents on Events from 1820 to 1860* (Westport, CT: Greenwood, 2003), 153.

26. Quoted in Harry Watson, *Liberty and Power: The Politics of Jacksonian America*, rev. ed. (New York: Hill and Wang, 2006), 151. See also Stephen W. Campbell, *The Bank War and the Partisan Press: Newspapers, Financial Institutions, and the Post Office in Jacksonian America* (Lawrence: University Press of Kansas, 2019).

27. Alasdair Roberts, *America's First Great Depression: Economic Crisis and Political Disorder after the Panic of 1837* (Ithaca, NY: Cornell University Press, 2012), 31, 36.

28. Quoted in ibid., 38.

29. "Great Public Meeting in Philadelphia," *Niles' Weekly Register* (May 27, 1837), 198.

30. Roberts, *America's First Great Depression*, 23.

31. Quoted in ibid., 21.

32. Ibid., 53. Also see Jessica Lepler, *The Many Panics of 1837: People, Politics, and the Creation of a Transatlantic Financial Crisis* (New York: Cambridge University Press, 2013).

33. Henry Clay to Francis Brooke, December 16, 1833, quoted in Michael F. Holt, *The Rise and Fall of the American Whig Party: Jacksonian Politics and the Onset of the Civil War* (New York: Oxford University Press, 1999), 29.

34. Joseph Nathan Kane, *Presidential Fact Book* (New York: Random House, 1998), 61.

35. William Morgan, *Illustrations of Masonry, by One of the Fraternity, Who Has Devoted Thirty Years to the Subject* (Batavia, NY: Miller, 1826). http://archive.org/details/illustrationsofm00morg.

36. William Preston Vaughn, *The Anti-Masonic Party in the United States: 1826–1843*, paperback ed. (Lexington: University Press of Kentucky, 2009), 31.

37. Rebecca Theresa Reed, *Six Months in a Convent, or, The Narrative of Rebecca Theresa Reed* (Boston: Russell, Odiorne and Metcalf, 1835). http://archive.org/details/sixmonthsinconve00reedr.

38. [Samuel F. B. Morse], *Foreign Conspiracy against the Liberties of the United States* (New York: Leavitt, Lord, 1835), 16, 127. http://archive.org/details/foreignconspira00mors.

39. Lyman Beecher, *A Plea for the West*, 2nd ed. (Cincinnati, OH: Truman and Smith, 1835), 54, http://archive.org/details/pleaforwest00beec.

40. Frederick Marryat, *Diary in America with Remarks on Its Institutions* (London: Longman, 1839), Vol. 1, 297, quoted in Eric Ledell Smith, "The End of Black Voting Rights in Pennsylvania: African Americans and the Pennsylvania Constitutional Convention of 1837–1838," *Pennsylvania History* 65, no. 3 (Summer 1998): 296.

41. Michael R. Haines, "Table Aa145-184: Population, by Sex and Race: 1790–1990," *Historical Statistics of the United States*, millennial ed. online, eds. Susan B. Carter, Scott Sigmund Gartner, Michael R. Haines, Alan L. Olmstead, Richard Sutch, and Gavin Wright (New York: Cambridge University Press, 2006). http://hsus.cambridge.org.

42. *Niles' Weekly Register* (August 23, 1834), 426.

RECOMMENDED READING

Allgor, Catherine. *Parlor Politics: In Which the Ladies of Washington Help Build a City and a Government.* Charlottesville: University Press of Virginia, 2000.

Burstein, Andrew. *The Passions of Andrew Jackson.* New York: Knopf, 2003.

Ellis, Richard E. *The Union at Risk: Jacksonian Democracy, States' Rights and the Nullification Crisis.* New York: Oxford University Press, 1987.

Feller, Daniel. *The Jacksonian Promise: America, 1815–1840.* Baltimore: Johns Hopkins University Press, 1995.

Foster, A. Kristen. *Moral Visions and Material Ambitions: Philadelphia Struggles to Define the Republic, 1776–1836.* Lanham, MD: Lexington Books, 2004.

Freeman, Joanne B. *Affairs of Honor: National Politics in the New Republic.* New Haven, CT: Yale University Press, 2002.

Hansen, Deborah Gold. *Strained Sisterhood: Gender and Class in the Boston Female Anti-Slavery Society.* Amherst: University of Massachusetts Press, 1993.

Holt, Michael F. *The Rise and Fall of the American Whig Party: Jacksonian Politics and the Onset of the Civil War.* New York: Oxford University Press, 1999.

Howe, Daniel Walker. *The Political Culture of the American Whigs.* Chicago: University of Chicago Press, 1979.

Jeffrey, Julie Roy. *The Great Silent Army of Abolitionism: Ordinary Women in the Antislavery Movement.* Chapel Hill: University of North Carolina Press, 1998.

Kamensky, Jane. *The Exchange Artist: A Tale of High-Flying Speculation and America's First Banking Collapse.* New York: Penguin, 2008.

Lepler, Jessica. *The Many Panics of 1837: People, Politics, and the Creation of a Transatlantic Financial Crisis.* New York: Cambridge University Press, 2013.

Lhamon, W. T., Jr. *Jump Jim Crow: Lost Plays, Lyrics, and Street Prose of the First Atlantic Popular Culture.* Cambridge, MA: Harvard University Press, 2003.

Malone, Christopher. *Between Freedom and Bondage: Race, Party, and Voting Rights in the Antebellum North.* New York: Routledge, 2008.

McInnis, Maurie D. *The Politics of Taste in Antebellum Charleston.* Chapel Hill: University of North Carolina Press, 2005.

Parsons, Lynn Hudson. *The Birth of Modern Politics: Andrew Jackson, John Quincy Adams, and the Election of 1828.* New York: Oxford University Press, 2009.

Roberts, Alasdair. *America's First Great Depression: Economic Crisis and Political Disorder After the Panic of 1837.* Ithaca, NY: Cornell University Press, 2012.

Roediger, David R. *The Wages of Whiteness: Race and the Making of the American Working Class,* rev. ed. New York: Verso, 1999.

Siddali, Silvana R. *Frontier Democracy: Constitutional Conventions in the Old Northwest.* New York: Cambridge University Press, 2016.

Stansel, Christine. *City of Women: Sex and Class in New York, 1789–1860.* New York: Knopf, 1986.

Varon, Elizabeth R. *We Mean to Be Counted: White Women and Politics in Antebellum Virginia.* Chapel Hill: University of North Carolina Press, 1998.

Vaughn, William Preston. *The Anti-Masonic Party in the United States: 1826–1843,* paperback ed. Lexington: University Press of Kentucky, 2009.

Watson, Harry. *Liberty and Power: The Politics of Jacksonian America,* rev. ed. New York: Hill and Wang, 2006.

Wellman, Judith. *Grassroots Reform in the Burned-Over District of Upstate New York: Religion, Abolitionism, and Democracy.* New York: Routledge, 2016.

Wilentz, Sean. *The Rise of American Democracy: Jefferson to Lincoln.* New York: Norton, 2005.

10
Religion and Reform

I. Introduction

The early nineteenth century was a period of immense change in the United States. Economic, political, demographic, and territorial transformations radically altered how Americans thought about themselves, their communities, and the rapidly expanding nation. It was a period of great optimism, with the possibilities of self-governance infusing everything from religion to politics. Yet it was also a period of great conflict, as the benefits of industrialization and democratization increasingly accrued along starkly uneven lines of gender, race, and class. Westward expansion distanced urban dwellers from frontier settlers more than ever before, even as the technological innovations of industrialization—like the telegraph and railroads—offered exciting new ways to maintain communication. The spread of democracy opened the franchise to nearly all

Camp Meeting of the Methodists in N. America, 1819. Library of Congress.

white men, but urbanization and a dramatic influx of European migration increased social tensions and class divides.

Americans looked on these changes with a mixture of enthusiasm and suspicion, wondering how the moral fabric of the new nation would hold up to emerging social challenges. Increasingly, many turned to two powerful tools to help understand and manage the various transformations: spiritual revivalism and social reform. Reacting to the rationalism of the eighteenth-century Enlightenment, the religious revivals of the Second Great Awakening reignited Protestant spirituality during the early nineteenth century. The revivals incorporated worshippers into an expansive religious community that crisscrossed all regions of the United States and armed them with a potent evangelical mission. Many emerged from these religious revivals with a conviction that human society could be changed to look more heavenly. They joined their spiritual networks to rapidly developing social reform networks that sought to alleviate social ills and eradicate moral vice. Tackling numerous issues, including alcoholism, slavery, and the inequality of women, reformers worked tirelessly to remake the world around them. While not all these initiatives were successful, the zeal of reform and the spiritual rejuvenation that inspired it were key facets of antebellum life and society.

II. Revival and Religious Change

In the early nineteenth century, a succession of religious revivals collectively known as the Second Great Awakening remade the nation's religious landscape. Revivalist preachers traveled on horseback, sharing the message of spiritual and moral renewal to as many as possible. Residents of urban centers, rural farmlands, and frontier territories alike flocked to religious revivals and camp meetings, where intense physical and emotional enthusiasm accompanied evangelical conversion.

The Second Great Awakening emerged in response to powerful intellectual and social currents. Camp meetings captured the democratizing spirit of the American Revolution, but revivals also provided a unifying moral order and new sense of spiritual community for Americans struggling with the great changes of the day. The market revolution, western expansion, and European immigration all challenged traditional bonds of authority, and evangelicalism promised equal measures of excitement and order. Revivals spread like wildfire throughout the United States, swelling church membership, spawning new Christian denominations, and inspiring social reform.

One of the earliest and largest revivals of the Second Great Awakening occurred in Cane Ridge, Kentucky, over a one-week period in August 1801. The Cane Ridge Revival drew thousands of people, and possibly as many as one of every ten residents of Kentucky.[1] Though large crowds had previously gathered annually in rural areas each late summer or fall to receive communion, this assembly was very different.[2] Methodist, Baptist, and Presbyterian preachers all delivered passionate sermons, exhorting the crowds to strive for their own salvation. They preached from inside buildings, evangelized outdoors under the open sky, and even used tree stumps as makeshift pulpits, all to reach their enthusiastic audiences in any way possible. Women, too, exhorted, in a striking break with common practice. Attendees, moved by the preachers' fervor, responded by crying, jumping, speaking in tongues, or even fainting.[3]

Events like the Cane Ridge Revival did spark significant changes in Americans' religious affiliations. Many revivalists abandoned the comparatively formal style of worship observed in the well-established Congregationalist and Episcopalian churches and instead embraced more impassioned forms of worship that included the spontaneous jumping, shouting, and gesturing found in new and alternative denominations. The ranks of Christian denominations such as the Methodists, Baptists, and Presbyterians swelled precipitously alongside new denominations such as the Seventh-Day Adventist Church. The evangelical fire reached such heights, in fact, that one swath of western and central New York state came to be known as the Burned-Over District. Charles Grandison Finney, the influential revivalist preacher who first coined the term, explained that the residents of this area had experienced so many revivals by different religious groups that there were no more souls to awaken to the fire of spiritual conversion.[4]

Removing the government support of churches created what historians call the American spiritual marketplace. Methodism achieved the most remarkable success, enjoying the most significant denominational increase in American history. By 1850, Methodism was by far the most popular American denomination. The Methodist denomination grew from fewer than one thousand members at the end of the eighteenth century to constitute 34 percent of all American church membership by the midnineteenth century.[5] After its leaders broke with the Church of England to form a new American denomination in 1784, the Methodist Episcopal Church (MEC) achieved its growth through innovation. Methodists used itinerant preachers, known as circuit riders. These men (and the occasional woman) won converts by pushing west with the expanding United States over the Alleghenies and into the Ohio River Valley, bringing religion to new settlers hungry to have their spiritual needs attended. Circuit riding took preachers into homes, meetinghouses, and churches, all mapped out at regular intervals that collectively took about two weeks to complete.

Revolutionary ideals also informed a substantial theological critique of orthodox Calvinism that had far-reaching consequences for religious individuals and for society as a whole. Calvinists believed that all of humankind was marred by sin, and God predestined only some for salvation. These attitudes began to seem too pessimistic for many American Christians. Worshippers increasingly began to take responsibility for their own spiritual fates by embracing theologies that emphasized human action in effecting salvation, and revivalist preachers were quick to recognize the importance of these cultural shifts. Radical revivalist preachers, such as Charles Grandison Finney, put theological issues aside and evangelized by appealing to worshippers' hearts and emotions. Even more conservative spiritual leaders, such as Lyman Beecher of the Congregational Church, appealed to younger generations of Americans by adopting a less orthodox approach to Calvinist doctrine.[6] Though these men did not see eye to eye, they both contributed to the emerging consensus that all souls are equal in salvation and that all people can be saved by surrendering to God. This idea of spiritual egalitarianism was one of the most important transformations to emerge out of the Second Great Awakening.

Spiritual egalitarianism dovetailed neatly with an increasingly democratic United States. In the process of winning independence from Britain, the revolution weakened the power of long-standing social hierarchies and the codes of conduct that went along with them. The democratizing ethos opened the door for a more egalitarian approach to spiritual leadership. Whereas preachers of long-standing denominations like the Congregationalists were required to have a divinity degree and at least some theological training in order to become spiritual leaders, many alternative denominations only required a conversion experience and a supernatural "call to preach." This meant, for example, that a twenty-year-old man could go from working in a mill to being a full-time circuit-riding preacher for the Methodists practically overnight. Indeed, their emphasis on spiritual egalitarianism over formal training enabled Methodists to outpace spiritual competition during this period. Methodists attracted more new preachers to send into the field, and the lack of formal training meant that individual preachers could be paid significantly less than a Congregationalist preacher with a divinity degree.

In addition to the divisions between evangelical and nonevangelical denominations wrought by the Second Great Awakening, the revivals and subsequent evangelical growth also revealed strains within the Methodist and Baptist churches. Each witnessed several schisms during the 1820s and 1830s as reformers advocated for a return to the practices and policies of an earlier generation. Many others left mainstream Protestantism altogether, opting instead to form their own churches. Some, like Alexander Campbell and Barton Stone, proposed a return to (or "restoration" of) New Testament Christianity, stripped of centuries of additional teachings and practices.[7] Other restorationists built on the foundation laid by the evangelical churches by using their methods and means to both critique the Protestant mainstream and move beyond the accepted boundaries of contemporary Christian orthodoxy. Self-declared prophets claimed that God had called them to establish new churches and introduce new (or, in their understanding, restore *lost*) teachings, forms of worship, and even scripture.

Mormon founder Joseph Smith, for example, claimed that God the Father and Jesus Christ appeared to him in a vision in a grove of trees near his boyhood home in upstate New York and commanded him to "join none of [the existing churches], for they are all wrong."[8] Subsequent visitations from angelic beings revealed to Smith the location of a buried record, purportedly containing the writings and histories of an ancient Christian civilization on the American continent. Smith published the Book of Mormon in early 1830 and organized the Church of Christ (later renamed the Church of Jesus Christ of Latter-day Saints) a short time later. Borrowing from the Methodists a faith in the abilities of itinerant preachers without formal training, Smith dispatched early converts as missionaries to take the message of the Book of Mormon throughout the United States, across the ocean to England and Ireland, and eventually even farther abroad. He attracted a sizable number of followers on both sides of the Atlantic and commanded them to gather to a center place, where they collectively anticipated the imminent second coming of Christ. Continued growth and near-constant opposition from both Protestant ministers and neighbors suspicious of their potential political power forced the Mormons to move several times, first from New York to Ohio, then to Missouri, and finally to Illinois, where they established a thriving community on the banks of the Mississippi River. In Nauvoo, as they called their city, Smith moved even further beyond the bounds of the Christian orthodoxy by continuing to pronounce additional revelations and introducing sacred rites to be performed only in front of church members in Mormon temples. Most controversially, Smith and a select group of his most loyal followers began taking additional wives (Smith himself married at least thirty women). Although Mormon polygamy was not publicly acknowledged and openly practiced until 1852 (when the Mormons had moved yet again, this time to the protective confines of the intermountain west on the shores of the Great Salt Lake), rumors of Smith's involvement circulated almost immediately after its quiet introduction and played a part in the motivations of the mob that eventually murdered the Mormon prophet in the summer of 1844.

Mormons were not the only religious community in antebellum America to challenge the domestic norms of the era through radical sexual experiments: Shakers strictly enforced celibacy in their several communes scattered throughout New England and the upper Midwest, while John Humphrey Noyes introduced free love (or "complex marriage") to his Oneida community in upstate New York. Others challenged existing cultural customs in less radical ways. For individual worshippers, spiritual egalitarianism in revivals and camp meetings could break down traditional social conventions. For example, revivals generally admitted both men and women. Furthermore, in an era when many American Protestants discouraged or outright forbade women from speaking in church meetings, some preachers provided women with new opportunities to openly express themselves and participate in spiritual communities. This was particularly true in the Methodist and Baptist traditions, though by the midnineteenth century most of these opportunities would be curtailed as these denominations attempted to move away from radical revivalism and toward the status of respectable denominations. Some preachers also promoted racial integration in religious gatherings, expressing equal concern for white and Black people's spiritual salvation and encouraging both enslavers and the enslaved to attend the same meetings. Historians have even suggested that the extreme physical and vocal manifestations of conversion seen at impassioned revivals and camp meetings offered the ranks of worshippers a way to enact a sort of social leveling by flouting the codes of self-restraint prescribed by upper-class elites. Although the revivals did not always live up to such progressive ideals in practice, particularly in the more conservative regions of the slaveholding South, the concept of spiritual egalitarianism nonetheless changed how Protestant Americans thought about themselves, their God, and one another.

As the borders of the United States expanded during the nineteenth century and as new demographic changes altered urban landscapes, revivalism also offered worshippers a source of social and religious structure to help cope with change. Revival meetings held by itinerant preachers offered community and collective spiritual purpose to migrant families and communities isolated from established social and religious institutions. In urban centers, where industrialization and European famines brought growing numbers of domestic and foreign migrants, evangelical preachers provided moral order and spiritual solace to an increasingly anonymous population. Additionally, and quite significantly, the Second Great Awakening armed evangelical Christians with a moral purpose to address and eradicate the many social problems they saw as arising from these dramatic demographic shifts.

Not all American Christians, though, were taken with the revivals. The early nineteenth century also saw the rise of Unitarianism as a group of ministers and their followers came to reject key aspects of "orthodox" Protestant belief including the divinity of Christ. Christians in New England were particularly involved in the debates surrounding Unitarianism as Harvard University became a hotly contested center of cultural authority between Unitarians and Trinitarians. Unitarianism had important effects on the world of reform when a group of Unitarian ministers founded the Transcendental Club in 1836.[9] The club met for four years and included Ralph Waldo Emerson, Bronson Alcott, Frederic Henry Hedge, George Ripley, Orestes Brownson, James Freeman Clarke, and Theodore Parker. While initially limited to ministers or former ministers—except for the eccentric Alcott—the club quickly expanded to include numerous literary intellectuals. Among these were the author Henry David Thoreau, the protofeminist and literary critic Margaret Fuller, and the educational reformer Elizabeth Peabody.

Transcendentalism had no established creed, but this was intentional. What united the Transcendentalists was their belief in a higher spiritual principle within each person that could be trusted to discover truth, guide moral action, and inspire art. They often referred to this principle as Soul, Spirit, Mind, or Reason. Deeply influenced by British Romanticism and German idealism's celebration of individual artistic inspiration, personal spiritual experience, and aspects of human existence not easily explained by reason or logic, the Transcendentalists established an enduring legacy precisely because they developed distinctly American ideas that emphasized individualism, optimism, oneness with nature, and a modern orientation toward the future rather than the past. These themes resonated in an American nineteenth century where political democracy and readily available land distinguished the United States from Europe.

Ralph Waldo Emerson espoused a religious worldview wherein God, "the eternal ONE," manifested through the special harmony between the individual soul and nature. In "The American Scholar" (1837) and "Self-Reliance" (1841), Emerson emphasized the utter reliability and sufficiency of the individual soul and exhorted his audience to overcome "our long apprenticeship to the learning of other lands."[10] Emerson believed that the time had come for Americans to declare their intellectual independence from Europe. Henry David Thoreau espoused a similar enthusiasm for simple living, communion with nature, and self-sufficiency. Thoreau's sense of rugged individualism, perhaps the strongest among even the Transcendentalists, also yielded "Resistance to Civil Government" (1849).[11] Several of the Transcendentalists also participated in communal living experiments. For example, in the mid-1840s, George Ripley and other members of the utopian Brook Farm community began to espouse Fourierism, a vision of society based on cooperative principles, as an alternative to capitalist conditions.[12]

Many of these different types of responses to the religious turmoil of the time had a similar endpoint in the embrace of voluntary associations and social reform work. During the antebellum period, many American Christians responded to the moral anxiety of industrialization and urbanization by organizing to address specific social needs. Social problems such as intemperance, vice, and crime assumed a new and distressing scale that older solutions, such as almshouses, were not equipped to handle. Moralists grew concerned about the growing mass of urban residents who did not attend church, and who, thanks to poverty or illiteracy, did not even have access to scripture. Voluntary benevolent societies exploded in number to tackle these issues. Led by ministers and dominated by middle-class women, voluntary societies printed and distributed Protestant tracts, taught Sunday school, distributed outdoor relief, and evangelized in both frontier towns and urban slums. These associations and their evangelical members also lent moral backing and workers to large-scale social reform projects, including the temperance movement designed to curb Americans' consumption of alcohol, the abolitionist campaign to eradicate slavery in the United States, and women's rights agitation to improve women's political and economic rights. As such wide-ranging reform projects combined with missionary zeal, evangelical Christians formed a "benevolent empire" that swiftly became a cornerstone of the antebellum period.

III. Atlantic Origins of Reform

The reform movements that emerged in the United States during the first half of the nineteenth century were not American inventions. Instead, these movements were rooted in a transatlantic world where both sides of the ocean faced similar problems and together collaborated to find similar solutions. Many of the same factors that spurred American reformers to action—such as urbanization, industrialization, and class struggle—equally affected Europe. Reformers on both sides of the Atlantic visited and corresponded with one another. Exchanging ideas and building networks proved crucial to shared causes like abolition and women's rights.

Improvements in transportation, including the introduction of the steamboat, canals, and railroads, connected people not just across the United States, but also with other like-minded reformers in Europe. (Ironically, the same technologies also helped ensure that even after the abolition of slavery in the British Empire, the British remained heavily invested in slavery, both directly and indirectly.) Equally important, the reduction of publication costs created by new printing technologies in the 1830s allowed reformers to reach new audiences across the world.[13] Almost immediately after its publication in the United States, for instance, Frederick Douglass's autobiography was republished in Europe and translated into French and Dutch. This abolitionist who escaped enslavement earned supporters across the Atlantic.[14]

Such exchanges began as part of the larger processes of colonialism and empire building. Missionary organizations from the colonial era had created many of these transatlantic links. The Atlantic travel of major figures during the First Great Awakening such as George Whitefield had built enduring networks. These networks changed as a result of the American Revolution but still revealed spiritual and personal connections between religious individuals and organizations in the United States and Great Britain. These connections can be seen in multiple areas. Mission work continued to be a joint effort, with American and European missionary societies in close correspondence throughout the early nineteenth century, as they coordinated domestic and foreign evangelistic missions. The transportation and print revolutions meant that news of British missionary efforts in India and Tahiti could be quickly printed in American religious periodicals, galvanizing American efforts to evangelize Native Americans, frontier settlers, immigrant groups, and even people overseas.

In addition to missions, antislavery work had a decidedly transatlantic cast from its very beginnings. American Quakers began to question slavery as early as the late seventeenth century and worked with British reformers in the successful campaign that ended the slave trade.[15] Before, during, and after the Revolution, many Americans continued to admire European thinkers. Influence extended both east and west. By foregrounding questions about rights, the American Revolution helped inspire British abolitionists, who in turn offered support to their American counterparts. American antislavery activists developed close relationships with abolitionists on the other side of the Atlantic, such as Thomas Clarkson, Daniel O'Connell, and Joseph Sturge. Prominent American abolitionists such as Theodore Dwight Weld, Lucretia Mott, and William Lloyd Garrison were converted to the antislavery idea of immediatism—that is, the demand for emancipation without delay—by British abolitionists Elizabeth Heyrick and Charles Stuart.[16] Although Anglo-American antislavery networks reached back to the late eighteenth century, they dramatically grew in support and strength over the antebellum period, as evidenced by the General Anti-Slavery Convention of 1840. This antislavery delegation consisted of more than five hundred abolitionists, mostly coming from France, England, and the United States. All met together in England, united by their common goal of ending slavery in their time. Although abolitionism was not the largest American reform movement of the antebellum period (that honor belongs to temperance), it did foster greater cooperation among reformers in England and the United States.

In the course of their abolitionist activities, many American women began to establish contact with their counterparts across the Atlantic, each group penning articles and contributing material support to the others' antislavery publications and fundraisers. The bonds between British and American reformers can be traced throughout the many social improvement projects of the nineteenth century. Transatlantic cooperation galvanized efforts to reform individuals' and societies' relationships to alcohol, labor, religion, education, commerce, and land ownership. This cooperation stemmed from the recognition that social problems on both sides of the Atlantic were strikingly similar. Atlantic activists helped American reformers conceptualize themselves as part of a worldwide moral mission to attack social ills and spread the gospel of Christianity.

This enormous painting documents the 1840 convention of the British and Foreign Anti-Slavery Society, established by both American and English antislavery activists to promote worldwide abolition. Benjamin Haydon, *The Anti-Slavery Society Convention*, 1840. Wikimedia.

IV. The Benevolent Empire

After religious disestablishment, citizens of the United States faced a dilemma: how to cultivate a moral and virtuous public without aid from state-sponsored religion. Most Americans agreed that a good and moral citizenry was essential for the national project to succeed, but many shared the perception that society's moral foundation was weakening. Narratives of moral and social decline, known as jeremiads, had long been embedded in Protestant story-telling traditions, but jeremiads took on new urgency in the antebellum period. In the years immediately following disestablishment, "traditional" Protestant Christianity was at low tide, while the Industrial Revolution and the spread of capitalism had led to a host of social problems associated with cities and commerce. The Second Great Awakening was in part a spiritual response to such changes, revitalizing Christian spirits through the promise of salvation. The revivals also provided an institutional antidote to the insecurities of a rapidly changing world by inspiring an immense and widespread movement for social reform. Growing directly out of nineteenth-century revivalism, reform societies proliferated throughout the United States between 1815 and 1861, melding religion and reform into a powerful force in American culture known as the *benevolent empire*.

The benevolent empire departed from revivalism's early populism, as middle-class ministers dominated the leadership of antebellum reform societies. Because of the economic forces of the market revolution, middle-class evangelicals had the time and resources to devote to reform campaigns. Often, their reforms focused on creating and maintaining respectable middle-class culture throughout the United States. Middle-class women, in particular, played a leading role in reform activity. They became increasingly responsible for the moral maintenance of their homes and communities, and their leadership signaled a dramatic departure from previous generations when such prominent roles for ordinary women would have been unthinkable.[17]

Different forces within evangelical Protestantism combined to encourage reform. One of the great lights of benevolent reform was Charles Grandison Finney, the radical revivalist, who promoted a movement known as "perfectionism." Premised on the belief that truly redeemed Christians would be motivated to live free of sin and reflect the perfection of God himself, his wildly popular revivals encouraged his converted followers to join reform movements and create God's kingdom on earth. The idea of "disinterested benevolence" also turned many evangelicals toward reform. Preachers championing disinterested benevolence argued that true Christianity requires that a person give up self-love in favor of loving others. Though perfectionism and disinterested benevolence were the most prominent forces encouraging benevolent societies, some preachers achieved the same end in their advocacy of postmillennialism. In this worldview, Christ's return was foretold to occur after humanity had enjoyed one thousand years' peace, and it was the duty of converted Christians to improve the world around them in order to pave the way for Christ's redeeming return. Though ideological and theological issues like these divided Protestants into more and more sects, church leaders often worked on an interdenominational basis to establish benevolent societies and draw their followers into the work of social reform.

Under the leadership of preachers and ministers, reform societies attacked many social problems. Those concerned about drinking could join

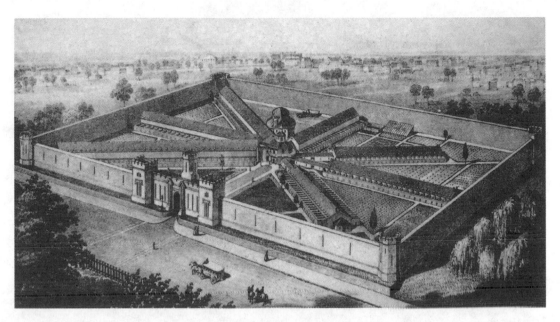

Eastern State Penitentiary changed the principles of imprisonment, focusing on reform rather than punishment. The structure itself used the panopticon surveillance system and was widely copied by prison systems around the world. P. S. Duval and Co., *The State Penitentiary for the Eastern District of Pennsylvania*, 1855. Wikimedia. Creative Commons Attribution 2.0 Generic.

temperance societies; other groups focused on eradicating dueling and gambling. Evangelical reformers might support home or foreign missions or Bible and tract societies. Sabbatarians fought tirelessly to end non-religious activity on the Sabbath. Moral reform societies sought to end prostitution and redeem "fallen women." Over the course of the antebellum period, voluntary associations and benevolent activists also worked to reform bankruptcy laws, prison systems, insane asylums, labor laws, and education. They built orphanages and free medical dispensaries and developed programs to provide professional services like social work, job placement, and day camps for children in the slums.

These organizations often shared membership as individuals found themselves interested in a wide range of reform movements. On Anniversary Week, many of the major reform groups coordinated the schedules of their annual meetings in New York or Boston to allow individuals to attend multiple meetings in a single trip.[18]

Among all the social reform movements associated with the benevolent empire, the temperance crusade was the most successful. Championed by prominent preachers like Lyman Beecher, the movement's effort to curb the consumption of alcohol galvanized widespread support among the middle class. Alcohol consumption became a significant social issue

THE TREE OF INTEMPERANCE.

THE TREE OF TEMPERANCE.

N. Currier, *Tree of Temperance* and *Tree of Intemperance*, 1849. Courtesy American Antiquarian Society.

after the American Revolution. Commercial distilleries produced readily available, cheap whiskey that was frequently more affordable than milk or beer and safer than water, and hard liquor became a staple beverage in many lower- and middle-class households. Consumption among adults skyrocketed in the early nineteenth century, and alcoholism had become an endemic problem across the United States by the 1820s. As alcoholism became an increasingly visible issue in towns and cities, most reformers escalated their efforts from advocating moderation in liquor consumption to full abstinence from all alcohol.

Many reformers saw intemperance as the biggest impediment to maintaining order and morality in the young republic. Temperance reformers saw a direct correlation between alcohol and other forms of vice and, most importantly, felt that it endangered family life. In 1826, evangelical ministers organized the American Temperance Society to help spread the crusade nationally. It supported lecture campaigns, produced temperance literature, and organized revivals specifically aimed at encouraging worshippers to give up the drink. It was so successful that within a decade, it established five thousand branches and grew to over a million members.[19] Temperance reformers pledged not to touch the bottle and canvassed their neighborhoods and towns to encourage others to join their

"Cold Water Army." They also influenced lawmakers in several states to prohibit the sale of liquor.

In response to the perception that heavy drinking was associated with men who abused, abandoned, or neglected their family obligations, women formed a significant presence in societies dedicated to eradicating liquor. Temperance became a hallmark of middle-class respectability among both men and women and developed into a crusade with a visible class character. Temperance, like many other reform efforts, was championed by the middle class and threatened to intrude on the private lives of lower-class workers, many of whom were Irish Catholics. Such intrusions by the Protestant middle class exacerbated class, ethnic, and religious tensions. Still, while the temperance movement made less substantial inroads into lower-class workers' drinking culture, the movement was still a great success for reformers. In the 1840s, Americans drank half of what they had in the 1820s, and per capita consumption continued to decline over the next two decades.[20]

Though middle-class reformers worked tirelessly to cure all manner of social problems through institutional salvation and voluntary benevolent work, they regularly participated in religious organizations founded

Nathaniel Currier, *The Drunkard's Progress*, 1846. Wikimedia.

explicitly to address the spiritual mission at the core of evangelical Protestantism. In fact, for many reformers, it was actually the experience of evangelizing among the poor and seeing firsthand the rampant social issues plaguing life in the slums that first inspired them to get involved in benevolent reform projects. Modeling themselves on the British and Foreign Bible Society, formed in 1804 to spread Christian doctrine to the British working class, urban missionaries emphasized the importance of winning the world for Christ, one soul at a time. For example, the American Bible Society and the American Tract Society used the efficient new steam-powered printing press to distribute Bibles and evangelizing religious tracts throughout the United States. For example, the New York Religious Tract Society alone managed to distribute religious tracts to all but 388 of New York City's 28,383 families.[21] In places like Boston, New York, and Philadelphia, middle-class women also established groups specifically to canvass neighborhoods and bring the gospel to lower-class "wards."

Such evangelical missions extended well beyond the urban landscape, however. Stirred by nationalism and moral purpose, evangelicals labored to make sure the word of God reached far-flung settlers on the new American frontier. The American Bible Society distributed thousands of Bibles to frontier areas where churches and clergy were scarce, while the American Home Missionary Society provided substantial financial assistance to frontier congregations struggling to achieve self-sufficiency. Missionaries worked to translate the Bible into Iroquois and other languages in order to more effectively evangelize Native American populations. As efficient printing technology and faster transportation facilitated new transatlantic and global connections, religious Americans also began to flex their missionary zeal on a global stage. In 1810, for example, Presbyterian and Congregationalist leaders established the American Board of Commissioners for Foreign Missions to evangelize in India, Africa, East Asia, and the Pacific.[22]

The potent combination of social reform and evangelical mission at the heart of the nineteenth century's benevolent empire produced reform agendas and institutional changes that have reverberated through the twentieth and twenty-first centuries. By devoting their time to the moral uplift of their communities and the world at large, middle-class reformers created many of the largest and most influential organizations in the nation's history. For the optimistic, religiously motivated American, no problem seemed too great to solve.

Difficulties arose, however, when the benevolent empire attempted to take up more explicitly political issues. The movement against Na-

tive American removal was the first major example of this. Missionary
work had first brought the Cherokee Nation to the attention of northeastern evangelicals in the early nineteenth century. Missionaries sent by the
American Board and other groups sought to introduce Christianity and
American cultural values to the Cherokee and celebrated when their efforts
seemed to be met with success. Evangelicals proclaimed that the Cherokee
were becoming "civilized," which could be seen in their adoption of a written language and of a constitution modeled on that of the U.S. government.
Mission supporters were shocked, then, when the election of Andrew Jackson brought a new emphasis on the removal of Native Americans from
the land east of the Mississippi River. The Indian Removal Act of 1830
was met with fierce opposition from within the affected Native American
communities as well as from the benevolent empire. Jeremiah Evarts, one
of the leaders of the American Board, wrote a series of essays under the
pen name William Penn urging Americans to oppose removal.[23] He used
the religious and moral arguments of the mission movement but added a
new layer of politics in his extensive discussion of the history of treaty law
between the United States and Native Americans. This political shift was
even more evident when American missionaries challenged Georgia state
laws asserting sovereignty over Cherokee territory in the Supreme Court
Case *Worcester v. Georgia*.[24] Although the case was successful, the federal
government did not enforce the Court's decision, and Indian removal was
accomplished through the Trail of Tears, the tragic, forced removal of Native Americans to territories west of the Mississippi River.

Anti-removal activism was also notable for the entry of ordinary
American women into political discourse. The first major petition campaign by American women focused on opposition to removal and was led
(anonymously) by Catharine Beecher. Beecher was already a leader in the
movement to reform women's education and came to her role in removal
through her connections to the mission movement. Inspired by a meeting with Jeremiah Evarts, Beecher echoed his arguments from the William Penn letters in her appeal to American women.[25] Beecher called on
women to petition the government to end the policy of Indian removal.
She used religious and moral arguments to justify women's entry into political discussion when it concerned an obviously moral cause. This effort
was ultimately unsuccessful but still introduced the kinds of arguments
that paved the way for women's political activism for abolitionism and
women's rights. The divisions that the anti-removal campaign revealed
became more dramatic with the next political cause of nineteenth century
reformers: abolitionism.

V. Antislavery and Abolitionism

The revivalist doctrines of salvation, perfectionism, and disinterested benevolence led many evangelical reformers to believe that slavery was the most God-defying of all sins and the most terrible blight on the moral virtue of the United States. While white interest in and commitment to abolition had existed for several decades, organized antislavery advocacy had been largely restricted to models of gradual emancipation (seen in several northern states following the American Revolution) and conditional emancipation (seen in colonization efforts to remove Black Americans to settlements in Africa). The colonizationist movement of the early nineteenth century had drawn together a broad political spectrum of Americans with its promise of gradually ending slavery in the United States by removing the free Black population from North America. By the 1830s, however, a rising tide of anticolonization sentiment among northern free Black Americans and middle-class evangelicals' flourishing commitment to social reform radicalized the movement. Baptists such as William Lloyd Garrison, Congregational revivalists like Arthur and Lewis Tappan and Theodore Dwight Weld, and radical Quakers including Lucretia Mott and John Greenleaf Whittier helped push the idea of immediate emancipation onto the center stage of northern reform agendas. Inspired by a strategy known as "moral suasion," these young abolitionists believed they could convince enslavers to voluntarily release their enslaved laborers by appealing to their sense of Christian conscience. The result would be national redemption and moral harmony.

William Lloyd Garrison's early life and career famously illustrated this transition toward immediatism. As a young man immersed in the reform culture of antebellum Massachusetts, Garrison had fought slavery in the 1820s by advocating for both Black colonization and gradual abolition. Fiery tracts penned by Black northerners David Walker and James Forten, however, convinced Garrison that colonization was an inherently racist project and that African Americans possessed a hard-won right to the fruits of American liberty.[26] So, in 1831, he established a newspaper called *The Liberator*, through which he organized and spearheaded an unprecedented interracial crusade dedicated to promoting immediate emancipation and Black citizenship. Then, in 1833, Garrison presided as reformers from ten states came together to create the American Anti-Slavery Society. They rested their mission for immediate emancipation "upon the Declaration of our Independence, and upon the

truths of Divine Revelation," binding their cause to both national and Christian redemption.[27] Abolitionists fought to save the enslaved and thereby save the nation.

The Liberator, April 17, 1857. Masthead designed by Hammatt Billings in 1850. Metropolitan State University.

In order to accomplish their goals, abolitionists employed every method of outreach and agitation. At home in the North, abolitionists established hundreds of antislavery societies and worked with long-standing associations of Black activists to establish schools, churches, and voluntary associations. Women and men of all colors were encouraged to associate together in these spaces to combat what they termed "color phobia." Harnessing the potential of steam-powered printing and mass communication, abolitionists also blanketed the free states with pamphlets and antislavery newspapers. They blared their arguments from lyceum podiums and broadsides. Prominent individuals such as Wendell Phillips and Angelina Grimké saturated northern media with shame-inducing exposés of northern complicity in the return of freedom-seeking fugitive enslaved people, and white reformers sentimentalized slave narratives that tugged at middle-class heartstrings. Abolitionists used the U.S. Postal Service in 1835 to inundate southern enslavers with calls to emancipate their enslaved laborers in order to save their souls, and, in 1836, they prepared thousands of petitions for Congress as part of the Great Petition Campaign. In the six years from 1831 to 1837, abolitionist activities reached dizzying heights.[28]

However, such efforts encountered fierce opposition, as most Americans did not share abolitionists' particular brand of nationalism. In fact, abolitionists remained a small, marginalized group detested by most white Americans in both the North and the South. Immediatists were attacked as the harbingers of disunion, rabble-rousers who would stir up sectional tensions and thereby imperil the American experiment of self-government. Particularly troubling to some observers was the public engagement of women as abolitionist speakers and activists. Fearful of disunion and outraged by the interracial nature of abolitionism, northern mobs smashed abolitionist printing presses and even killed a prominent antislavery newspaper editor named Elijah Lovejoy. White southerners, believing that abolitionists had incited Nat Turner's rebellion in 1831, aggressively purged antislavery dissent from the region. Violent harassment threatened abolitionists' personal safety. In Congress, Whigs and Democrats joined forces in 1836 to pass an unprecedented restriction on freedom of political expression known as the gag rule, prohibiting all discussion of abolitionist petitions in the House of Representatives. Two years later, mobs attacked the Anti-Slavery Convention of American Women, throwing rocks through the windows and burning the newly constructed Pennsylvania Hall to the ground.[29]

In the face of such substantial external opposition, the abolitionist movement began to splinter. In 1839, an ideological schism shook the foundations of organized antislavery. Moral suasionists, led most prominently by William Lloyd Garrison, felt that the U.S. Constitution was a fundamentally pro-slavery document, and that the present political system was irredeemable. They dedicated their efforts exclusively toward persuading the public to redeem the nation by reestablishing it on antislavery grounds. However, many abolitionists, reeling from the level of entrenched opposition met in the 1830s, began to feel that moral suasion was no longer realistic. Instead, they believed, abolition would have to be effected through existing political processes. So, in 1839, political abolitionists formed the Liberty Party under the leadership of James G. Birney. This new abolitionist society was predicated on the belief that the U.S. Constitution was actually an antislavery document that could be used to abolish the stain of slavery through the national political system.[30]

Women's rights, too, divided abolitionists. Many abolitionists who believed full-heartedly in moral suasion nonetheless felt compelled to leave the American Anti-Slavery Society because, in part, it elevated women to leadership positions and endorsed women's suffrage. This question came to a head when, in 1840, Abby Kelly was elected to the business committee of the society. The elevation of women to full leadership roles was too much for some conservative members who saw this as evidence that the society had lost sight of its most important goal. Under the leadership of Arthur Tappan, they left to form the American and Foreign Anti-Slavery

Society. These disputes became so bitter and acrimonious that former friends cut social ties and traded public insults.

Another significant shift stemmed from the disappointments of the 1830s. Abolitionists in the 1840s increasingly moved from agendas based on reform to agendas based on resistance. Moral suasionists continued to appeal to hearts and minds, and political abolitionists launched sustained campaigns to bring abolitionist agendas to the ballot box. Meanwhile the entrenched and violent opposition of both enslavers and the northern public encouraged abolitionists to find other avenues of fighting the slave power. Increasingly, for example, abolitionists aided runaway enslaved people and established international antislavery networks to pressure the United States to abolish slavery. Frederick Douglass represented the intersection of these two trends. After escaping from slavery, Douglass came to the fore of the abolitionist movement as a naturally gifted orator and a powerful narrator of his experiences in slavery. His first autobiography, published in 1845, was so widely read that it was reprinted in nine editions and translated into several languages.[31] Douglass traveled to Great Britain in 1845 and met with famous British abolitionists like Thomas Clarkson, drumming up moral and financial support from Brit-

Frederick Douglass was perhaps the most famous African American abolitionist, fighting tirelessly not only for the end of slavery but for equal rights of all American citizens. This copy of a daguerreotype shows him as a young man, around the age of twenty-nine and soon after his self-emancipation. Print, c. 1850 after c. 1847 daguerreotype. Wikimedia.

ish and Irish antislavery societies. His great success abroad contributed significantly to rousing morale among weary abolitionists at home.

The model of resistance to the slave power only became more pronounced after 1850, when a long-standing Fugitive Slave Act was given new teeth. Though a legal mandate to return runaway enslaved people had existed in U.S. federal law since 1793, the Fugitive Slave Act of 1850 upped the ante by harshly penalizing officials who failed to arrest runaways and private citizens who tried to help them. This law, coupled with growing concern over the possibility that slavery would be allowed in Kansas when it was admitted as a state, made the 1850s a highly volatile and violent period of American antislavery. Reform took a backseat as armed mobs protected freedom-seeking enslaved people in the North and fortified abolitionists engaged in bloody skirmishes in the West. Culminating in John Brown's raid on Harper's Ferry, the violence of the 1850s convinced many Americans that the issue of slavery was pushing the nation to the brink of sectional cataclysm. After two decades of immediatist agitation, the idealism of revivalist perfectionism had given way to a protracted battle for the moral soul of the country.

For all of the problems that abolitionism faced, the movement was far from a failure. The prominence of African Americans in abolitionist organizations offered a powerful, if imperfect, model of interracial coexistence. While immediatists always remained a minority, their efforts paved the way for the moderately antislavery Republican Party to gain traction in the years preceding the Civil War. It is hard to imagine that Abraham Lincoln could have become president in 1860 without the ground prepared by antislavery advocates and without the presence of radical abolitionists against whom he could be cast as a moderate alternative. Though it ultimately took a civil war to break the bonds of slavery in the United States, the evangelical moral compass of revivalist Protestantism provided motivation for the embattled abolitionists.

VI. Women's Rights in Antebellum America

In the era of revivalism and reform, Americans understood the family and home as the hearthstones of civic virtue and moral influence. This increasingly confined middle-class white women to the domestic sphere, where they were responsible for educating children and maintaining household virtue. Yet women took the very ideology that defined their place in the home and managed to use it to fashion a public role for themselves. As a result, women actually became more visible and active in the public sphere than ever before. The influence of the Second Great Awakening, coupled with new educational opportunities available to girls and young women, enabled white middle-class women to leave their homes en masse, joining and forming societies dedicated to everything from literary interests to the antislavery movement.

In the early nineteenth century, the dominant understanding of gender claimed that women were the guardians of virtue and the spiritual heads of the home. Women were expected to be pious, pure, submissive, and domestic, and to pass these virtues on to their children. Historians have described these expectations as the "Cult of Domesticity," or the "Cult of True Womanhood," and they developed in tandem with industrialization, the market revolution, and the Second Great Awakening.[32] These economic and religious transformations increasingly seemed to divide the world into the public space of work and politics and the domestic space of leisure and morality. Voluntary work related to labor laws, prison reform, and antislavery applied women's roles as guardians of moral virtue to address all forms of social issues that they felt contributed to the moral decline of society. In spite of this apparent valuation of women's position in society, there were clear limitations. Under the terms of coverture, men gained legal control over their wives' property, and women with children had no legal rights over their offspring. Additionally, women could not initiate divorce, make wills, sign contracts, or vote.

Female education provides an example of the great strides made by and for women during the antebellum period. As part of a larger education reform movement in the early republic, several female reformers worked tirelessly to increase women's access to education. They argued that if women were to take charge of the education of their children, they needed to be well educated themselves. While the women's education movement did not generally push for women's political or social equality, it did assert women's intellectual equality with men, an idea that would eventually have important effects. Educators such as Emma Willard, Catharine Beecher, and Mary Lyon (founders of the Troy Female Seminary, Hartford Female Seminary, and Mount Holyoke Seminary, respectively) adopted the same rigorous curriculum that was used for boys. Many of these schools had the particular goal of training women to be teachers. Many graduates of these prominent seminaries would found their own schools, spreading women's education across the country, and with it ideas about women's potential to take part in public life.

The abolitionist movement was another important school for women's public engagement. Many of the earliest women's rights advocates began their activism by fighting the injustices of slavery, including Angelina and Sarah Grimké, Lucretia Mott, Sojourner Truth, Elizabeth Cady Stanton, and Susan B. Anthony. In the 1830s, women in cities such as Boston, New York, and Philadelphia established female societies dedicated to the antislavery cause. Initially, these societies were similar to the prayer and fund-raising-based projects of other reform societies. As such societies proliferated, however, their strategies changed. Women could not vote, for example, but they increasingly used their right to petition to express their antislavery grievances to the government. Impassioned women like the Grimké sisters even began to travel on lecture circuits. This latter strategy, born of fervent antislavery advocacy, ultimately tethered the cause of women's rights to abolitionism.

Sarah Moore Grimké and Angelina Emily Grimké were born to a wealthy family in Charleston, South Carolina, where they witnessed the horrors of slavery firsthand. Repulsed by the treatment of the enslaved laborers on the Grimké plantation, they decided to support the antislavery movement by sharing their experiences on northern lecture tours. At first speaking to female audiences, they soon attracted "promiscuous" crowds of both men and women. They were among the earliest and most famous American women to take such a public role in the name of reform. When the Grimké sisters met substantial harassment and opposition to their public speaking on antislavery, they were inspired to speak out against more than the slave system. They began to see that they would need to fight for women's rights in order to fight for the rights of enslaved people.[33] Other female abolitionists soon joined them in linking the issues of women's rights and abolitionism by drawing direct comparisons between the condition of free women in the United States and the condition of the slave.

As the antislavery movement gained momentum in northern states in the 1830s and 1840s, so too did efforts for women's rights. These efforts came to a head at an event that took place in London in 1840. That year, Lucretia Mott was among the American delegates attending the World Anti-Slavery Convention in London. Because of ideological disagreements between some of the abolitionists, the convention's organizers refused to seat the female delegates or allow them to vote during the proceedings. Angered by such treatment, Mott and Elizabeth Cady Stanton, whose husband was also a delegate, returned to the United States with a renewed interest in pursuing women's rights. In 1848, they organized the

Lucretia Mott campaigned for women's rights, abolition, and equality in the United States. Joseph Kyle (artist), *Lucretia Mott*, 1842. Wikimedia.

Seneca Falls Convention, a two-day summit in New York state in which women's rights advocates came together to discuss the problems facing women.

Stanton wrote the Declaration of Sentiments for the Seneca Falls Convention to capture the wide range of issues embraced by the early women's rights movement. She modeled the document on the Declaration of Independence to make explicit the connection between women's liberty and the rhetoric of America's founding. The Declaration of Sentiments outlined fifteen grievances and eleven resolutions. They championed property rights, access to the professions, and, most controversially, the right to vote. Sixty-eight women and thirty-two men, all of whom were already involved in some aspect of reform, signed the Declaration of Sentiments.[34]

Antebellum women's rights fought what they perceived as senseless gender discrimination, such as the barring of women from college and inferior pay for female teachers. They also argued that men and women should be held to the same moral standards. The Seneca Falls Convention was the first of many such gatherings promoting women's rights, held almost exclusively in the northern states. Yet the women's rights movement grew slowly and experienced few victories. Few states reformed married women's property laws before the Civil War, and no state was prepared to offer women the right to vote during the antebellum period. At the onset of the Civil War, women's rights advocates temporarily threw the bulk of their support behind abolition, allowing the cause of racial equality to temporarily trump that of gender equality. But the words of the Seneca Falls convention continued to inspire generations of activists.

VII. Conclusion

By the time civil war erupted in 1861, the revival and reform movements of the antebellum period had made an indelible mark on the American landscape. The Second Great Awakening ignited Protestant spirits by connecting evangelical Christians in national networks of faith. Social reform spurred members of the middle class to promote national morality and the public good. Not all reform projects were equally successful, however. While the temperance movement made substantial inroads against the excesses of alcohol consumption, the abolitionist movement proved so divisive that it paved the way for sectional crisis. Yet participation in reform movements, regardless of their ultimate success, encouraged many Americans to see themselves in new ways. Black activists became a powerful voice in antislavery societies, for example, developing domestic and transnational connections to pursue the cause of liberty. Middle-class women's dominant presence in the benevolent empire encouraged them to pursue a full-fledged women's right movement that has lasted in various forms up through the present day. In their efforts to make the United States a more virtuous and moral nation, nineteenth-century reform activists developed cultural and institutional foundations for social change that have continued to reverberate through the twentieth and twenty-first centuries.

VIII. Reference Material

This chapter was edited by Emily Conroy-Krutz, with content contributions by Elena Abbott, Cameron Blevins, Frank Cirillo, Justin Clark, Emily Conroy-Krutz, Nicolas Hoffmann, Christopher C. Jones, Jonathan Koefoed, Charles McCrary, William E. Skidmore, Megan Stanton, Kelly Weber, and Ben Wright.

Recommended citation: Elena Abbott et al., "Religion and Reform," Emily Conroy-Krutz, ed., in *The American Yawp*, eds. Joseph Locke and Ben Wright (Stanford, CA: Stanford University Press, 2019).

NOTES TO CHAPTER 10

1. Sam Haselby, *The Origins of American Religious Nationalism* (New York: Oxford University Press, 2015), 170.

2. Leigh Eric Schmidt, *Holy Fairs: Scotland and the Making of American Revivalism* (Grand Rapids, MI: Eerdmans, 2001).

3. John B. Boles, *The Great Revival: The Origins of the Southern Evangelical Mind* (Lexington: University Press of Kentucky, 1972).

4. Charles G. Finney, *Memoirs of Charles G. Finney* (New York: Revell, 1876), 78.

5. John H. Wigger, *Taking Heaven by Storm: Methodism and the Rise of Popular Christianity in America* (New York: Oxford University Press, 1998), 3, 197–200, 201n1.

6. Gary J. Dorrien, *The Making of American Liberal Theology: Imagining Progressive Religion, 1805–1900, Volume 1* (Louisville, KY: Westminster John Knox Press, 2001), 119.

7. David Edwin Harrell, *A Social History of the Disciples Christ: Quest for a Christian America, 1800–1865* (Tuscaloosa: University of Alabama Press, 1966).

8. Joseph Smith, "History, 1838–1856, volume A-1, 23 December 1805–30 August 1834," Joseph Smith Papers. http://josephsmithpapers.org/paper Summary/history-1838-1856-volume-a-1-23-december-1805-30-august-1834, accessed July 8, 2015.

9. Philip F. Gura, *American Transcendentalism: A History* (New York: Hill and Wang, 2008), 5.

10. Ralph Waldo Emerson, "The American Scholar." http://digitalemerson .wsulibs.wsu.edu/exhibits/show/text/the-american-scholar, accessed May 6, 2018; Ralph Waldo Emerson, "Self Reliance," in *Essays, First Series*. http://digitalemerson .wsulibs.wsu.edu/exhibits/show/text/first-series/self-reliance, accessed May 6, 2018.

11. Henry David Thoreau, *Walden, and On the Duty of Civil Disobedience*. http://www.gutenberg.org/files/205/205-h/205-h.htm, accessed May 6, 2018.

12. Sterling F. Delano, *Brook Farm: The Dark Side of Utopia* (Cambridge, MA: Harvard University Press, 2009).

13. Robert A. Gross and Mary Kelley, eds., *A History of the Book in America: Volume 2: An Extensive Republic: Print Culture, and Society in the New Nation, 1790–1840* (Chapel Hill: University of North Carolina Press, 2010), 112.

14. Frederick Douglass, *Narrative of the Life of Frederick Douglass, an American Slave, Written by Himself* (Boston: Anti-Slavery Office, 1845). http:// docsouth.unc.edu/neh/douglass/douglass.html.

15. Christopher Leslie Brown, *Moral Capital: Foundations of British Abolitionism* (Chapel Hill: University of North Carolina Press, 2012).

16. David Brion Davis, "The Emergence of Immediatism in British and American Antislavery Thought," *Journal of American History* 49, no. 2 (September 1962): 209–230.

17. Lori D. Ginzberg, *Women and the Work of Benevolence: Morality, Politics, and Class in the Nineteenth Century* (New Haven, CT: Yale University Press, 1990).

18. Michael P. Young, *Bearing Witness Against Sin: The Evangelical Birth of the American Social Movement* (Chicago: University of Chicago Press, 2006), 74–75.

19. Milton A. Maxwell, "Washingtonian Movement," *Quarterly Journal of Studies on Alcohol* 11 (1950): 410.

20. Jack S. Blocker, *American Temperance Movements: Cycles of Reform* (Boston: Hall, 1989).

21. David Paul Nord, *Faith in Reading: Religious Publishing and the Birth of Mass Media in America* (New York: Oxford University Press, 222), 85.

22. Emily Conroy-Krutz, *Christian Imperialism: Converting the World in the Early American Republic* (Ithaca, NY: Cornell University Press, 2015).

23. Jeremiah Evarts, *Essays on the Present Crisis in the Condition of the American Indians: First Published in the National Intelligencer, Under the Signature of William Penn* (Boston: Perkins and Marvin, 1829). http://eco.canadiana.ca/view/oocihm.51209/3?r=0&s=1.

24. *Worcester v. Georgia* (1832). https://www.law.cornell.edu/supremecourt/text/31/515.

25. Catharine Beecher, "Circular Addressed to the Benevolent Ladies of the U. States," December 25, 1829, in *The Cherokee Removal: A Brief History with Documents*, 2nd ed., ed. Theda Purdue and Michael D. Green (Boston: Bedford St. Martin's, 2005), 111–114.

26. See, for example, David Walker, *Walker's Appeal* (Boston: Walker, 1829) and James Forten, *Letters from A Man of Colour* (Philadelphia: s.n., 1813).

27. Paul Goodman, *Of One Blood: Abolitionism and the Origins of Racial Equality* (Berkeley: University of California Press, 1998), 105.

28. James Brewer Stewart, *Abolitionist Politics and the Coming of the Civil War* (Amherst: University of Massachusetts Press, 2008), 13–14.

29. Beverly C. Tomek, *Pennsylvania Hall: A "Legal Lynching" in the Shadow of the Liberty Bell* (New York: Oxford University Press, 2013).

30. Reinhard O. Johnson, *The Liberty Party, 1840–1848: Antislavery Third-Party Politics in the United States* (Baton Rouge: LSU Press, 2009).

31. Philip Gould, "The Rise, Development, and Circulation of the Slave Narrative," in *The Cambridge Companion to the African American Slave Narrative*, ed. Audrey Fisch (Cambridge, UK: Cambridge University Press, 2007), 24.

32. Barbara Welter, "The Cult of True Womanhood: 1820–1860," *American Quarterly* 18, no. 2 (1966): 151–174.

33. Gerda Lerner, *The Grimké Sisters from South Carolina: Pioneers for Women's Rights and Abolition* (Chapel Hill: University of North Carolina Press, 2009).

34. "Declaration of Sentiments," in Elizabeth Cady Stanton, Susan B. Anthony, and Matilda Joslyn Gage, *History of Woman Suffrage*, vol. 1 (Rochester, NY: Fowler and Wells, 1889), 70–71. http://legacy.fordham.edu/halsall/mod/senecafalls.asp.

RECOMMENDED READING

Berg, Barbara J. *The Remembered Gates: Origins of American Feminism, The Woman and the City 1800–1860*. New York: Oxford University Press, 1978.

Boylan, Anne. *The Origins of Women's Activism: New York and Boston, 1797–1840*. Chapel Hill: University of North Carolina Press, 2002.

Brekus, Catherine A. *Strangers and Pilgrims: Female Preaching in America, 1740–1845*. Chapel Hill: University of North Carolina Press, 1998.

Conroy-Krutz, Emily. *Christian Imperialism: Converting the World in the Early American Republic*. Ithaca, NY: Cornell University Press, 2015.

Dorsey, Bruce. *Reforming Men and Women: Gender in the Antebellum City*. Ithaca, NY: Cornell University Press, 2002.

DuBois, Ellen. *Feminism and Suffrage: The Emergence of an Independent Women's Movement in America, 1848–1869*. Ithaca, NY: Cornell University Press, 1999.

Ginzberg, Lori D. *Untidy Origins: A Story of Woman's Rights in Antebellum New York*. Chapel Hill: University of North Carolina Press, 2005.

Ginzberg, Lori. *Women and the Work of Benevolence: Morality, Politics, and Class in the 19th Century United States*. New Haven, CT: Yale University Press, 1990.

Hatch, Nathan O. *The Democratization of American Christianity*. New Haven, CT: Yale University Press, 1989.

Haynes, April R. *Riotous Flesh: Women, Physiology, and the Solitary Vice in Nineteenth Century America*. Chicago: University of Chicago Press, 2015.

Hempton, David. *Methodism: Empire of the Spirit*. New Haven, CT: Yale University Press, 2005.

Hewitt, Nancy. *Women's Activism and Social Change: Rochester, New York 1822–1872*. Ithaca, NY: Cornell University Press, 1984.

Jeffrey, Julie Roy. *The Great Silent Army of Abolitionism: Ordinary Women in the Antislavery Movement*. Chapel Hill: University of North Carolina Press, 1998.

Johnson, Paul. *A Shopkeepers Millennium: Society and Revivals in Rochester, New York, 1815–1837*. New York: Hill and Wang, 2004.

Juster, Susan. *Disorderly Women: Sexual Politics and Evangelicalism in Revolutionary New England*. Ithaca, NY: Cornell University Press, 1994.

Lerner, Gerda. *The Grimké Sisters from South Carolina: Pioneers for Women's Rights and Abolition*. Chapel Hill: University of North Carolina Press, 2009.

Makdisi, Ussama. *Artillery of Heaven: American Missionaries and the Failed Conversion of the Middle East*. Ithaca, NY: Cornell University Press, 2008.

McDaniel, W. Caleb. *The Problem of Democracy in the Age of Slavery: Garrisonian Abolitionists and Transatlantic Reform*. Baton Rouge: LSU Press, 2013.

Muncy, Raymond Lee. *Sex and Marriage in Utopian Communities: 19th Century America*. Bloomington: Indiana University Press, 1973.

Newman, Richard S., *The Transformation of American Abolitionism: Fighting Slavery in the Early Republic*. Chapel Hill: University of North Carolina Press, 2002.

Ryan, Mary P. *Cradle of the Middle Class: The Family in Oneida County, New York, 1790–1865*. New York: Cambridge University Press, 1981.

Ryan, Susan M. *The Grammar of Good Intentions: Race and the Antebellum Culture of Benevolence*. Ithaca, NY: Cornell University Press, 2003.

Sinha, Manisha. *The Slave's Cause: A History of Abolition*. New Haven, CT: Yale University Press, 2016.

Stewart, James Brewer. *Holy Warriors: The Abolitionists and American Slavery*. New York: Hill and Wang, 1996.

Tomek, Beverly C. *Colonization and Its Discontents: Emancipation, Emigration, and Antislavery in Antebellum Pennsylvania*. New York: New York University Press, 2011.

Walters, Ronald. *American Reformers, 1815–1860*. New York: Hill and Wang, 1997.

11

The Cotton Revolution

I. Introduction

In the decades leading up to the Civil War, the southern states experienced extraordinary change that would define the region and its role in American history for decades, even centuries, to come. Between the 1830s and the beginning of the Civil War in 1861, the American South expanded its wealth and population and became an integral part of an increasingly global economy. It did not, as previous generations of histories have told, sit back on its cultural and social traditions and insulate itself from an ex-

Eyre Crowe, *Slaves Waiting for Sale, Richmond, Virginia*, 1861. University of Virginia, The Atlantic Slave Trade and Slave Life in the Americas.

panding system of communication, trade, and production that connected Europe and Asia to the Americas. Quite the opposite; the South actively engaged new technologies and trade routes while also seeking to assimilate and upgrade its most "traditional" and culturally ingrained practices— such as slavery and agricultural production—within a modernizing world.

Beginning in the 1830s, merchants from the Northeast, Europe, Canada, Mexico, and the Caribbean flocked to southern cities, setting up trading firms, warehouses, ports, and markets. As a result, these cities— Richmond, Charleston, St. Louis, Mobile, Savannah, and New Orleans, to name a few—doubled and even tripled in size and global importance. Populations became more cosmopolitan, more educated, and wealthier. Systems of class—lower-, middle-, and upper-class communities— developed where they had never clearly existed. Ports that had once focused entirely on the importation of enslaved laborers and shipped only regionally became home to daily and weekly shipping lines to New York City, Liverpool, Manchester, Le Havre, and Lisbon. The world was slowly but surely coming closer together, and slavery was right in the middle.

II. The Importance of Cotton

In November 1785, the Liverpool firm of Peel, Yates & Co. imported the first seven bales of American cotton ever to arrive in Europe. Prior to this unscheduled, and frankly unwanted, delivery, European merchants saw cotton as a product of the colonial Caribbean islands of Barbados, Saint-Domingue (now Haiti), Martinique, Cuba, and Jamaica. The American South, though relatively wide and expansive, was the go-to source for rice and, most importantly, tobacco.

Few knew that the seven bales sitting in Liverpool that winter of 1785 would change the world. But they did. By the early 1800s, the American South had developed a niche in the European market for "luxurious" long-staple cotton grown exclusively on the Sea Islands off the coast of South Carolina, Georgia, and Florida.[1] But this was only the beginning of a massive flood to come and the foundation of the South's astronomical rise to global prominence. Before long, botanists, merchants, and planters alike set out to develop strains of cotton seed that would grow farther west on the southern mainland, especially in the new lands opened up by the Louisiana Purchase of 1803—an area that stretched from New Orleans in the South to what is today Minnesota, parts of the Dakotas, and Montana.

American and global cotton markets changed forever after Rush Nutt of Rodney, Mississippi, developed a hybrid strain of cotton in 1833 that he named Petit Gulf.[2] Petit Gulf, it was said, slid through the cotton gin—a machine developed by Eli Whitney in 1794 for deseeding cotton—more easily than any other strain. It also grew tightly, producing more usable cotton than anyone had imagined to that point. Perhaps most importantly, though, it came up at a time when Native peoples were removed from the Southwest—southern Georgia, Alabama, Mississippi, and northern Louisiana. After Indian removal, land became readily available for white men with a few dollars and big dreams. Throughout the 1820s and 1830s, the federal government implemented several forced migrations of Native Americans, establishing a system of reservations west of the Mississippi River on which all eastern peoples were required to relocate and settle. This system, enacted through the Indian Removal Act of 1830, allowed the federal government to survey, divide, and auction off millions of acres of land for however much bidders were willing to pay. Suddenly, farmers with dreams of owning a large plantation could purchase dozens, even hundreds, of acres in the fertile Mississippi River Delta for cents on the dollar. Pieces of land that would cost thousands of dollars elsewhere sold in the 1830s for several hundred, at prices as low as 40¢ per acre.[3]

Thousands rushed into the Cotton Belt. Joseph Holt Ingraham, a writer and traveler from Maine, called it a "mania."[4] William Henry

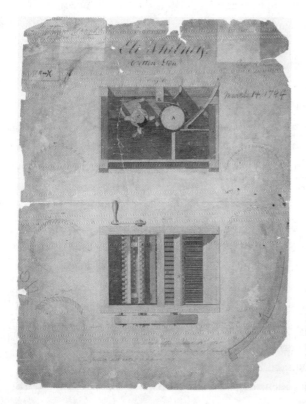

Eli Whitney's mechanical cotton gin revolutionized cotton production and expanded and strengthened slavery throughout the South. Eli Whitney's patent for the cotton gin, March 14, 1794; Records of the Patent and Trademark Office; Record Group 241. Wikimedia.

A nineteenth-century cotton gin on display at the Eli Whitney Museum. Wikimedia.

Sparks, a lawyer living in Natchez, Mississippi, remembered it as "a new El Dorado" in which "fortunes were made in a day, without enterprise or work." The change was astonishing. "Where yesterday the wilderness darkened over the land with her wild forests," he recalled, "to-day the cotton plantations whitened the earth."[5] Money flowed from banks, many newly formed, on promises of "other-worldly" profits and overnight returns. Banks in New York City, Baltimore, Philadelphia, and even London offered lines of credit to anyone looking to buy land in the Southwest. Some even sent their own agents to purchase cheap land at auction for the express purpose of selling it, sometimes the very next day, at double and triple the original value, a process known as speculation.

The explosion of available land in the fertile Cotton Belt brought new life to the South. By the end of the 1830s, Petit Gulf cotton had been perfected, distributed, and planted throughout the region. Advances in steam power and water travel revolutionized southern farmers' and planters' ability to deseed and bundle their products and move them to ports popping up along the Atlantic seaboard. Indeed, by the end of the 1830s, cotton had become the primary crop not only of the southwestern states but of the entire nation.

The numbers were staggering. In 1793, just a few years after the first, albeit unintentional, shipment of American cotton to Europe, the South produced around five million pounds of cotton, again almost exclusively the product of South Carolina's Sea Islands. Seven years later, in 1800, South Carolina remained the primary cotton producer in the South, sending 6.5 million pounds of the luxurious long-staple blend to markets in Charleston, Liverpool, London, and New York.[6] But as the tighter, more abundant, and vibrant Petit Gulf strain moved west with the dreamers, schemers, and speculators, the American South quickly became the world's leading cotton producer. By 1835, the five main cotton-growing states—South Carolina, Georgia, Alabama, Mississippi, and Louisiana—produced more than five hundred million pounds of Petit Gulf for a global market stretching from New Orleans to New York and to London, Liverpool, Paris and beyond. That five hundred million pounds of cotton made up nearly 55 percent of the entire United States export market, a trend that continued nearly every year until the outbreak of the Civil War. Indeed, the two billion pounds of cotton produced in 1860 alone amounted to more than 60 percent of the United States' total exports for that year.[7]

The astronomical rise of American cotton production came at the cost of the South's first staple crop—tobacco. Perfected in Virginia but grown and sold in nearly every southern territory and state, tobacco served as the South's main economic commodity for more than a century. But tobacco was a rough crop. It treated the land poorly, draining the soil of nutrients. Tobacco fields did not last forever. In fact, fields rarely survived more than four or five cycles of growth, which left them dried and barren, incapable of growing much more than patches of grass. Of course, tobacco is, and was, an addictive substance, but because of its declining yields, farmers had to move around, purchasing new lands, developing new methods of production, and even creating new fields through deforestation and westward expansion. Tobacco, then, was expensive to produce—and not only because of the ubiquitous use of slave labor. It required massive, temporary fields, large numbers of laborers, and constant movement.

Cotton was different, and it arrived at a time best suited for its success. Petit Gulf cotton, in particular, grew relatively quickly on cheap, widely available land. With the invention of the cotton gin in 1794, and the emergence of steam power three decades later, cotton became the common person's commodity, the product with which the United States could expand westward, producing and reproducing Thomas Jefferson's vision of an idyllic republic of small farmers—a nation in control of its land, reaping the benefits of honest, free, and self-reliant work, a nation of families and farmers, expansion and settlement. But this all came at a violent

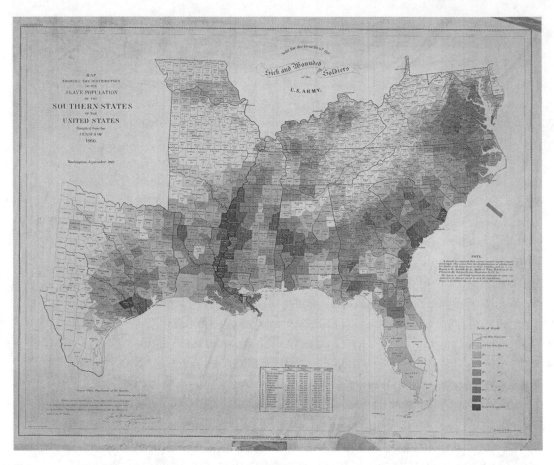

This map, published by the U.S. Coast Guard, shows the percentage of enslaved people in the population in each county of the slave-holding states in 1860. The highest percentages lie along the Mississippi River, in the "Black Belt" of Alabama, and coastal South Carolina, all of which were centers of agricultural production (cotton and rice) in the United States. E. Hergesheimer (cartographer) and Th. Leonhardt (engraver), *Map Showing the Distribution of the Slave Population of the Southern States of the United States Compiled from the Census of 1860*, c. 1861. Wikimedia.

cost. With the democratization of land ownership through Native American removal, federal auctions, readily available credit, and the seemingly universal dream of cotton's immediate profit, one of the South's lasting traditions became normalized and engrained. And by the 1860s, that very tradition, seen as the backbone of southern society and culture, would split the nation in two. The heyday of American slavery had arrived.

III. Cotton and Slavery

The rise of cotton and the resulting upsurge in the United States' global position wed the South to slavery. Without slavery there could be no Cotton Kingdom, no massive production of raw materials stretching across thousands of acres worth millions of dollars. Indeed, cotton grew alongside slavery. The two moved hand-in-hand. The existence of slavery and its importance to the southern economy became the defining factor in what would be known as the Slave South. Although slavery arrived in the Americas long before cotton became a profitable commodity, the use and purchase of enslaved laborers, the moralistic and economic justifications for the continuation of slavery, and even the urgency to protect the practice from extinction before the Civil War all received new life from the rise of cotton and the economic, social, and cultural growth spurt that accompanied its success.

Slavery had existed in the South since at least 1619, when a group of Dutch traders arrived at Jamestown with twenty Africans. Although these Africans remained under the ambiguous legal status of "unfree" rather than being actually enslaved, their arrival set in motion a practice that would stretch across the entire continent over the next two centuries. Slavery was everywhere by the time the American Revolution created the United States, although northern states began a process of gradually abolishing the practice soon thereafter. In the more rural, agrarian South, slavery became a way of life, especially as farmers expanded their lands, planted more crops, and entered the international trade market. By 1790, two years after the ratification of the Constitution, 654,121 enslaved people lived in the South—then just Maryland, Virginia, North Carolina, South Carolina, Georgia, and the Southwest Territory (now

Though taken after the end of slavery, these stereographs show various stages of cotton production. The fluffy white staple fiber is first extracted from the boll (a prickly, sharp protective capsule), after which the seed is separated in the ginning and taken to a storehouse. Unknown, *Picking cotton in a great plantation in North Carolina, U.S.A.*, c. 1865–1903. Wikimedia.

Tennessee). Just twenty years later, in 1810, that number had increased to more than 1.1 million individuals in bondage.[8]

The massive change in the South's enslaved population between 1790 and 1810 makes historical sense. During that time, the South advanced from a region of four states and one rather small territory to a region of six states (Virginia, North and South Carolina, Georgia, Kentucky, and Tennessee) and three rather large territories (Mississippi, Louisiana, and Orleans). The free population of the South also nearly doubled over that period—from around 1.3 million in 1790 to more than 2.3 million in 1810. The enslaved population of the South did not increase at any rapid rate over the next two decades, until the cotton boom took hold in the mid-1830s. Indeed, following the constitutional ban on the international slave trade in 1808, the number of enslaved people in the South increased by just 750,000 in twenty years.

But then cotton came, and grew, and changed everything. Over the course of the 1830s, 1840s, and 1850s, slavery became so endemic to the Cotton Belt that travelers, writers, and statisticians began referring to the area as the Black Belt, not only to describe the color of the rich land but also to describe the skin color of those forced to work its fields, line its docks, and move its products.

Perhaps the most important aspect of southern slavery during this so-called Cotton Revolution was the value placed on both the work and the bodies of the enslaved themselves. Once the fever of the initial land rush subsided, land values became more static and credit less free-flowing. For Mississippi land that in 1835 cost no more than $600, a farmer or investor would have to shell out more than $3,000 in 1850. By 1860, that same land, depending on its record of production and location, could cost as much as $100,000.[9] In many cases, cotton growers, especially planters with large lots and enslaved workforces, put up enslaved laborers as collateral for funds dedicated to buying more land. If that land, for one reason or another, be it weevils, a late freeze, or a simple lack of nutrients, did not produce a viable crop within a year, the planter would lose not only the new land but also the enslaved laborers he or she put up as a guarantee of payment.

So much went into the production of cotton, the expansion of land, and the maintenance of enslaved workforces that by the 1850s, nearly every ounce of credit offered by southern, and even northern, banks dealt directly with some aspect of the cotton market. Millions of dollars changed hands. Enslaved people, the literal and figurative backbone of the southern cotton economy, served as the highest and most important

SALE OF ESTATES, PICTURES AND SLAVES IN THE ROTUNDA, NEW ORLEANS.

The slave markets of the South varied in size and style, but the St. Louis Exchange in New Orleans was so frequently described that it became a kind of representation for all southern slave markets. Indeed, the St. Louis Hotel rotunda was cemented in the literary imagination of nineteenth-century Americans after Harriet Beecher Stowe chose it as the site for the sale of Uncle Tom in her 1852 novel, *Uncle Tom's Cabin*. After the ruin of the St. Clare plantation, Tom and his fellow enslaved people were suddenly property that had to be liquidated. Brought to New Orleans to be sold to the highest bidder, Tom found himself "beneath a splendid dome" where "men of all nations" scurried about. J. M. Starling (engraver), *Sale of estates, pictures and slaves in the rotunda, New Orleans*, 1842. Wikimedia.

expense for any successful cotton grower. Prices for enslaved laborers varied drastically, depending on skin color, sex, age, and location, both of purchase and birth. In Virginia in the 1820s, for example, a single enslaved woman of childbearing age sold for an average of $300; an unskilled man above age eighteen sold for around $450; and boys and girls below age thirteen sold for between $100 and $150.[10]

By the 1840s and into the 1850s, prices had nearly doubled—a result of both standard inflation and the increasing importance of enslaved laborers in the cotton market. In 1845, "plow boys" under age eighteen sold for more than $600 in some areas, measured at "five or six dollars per pound."[11] "Prime field hands," as they were called by merchants and traders, averaged $1,600 at market by 1850, a figure that fell in line with the rising prices of the cotton they picked. For example, when cotton sat at 7¢ per pound in 1838, the average "field hand" cost around $700. As the price of cotton increased to 9¢, 10¢, then 11¢ per pound over the next ten years, the average cost of an enslaved male laborer likewise rose to $775, $900, and then more than $1,600.[12]

The key is that cotton and enslaved labor helped define each other, at least in the cotton South. By the 1850s, slavery and cotton had become so intertwined that the very idea of change—be it crop diversity, antislavery ideologies, economic diversification, or the increasingly staggering cost of purchasing and maintaining enslaved laborers—became anathema to the southern economic and cultural identity. Cotton had become the foundation of the southern economy. Indeed, it was the only major product, besides perhaps sugarcane in Louisiana, that the South could effectively market internationally. As a result, southern planters, politicians, merchants, and traders became more and more dedicated—some would say "obsessed"—to the means of its production: slavery. In 1834, Joseph Ingraham wrote that "to sell cotton in order to buy negroes—to make more cotton to buy more negroes, 'ad infinitum,' is the aim and direct tendency of all the operations of the thorough going cotton planter; his whole soul is wrapped up in the pursuit."[13] Twenty-three years later, such pursuit had taken a seemingly religious character, as James Stirling, an Englishman traveling through the South, observed, "[slaves] and cotton—cotton and [slaves]; these are the law and the prophets to the men of the South."[14]

The Cotton Revolution was a time of capitalism, panic, stress, and competition. Planters expanded their lands, purchased enslaved laborers, extended lines of credit, and went into massive amounts of debt because they were constantly working against the next guy, the newcomer, the social mover, the speculator, the trader. A single bad crop could cost even the most wealthy planter his or her entire life, along with those of his or her enslaved laborers and their families. Although the cotton market was large and profitable, it was also fickle, risky, and cost intensive. The more wealth one gained, the more land one needed to procure, which led to more enslaved laborers, more credit, and more mouths to feed. The decades before the Civil War in the South, then, were not times of slow, simple tradition. They were times of high competition, high risk, and high reward, no matter where one stood in the social hierarchy. But the risk was not always economic.

The most tragic, indeed horrifying, aspect of slavery was its inhumanity. All enslaved people had memories, emotions, experiences, and thoughts. They saw their experiences in full color, felt the pain of the lash, the heat of the sun, and the heartbreak of loss, whether through

In southern cities like Norfolk, Virginia, markets sold not only vegetables, fruits, meats, and sundries, but also enslaved people. Enslaved men and women, like the two walking in the direct center, lived and labored next to free people, Black and white. S. Weeks, *Market Square, Norfolk*, from Henry Howe's Historical Collections of Virginia, 1845. Wikimedia.

death, betrayal, or sale. Communities developed on a shared sense of suffering, common work, and even family ties. Enslaved people communicated in the slave markets of the urban South and worked together to help their families, ease their loads, or simply frustrate their enslavers. Simple actions of resistance, such as breaking a hoe, running a wagon off the road, causing a delay in production due to injury, running away, or even pregnancy provided a language shared by nearly all enslaved laborers, a sense of unity that remained unsaid but was acted out daily.

Beyond the basic and confounding horror of it all, the problem of slavery in the cotton South was twofold. First and most immediate was the fear and risk of rebellion. With nearly four million individual enslaved people residing in the South in 1860, and nearly 2.5 million living in the Cotton Belt alone, the system of communication, resistance, and potential violence among enslaved people did not escape the minds of enslavers across the region and the nation as a whole. As early as 1785, Thomas Jefferson wrote in his *Notes on the State of Virginia* that the enslaved should be freed, but then they should be colonized to another country, where they could become an "independant people." White people's prejudices, and Black people's "recollections . . . of the injuries they have sustained" under slavery, would keep the two races from successfully living together in America. If freed people were not colonized, eventually there would be "convulsions which will probably never end but in the extermination of the one or the other race."[15]

Southern writers, planters, farmers, merchants, and politicians expressed the same fears more than a half century later. "The South cannot recede," declared an anonymous writer in an 1852 issue of the New Orleans–based *De Bow's Review*. "She must fight *for* her slaves or *against* them. Even cowardice would not save her."[16] To many enslavers in the South, slavery was the saving grace of not only their own economic stability but also the maintenance of peace and security in everyday life. Much of pro-slavery ideology rested on the notion that slavery provided a sense of order, duty, and legitimacy to the lives of individual enslaved people, feelings that Africans and African Americans, it was said, could not otherwise experience. Without slavery, many thought, "blacks" (the word most often used for "slaves" in regular conversation) would become violent, aimless, and uncontrollable.

Some commentators recognized the problem in the 1850s as the internal slave trade, the legal trade of enslaved laborers between states, along rivers, and along the Atlantic coastline. The internal trade picked up in the decade before the Civil War. The problem was rather simple. The more enslaved laborers one owned, the more money it cost to maintain them and to extract product from their work. As planters and cotton growers expanded their lands and purchased more enslaved laborers, their expectations increased.

And productivity, in large part, did increase. But it came on the backs of enslaved laborers with heavier workloads, longer hours, and more intense punishments. "The great limitation to *production is labor*," wrote one commentator in the *American Cotton Planter* in 1853. And many planters recognized this limitation and worked night and day, sometimes literally, to find the furthest extent of that limit.[17] According to some contemporary accounts, by the mid-1850s, the expected production of an individual enslaved person in Mississippi's Cotton Belt had increased from between four and five bales (weighing about 500 pounds each) per day to between eight and ten bales per day, on average.[18] Other, perhaps more reliable sources, such as the account book of Buena Vista Plantation in Tensas Parish, Louisiana, list average daily production at between 300 and 500 pounds "per hand," with weekly averages ranging from 1,700 to 2,100 pounds "per hand." Cotton production "per hand" increased by 600 percent in Mississippi between 1820 and 1860.[19] Each slave, then, was working longer, harder hours to keep up with his or her enslaver's expected yield.

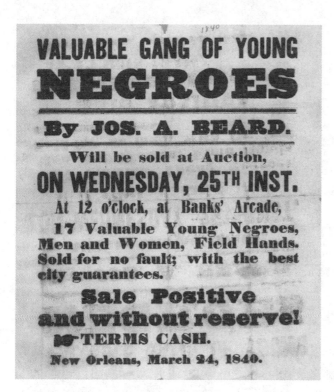

The slave trade sold bondspeople—men, women, and children—like mere pieces of property, as seen in the advertisements produced during the era. 1840 poster advertising enslaved laborers for sale in New Orleans. Wikimedia.

Here was capitalism with its most colonial, violent, and exploitative face. Humanity became a commodity used and worked to produce profit for a select group of investors, regardless of its shortfalls, dangers, and immoralities. But slavery, profit, and cotton did not exist only in the rural South. The Cotton Revolution sparked the growth of an urban South, cities that served as southern hubs of a global market, conduits through which the work of enslaved people and the profits of planters met and funded a wider world.

IV. The South and the City

Much of the story of slavery and cotton lies in the rural areas where cotton actually grew. Enslaved laborers worked in the fields, and planters and farmers held reign over their plantations and farms. But the 1830s, 1840s, and 1850s saw an extraordinary spike in urban growth across the South. For nearly a half century after the Revolution, the South existed as a series of plantations, county seats, and small towns, some connected by roads, others connected only by rivers, streams, and lakes. Cities certainly existed, but they served more as local ports than as regional, or national, commercial hubs. For example, New Orleans, then the capital of Louisiana, which entered the union in 1812, was home to just over 27,000 people in 1820; and even with such a seemingly small population, it was the second-largest city in the South—Baltimore had more than 62,000 people in 1820.[20] Given the standard nineteenth-century measurement of an urban space (2,500+ people), the South had just ten in that year, one of which—Mobile, Alabama—contained only 2,672 individuals, nearly half of whom were enslaved.[21]

As late as the 1820s, southern life was predicated on a rural lifestyle—farming, laboring, acquiring land and enslaved laborers, and producing whatever that land and those enslaved laborers could produce. The market, often located in the nearest town or city, rarely stretched beyond state lines. Even in places like New Orleans, Charleston, and Norfolk, Virginia, which had active ports as early as the 1790s, shipments rarely, with some notable exceptions, left American waters or traveled farther than the closest port down the coast. In the first decades of the nineteenth century, American involvement in international trade was largely confined to ports in New York, Boston, Philadelphia, and sometimes Baltimore—which loosely falls under the demographic category of the South. Imports dwarfed exports. In 1807, U.S. imports outnumbered exports by nearly $100 million, and even as the Napoleonic Wars broke out in Europe, causing a drastic decrease in European production and trade, the United States still took in almost $50 million more than it sent out.[22]

Cotton changed much of this, at least with respect to the South. Before cotton, the South had few major ports, almost none of which actively maintained international trade routes or even domestic supply routes. Internal travel and supply was difficult, especially on the waters of the Mississippi River, the main artery of the North American continent, and the eventual gold mine of the South. With the Mississippi's strong current, deadly undertow, and constant sharp turns, sandbars, and subsystems, navigation was difficult and dangerous. The river promised a revolution in trade, transportation, and commerce only *if* the technology existed to handle its impossible bends and fight against its southbound current. By the 1820s and into the 1830s, small ships could successfully navigate their way to New Orleans from as far north as Memphis and even St. Louis, if they so dared. But the problem was getting back. Most often, traders and sailors scuttled their boats on landing in New Orleans, selling the wood for a quick profit or a journey home on a wagon or caravan.

The rise of cotton benefited from a change in transportation technology that aided and guided the growth of southern cotton into one of the world's leading commodities. In January 1812, a 371-ton ship called the

New Orleans arrived at its namesake city from the distant internal port of Pittsburgh, Pennsylvania. This was the first steamboat to navigate the internal waterways of the North American continent from one end to the other and remain capable of returning home. The technology was far from perfect—the *New Orleans* sank two years later after hitting a submerged sandbar covered in driftwood—but its successful trial promised a bright, new future for river-based travel.

And that future was, indeed, bright. Just five years after the *New Orleans* arrived in its city, 17 steamboats ran regular upriver lines. By the mid-1840s, more than 700 steamboats did the same. In 1860, the port of New Orleans received and unloaded 3,500 steamboats, all focused entirely on internal trade. These boats carried around 160,000 tons of raw product that merchants, traders, and agents converted into nearly $220 million in trade, all in a single year.[23] More than 80 percent of the yield was from cotton alone, the product of the same fields tilled, expanded, and sold over the preceding three decades. Only now, in the 1840s and 1850s, could those fields, plantations, and farms simply load

Gordon, pictured here, endured terrible brutality from his enslaver before escaping to Union Army lines in 1863. He would become a soldier and help fight to end the violent system that produced the horrendous scars on his back. Matthew Brady, *Gordon*, 1863. Wikimedia.

their products onto a boat and wait for the profit, credit, or supplies to return from downriver.

The explosion of steam power changed the face of the South, and indeed the nation as a whole. Everything that could be steam-powered was steam-powered, sometimes with mixed results. Cotton gins, wagons, grinders, looms, and baths, among countless others, all fell under the net of this new technology. Most importantly, the South's rivers, lakes, and bays were no longer barriers and hindrances to commerce. Quite the opposite; they had become the means by which commerce flowed, the roads of a modernizing society and region. And most importantly, the ability to use internal waterways connected the rural interior to increasingly urban ports, the sources of raw materials—cotton, tobacco, wheat, and so on—to an eager global market.

Coastal ports like New Orleans, Charleston, Norfolk, and even Richmond became targets of steamboats and coastal carriers. Merchants, traders, skilled laborers, and foreign speculators and agents flooded the towns. In fact, the South experienced a a greater rate of urbanization between 1820 and 1860 than the seemingly more industrial, urban-based North. Urbanization of the South simply looked different from that seen in the North and in Europe. Where most northern and some European cities (most notably London, Liverpool, Manchester, and Paris) developed along the lines of industry, creating public spaces to boost the morale of wage laborers in factories, on the docks, and in storehouses, southern cities developed within the cyclical logic of sustaining the trade in cotton that justified and paid for the maintenance of an enslaved labor force. The growth of southern cities, then, allowed slavery to flourish and brought the South into a more modern world.

Between 1820 and 1860, quite a few southern towns experienced dramatic population growth, which paralleled the increase in cotton production and international trade to and from the South. The 27,176 people New Orleans claimed in 1820 expanded to more than 168,000 by 1860. In fact, in New Orleans, the population nearly quadrupled from 1830 to 1840 as the Cotton Revolution hit full stride. At the same time, Charleston's population nearly doubled, from 24,780 to 40,522; Richmond expanded threefold, growing from a town of 12,067 to a capital city of 37,910; and St. Louis experienced the largest increase of any city in the nation, expanding from a frontier town of 10,049 to a booming Mississippi River metropolis of 160,773.[24]

The city and the field, the urban center and the rural space, were inextricably linked in the decades before the Civil War. And that relationship connected the region to a global market and community. As southern cities grew, they became more cosmopolitan, attracting types of people either unsuited for or uninterested in rural life. These people—merchants, skilled laborers, traders, sellers of all kinds and colors—brought rural goods to a market desperate for raw materials. Everyone, it seemed, had a place in the cotton trade. Agents, many of them transients from the North, and in some cases Europe, represented the interests of planters and cotton farmers in the cities, making connections with traders who in turn made deals with manufactories in the Northeast, Liverpool, and Paris.

Among the more important aspects of southern urbanization was the development of a middle class in the urban centers, something that never fully developed in the more rural areas. In a very general sense, the rural South fell under a two-class system in which a landowning elite controlled the politics and most of the capital, and a working poor survived on subsistence farming or basic, unskilled labor funded by the elite. The development of large urban centers founded on trade, and flush with transient populations of sailors, merchants, and travelers, gave rise to a large, highly developed middle class in the South. Predicated on the idea of separation from those above and below them, middle-class men and women in the South thrived in the active, feverish rush of port city life.

Skilled craftsmen, merchants, traders, speculators, and store owners made up the southern middle class. Fashion trends that no longer served their original purpose—such as a broad-brimmed hat to protect one from the sun, knee-high boots for horse riding, and linen shirts and trousers to fight the heat of an unrelenting sun—lost popularity at an astonishing rate. Silk, cotton, and bright colors came into vogue, especially in coastal cities like New Orleans and Charleston; cravats, golden brooches, diamonds, and "the best stylings of Europe" became the standards of urban middle-class life in the South.[25] Neighbors, friends, and business partners formed and joined the same benevolent societies. These societies worked to aid the less fortunate in society, the orphans, the impoverished, the destitute. But in many cases these benevolent societies simply served as a way to keep other people out of middle-class circles, sustaining both wealth and social prestige within an insular, well-regulated community. Members and partners married each other's sisters, stood as godparents for each other's children, and served, when the time came, as executors of fellow members' wills.

The city bred exclusivity. That was part of the rush, part of the fever of the time. Built upon the cotton trade, funded by European and northeastern merchants, markets, and manufactories, southern cities became the headquarters of the nation's largest and most profitable commodities—cotton and enslaved people. And they welcomed the world with open checkbooks and open arms.

V. Southern Cultures

To understand the global and economic functions of the South, we also must understand the people who made the whole thing work. The South, more than perhaps any other region in the United States, had a great diversity of cultures and situations. The South still relied on the existence of slavery; as a result, it was home to nearly four million enslaved people by 1860, amounting to more than 45 percent of the entire Southern population.[26] Naturally, these people, though fundamentally unfree in their movement, developed a culture all their own. They created kinship and family networks, systems of (often illicit) trade, linguistic codes, religious congregations, and even benevolent and social aid organizations—all within the grip of slavery, a system dedicated to extraction rather than development, work and production rather than community and emotion.

The concept of family, more than anything else, played a crucial role in the daily lives of enslaved people. Family and kinship networks, and the benefits they carried, represented an institution through which enslaved people could piece together a sense of community, a sense of feeling and dedication, separate from the forced system of production that defined their daily lives. The creation of family units, distant relations, and communal traditions allowed enslaved people to maintain religious beliefs, ancient ancestral traditions, and even names passed down from generation to generation in a way that challenged enslavement. Ideas passed between relatives on different plantations, names given to children in honor of the deceased, and basic forms of love and devotion created a sense of individuality, an identity that assuaged the loneliness and desperation of enslaved life. Family defined how each plantation, each community, functioned, grew, and labored.

Nothing under slavery lasted long, at least not in the same form. Enslaved families and networks were no exceptions to this rule. African-born enslaved people during the seventeenth and eighteenth centuries engaged in marriages—sometimes polygamous—with those of the same ethnic groups whenever possible. This, most importantly, allowed for the maintenance of cultural traditions, such as language, religion, name practices, and even the rare practice of bodily scarring. In some parts of the South, such as Louisiana and coastal South Carolina, ethnic homogeneity thrived, and as a result, traditions and networks survived relatively unchanged for decades. As the number of enslaved people arriving in the United States increased, and generations of American-born enslaved laborers overtook the original African-born populations, the practice of marriage, especially among members of the same ethnic group or even simply the same plantation, became vital to the continuation of aging traditions. Marriage served as the single most important aspect of cultural and identity formation, as it connected enslaved people to their own pasts and gave some sense of protection for the future.[27] By the start of the Civil War, approximately two thirds of enslaved people were members of nuclear households, each household averaging six people— mother, father, children, and often a grandparent, elderly aunt or uncle, and even "in-laws." Those who did not have a marriage bond, or even a nuclear family, still maintained family ties, most often living with a single parent, brother, sister, or grandparent.[28]

Many marriages between enslaved people endured for many years. But the threat of disruption, often through sale, always loomed. As the internal slave trade increased following the constitutional ban on slave importation in 1808 and the rise of cotton in the 1830s and 1840s, enslaved families, especially those established prior to arriving in the United

Free people of color were present throughout the American South, particularly in urban areas like Charleston and New Orleans. Some were relatively well off, like this *femme de couleur libre* who posed with her mixed-race child in front of her New Orleans home, maintaining a middling position between free white people and enslaved Black people. Free woman of color with quadroon daughter; late eighteenth-century collage painting, New Orleans. Wikimedia.

States, came under increased threat. Hundreds of thousands of marriages, many with children, fell victim to sale "downriver"—a euphemism for the near-constant flow of enslaved laborers down the Mississippi River to the developing cotton belt in the Southwest.[29] In fact, during the Cotton Revolution alone, between one fifth and one third of all marriages between enslaved people were broken up through sale or forced migration. But this was not the only threat. Planters and enslavers of all shapes and sizes recognized that marriage was, in the most basic and tragic sense, a privilege granted and defined by them for their enslaved laborers. And as a result, many enslavers used marriages, or the threats thereto, to squeeze out more production, counteract disobedience, or simply make a gesture of power and superiority.

Threats to family networks, marriages, and household stability did not stop with the death of an enslaver. An enslaved couple could live their entire lives together, even having been born, raised, and married on the slave plantation, and, following the death of their enslaver, find themselves at opposite sides of the known world. It only took a single relative, executor, creditor, or friend of the deceased to make a claim against the estate to cause the sale and dispersal of an entire enslaved community.

Enslaved women were particularly vulnerable to the shifts of fate attached to slavery. In many cases, enslaved women did the same work as men, spending the day—from sunup to sundown—in the fields picking and bundling cotton. In some rare cases, especially among the larger plantations, planters tended to use women as house servants more than men, but this was not universal. In both cases, however, enslaved women's experiences were different than their male counterparts, husbands, and neighbors. Sexual violence, unwanted pregnancies, and constant child-rearing while continuing to work the fields all made life as an enslaved woman more prone to disruption and uncertainty. Harriet Jacobs, an enslaved woman from North Carolina, chronicled her enslaver's attempts to sexually abuse her in her narrative, *Incidents in the Life of a Slave Girl*. Jacobs suggested that her successful attempts to resist sexual assault and her determination to love whom she pleased was "something akin to freedom."[30] But this "freedom," however empowering and contextual, did not cast a wide net. Many enslaved women had no choice concerning love, sex, and motherhood. On plantations and small farms, and even in cities, rape was ever-present. Like the splitting of families, enslavers used sexual violence as a form of terrorism, a way to promote increased production, obedience, and power relations. And this was not restricted to unmarried women. In numerous contemporary accounts, particularly violent enslavers forced men to witness the rape of their wives, daughters, and relatives, often as punishment, but occasionally as a sadistic expression of power and dominance.[31]

As property, enslaved women had no recourse, and society, by and large, did not see a crime in this type of violence. Racist pseudoscientists claimed that whites could not physically rape Africans or African Americans, as the sexual organs of each were not compatible in that way. State law, in some cases, supported this view, claiming that rape could only occur between either two white people or a Black man and a white woman. All other cases fell under a silent acceptance.[32] The consequences of rape, too, fell to enslaved victims. Pregnancies that resulted from rape did not always lead to a lighter workload for the mother. And if an enslaved woman acted out against a rapist, whether that be her enslaver or any other white attacker, her actions were seen as crimes rather than desperate acts of survival. For example, a nineteen-year-old enslaved woman named Celia fell victim to repeated rape by her enslaver in Callaway County, Missouri. Between 1850 and 1855, Robert Newsom raped Celia hundreds of times, producing two children and several miscarriages. Sick and desperate in the fall of 1855, Celia took a club and struck her enslaver in the head, killing him. But instead of sympathy and aid, or even an honest attempt to understand and empathize, the community called for the execution of Celia. On November 16, 1855, after a trial of ten

The women in this photograph are Selina Gray and two of her daughters. Gray was the enslaved housekeeper to Robert E. Lee. National Park Service.

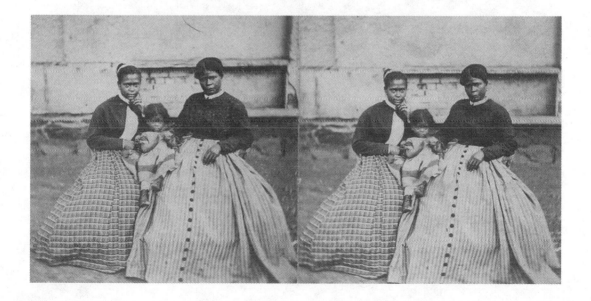

days, Celia, the nineteen-year-old enslaved rape victim, was hanged for her crimes against her enslaver.[33]

Gender inequality did not always fall along the same lines as racial inequality. Southern society, especially in the age of cotton, deferred to white men, under whom laws, social norms, and cultural practices were written, dictated, and maintained. White and free women of color lived in a society dominated, in nearly every aspect, by men. Denied voting rights, women of all statuses and colors had no direct representation in the creation and discussion of law. Husbands, it was said, represented their wives, as the public sphere was too violent, heated, and high-minded for women. Society expected women to represent the foundations of the republic, gaining respectability through their work at home, in support of their husbands and children, away from the rough and boisterous realm of masculinity. In many cases, too, law did not protect women the same

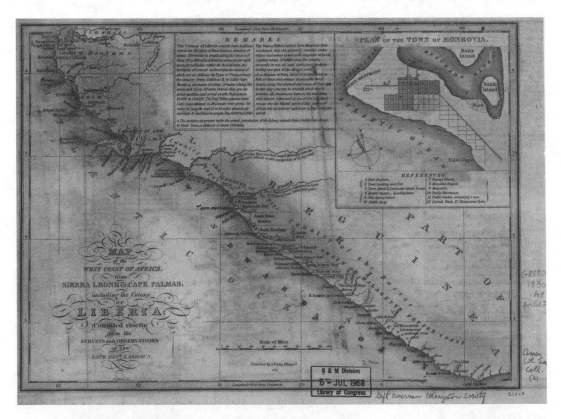

The issue of emigration elicited disparate reactions from African Americans. Tens of thousands left the United States for Liberia, a map of which is shown here, to pursue greater freedoms and prosperity. Most emigrants did not experience such success, but Liberia continued to attract Black settlers for decades. J. Ashmun, *Map of the West Coast of Africa from Sierra Leone to Cape Palmas, including the colony of Liberia,* . . . 1830. Library of Congress.

way it protected men. In most states, marriage, an act expected of any self-respecting, reasonable woman of any class, effectively transferred all of a woman's property to her husband, forever, regardless of claim or command. Divorce existed, but it hardly worked in a woman's favor, and often, if successful, it ruined the wife's standing in society and even led to well-known instances of death by suicide.[34]

Life on the ground in the cotton South, like the cities, systems, and networks within which it rested, defied the standard narrative of the Old South. Slavery existed to dominate, yet enslaved people formed bonds, maintained traditions, and crafted new culture. They fell in love, had children, and protected one another using the privileges granted them by their captors and the basic intellect allowed all human beings. They were resourceful, brilliant, and vibrant, and they created freedom where freedom seemingly could not exist. And within those communities, resilience and dedication often led to cultural sustenance. Among the enslaved, women, and the impoverished-but-free, culture thrived in ways that are difficult to see through the bales of cotton and the stacks of money sitting on the docks and in the countinghouses of the South's urban centers. But religion, honor, and pride transcended material goods, especially among those who could not express themselves that way.

VI. Religion and Honor in the Slave South

Economic growth, violence, and exploitation coexisted and mutually reinforced evangelical Christianity in the South. The revivals of the Second Great Awakening established the region's prevailing religious culture. Led by Methodists, Baptists, and to a lesser degree, Presbyterians, this intense period of religious regeneration swept the southern backcountry. By the outbreak of the Civil War, the vast majority of southerners who affiliated with a religious denomination belonged to either the Baptist or Methodist faith.[35] Both churches in the South briefly attacked slavery before transforming into some of the most vocal defenders of slavery and the southern social order.

Southern ministers contended that God himself had selected Africans for bondage but also considered the evangelization of enslaved people to be one of their greatest callings.[36] Missionary efforts among enslaved southerners largely succeeded and Protestantism spread rapidly among African Americans, leading to a proliferation of biracial congregations and prominent independent Black churches. Some Black and white southerners forged positive and rewarding biracial connections; however, more often Black and white southerners described strained or superficial religious relationships.

As the institution of slavery hardened racism in the South, relationships between missionaries and Native Americans transformed as well. Missionaries of all denominations were among the first to represent themselves as "pillars of white authority." After the Louisiana Purchase in 1803, plantation culture expanded into the Deep South, and mission work became a crucial element of Christian expansion. Frontier mission schools carried a continual flow of Christian influence into Native American communities. Some missionaries learned Indigenous languages, but many more worked to prevent Indigenous children from speaking their native tongues, insisting on English for Christian understanding. By the Indian removals of 1835 and the Trail of Tears in 1838, missionaries in the South preached a pro-slavery theology that emphasized obedience to enslavers, the biblical basis of racial slavery via the curse of Ham, and the "civilizing" paternalism of enslavers.

Enslaved people most commonly received Christian instruction from white preachers or enslavers, whose religious message typically stressed the subservience of enslaved people. Anti-literacy laws ensured that most enslaved people would be unable to read the Bible in its entirety and thus could not acquaint themselves with such inspirational stories as Moses delivering the Israelites out of slavery. Contradictions between God's Word and enslavers' cruelty did not pass unnoticed by many enslaved African Americans. As formerly enslaved person William Wells Brown declared, "slaveholders hide themselves behind the Church," adding that "a more praying, preaching, psalm-singing people cannot be found than the slaveholders of the South."[37]

Many enslaved people chose to create and practice their own versions of Christianity, one that typically incorporated aspects of traditional African religions with limited input from the white community. Nat Turner, the leader of the great slave rebellion, found inspiration from religion early in life. Adopting an austere Christian lifestyle during his adolescence, Turner claimed to have been visited by "spirits" during his twenties and considered himself something of a prophet. He claimed to have had visions, in which he was called on to do the work of God, leading some contemporaries (as well as historians) to question his sanity.[38]

Inspired by his faith, Turner led the most deadly slave rebellion in the antebellum South. On the morning of August 22, 1831, in Southampton County, Virginia, Nat Turner and six collaborators attempted to free the region's enslaved population. Turner initiated the violence by killing his

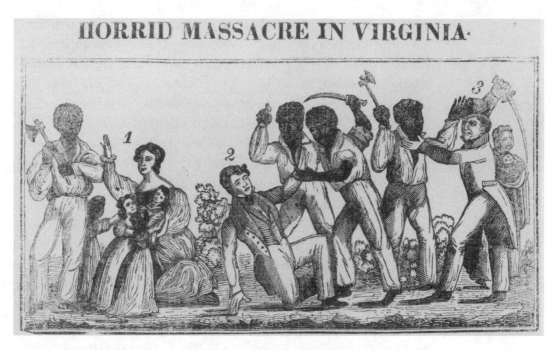

This woodcut captured the terror felt by white southerners in the aftermath of Nat Turner's rebellion. After the rebellion, fearful white reactionaries killed hundreds of enslaved people—most of whom were unconnected to the rebellion—and the state created stricter, more limiting laws concerning slavery. African American Intellectual History Society.

enslaver with an ax blow to the head. By the end of the day, Turner and his band, which had grown to over fifty men, killed fifty-seven white men, women, and children on eleven farms. By the next day, the local militia and white residents had captured or killed all of the participants except Turner, who hid for a number of weeks in nearby woods before being captured and executed. The white terror that followed Nat Turner's rebellion transformed southern religion, as anti-literacy laws increased and Black-led churches were broken up and placed under the supervision of white ministers.

Evangelical religion also shaped understandings of what it meant to be a southern man or a southern woman. Southern manhood was largely shaped by an obsession with masculine honor, whereas southern womanhood centered on expectations of sexual virtue or purity. Honor prioritized the public recognition of white masculine claims to reputation and authority. Southern men developed a code to ritualize their interactions with each other and to perform their expectations of honor. This code structured language and behavior and was designed to minimize conflict. But when conflict did arise, the code also provided rituals that would reduce the resulting violence.

The formal duel exemplified the code in action. If two men could not settle a dispute through the arbitration of their friends, they would exchange pistol shots to prove their equal honor status. Duelists arranged a secluded meeting, chose from a set of deadly weapons, and risked their lives as they clashed with swords or fired pistols at one another. Some of the most illustrious men in American history participated in a duel at some point during their lives, including President Andrew Jackson, Vice President Aaron Burr, and U.S. senators Henry Clay and Thomas Hart Benton. In all but Burr's case, dueling helped elevate these men to prominence.

Violence among the lower classes, especially those in the backcountry, involved fistfights and shoot-outs. Tactics included the sharpening of fingernails and filing of teeth into razor-sharp points, which would be used to gouge eyes and bite off ears and noses. In a duel, a gentleman achieved recognition by risking his life rather than killing his opponent, whereas those involved in rough-and-tumble fighting achieved victory through maiming their opponent.

The legal system was partially to blame for the prevalence of violence in the Old South. Although states and territories had laws against murder, rape, and various other forms of violence, including specific laws against dueling, upper-class southerners were rarely prosecuted, and juries often acquitted the accused. Despite the fact that hundreds of duelists fought and killed one another, there is little evidence that many duelists faced prosecution, and only one, Timothy Bennett (of Belleville, Illinois), was ever executed. By contrast, prosecutors routinely sought cases against lower-class southerners, who were found guilty in greater numbers than their wealthier counterparts.

The southern emphasis on honor affected women as well. While southern men worked to maintain their sense of masculinity; so too southern women cultivated a sense of femininity. Femininity in the South was intimately tied to the domestic sphere, even more so than for women in the North. The cult of domesticity strictly limited the ability of wealthy southern women to engage in public life. While northern women began to organize reform societies, southern women remained bound to the home, where they were instructed to cultivate their families' religious sensibility and manage their household. Managing the household was not easy work, however. For women on large plantations, managing the household would include directing a large bureaucracy of potentially rebellious enslaved people. For most southern women who did not live on plantations, managing the household included nearly constant work in keeping families clean, fed, and well-behaved. On top of these duties, many southern women were required to help with agricultural tasks.

Female labor was an important aspect of the southern economy, but the social position of women in southern culture was understood not through economic labor but rather through moral virtue. While men fought to get ahead in the turbulent world of the cotton boom, women were instructed to offer a calming, moralizing influence on husbands and children. The home was to be a place of quiet respite and spiritual solace. Under the guidance of a virtuous woman, the southern home would foster the values required for economic success and cultural refinement. Female virtue came to be understood largely as a euphemism for sexual purity, and southern culture, southern law, and southern violence largely centered on protecting that virtue of sexual purity from any possible imagined threat. In a world saturated with the sexual exploitation of Black women, southerners developed a paranoid obsession with protecting the sexual purity of white women. Black men were presented as an insatiable sexual threat. Racial systems of violence and domination were wielded with crushing intensity for generations, all in the name of keeping white womanhood as pure as the cotton that anchored southern society.

VII. Conclusion

Cotton created the antebellum South. The wildly profitable commodity opened a previously closed society to the grandeur, the profit, the exploitation, and the social dimensions of a larger, more connected, global community. In this way, the South, and the world, benefited from the Cotton Revolution and the urban growth it sparked. But not all that glitters is gold. Slavery remained and the internal slave trade grew to untold heights as the 1860s approached. Politics, race relations, and the burden of slavery continued beneath the roar of steamboats, counting-houses, and the exchange of goods. Underneath it all, many questions remained—chief among them, what to do if slavery somehow came under threat.

VIII. Reference Material

This chapter was edited by Andrew Wegmann, with content contributions by Ian Beamish, Amanda Bellows, Marjorie Brown, Matthew Byron, Steffi Cerato, Kristin Condotta, Mari Crabtree, Jeff Fortney, John Harris, Robert Gudmestad, John

Marks, Maria Montalvo, James Anthony Owen, Katherine Rohrer, Marie Stango, James Wellborn, Ben Wright, and Ashley Young.

Recommended citation: Ian Beamish et al., "The Cotton Revolution," Andrew Wegmann, ed., in *The American Yawp*, eds. Joseph Locke and Ben Wright (Stanford, CA: Stanford University Press, 2019).

NOTES TO CHAPTER 11

1. See Sven Beckert, *Empire of Cotton: A Global History* (New York: Knopf, 2014), 103; and Angela Lakwete, *Inventing the Cotton Gin: Machine and Myth in Antebellum America* (Baltimore: Johns Hopkins University Press, 2003), 148–151.

2. D. Clayton James, *Antebellum Natchez* (Baton Rouge: Louisiana State University Press, 1968), 156; Walter Johnson, *River of Dark Dreams: Slavery and Empire in the Cotton Kingdom* (Cambridge, MA: Belknap Press, 2013), 151–152; John Solomon Otto, *The Southern Frontiers, 1607–1860: The Agricultural Evolution of the Colonial and Antebellum South* (Westport, CT: Greenwood, 1989), 94–96.

3. Joshua D. Rothman, *Flush Times and Fever Dreams: A Story of Capitalism and Slavery in the Age of Jackson* (Athens: University of Georgia Press, 2012), 6–7; David J. Libby, *Slavery and Frontier Mississippi, 1720–1835* (Jackson: University Press of Mississippi, 2004), 30–36; Scott Reynolds Nelson, *A Nation of Deadbeats: An Uncommon History of America's Financial Disasters* (New York: Knopf, 2012), 115–118.

4. Joseph Holt Ingraham, quoted in Rothman, *Flush Times and Fever Dreams*, 5.

5. W. H. Sparks, *Memories of Fifty Years* (Philadelphia: Claxton, Remsen and Haffelfinger, 1870), 364.

6. Beckert, *Empire of Cotton*, 102–103.

7. For more cotton statistics, see Rothman, *Flush Times and Fever Dreams*, 3–5, 96–103; Johnson, *River of Dark Dreams*, 254–260; Beckert, *Empire of Cotton*, 102–104; Avery Plaw, "Slavery," in *The American Economy: A Historical Encyclopedia*, ed. Cynthia Clark (Santa Barbara, CA: ABC-Clio, 2011), 108–109, 787–798; William J. Phalen, *The Consequences of Cotton in Antebellum America* (Jefferson, NC: McFarland, 2014), 110–114; and Gene Dattel, *Cotton and Race in the Making of America: The Human Costs of Economic Power* (Lanham, MD: Rowman and Littlefield, 2009), 370–371.

8. For a valuable and approachable rundown of American slavery statistics, see Jenny Bourne, "Slavery in the United States," https://eh.net/encyclopedia/slavery-in-the-united-states/, accessed May 7, 2018. For statistics earlier than 1790, see Edmund S. Morgan, *American Slavery, American Freedom: The Ordeal of Colonial Virginia* (New York: Norton, 1975), appendix; and Peter Kolchin, *American Slavery: 1619–1877* (New York: Hill and Wang, 1993), 252–257. All slavery statistics hereafter refer to Bourne's "Slavery in the United States" unless otherwise noted.

9. On antebellum land prices, especially in the Cotton Belt, see Phalen, *Consequences of Cotton*, 157–160; Otto, *The Southern Frontiers*, 86–99; Beth

English, *A Common Thread: Labor, Politics, and Capital Mobility in the Textile Industry* (Athens: University of Georgia Press, 2006), 40–44; and Harold D. Woodman, *King Cotton and His Retainers: Financing and Marketing the Cotton Crop of the South, 1800–1925* (Columbia: University of South Carolina Press, 1990), chap. 11.

10. See Brenda E. Stevenson, *Life in Black and White: Family and Community in the Slave South* (New York: Oxford University Press, 1996), 171–181.

11. See Walter Johnson, *Soul by Soul: Life Inside the Antebellum Slave Market* (Cambridge, MA: Harvard University Press, 1999), 140–141; and John Brown, *Slave Life in Georgia: A Narrative of the Life, Sufferings, and Escapes of John Brown, a Fugitive Now in England* (London: Chamerovzow, 1855), 16–17.

12. James L. Huston, "The Pregnant Economies of the Border South, 1840-1860: Virginia, Kentucky, Tennessee, and the Possibilities of Slave-Labor Expansion," in *The Old South's Modern Worlds: Slavery, Region, and Nation in the Age of Progress*, ed. L. Diane Barnes, Brian Schoen, and Frank Towers (New York: Oxford University Press, 2011), 132–134.

13. See Joseph Holt Ingraham, *The Southwest, by a Yankee* (New York: Harper, 1835), Vol. 2, 91, quoted in Woodman, *King Cotton and His Retainers*, 135. A similar quote, recorded in 1854 and attributed to Edward Russell, appears in Johnson, *River of Dark Dreams*, 12.

14. James Stirling, *Letters from the Slaves States* (London: Parker, 1857), 179–180.

15. Thomas Jefferson, *Notes on the State of Virginia*, ed. Frank Shuffelton (New York: Penguin, 1999), 145.

16. See "Excessive Slave Population: The Remedy," *De Bow's Review* 12, no. 2 (February 1852): 184–185, also quoted in Johnson, *River of Dark Dreams*, 13.

17. See Anonymous, "Cotton and Its Prospects," *American Cotton Planter* 1, no. 8 (August 1853): 226, also quoted in Johnson, *River of Dark Dreams*, 246.

18. See Thomas Prentice Kettel, *Southern Wealth and Northern Profits, as Exhibited in Statistical Facts and Official Figures* (New York: Wood, 1860), 23.

19. Johnson, *River of Dark Dreams*, 247, 244.

20. On the populations of southern cities, see Richard C. Wade, *Slavery in the Cities: The South, 1820–1860* (New York: Oxford University Press, 1964), 325–327. The top three southern cities, in terms of population in 1820, were Baltimore (62,738), New Orleans (27,176), and Charleston (24,780).

21. See Wade, *Slavery in the Cities*, 326.

22. For American import-export statistics, see Spencer C. Tucker, ed., *The Encyclopedia of the Wars of the Early American Republic, 1783–1812* (Santa Barbara, CA: ABC–Clio, 2014), 670–671; and, among others, J. Bradford De Long, "Trade Policy and America's Standard of Living: A Historical Perspective," in Susan M. Collins, ed., *Exports, Imports, and the American Worker* (Washington, DC: Brookings Institution, 1998), 354–357.

23. See Johnson, *River of Dark Dreams*, 6, 73–88; Paul F. Paskoff, *Troubled Waters: Steamboat Disasters, River Improvements, and American Public Policy,*

1821–1860 (Baton Rouge: LSU Press, 2007), 13–19; and Robert H. Gudmestad, *Steamboats and the Rise of the Cotton Kingdom* (Baton Rouge: LSU Press, 2011), chap. 1, 174–180.

24. See Scott P. Marler, *The Merchants' Capital: New Orleans and the Political Economy of the Nineteenth-Century South* (New York: Cambridge University Press, 2013), part I; and Wade, *Slavery in the Cities*, 326–327.

25. On the fashion of the southern middle class, see Andrew N. Wegmann, "Skin Color and Social Practice: The Problem of Race and Class Among New Orleans Creoles and Across the South, 1718–1862," PhD diss., Louisiana State University, 2015, chap. 4; Jonathan D. Wells, *The Origins of the Southern Middle Class, 1800–1861* (Chapel Hill: University of North Carolina Press, 2004), 74–80; and John G. Deal, "Middle-Class Benevolent Societies in Antebellum Norfolk, Virginia," in *The Southern Middle Class in the Long Nineteenth Century*, ed. Jonathan Daniel Wells and Jennifer R. Green (Baton Rouge: LSU Press, 2011), 92–95.

26. The enslaved population of the South in 1860 was 3,950,511; the free, 8,289,782. For statistics on slavery, see Bourne, "Slavery in the United States."

27. See Stevenson, *Life in Black and White*, chap. 8, especially 231–238; and Emily West, *Chains of Love: Slave Couples in Antebellum South Carolina* (Urbana: University of Illinois Press, 2004), particularly 21–33.

28. See Stephen Crawford, "The Slave Family: A View from the Slave Narratives," in *Strategic Factors in Nineteenth Century American Economic History: A Volume to Honor Robert W. Fogel*, ed. Claudia Goldin and Hugh Rockoff (Chicago: University of Chicago Press, 1992), 331–350.

29. For a fascinating, visual treatment of "downriver" sales of enslaved people, see Maurie D. McInnis, *Slaves Waiting for Sale: Abolitionist Art and the American Slave Trade* (Chicago: University of Chicago Press, 2011), chap. 3. More generally, see Johnson, *River of Dark Dreams*, 144–147; and Kolchin, *American Slavery*, 95–98.

30. Harriet Jacobs, *Incidents in the Life of a Slave Girl* (Boston: n.p., 1861), 85.

31. Kevin Bales and Jody Sarich, "The Paradox of Women, Children, and Slavery," in *Trafficking in Slavery's Wake: Law and the Experience of Women and Children in Africa*, ed. Benjamin N. Lawrence and Richard L. Roberts (Athens: Ohio University Press, 2012), 241–243; Diane Miller Sommerville, *Rape and Race in the Nineteenth-Century South* (Chapel Hill: University of North Carolina Press, 2004), 44–48; and Jacqueline Jones, *Labor of Love, Labor of Sorrow: Black Women, Work, and the Family, from Slavery to the Present* (New York: Basic Books, 2010), 35–38.

32. See Clarence Walker, *Mongrel Nation: The America Begotten by Thomas Jefferson and Sally Hemings* (Charlottesville: University of Virginia Press, 2009), 30–46; and, among others, Hannah Rosen, *Terror in the Heart of Freedom: Citizenship, Sexual Violence, and the Meaning of Race in the Postemancipation South* (Chapel Hill: University of North Carolina Press, 2009), 9–11, 75–82.

33. See Melton A. McLaurin, *Celia, a Slave: A True Story of Violence and Retribution in Antebellum Missouri* (Athens: University of Georgia Press, 1991), chaps. 2, 5, and 6.

34. On divorce, see Carol Lasser and Stacey Robertson, *Antebellum Women: Private, Public, Partisan* (Lanham, MD: Rowman and Littlefield, 2010), 5–8; Nancy Isenberg, *Sex and Citizenship in Antebellum America* (Chapel Hill: University of North Carolina Press, 1998), 200–204; and David Silkenat, *Moments of Despair: Suicide, Divorce, and Debt in Civil War Era North Carolina* (Chapel Hill: University of North Carolina Press, 2011), chap. 4, particularly 77–88.

35. Samuel S. Hill, *Southern Churches in Crisis Revisited* (Tuscaloosa: University of Alabama Press, 1999), 33.

36. Charles Irons, *The Origins of Proslavery Christianity: White and Black Evangelicals in Colonial and Antebellum Virginia* (Chapel Hill: University of North Carolina Press, 2008).

37. William Wells Brown, *Narrative of William W. Brown, a Fugitive Slave. Written by Himself* (Reading, MA: Addison Wesley, 1969), 56.

38. Nat Turner, *The Confessions of Nat Turner, the Leader of the Late Insurrection in Southampton, Va.* (Baltimore: Gray, 1831), 9–11.

RECOMMENDED READING

Baptist, Edward E. *The Half Has Never Been Told: Slavery and the Making of American Capitalism.* New York: Basic Books, 2014.

Beckert, Sven. *Empire of Cotton: A Global History.* New York: Knopf, 2014.

Blassingame, John W. *The Slave Community: Plantation Life in the Antebellum South.* New York: Oxford University Press, 1979.

Camp, Stephanie M. H. *Closer to Freedom: Enslaved Women and Everyday Resistance in the Plantation South.* Chapel Hill: University of North Carolina Press, 2004.

Dunaway, Wilma A. *The African-American Family in Slavery and Emancipation.* Cambridge, UK: Cambridge University Press, 2003.

Einhorn, Robin. *American Taxation, American Slavery.* Chicago: University of Chicago Press, 2006.

English, Beth. *A Common Thread: Labor, Politics, and Capital Mobility in the Textile Industry.* Athens: University of Georgia Press, 2006.

Ford, Lacy K. *Deliver Us from Evil: The Slavery Question in the Old South.* New York: Oxford University Press, 1999.

Genovese, Eugene D. *Roll, Jordan, Roll: The World the Slaves Made.* New York: Vintage Books, 1974.

Hahn, Barbara. *Making Tobacco Bright: Creating an American Commodity, 1617–1937.* Baltimore: Johns Hopkins University Press, 2011.

Hall, Gwendolyn Midlo. *Slavery and African Ethnicities in the Americas: Restoring the Links.* Chapel Hill: University of North Carolina Press, 2005.

Johnson, Walter. *River of Dark Dreams: Slavery and Empire in the Cotton Kingdom.* Cambridge, MA: Belknap Press, 2013.

Jones, Jacqueline. *Labor of Love, Labor of Sorrow: Black Women, Work, and the Family, from Slavery to the Present.* New York: Basic Books, 2010.

Kolchin, Peter. *American Slavery: 1619–1877.* New York: Hill and Wang, 1993.

Lakwete, Angela. *Inventing the Cotton Gin: Machine and Myth in Antebellum America.* Baltimore: Johns Hopkins University Press, 2003.

Marler, Scott P. *The Merchants' Capital: New Orleans and the Political Economy of the Nineteenth-Century South*. New York: Cambridge University Press, 2013.

McDonald, Robin, and Valerie Pope Burnes. *Visions of the Black Belt: A Cultural Survey of the Heart of Alabama*. Tuscaloosa: The University of Alabama Press, 2015.

McInnis, Maurie D. *Slaves Waiting for Sale: Abolitionist Art and the American Slave Trade*. Chicago: University of Chicago Press, 2011.

Penningroth, Dylan C. *The Claims of Kinfolk: African American Property and Community in the Nineteenth-Century South*. Chapel Hill: University of North Carolina Press, 2003.

Rothman, Joshua D. *Flush Times and Fever Dreams: A Story of Capitalism and Slavery in the Age of Jackson*. Athens: University of Georgia Press, 2012.

Sommerville, Diane Miller. *Rape and Race in the Nineteenth-Century South*. Chapel Hill: University of North Carolina Press, 2004.

Tise, Larry E. *Proslavery: A History of the Defense of Slavery in America, 1701–1840*. Athens: University of Georgia Press, 1987.

Tyler-McGraw, Marie. *At the Falls: Richmond, Virginia, and Its People*. Chapel Hill: University of North Carolina Press, 1994.

West, Emily. *Chains of Love: Slave Couples in Antebellum South Carolina*. Urbana: University of Illinois Press, 2004.

White, Deborah Gray. *Ar'n't I a Woman?: Female Slaves in the Plantation South*. Norton, 1999.

Wood, Betty. *The Origins of American Slavery: Freedom and Bondage in the English Colonies*. New York: Hill and Wang, 1997.

12

Manifest Destiny

I. Introduction

John Louis O'Sullivan, a popular editor and columnist, articulated the long-standing American belief in the God-given mission of the United States to lead the world in the peaceful transition to democracy. In a little-read essay printed in *The United States Magazine and Democratic Review*, O'Sullivan outlined the importance of annexing Texas to the United States:

> Why, were other reasoning wanting, in favor of now elevating this question of the reception of Texas into the Union, out of the lower region of our past party dissensions, up to its proper level of a high and broad nationality, it surely is to be found, found abundantly, in the manner in which other nations have undertaken to intrude themselves into it, between us and the proper parties to the case, in a spirit of hostile interference against us, for the avowed object of thwarting our policy and

Emanuel Gottlieb Leutze, *Westward the Course of Empire Takes Its Way*, 1862. Mural, United States Capitol.

hampering our power, limiting our greatness and checking the fulfillment of our manifest destiny to overspread the continent allotted by Providence for the free development of our yearly multiplying millions.[1]

O'Sullivan and many others viewed expansion as necessary to achieve America's destiny and to protect American interests. The quasi-religious call to spread democracy coupled with the reality of thousands of settlers pressing westward. Manifest destiny was grounded in the belief that a democratic, agrarian republic would save the world.

Although called into name in 1845, manifest destiny was a widely held but vaguely defined belief that dated back to the founding of the nation. First, many Americans believed that the strength of American values and institutions justified moral claims to hemispheric leadership. Second, the lands on the North American continent west of the Mississippi River (and later into the Caribbean) were destined for American-led political and agricultural improvement. Third, God and the Constitution ordained an irrepressible destiny to accomplish redemption and democratization throughout the world. All three of these claims pushed many Americans, whether they uttered the words *manifest destiny* or not, to actively seek the expansion of democracy. These beliefs and the resulting

John O'Sullivan, shown here in an 1874 *Harper's Weekly* sketch, coined the phrase "manifest destiny" in an 1845 newspaper article. Wikimedia.

actions were often disastrous to anyone in the way of American expansion. The new religion of American democracy spread on the feet and in the wagons of those who moved west, imbued with the hope that their success would be the nation's success.

The Young America movement, strongest among members of the Democratic Party but spanning the political spectrum, downplayed divisions over slavery and ethnicity by embracing national unity and emphasizing American exceptionalism, territorial expansion, democratic participation, and economic interdependence.[2] Poet Ralph Waldo Emerson captured the political outlook of this new generation in a speech he delivered in 1844 titled "The Young American":

> In every age of the world, there has been a leading nation, one of a more generous sentiment, whose eminent citizens were willing to stand for the interests of general justice and humanity, at the risk of being called, by the men of the moment, chimerical and fantastic. Which should be that nation but these States? Which should lead that movement, if not New England? Who should lead the leaders, but the Young American?[3]

However, many Americans, including Emerson, disapproved of aggressive expansion. For opponents of manifest destiny, the lofty rhetoric of the Young Americans was nothing other than a kind of imperialism that the American Revolution was supposed to have repudiated.[4] Many members of the Whig Party (and later the Republican Party) argued that the United States' mission was to lead by example, not by conquest. Abraham Lincoln summed up this criticism with a fair amount of sarcasm during a speech in 1859:

> He (the Young American) owns a large part of the world, by right of possessing it; and all the rest by right of wanting it, and intending to have it. . . . Young America had "a pleasing hope—a fond desire—a longing after" territory. He has a great passion—a perfect rage—for the "new"; particularly new men for office, and the new earth mentioned in the revelations, in which, being no more sea, there must be about three times as much land as in the present. He is a great friend of humanity; and his desire for land is not selfish, but merely an impulse to extend the area of freedom. He is very anxious to fight for the liberation of enslaved nations and colonies, provided, always, they have land. . . . As to those who have no land, and would be glad of help from any quarter, he considers they can afford to wait a few hundred years longer. In knowledge he is particularly rich. He knows all that can possibly be known; inclines to believe in spiritual trappings, and is the unquestioned inventor of "Manifest Destiny."[5]

Artistic propaganda like this promoted the national project of manifest destiny. Columbia, the female figure of America, leads Americans into the West and into the future by carrying the values of republicanism (as seen through her Roman garb) and progress (shown through the inclusion of technological innovations like the telegraph) and clearing native peoples and animals, seen being pushed into the darkness. John Gast, *American Progress*, 1872. Wikimedia.

But Lincoln and other anti-expansionists would struggle to win popular opinion. The nation, fueled by the principles of manifest destiny, would continue westward. Along the way, Americans battled both native peoples and foreign nations, claiming territory to the very edges of the continent. But westward expansion did not come without a cost. It exacerbated the slavery question, pushed Americans toward civil war, and, ultimately, threatened the very mission of American democracy it was designed to aid.

II. Antebellum Western Migration and Indian Removal

After the War of 1812, Americans settled the Great Lakes region rapidly thanks in part to aggressive land sales by the federal government.[6] Missouri's admission as a slave state presented the first major crisis over westward migration and American expansion in the antebellum period. Farther north, lead and iron ore mining spurred development in Wisconsin.[7] By the 1830s and 1840s, increasing numbers of German and Scandinavian immigrants joined easterners in settling the Upper Mississippi watershed.[8] Little settlement occurred west of Missouri as migrants viewed the Great Plains as a barrier to farming. Farther west, the Rocky Mountains loomed as undesirable to all but fur traders, and all Native Americans west of the Mississippi appeared too powerful to allow for white expansion.

"Do not lounge in the cities!" commanded publisher Horace Greeley in 1841, "There is room and health in the country, away from the crowds of idlers and imbeciles. Go west, before you are fitted for no life but that of the factory."[9] The *New York Tribune* often argued that American exceptionalism required the United States to benevolently conquer the continent as the prime means of spreading American capitalism and American democracy. However, the vast West was not empty. Native Americans controlled much of the land east of the Mississippi River and almost all of the West. Expansion hinged on a federal policy of Indian removal.

The harassment and dispossession of Native Americans—whether driven by official U.S. government policy or the actions of individual Americans and their communities—depended on the belief in manifest destiny. Of course, a fair bit of racism was part of the equation as well. The political and legal processes of expansion always hinged on the belief that white Americans could best use new lands and opportunities. This belief rested on the idea that only Americans embodied the democratic ideals of yeoman agriculturalism extolled by Thomas Jefferson and expanded under Jacksonian democracy.

Florida was an early test case for the Americanization of new lands. The territory held strategic value for the young nation's growing economic and military interests in the Caribbean. The most important factors that led to the annexation of Florida included anxieties over runaway slaves, Spanish neglect of the region, and the desired defeat of Native American tribes who controlled large portions of lucrative farm territory.

During the early nineteenth century, Spain wanted to increase productivity in Florida and encouraged migration of mostly southern enslavers. By the second decade of the 1800s, Anglo settlers occupied plantations along the St. Johns River, from the border with Georgia to Lake George a hundred miles upstream. Spain began to lose control as the area quickly became a haven for slave smugglers bringing illicit human cargo into the United States for lucrative sale to Georgia planters. Plantation owners grew apprehensive about the growing numbers of enslaved laborers running to the swamps and Native American–controlled areas of Florida. American enslavers pressured the U.S. government to confront the Spanish authorities. Southern enslavers refused to quietly accept the continued presence of armed Black men in Florida. During the War of 1812, a ragtag assortment of Georgia enslavers joined by a plethora of armed opportunists raided Spanish and British-owned plantations along the St. Johns River. These private citizens received U.S. government help on July 27, 1816, when U.S. army regulars attacked the Negro Fort (established as an armed outpost during the war by the British and located about sixty miles south of the Georgia border). The raid killed 270 of the fort's inhabitants as a result of a direct hit on the fort's gunpowder stores. This conflict set the stage for General Andrew Jackson's invasion of Florida in 1817 and the beginning of the First Seminole War.[10]

Americans also held that Creek and Seminole people, occupying the area from the Apalachicola River to the wet prairies and hammock islands of central Florida, were dangers in their own right. These tribes, known to the Americans collectively as Seminoles, migrated into the region over the course of the eighteenth century and established settlements, tilled fields, and tended herds of cattle in the rich floodplains and grasslands that dominated the northern third of the Florida peninsula. Envious eyes looked upon these lands. After bitter conflict that often pitted Americans against a collection of Native Americans and formerly enslaved people, Spain eventually agreed to transfer the territory to the United States. The resulting Adams-Onís Treaty exchanged Florida for $5 million and other territorial concessions elsewhere.[11]

After the purchase, planters from the Carolinas, Georgia, and Virginia entered Florida. However, the influx of settlers into the Florida territory was temporarily halted in the mid-1830s by the outbreak of the Second Seminole War (1835–1842). Free Black men and women and enslaved laborers also occupied the Seminole district, a situation that deeply troubled enslavers. Indeed, General Thomas Sidney Jesup, U.S. commander during the early stages of the Second Seminole War, labeled that conflict "a negro, not an Indian War," fearful as he was that if the revolt "was not speedily put down, the South will feel the effect of it on their slave population before the end of the next season."[12] Florida became a state in 1845 and settlement expanded.

American action in Florida seized Indigenous people's eastern lands, reduced lands available for freedom-seeking enslaved people, and killed entirely or removed Native American peoples farther west. This became the template for future action. Presidents, since at least Thomas Jefferson, had long discussed removal, but President Andrew Jackson took the most dramatic action. Jackson believed, "It [speedy removal] will place a dense and civilized population in large tracts of country now occupied by a few savage hunters."[13] Desires to remove Native Americans from valuable farmland motivated state and federal governments to cease trying to assimilate Native Americans and instead plan for forced removal.

Congress passed the Indian Removal Act in 1830, thereby granting the president authority to begin treaty negotiations that would give Native Americans land in the West in exchange for their lands east of the Mississippi. Many advocates of removal, including President Jackson, paternalistically claimed that it would protect Native Americans communities from outside influences that jeopardized their chances of becoming "civilized" farmers. Jackson emphasized this paternalism—the belief that the government was acting in the best interest of Native peoples—in his 1830 State of the Union Address. "It [removal] will separate the Indians from immediate contact with settlements of whites . . . and perhaps cause them gradually, under the protection of the Government and through the influence of good counsels, to cast off their savage habits and become an interesting, civilized, and Christian community."[14]

The experience of the Cherokee was particularly brutal. Despite many tribal members adopting some Euro-American ways, including intensified agriculture, slaving, and Christianity, state and federal governments pressured the Choctaw, Chickasaw, Creek, and Cherokee Nations to sign treaties and surrender land. Many of these tribal nations used the law in hopes of protecting their lands. Most notable among these efforts was the Cherokee Nation's attempt to sue the state of Georgia.

Beginning in 1826, Georgian officials asked the federal government to negotiate with the Cherokee to secure lucrative lands. The Adams administration resisted the state's request, but harassment from local settlers against the Cherokee forced the Adams and Jackson administrations to begin serious negotiations with the Cherokee. Georgia grew impatient with the process of negotiation and abolished existing state agreements with the Cherokee that had guaranteed rights of movement and jurisdiction of tribal law. Andrew Jackson penned a letter soon after taking office that encouraged the Cherokee, among others, to voluntarily relocate to the West. The discovery of gold in Georgia in the fall of 1829 further antagonized the situation.

The Cherokee defended themselves against Georgia's laws by citing treaties signed with the United States that guaranteed the Cherokee Nation both their land and independence. The Cherokee appealed to the Supreme Court against Georgia to prevent dispossession. The Court, while sympathizing with the Cherokee's plight, ruled that it lacked jurisdiction to hear the case (*Cherokee Nation v. Georgia* [1831]). In an associated case, *Worcester v. Georgia* (1832), the Supreme Court ruled that Georgia laws did not apply within Cherokee territory.[15] Regardless of these rulings, the state government ignored the Supreme Court and did little to prevent conflict between settlers and the Cherokee.

Jackson wanted a solution that might preserve peace and his reputation. He sent secretary of war Lewis Cass to offer title to western lands and the promise of tribal governance in exchange for relinquishing of the Cherokee's eastern lands. These negotiations opened a rift within the Cherokee Nation. Cherokee leader John Ridge believed removal was inevitable and pushed for a treaty that would give the best terms. Others, called nationalists and led by John Ross, refused to consider removal in negotiations. The Jackson administration refused any deal that fell short of large-scale removal of the Cherokee from Georgia, thereby fueling a devastating and violent intratribal battle between the two factions. Eventually tensions grew to the point that several treaty advocates were assassinated by members of the national faction.[16]

In 1835, a portion of the Cherokee Nation led by John Ridge, hoping to prevent further tribal bloodshed, signed the Treaty of New Echota. This treaty ceded lands in Georgia for $5 million and, the signatories hoped, would limit future conflicts between the Cherokee and white settlers. However, most of the tribe refused to adhere to the terms, viewing the treaty as illegitimately negotiated. In response, John Ross pointed out the U.S. government's hypocrisy. "You asked us to throw off the hunter and warrior state: We did so—you asked us to form a republican government: We did so. Adopting your own as our model. You asked us to cultivate the earth, and learn the mechanic arts. We did so. You asked us to learn to read. We did so. You asked us to cast away our idols and worship your god. We did so. Now you demand we cede to you our lands. That we will not do."[17]

President Martin van Buren, in 1838, decided to press the issue beyond negotiation and court rulings and used the New Echota Treaty provisions to order the army to forcibly remove those Cherokee not obeying the treaty's cession of territory. Harsh weather, poor planning, and difficult travel compounded the tragedy of what became known as the Trail of Tears. Sixteen thousand Cherokee embarked on the journey; only ten thousand completed it.[18] Not every instance of removal was as treacherous or demographically disastrous as the Cherokee example. Furthermore, tribes responded in a variety of ways. Some tribes violently resisted removal. Ultimately, over sixty thousand Native Americans were forced west prior to the Civil War.[19]

The allure of manifest destiny encouraged expansion regardless of terrain or locale, and Indian removal also took place, to a lesser degree, in northern lands. In the Old Northwest, Odawa and Ojibwe communities in Michigan, Wisconsin, and Minnesota resisted removal as many lived on land north of desirable farming land. Moreover, some Ojibwe and Odawa individuals purchased land independently. They formed successful alliances with missionaries to help advocate against removal, as well as with some traders and merchants who depended on trade with Native peoples. Yet Indian removal occurred in the North as well—the Black Hawk War in 1832, for instance, led to the removal of many Sauk to Kansas.[20]

Despite the disaster of removal, tribal nations slowly rebuilt their cultures and in some cases even achieved prosperity in new territories. Tribal nations blended traditional cultural practices, including common land systems, with western practices including constitutional governments, common school systems, and creating an elite enslaving class.

Some Native American groups remained too powerful to remove. Beginning in the late eighteenth century, the Comanche rose to power in the Southern Plains region of what is now the southwestern United States. By quickly adapting to the horse culture first introduced by the Spanish, the Comanche transitioned from a foraging economy into a mixed hunting and pastoral society. After 1821, the new Mexican nation-state claimed the region as part of the northern Mexican frontier, but they had little control. Instead, the Comanche remained in power and controlled the economy of the Southern Plains. A flexible political structure allowed the Comanche to dominate other Native American groups as well as Mexican and American settlers.

In the 1830s, the Comanche launched raids into northern Mexico, ending what had been an unprofitable but peaceful diplomatic relationship with Mexico. At the same time, they forged new trading relationships with Anglo-American traders in Texas. Throughout this period, the Comanche and several other independent Native groups, particularly the Kiowa, Apache, and Navajo, engaged in thousands of violent encounters with northern Mexicans. Collectively, these encounters comprised an ongoing war during the 1830s and 1840s as tribal nations vied for power and wealth. By the 1840s, Comanche power peaked with an empire that controlled a vast territory in the trans-Mississippi west known as Comancheria. By trading in Texas and raiding in northern Mexico, the Comanche controlled the flow of commodities, including captives, livestock, and trade goods. They practiced a fluid system of captivity and captive trading, rather than a rigid chattel system. The Comanche used captives for economic exploitation but also adopted captives into kinship networks. This allowed for the assimilation of diverse peoples in the region into the empire. The ongoing conflict in the region had sweeping consequences on both Mexican and American politics. The U.S.-Mexican War, beginning in 1846, can be seen as a culmination of this violence.[21]

Map of the Plains Indians, undated. Smithsonian Institution.

In the Great Basin region, Mexican independence also escalated patterns of violence. This region, on the periphery of the Spanish empire,

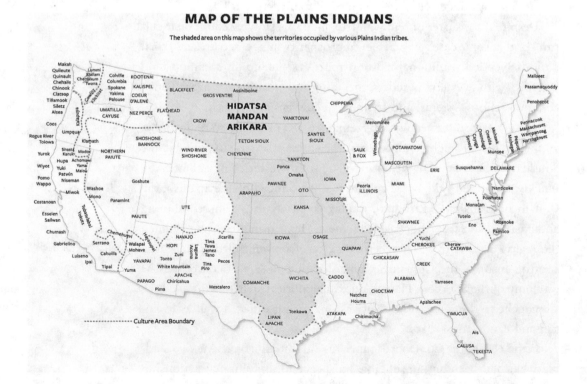

MAP OF THE PLAINS INDIANS

The shaded area on this map shows the territories occupied by various Plains Indian tribes.

was nonetheless integrated in the vast commercial trading network of the West. Mexican officials and Anglo-American traders entered the region with their own imperial designs. New forms of violence spread into the homelands of the Paiute and Western Shoshone. Traders, settlers, and Mormon religious refugees, aided by U.S. officials and soldiers, committed daily acts of violence and laid the groundwork for violent conquest. This expansion of the American state into the Great Basin meant groups such as the Ute, Cheyenne, and Arapahoe had to compete over land, resources, captives, and trade relations with Anglo-Americans. Eventually, white incursion and ongoing wars against Native Americans resulted in traumatic dispossession of land and the struggle for subsistence.

The federal government attempted more than relocation of Native Americans. Policies to "civilize" Native Americans coexisted along with forced removal and served an important "Americanizing" vision of expansion that brought an ever-increasing population under the American flag and sought to balance aggression with the uplift of paternal care. Thomas L. McKenney, superintendent of Indian trade from 1816 to 1822 and the Superintendent of Indian Affairs from 1824 to 1830, served as the main architect of the civilization policy. He asserted that Native Americans were morally and intellectually equal to whites. He sought to establish a national Indian school system.

Congress rejected McKenney's plan but instead passed the Civilization Fund Act in 1819. This act offered $10,000 annually to be allocated toward societies that funded missionaries to establish schools among Native American tribes. However, providing schooling for Native Americans under the auspices of the civilization program also allowed the federal government to justify taking more land. Treaties, such as the 1820 Treaty of Doak's Stand made with the Choctaw nation, often included land cessions as requirements for education provisions. Removal and Americanization reinforced Americans' sense of cultural dominance.[22]

After removal in the 1830s, the Cherokee, Choctaw, and Chickasaw began to collaborate with missionaries to build school systems of their own. Leaders hoped education would help ensuing generations to protect political sovereignty. In 1841, the Cherokee Nation opened a public school system that within two years included eighteen schools. By 1852, the system expanded to twenty-one schools with a national enrollment of 1,100 pupils.[23] Many of the students educated in these tribally controlled schools later served their nations as teachers, lawyers, physicians, bureaucrats, and politicians.

III. Life and Culture in the West

The dream of creating a democratic utopia in the West ultimately rested on those who picked up their possessions and their families and moved west. Western settlers usually migrated as families and settled along navigable and potable rivers. Settlements often coalesced around local traditions, especially religion, carried from eastern settlements. These shared understandings encouraged a strong sense of cooperation among western settlers that forged communities on the frontier.

Before the Mexican War, the West for most Americans still referred to the fertile area between the Appalachian Mountains and the Mississippi River with a slight amount of overspill beyond its banks. With soil exhaustion and land competition increasing in the East, most early western migrants sought a greater measure of stability and self-sufficiency by engaging in small-scale farming. Boosters of these new agricultural areas along with the U.S. government encouraged perceptions of the West as a land of hard-built opportunity that promised personal and national bounty.

Women migrants bore the unique double burden of travel while also being expected to conform to restrictive gender norms. The key virtues of femininity, according to the "cult of true womanhood," included piety, purity, domesticity, and submissiveness. The concept of "separate spheres" expected women to remain in the home. These values accompanied men and women as they traveled west to begin their new lives.

While many of these societal standards endured, there often existed an openness of frontier society that resulted in modestly more opportunities for women. Husbands needed partners in setting up a homestead and working in the field to provide food for the family. Suitable wives were often in short supply, enabling some to informally negotiate more power in their households.[24]

Americans debated the role of government in westward expansion. This debate centered on the proper role of the U.S. government in paying for the internal improvements that soon became necessary to encourage and support economic development. Some saw frontier development as a self-driven undertaking that necessitated private risk and investment devoid of government interference. Others saw the federal government's role as providing the infrastructural development needed to give migrants the push toward engagement with the larger national economy. In the end, federal aid proved essential for the conquest and settlement of the region.

American artist George Catlin traveled west to paint Native Americans. In 1832, he painted Eeh-nís-kim, Crystal Stone, wife of a Blackfoot leader. Smithsonian American Art Museum.

Economic busts constantly threatened western farmers and communities. The economy worsened after the Panic of 1819. Falling prices and depleted soil meant farmers were unable to make their loan payments. The dream of subsistence and stability abruptly ended as many migrants lost their land and felt the hand of the distant market economy forcing them even farther west to escape debt. As a result, the federal government consistently sought to increase access to land in the West, including efforts to lower the amount of land required for purchase. Smaller lots made it easier for more farmers to clear land and begin farming faster.[25]

More than anything else, new roads and canals provided conduits for migration and settlement. Improvements in travel and exchange fueled economic growth in the 1820s and 1830s. Canal improvements expanded in the East, while road building prevailed in the West. Congress continued to allocate funds for internal improvements. Federal money pushed the National Road, begun in 1811, farther west every year. Laborers needed to construct these improvements increased employment opportunities and encouraged nonfarmers to move to the West. Wealth promised by engagement with the new economy was hard to reject.

However, roads were expensive to build and maintain, and some Americans strongly opposed spending money on these improvements.

The use of steamboats grew quickly throughout the 1810s and into the 1820s. As water trade and travel grew in popularity, local, state, and federal funds helped connect rivers and streams. Hundreds of miles of new canals cut through the eastern landscape. The most notable of these early projects was the Erie Canal. That project, completed in 1825, linked the Great Lakes to New York City. The profitability of the canal helped New York outpace its East Coast rivals to become the center for commercial import and export in the United States.[26]

Early railroads like the Baltimore and Ohio line hoped to link mid-Atlantic cities with lucrative western trade routes. Railroad boosters encouraged the rapid growth of towns and cities along their routes. Not only did rail lines promise to move commerce faster, but the rails also encouraged the spreading of towns farther away from traditional waterway locations. Technological limitations, constant repairs, conflicts with Native Americans, and political disagreements all hampered railroading and kept canals and steamboats as integral parts of the transportation system. Nonetheless, this early establishment of railroads enabled a rapid expansion after the Civil War.

Economic chains of interdependence stretched over hundreds of miles of land and through thousands of contracts and remittances. America's manifest destiny became wedded not only to territorial expansion but also to economic development.[27]

IV. Texas, Mexico, and the United States

The debate over slavery became one of the prime forces behind the Texas Revolution and the resulting republic's annexation to the United States. After gaining its independence from Spain in 1821, Mexico hoped to attract new settlers to its northern areas to create a buffer between it and the powerful Comanche. New immigrants, mostly from the southern United States, poured into Mexican Texas. Over the next twenty-five years, concerns over growing Anglo influence and possible American designs on the area produced great friction between Mexicans and the former Americans in the area. In 1829, Mexico, hoping to quell both anger and immigration, outlawed slavery and required all new immigrants to convert to Catholicism. American immigrants, eager to expand their agricultural fortunes, largely ignored these requirements. In response, Mexican authorities closed their territory to any new immigration in 1830—a prohibition ignored by Americans who often squatted on public lands.[28]

In 1834, an internal conflict between federalists and centralists in the Mexican government led to the political ascendency of General Antonio López de Santa Anna. Santa Anna, governing as a dictator, repudiated the federalist Constitution of 1824, pursued a policy of authoritarian central control, and crushed several revolts throughout Mexico. Anglo settlers in Mexican Texas, or Texians as they called themselves, opposed Santa Anna's centralizing policies and met in November. They issued a statement of purpose that emphasized their commitment to the Constitution of 1824 and declared Texas to be a separate state within Mexico. After the Mexican government angrily rejected the offer, Texian leaders soon abandoned their fight for the Constitution of 1824 and declared independence on March 2, 1836.[29] The Texas Revolution of 1835–1836 was a successful secessionist movement in the northern district of the Mexican state of Coahuila y Tejas that resulted in an independent Republic of Texas.

At the Alamo and Goliad, Santa Anna crushed smaller rebel forces and massacred hundreds of Texian prisoners. The Mexican army pursued the retreating Texian army deep into East Texas, spurring a mass panic and evacuation by American civilians known as the Runaway Scrape. The confident Santa Anna consistently failed to make adequate defensive preparations, an oversight that eventually led to a surprise attack from the outnumbered Texian army led by Sam Houston on April 21, 1836. The battle of San Jacinto lasted only eighteen minutes and resulted in a decisive victory for the Texians, who retaliated for previous Mexican atrocities by killing fleeing and surrendering Mexican soldiers for hours after the initial assault. Santa Anna was captured in the aftermath and compelled to sign the Treaty of Velasco on May 14, 1836, by which he agreed to withdraw his army from Texas and acknowledged Texas independence. Although a new Mexican government never recognized the Republic of Texas, the United States and several other nations gave the new country diplomatic recognition.[30]

Texas annexation had remained a political landmine since the Republic declared independence from Mexico in 1836. American politicians feared that adding Texas to the Union would provoke a war with Mexico and reignite sectional tensions by throwing off the balance between free and slave states. However, after his expulsion from the Whig party, President John Tyler saw Texas statehood as the key to saving his political

career. In 1842, he began work on opening annexation to national debate. Harnessing public outcry over the issue, Democrat James K. Polk
rose from virtual obscurity to win the presidential election of 1844. Polk
and his party campaigned on promises of westward expansion, with eyes
toward Texas, Oregon, and California. In the final days of his presidency,
Tyler at last extended an official offer to Texas on March 3, 1845. The
republic accepted on July 4, becoming the twenty-eighth state.

Mexico denounced annexation as "an act of aggression, the most un-
just which can be found recorded in the annals of modern history."[31]
Beyond the anger produced by annexation, the two nations both laid
claim over a narrow strip of land between two rivers. Mexico drew the
southwestern border of Texas at the Nueces River, but Texans claimed
that the border lay roughly 150 miles farther west at the Rio Grande.
Neither claim was realistic since the sparsely populated area, known as
the Nueces strip, was in fact controlled by Native Americans.

In November 1845, President Polk secretly dispatched John Slidell
to Mexico City to purchase the Nueces strip along with large sections
of New Mexico and California. The mission was an empty gesture, designed largely to pacify those in Washington who insisted on diplomacy
before war. Predictably, officials in Mexico City refused to receive Slidell.
In preparation for the assumed failure of the negotiations, Polk preemp-
tively sent a four-thousand-man army under General Zachary Taylor to
Corpus Christi, Texas, just northeast of the Nueces River. Upon word of
Slidell's rebuff in January 1846, Polk ordered Taylor to cross into the disputed territory. The president hoped that this show of force would push
the lands of California onto the bargaining table as well. Unfortunately,
he badly misread the situation. After losing Texas, the Mexican public
strongly opposed surrendering any more ground to the United States.
Popular opinion left the shaky government in Mexico City without room
to negotiate. On April 24, Mexican cavalrymen attacked a detachment
of Taylor's troops in the disputed territory just north of the Rio Grande,
killing eleven U.S. soldiers.

It took two weeks for the news to reach Washington. Polk sent a
message to Congress on May 11 that summed up the assumptions and
intentions of the United States.

> Instead of this, however, we have been exerting our best efforts to propiti-
> ate her good will. Upon the pretext that Texas, a nation as independent
> as herself, thought proper to unite its destinies with our own, she has
> affected to believe that we have severed her rightful territory, and in of-
> ficial proclamations and manifestoes has repeatedly threatened to make

war upon us for the purpose of reconquering Texas. In the meantime we have tried every effort at reconciliation. The cup of forbearance had been exhausted even before the recent information from the frontier of the Del Norte. But now, after reiterated menaces, Mexico has passed the boundary of the United States, has invaded our territory and shed American blood upon the American soil. She has proclaimed that hostilities have commenced, and that the two nations are now at war.[32]

The cagey Polk knew that since hostilities already existed, political dissent would be dangerous—a vote against war became a vote against supporting American soldiers under fire. Congress passed a declaration of war on May 13. Only a few members of both parties, notably John Quincy Adams and John C. Calhoun, opposed the measure. Upon declaring war in 1846, Congress issued a call for fifty thousand volunteer soldiers. Spurred by promises of adventure and conquest abroad, thousands of eager men flocked to assembly points across the country.[33] However, opposition to "Mr. Polk's War" soon grew.

In the early fall of 1846, the U.S. Army invaded Mexico on multiple fronts and within a year's time General Winfield Scott's men took control of Mexico City. However, the city's fall did not bring an end to the war. Scott's men occupied Mexico's capital for over four months while the two countries negotiated. In the United States, the war had been controversial from the beginning. Embedded journalists sent back detailed reports from the front lines, and a divided press viciously debated the news. Volunteers found that war was not as they expected. Disease killed seven times as many American soldiers as combat.[34] Harsh discipline, conflict within the ranks, and violent clashes with civilians led soldiers to desert in huge numbers. Peace finally came on February 2, 1848 with the signing of the Treaty of Guadalupe Hidalgo.

The United States gained lands that would become the future states of California, Utah, and Nevada; most of Arizona; and parts of New Mexico, Colorado, and Wyoming. Mexican officials would also have to surrender their claims to Texas and recognize the Rio Grande as its southern boundary. The United States offered $15 million for all of it. With American soldiers occupying their capital, Mexican leaders had no choice but to sign.

The new American Southwest attracted a diverse group of entrepreneurs and settlers to the commercial towns of New Mexico, the fertile lands of eastern Texas, the famed gold deposits of California, and the Rocky Mountains. This postwar migration built earlier paths dating back to the 1820s, when the lucrative Santa Fe trade enticed merchants to New Mexico

General Scott's entrance into Mexico. Lithograph. 1851. Originally published in George Wilkins Kendall and Carl Nebel, *The War between the United States and Mexico Illustrated, Embracing Pictorial Drawings of all the Principal Conflicts* (New York: D. Appleton), 1851. Wikimedia Commons.

and generous land grants brought numerous settlers to Texas. The Gadsden Purchase of 1854 further added to American gains north of Mexico.

The U.S.-Mexican War had an enormous impact on both countries. The American victory helped set the United States on the path to becoming a world power. It elevated Zachary Taylor to the presidency and served as a training ground for many of the Civil War's future commanders. Most significantly, however, Mexico lost roughly half of its territory. Yet the United States' victory was not without danger. Ralph Waldo Emerson, an outspoken critic, predicted ominously at the beginning of the conflict, "We will conquer Mexico, but it will be as the man who swallows the arsenic which will bring him down in turn. Mexico will poison us."[35] Indeed, the conflict over whether to extend slavery into the newly won territory pushed the nation ever closer to disunion and civil war.

V. Manifest Destiny and the Gold Rush

California, belonging to Mexico prior to the war, was at least three arduous months' travel from the nearest American settlements. There was some sparse settlement in the Sacramento Valley, and missionaries made the trip occasionally. The fertile farmland of Oregon, like the black dirt lands of the Mississippi Valley, attracted more settlers than California.

The great environmental and economic potential of the Oregon Territory led many to pack up their families and head west along the Oregon Trail. The Trail represented the hopes of many for a better life, represented and reinforced by images like Bierstadt's idealistic Oregon Trail. Albert Bierstadt, *Oregon Trail (Campfire)*, 1863. Wikimedia.

Dramatized stories of Native American attacks filled migrants with a sense of foreboding, although most settlers encountered no violence and often no Native Americans at all. The slow progress, disease, human and oxen starvation, poor trails, terrible geographic preparations, lack of guidebooks, threatening wildlife, vagaries of weather, and general confusion were all more formidable and frequent than attacks from Native Americans. Despite the harshness of the journey, by 1848 approximately twenty thousand Americans were living west of the Rockies, with about three fourths of that number in Oregon.

Many who moved nurtured a romantic vision of life, attracting more Americans who sought more than agricultural life and familial responsibilities. The rugged individualism and military prowess of the West, encapsulated for some by service in the Mexican war, drew a growing new breed west of the Sierra Nevada to meet with the Californians already there: a breed of migrants different from the modest agricultural communities of the near West.

If the great draw of the West served as manifest destiny's kindling, then the discovery of gold in California was the spark that set the fire ablaze. On January 24, 1848, James W. Marshall, a contractor hired by John Sutter, discovered gold on Sutter's sawmill land in the Sacramento Valley area of the California Territory. Most western settlers sought land ownership, but the lure of getting rich quick drew younger single men (with some women) to gold towns throughout the West. These adventurers and fortune-seekers then served as magnets for the arrival of others providing services associated with the gold rush. Towns and cities grew rapidly throughout the West, notably San Francisco, whose population grew from about five hundred in 1848 to almost fifty thousand by 1853. Lawlessness, predictable failure of most fortune seekers, racial conflicts, and the slavery question all threatened manifest destiny's promises.

Throughout the 1850s, Californians beseeched Congress for a transcontinental railroad to provide service for both passengers and goods from the Midwest and the East Coast. The potential economic benefits for communities along proposed railroads made the debate over the route rancorous. Growing dissent over the slavery issue also heightened tensions.

The great influx of diverse people clashed in a combative and aggrandizing atmosphere of individualistic pursuit of fortune.[36] Linguistic, cultural, economic, and racial conflict roiled both urban and rural areas. By the end of the 1850s, Chinese and Mexican immigrants made up one fifth of the mining population in California. The ethnic patchwork of these frontier towns belied a clearly defined socioeconomic arrangement that saw whites on top as landowners and managers, with poor whites and ethnic minorities working the mines and assorted jobs. The competition for land, resources, and riches furthered individual and collective abuses, particularly against Native Americans and older Mexican communities. California's towns, as well as those dotting the landscape throughout the West, struggled to balance security with economic development and the protection of civil rights and liberties.

VI. The Monroe Doctrine and Manifest Destiny

The expansion of influence and territory off the continent became an important corollary to westward expansion. The U.S. government sought to keep European countries out of the Western Hemisphere and applied the principles of manifest destiny to the rest of the hemisphere. As secretary of state for President James Monroe, John Quincy Adams held the

This cartoon depicts a highly racialized image of a Chinese immigrant and Irish immigrant "swallowing" the United States—in the form of Uncle Sam. Networks of railroads and the promise of American expansion can be seen in the background. *The great fear of the period That Uncle Sam may be swallowed by foreigners: The problem solved*, 1860–1869. Library of Congress.

responsibility for the satisfactory resolution of ongoing border disputes between the United States, England, Spain, and Russia. Adams's view of American foreign policy was put into clearest practice in the Monroe Doctrine, which he had great influence in crafting.

Increasingly aggressive incursions from Russians in the Northwest, ongoing border disputes with the British in Canada, the remote possibility of Spanish reconquest of South America, and British abolitionism in the Caribbean all triggered an American response. In a speech before the U.S. House of Representatives on July 4, 1821, Secretary of State Adams acknowledged the American need for a robust foreign policy that simultaneously protected and encouraged the nation's growing and increasingly dynamic economy.

> America . . . in the lapse of nearly half a century, without a single exception, respected the independence of other nations while asserting and maintaining her own. . . . She is the well-wisher to the freedom and independence of all. . . . She well knows that by once enlisting under other banners than her own, were they even the banners of foreign independence, she would involve herself beyond the power of extrication, in all the wars of interest and intrigue, of individual avarice, envy, and ambition, which assume the colors and usurp the standard of freedom. The fundamental maxims of her policy would insensibly change from liberty to force. The frontlet on her brows would no longer beam with the ineffable splendor of freedom and independence; but in its stead would soon be substituted an imperial diadem, flashing in false and tarnished lustre the murky radiance of dominion and power. She might become the dictatress of the world; she would be no longer the ruler of her own spirit. . . . Her glory is not dominion, but liberty. Her march is the march of the mind. She has a spear and a shield: but the motto upon her shield is, Freedom, Independence, Peace. This has been her Declaration: this has been, as far as her necessary intercourse with the rest of mankind would permit, her practice.[37]

Adams's great fear was not territorial loss. He had no doubt that Russian and British interests in North America could be arrested. Adams held no reason to antagonize the Russians with grand pronouncements, nor was he generally called upon to do so. He enjoyed a good relationship with the Russian ambassador and stewarded through Congress most-favored trade status for the Russians in 1824. Rather, Adams worried gravely about the ability of the United States to compete commercially with the British in Latin America and the Caribbean. This concern deepened with the valid concern that America's chief Latin American trading partner, Cuba, dangled perilously close to outstretched British claws. Cabinet debates surrounding establishment of the Monroe Doctrine and geopolitical events in the Caribbean focused attention on that part of the world as key to the future defense of U.S. military and commercial interests, the main threat to those interests being the British. Expansion of economic opportunity and protection from foreign pressures became the overriding goals of U.S. foreign policy.[38] But despite the philosophical confidence present in the Monroe administration's decree, the reality of limited military power kept the Monroe Doctrine as an aspirational assertion.

Bitter disagreements over the expansion of slavery into the new lands won from Mexico began even before the war ended. Many northern businessmen and southern enslavers supported the idea of expanding slavery into the Caribbean as a useful alternative to continental expansion, since slavery already existed in these areas. Some were critical of these attempts, seeing them as evidence of a growing slave-power conspiracy. Many others supported attempts at expansion, like those previously seen in eastern Florida, even if these attempts were not exactly legal. Filibustering, as it was called, involved privately financed schemes directed at capturing and occupying foreign territory without the approval of the U.S. government.

Filibustering took greatest hold in the imagination of Americans as they looked toward Cuba. Fears of racialized revolution in Cuba (as in Haiti and Florida before it) as well as the presence of an aggressive British abolitionist influence in the Caribbean energized the movement to annex Cuba and encouraged filibustering as expedient alternatives to lethargic official negotiations. Despite filibustering's seemingly chaotic planning and destabilizing repercussions, those intellectually and economically guiding the effort imagined a willing and receptive Cuban population and expected an agreeable American business class. In Cuba, manifest destiny for the first time sought territory off the continent and hoped to put a unique spin on the story of success in Mexico. Yet the annexation of Cuba, despite great popularity and some military attempts led by Narciso López, a Cuban dissident, never succeeded.[39]

Other filibustering expeditions were launched elsewhere, including two by William Walker, a former American soldier. Walker seized portions of the Baja peninsula in Mexico and then later took power and established a slaving regime in Nicaragua. Eventually Walker was executed in Honduras.[40] These missions violated the laws of the United States, but wealthy Americans financed various filibusters, and less-wealthy adventurers were all too happy to sign up. Filibustering enjoyed its brief popularity into the late 1850s, at which point slavery and concerns over secession came to the fore. By the opening of the Civil War, most saw these attempts as simply territorial theft.

VII. Conclusion

Debates over expansion, economics, diplomacy, and manifest destiny exposed some of the weaknesses of the American system. The chauvinism of policies like Native American removal, the Mexican War, and filibus-tering existed alongside growing anxiety. Manifest destiny attempted to make a virtue of America's lack of history and turn it into the very basis of nationhood. To locate such origins, John O'Sullivan and other cham-pions of manifest destiny grafted biological and territorial imperatives—common among European definitions of nationalism—onto American political culture. The United States was the embodiment of the demo-cratic ideal, they said. Democracy had to be timeless, boundless, and portable. New methods of transportation and communication, the rapid-ity of the railroad and the telegraph, the rise of the international mar-ket economy, and the growth of the American frontier provided shared platforms to help Americans think across local identities and reaffirm a national character.

VIII. Reference Material

This chapter was edited by Joshua Beatty and Gregg Lightfoot, with content con-tributions by Ethan Bennett, Michelle Cassidy, Jonathan Grandage, Gregg Light-foot, Jose Juan Perez Melendez, Jessica Moore, Nick Roland, Matthew K. Saionz, Rowan Steinecker, Patrick Troester, and Ben Wright.

Recommended citation: Ethan Bennett et al., "Manifest Destiny," Joshua Be-atty and Gregg Lightfoot, eds., in *The American Yawp*, eds. Joseph Locke and Ben Wright (Stanford, CA: Stanford University Press, 2019).

NOTES TO CHAPTER 12

1. John O'Sullivan, "Annexation," *United States Magazine and Democratic Review* 17, no. 1 (July–August 1845): 5.

2. Yonatan Eyal, *The Young America Movement and the Transformation of the Democratic Party, 1828–1861* (New York: Cambridge University Press, 2007).

3. Ralph Waldo Emerson, "The Young American: A Lecture Read Before the Mercantile Library Association, Boston, February 7, 1844." http://www.emersoncentral.com/youngam.htm, accessed May 18, 2015.

4. See Peter S. Onuf, "Imperialism and Nationalism in the Early American Republic," in *Empire's Twin: U.S. Anti-imperialism from the Founding Era to the Age of Terrorism*, ed. Ian Tyrell and Jay Sexton (Ithaca, NY: Cornell University Press, 2015), 21–40.

5. Abraham Lincoln, "Lecture on Discoveries and Inventions: First Delivered April 6, 1858." http://www.abrahamlincolnonline.org/lincoln/speeches/discoveries.htm, accessed May 18, 2015.

6. Edmund Jefferson Danziger, *Great Lakes Indian Accommodation and Re-sistance During the Early Reservation* (Ann Arbor: University of Michigan Press, 2009), 11–13.

7. Malcolm J. Rohrbough, *Trans-Appalachian Frontier, Third Edition: People, Societies, and Institutions, 1775–1850* (Bloomington: Indiana University Press, 2008), 474–479.

8. Mark Wyman, *Immigrants in the Valley: Irish, Germans, and Americans in the Upper Mississippi Country, 1830–1860* (Carbondale: Southern Illinois University Press, 2016), 128, 148–149.

9. Horace Greeley, *New York Tribune*, 1841. Although the phrase "Go west, young man," is often attributed to Greeley, the exhortation was most likely only popularized by the newspaper editor in numerous speeches, letters, and editorials and always in the larger context of the comparable and superior health, wealth, and advantages to be had in the West.

10. Robert V. Remini, *Andrew Jackson: The Course of American Empire, 1767–1821* (Baltimore: Johns Hopkins University Press, 1977), 344–355.

11. Francis Newton Thorpe, ed., *The Federal and State Constitutions, Colonial Charters, and Other Organic Laws of the States, Territories, and Colonies Now or Heretofore Forming the United States of America Compiled and Edited Under the Act of Congress of June 30, 1906* (Washington, DC: U.S. Government Printing Office, 1909).

12. Thomas Sidney Jesup, quoted in Kenneth Wiggins Porter, "Negroes and the Seminole War, 1835–1842," *Journal of Southern History* 30, no. 4 (November 1964): 427.

13. "President Andrew Jackson's Message to Congress 'On Indian Removal' (1830)." http://www.ourdocuments.gov/doc.php?flash=true&doc=25&page=transcript, accessed May 26, 2015.

14. Ibid.

15. Tim A. Garrison, "*Worcester v. Georgia* (1832)," New Georgia Encyclopedia. http://www.georgiaencyclopedia.org/articles/government-politics/worcester-v-georgia-1832.

16. Fay A. Yarbrough, *Race and the Cherokee Nation: Sovereignty in the Nineteenth Century* (Philadelphia: University of Pennsylvania Press, 2008), 15–21.

17. John Ross, quoted in Brian Hicks, *Toward the Setting Sun: John Ross, the Cherokees, and the Trail of Tears* (New York: Atlantic Monthly Press, 2011), 210.

18. Russell Thornton, *The Cherokees: A Population History* (Lincoln: University of Nebraska Press, 1990), 76.

19. Senate Document #512, 23 Cong., 1 Sess. Vol. IV, p. x. https://books.google.com/books?id=KST1vxxCOkcC&dq=60,000+removal+indian&source=gbs_navlinks_s.

20. John P. Bowes, *Land Too Good for Indians: Northern Indian Removal* (Norman: University of Oklahoma Press, 2016).

21. Pekka Hämäläinen, *The Comanche Empire* (New Haven, CT: Yale University Press, 2008).

22. Samuel J. Wells, "Federal Indian Policy: From Accommodation to Removal," in Carolyn Reeves, ed., *The Choctaw Before Removal* (Jackson: University Press of Mississippi, 1985), 181–211.

23. William C. Sturtevant, *Handbook of North American Indians: History of Indian-White Relations*, Vol. 4 (Washington, DC: Smithsonian Institution, 1988), 289.

24. Adrienne Caughfield, *True Women and Westward Expansion* (College Station: Texas A&M University Press, 2005).

25. Murray Newton Rothbard, *Panic of 1819: Reactions and Policies* (New York: Columbia University Press, 1962).

26. Carol Sheriff, *The Artificial River: The Erie Canal and the Paradox of Progress, 1817–1862* (New York: Hill and Wang, 1996).

27. For more on the technology and transportation revolutions, see Daniel Walker Howe, *What Hath God Wrought: The Transformation of America, 1815–1848* (Oxford, UK: Oxford University Press, 2007).

28. David Reimers, *Other Immigrants: The Global Origins of the American People* (New York: New York University Press, 2005), 27.

29. H. P. N. Gammel, ed., *The Laws of Texas, 1822–1897*, Vol. 1 (Austin, TX: Gammel, 1898), 1063. https://texashistory.unt.edu/ark:/67531/metapth5872/m1/1071/.

30. Randolph B. Campbell, *An Empire for Slavery: The Peculiar Institution in Texas, 1821–1865* (Baton Rouge: LSU Press, 1989).

31. Quoted in *The Annual Register, or, a View of the History and Politics of the Year 1846, Volume 88* (Washington, DC: Rivington, 1847), 377.

32. James K. Polk, "President Polk's Mexican War Message," quoted in *The Statesmen's Manual: The Addresses and Messages of the Presidents of the United States, Inaugural, Annual, and Special, from 1789 to 1846: With a Memoir of Each of the Presidents and a History of Their Administrations; Also the Constitution of the United States, and a Selection of Important Documents and Statistical Information*, Vol. 2 (New York: Walker, 1847), 1489.

33. Amy S. Greenberg, *Manifest Manhood and the Antebellum American Empire* (Cambridge, UK: Cambridge University Press, 2005).

34. James M. McCaffrey, *Army of Manifest Destiny: The American Soldier in the Mexican War, 1846–1848* (New York: New York University Press, 1992), 53.

35. Ralph Waldo Emerson, quoted in James McPherson, *Battle Cry of Freedom: The Civil War Era* (New York: Oxford University Press, 1988), 51.

36. Susan Lee Johnson, *Roaring Camp: The Social World of the California Gold Rush* (New York: Norton, 2000).

37. John Quincy Adams, "Mr. Adams Oration, July 21, 1821," quoted in *Niles' Weekly Register* 20, (Baltimore: H. Niles, 1821), 332.

38. Gretchen Murphy, *Hemispheric Imaginings: The Monroe Doctrine and Narratives of U.S. Empire* (Durham, NC: Duke University Press, 2009).

39. Tom Chaffin, *Fatal Glory: Narciso López and the First Clandestine U.S. War Against Cuba* (Baton Rouge: LSU Press, 1996).

40. Anne F. Hyde, *Empires, Nations, and Families: A History of the North American West, 1800–1860* (Lincoln: University of Nebraska Press, 2011), 471.

RECOMMENDED READING

Blackhawk, Ned. *Violence over the Land: Indians and Empires in the Early American West*. Cambridge, MA: Harvard University Press, 2008.

Brooks, James F. *Captives and Cousins: Slavery, Kinship, and Community in the Southwest Borderlands*. Chapel Hill: University of North Carolina Press, 2003.

Cusick, James G. *The Other War of 1812: The Patriot War and the American Invasion of Spanish East Florida*. Athens: University of Georgia Press, 2007.

DeLay, Brian. *War of a Thousand Deserts: Indian Raids and the U.S.-Mexican War*. New Haven, CT: Yale University Press, 2009.

Exley, Jo Ella Powell. *Frontier Blood: The Saga of the Parker Family*. College Station: Texas A&M University Press, 2005.

Gómez, Laura E. *Manifest Destinies: The Making of the Mexican American Race*. New York: New York University Press, 2008.

Gordon, Sarah Barringer. *The Mormon Question: Polygamy and Constitutional Conflict in Nineteenth-Century America*. Chapel Hill: University of North Carolina Press, 2001.

Greenberg, Amy S. *Manifest Manhood and the Antebellum American Empire*. Cambridge, UK: Cambridge University Press, 2005.

Haas, Lisbeth. *Conquest and Historical Identities in California, 1769–1936*. Berkeley: University of California Press, 1995.

Hämäläinen, Pekka. *The Comanche Empire*. New Haven, CT: Yale University Press, 2008.

Holmes, Kenneth L. *Covered Wagon Women: Diaries & Letters from the Western Trails, 1840–1849*. Lincoln: University of Nebraska Press, 1995.

Horsman, Reginald. *Race and Manifest Destiny: The Origins of American Racial Anglo-Saxonism*. Cambridge, MA: Harvard University Press, 2009.

Hyde, Anne F. *Empires, Nations, and Families: A History of the North American West, 1800–1860*. Lincoln: University of Nebraska Press, 2011.

Johnson, Susan Lee. *Roaring Camp: The Social World of the California Gold Rush*. New York: Norton, 2000.

Larson, John Lauritz. *Internal Improvement: National Public Works and the Promise of Popular Government in the Early United States*. Chapel Hill: University of North Carolina Press, 2001.

Lazo, Rodrigo. *Writing to Cuba: Filibustering and Cuban Exiles in the United States*. Chapel Hill: University of North Carolina Press, 2006.

May, Robert E. *Manifest Destiny's Underworld: Filibustering in Antebellum America*. Chapel Hill: University of North Carolina Press, 2002.

Merry, Robert W. *A Country of Vast Designs: James K. Polk, the Mexican War and the Conquest of the American Continent*. New York: Simon and Schuster, 2009.

Namias, June. *White Captives: Gender and Ethnicity on the American Frontier*. Chapel Hill: University of North Carolina Press, 2005.

Perdue, Theda. *"Mixed Blood" Indians: Racial Construction in the Early South*. Athens: University of Georgia Press, 2005.

Peters, Virginia Pergman. *Women of the Earth Lodges: Tribal Life on the Plains.* Norman: University of Oklahoma Press, 2000.

Peterson, Dawn. *Indians in the Family: Adoption and the Politics of Antebellum Expansion.* Cambridge, MA: Harvard University Press, 2017.

Richter, Daniel K. *Facing East from Indian Country: A Native History of Early America.* Cambridge, MA: Harvard University Press, 2009.

Wilkins, David E. *Hollow Justice: A History of Indigenous Claims in the United States.* New Haven, CT: Yale University Press, 2013.

Yarbrough, Faye. *Race and the Cherokee Nation: Sovereignty in the Nineteenth Century.* Philadelphia: University of Pennsylvania Press, 2008.

13

The Sectional Crisis

I. Introduction

Slavery's western expansion created problems for the United States from the very start. Battles emerged over the westward expansion of slavery and over the role of the federal government in protecting the interests of enslavers. Northern workers felt that slavery suppressed wages and stole land that could have been used by poor white Americans to achieve economic independence. Southerners feared that without slavery's expansion, the abolitionist faction would come to dominate national politics and an increasingly dense population of enslaved people would lead to bloody insurrection and race war. Constant resistance from enslaved men and women required a strong pro-slavery government to maintain order. As the North gradually abolished human bondage, enslaved men and women headed north on an underground railroad of hideaways and safe houses. Northerners and southerners came to disagree sharply on the role of the federal government

This mural, created more than eighty years after John Brown's death, captures the violence and religious fervor of the man and his era. John Steuart Curry, *Tragic Prelude*, 1938–1940. Kansas State Capitol.

in capturing and returning these freedom seekers. While northerners appealed to their states' rights to refuse to capture people escaping slavery, white southerners demanded a national commitment to slavery. Enslaved laborers meanwhile remained vitally important to the nation's economy, fueling not only the southern plantation economy but also providing raw materials for the industrial North. Differences over the fate of slavery remained at the heart of American politics, especially as the United States expanded. After decades of conflict, Americans north and south began to fear that the opposite section of the country had seized control of the government. By November 1860, an opponent of slavery's expansion arose from within the Republican Party. During the secession crisis that followed, fears nearly a century in the making at last devolved into bloody war.

II. Sectionalism in the Early Republic

Prior to the American Revolution, nearly everyone in the world accepted slavery as a natural part of life.[1] English colonies north and south relied on enslaved workers who grew tobacco, harvested indigo and sugar, and worked in ports. They generated tremendous wealth for the British crown. That wealth and luxury fostered seemingly limitless opportunities and inspired seemingly boundless imaginations. Enslaved workers also helped give rise to revolutionary new ideals that in time became the ideological foundations of the sectional crisis. English political theorists, in particular, began to rethink natural-law justifications for slavery. They rejected the long-standing idea that slavery was a condition that naturally suited some people. A new transatlantic antislavery movement began to argue that freedom was the natural condition of humankind.[2]

Revolutionaries seized onto these ideas to stunning effect in the late eighteenth century. In the United States, France, and Haiti, revolutionaries began the work of splintering the old order. Each revolution seemed to radicalize the next. Bolder and more expansive declarations of equality and freedom followed one after the other. Revolutionaries in the United States declared, "All men are created equal," in the 1770s. French visionaries issued the "Declaration of Rights and Man and Citizen" by 1789. But the most startling development came in 1803 in Haiti. A revolution led by the island's rebellious enslaved people turned France's most valuable sugar colony into an independent country administered by the formerly enslaved.

The Haitian Revolution marked an early origin of the sectional crisis. It helped splinter the Atlantic basin into clear zones of freedom and

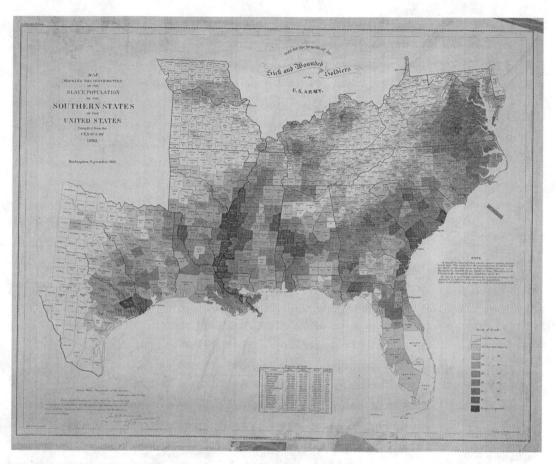

This map, published by the U.S. Coast Guard, shows the percentage of enslaved people in the population in each county of the slave-holding states in 1860. The highest percentages lie along the Mississippi River, in the "Black Belt" of Alabama, and in coastal South Carolina, all of which were centers of agricultural production (cotton and rice) in the United States. E. Hergesheimer (cartographer) and Th. Leonhardt (engraver), *Map Showing the Distribution of the Slave Population of the Southern States of the United States Compiled from the Census of 1860*, c. 1861. Wikimedia.

unfreedom, shattering the long-standing assumption that African-descended enslaved people could not also be rulers. Despite the clear limitations of the American Revolution in attacking slavery, the era marked a powerful break in slavery's history. Military service on behalf of both the English and the American army freed thousands of enslaved people. Many others simply used the turmoil of war to make their escape. As a result, free Black communities emerged—communities that would continually reignite the antislavery struggle. For nearly a century, most white Americans were content to compromise over the issue of slavery, but the constant agitation of Black Americans, both enslaved and free, kept the issue alive.[3]

The national breakdown over slavery occurred over a long timeline and across a broad geography. Debates over slavery in the American

West proved especially important. As the United States pressed westward, new questions arose as to whether those lands ought to be slave or free. The framers of the Constitution did a little, but not much, to help resolve these early questions. Article VI of the 1787 Northwest Ordinance banned slavery north and west of the Ohio River.[4] Many took it to mean that the founders intended for slavery to die out, as why else would they prohibit its spread across such a huge swath of territory?

Debates over the framers' intentions often led to confusion and bitter debate, but the actions of the new government left better clues as to what the new nation intended for slavery. Congress authorized the admission of Vermont (1791) and Kentucky (1792), with Vermont coming into the Union as a free state and Kentucky coming in as a slave state. Though Americans at the time made relatively little of the balancing act suggested by the admission of a slave state and a free state, the pattern became increasingly important, particularly when considering power in the United States Senate. By 1820, preserving the balance of free states and slave states would be seen as an issue of national security.

New pressures challenging the delicate balance again arose in the West. The Louisiana Purchase of 1803 more than doubled the size of the United States. Questions immediately arose as to whether these lands would be made slave or free. Complicating matters further was the rapid expansion of plantation slavery fueled by the invention of the cotton gin in 1793. Yet even with the booming cotton economy, many Americans, including Thomas Jefferson, believed that slavery was a temporary institution and would soon die out. Tensions rose with the Louisiana Purchase, but a truly sectional national debate remained mostly dormant.

That debate, however, came quickly. Sectional differences tied to the expansion of plantation slavery in the West were especially important after 1803. The Ohio River Valley became an early fault line in the coming sectional struggle. Kentucky and Tennessee emerged as slave states, while free states Ohio, Indiana (1816), and Illinois (1818) gained admission along the river's northern banks. Borderland negotiations and accommodations along the Ohio River fostered a distinctive kind of white supremacy, as laws tried to keep Black people out of the West entirely. Ohio's so-called Black Laws of 1803 foreshadowed the exclusionary cultures of Indiana, Illinois, and several subsequent states of the Old Northwest and later, the Far West.[5] These laws often banned African American voting, denied Black Americans access to public schools, and made it impossible for nonwhites to serve on juries and in local militias, among a host of other restrictions and obstacles.

The Missouri Territory, by far the largest section of the Louisiana Territory, marked a turning point in the sectional crisis. St. Louis, a bustling Mississippi River town filled with powerful enslavers, loomed large as an important trade headquarters for networks in the northern Mississippi Valley and the Greater West. In 1817, eager to put questions of whether this territory would be slave or free to rest, Congress opened its debate over Missouri's admission to the Union. Congressman James Tallmadge of New York proposed laws that would gradually abolish slavery in the new state. Southern states responded with unanimous outrage, and the nation shuddered at an undeniable sectional controversy.[6]

Congress reached a "compromise" on Missouri's admission, largely through the work of Kentuckian Henry Clay. Maine would be admitted to the Union as a free state. In exchange, Missouri would come into the Union as a slave state. Legislators sought to prevent future conflicts by making Missouri's southern border at 36°30' the new dividing line between slavery and freedom in the Louisiana Purchase lands. South of that line, running east from Missouri to the western edge of the Louisiana Purchase lands (near the present-day Texas panhandle), slavery could expand. North of it, encompassing what in 1820 was still "unorganized territory," there would be no slavery.[7]

The Missouri Compromise marked a major turning point in America's sectional crisis because it exposed to the public just how divisive the slavery issue had grown. The debate filled newspapers, speeches, and congressional records. Antislavery and pro-slavery positions from that point forward repeatedly returned to points made during the Missouri debates. Legislators battled for weeks over whether the Constitutional framers intended slavery's expansion, and these contests left deep scars. Even seemingly simple and straightforward phrases like "all men are created equal" were hotly contested all over again. Questions over the expansion of slavery remained open, but nearly all Americans concluded that the Constitution protected slavery where it already existed.

Southerners were not yet advancing arguments that said slavery was a positive good, but they did insist during the Missouri Debate that the framers supported slavery and wanted to see it expand. In Article I, Section 2, for example, the Constitution enabled representation in the South to be based on rules defining an enslaved person as three fifths of a voter, meaning southern white men would be overrepresented in Congress. The Constitution also stipulated that Congress could not interfere with the slave trade before 1808 and enabled Congress to draft fugitive slave laws.

Antislavery participants in the Missouri debate argued that the framers never intended slavery to survive the Revolution and in fact hoped it would disappear through peaceful means. The framers of the Constitution never used the word *slave*. Enslaved people were referred to as "persons held in service," perhaps referring to English common law precedents that questioned the legitimacy of "property in man." Antislavery activists also pointed out that while Congress could not pass a law limiting the slave trade before 1808, the framers had also recognized the flip side of the debate and had thus opened the door to legislating the slave trade's end once the deadline arrived. Language in the Tenth Amendment, they claimed, also said slavery could be banned in the territories. Finally, they pointed to the due process clause of the Fifth Amendment, which said that property could be seized through appropriate legislation.[8] The bruising Missouri debates ultimately transcended arguments about the Constitution. They became an all-encompassing referendum on the American past, present, and future.

Despite the furor, the Missouri crisis did not yet inspire hardened defenses of either slave or free labor. Those would come in the coming decades. In the meantime, the uneasy consensus forged by the Missouri debate managed to bring a measure of calm.

The Missouri debate had also deeply troubled the nation's African Americans and Native Americans. By the time of the Missouri Compromise debate, both groups saw that whites never intended them to be citizens of the United States. In fact, the debates over Missouri's admission had offered the first sustained debate on the question of Black citizenship, as Missouri's state constitution wanted to impose a hard ban on any future Black migrants. Legislators ultimately agreed that this hard ban violated the U.S. Constitution but reaffirmed Missouri's ability to deny citizenship to African Americans. Americans by 1820 had endured a broad challenge, not only to their cherished ideals but also more fundamentally to their conceptions of self.

III. The Crisis Joined

Missouri's admission to the Union in 1821 exposed deep fault lines in American society. But the compromise created a new sectional consensus that most white Americans, at least, hoped would ensure a lasting peace. Through sustained debates and arguments, white Americans agreed that the Constitution could do little about slavery where it already existed and that slavery, with the State of Missouri as the key exception, would never expand north of the 36°30′ line.

Once again westward expansion challenged this consensus, and this time the results proved even more damaging. Tellingly, enslaved southerners were among the first to signal their discontent. A rebellion led by Denmark Vesey in 1822 threatened lives and property throughout the Carolinas. The nation's religious leaders also expressed a rising discontent with the new status quo.[9] The Second Great Awakening further sharpened political differences by promoting schisms within the major Protestant churches, schisms that also became increasingly sectional in nature. Between 1820 and 1846, sectionalism drew on new political parties, new religious organizations, and new reform movements.

As politics grew more democratic, leaders attacked old inequalities of wealth and power, but in doing so many pandered to a unity under white supremacy. Slavery briefly receded from the nation's attention in the early 1820s, but that would change quickly. By the last half of the decade, slavery was back, and this time it appeared even more threatening.

Inspired by the social change of Jacksonian democracy, white men regardless of status would gain not only land and jobs but also the right to vote, the right to serve on juries, the right to attend public schools, and the right to serve in the militia and armed forces. In this post-Missouri context, leaders arose to push the country's new expansionist desires in aggressive new directions. As they did so, however, the sectional crisis again deepened.

The Democratic Party initially seemed to offer a compelling answer to the problems of sectionalism by promising benefits to white working men of the North, South, and West, while also uniting rural, small-town, and urban residents. Indeed, huge numbers of western, southern, and northern workingmen rallied behind Andrew Jackson during the 1828 presidential election. The Democratic Party tried to avoid the issue of slavery and instead sought to unite Americans around shared commitments to white supremacy and desires to expand the nation.

Democrats were not without their critics. Northerners seen as especially friendly to the South had become known as "Doughfaces" during the Missouri debates, and as the 1830s wore on, more and more Doughfaced Democrats became vulnerable to the charge that they served the southern slaving oligarchs better than they served their own northern communities. Whites discontented with the direction of the country used the slur and other critiques to help chip away at Democratic Party majorities. The accusation that northern Democrats were lapdogs for southern enslavers had real power.[10]

The Whigs offered an organized major-party challenge to the Democrats. Whig strongholds often mirrored the patterns of westward migrations out of New England. Whigs drew from an odd coalition of wealthy merchants, middle- and upper-class farmers, planters in the Upland South, and settlers in the Great Lakes. Because of this motley coalition, the party struggled to bring a cohesive message to voters in the 1830s. Their strongest support came from places like Ohio's Western Reserve, the rural and Protestant-dominated areas of Michigan, and similar parts of Protestant and small-town Illinois, particularly the fast-growing towns and cities of the state's northern half.[11]

Whig leaders stressed Protestant culture and federal-sponsored internal improvements and courted the support of a variety of reform movements, including temperance, nativism, and even antislavery, though few Whigs believed in racial equality. These positions attracted a wide range of figures, including a young convert to politics named Abraham Lincoln. Lincoln admired Whig leader Henry Clay of Kentucky, and by the early 1830s, Lincoln certainly fit the image of a developing Whig. A veteran of the Black Hawk War, Lincoln had relocated to New Salem, Illinois, where he worked a variety of odd jobs, living a life of thrift, self-discipline, and sobriety as he educated himself in preparation for a professional life in law and politics.

The Whig Party blamed Democrats for defending slavery at the expense of the American people, but antislavery was never a core component of the Whig platform. Several abolitionists grew so disgusted with the Whigs that they formed their own party, a true antislavery party. Activists in Warsaw, New York, organized the antislavery Liberty Party in 1839. Liberty leaders demanded the end of slavery in the District of Columbia, the end of the interstate slave trade, and the prohibition of slavery's expansion into the West. But the Liberty Party also shunned women's participation in the movement and distanced themselves from visions of true racial egalitarianism. Few Americans voted for the party. The Democrats and Whigs continued to dominate American politics.

Democrats and Whigs fostered a moment of relative calm on the slavery debate, partially aided by gag rules prohibiting discussion of antislavery petitions. Arkansas (1836) and Michigan (1837) became the newest states admitted to the Union, with Arkansas coming in as a slave state, and Michigan coming in as a free state. Michigan gained admission through provisions established in the Northwest Ordinance, while Arkansas came in under the Missouri Compromise. Since its lands were below the line at 36°30′, the admission of Arkansas did not threaten the Missouri consensus. The balancing act between slavery and freedom continued.

Events in Texas would shatter the balance. Independent Texas soon gained recognition from a supportive Andrew Jackson administration in 1837. But Jackson's successor, President Martin Van Buren, also a Democrat, soon had reasons to worry about the Republic of Texas. Texas struggled with ongoing conflicts with Mexico and raids from the powerful Comanche. The 1844 democratic presidential candidate James K. Polk sought to bridge the sectional divide by promising new lands to whites north and south. Polk cited the annexation of Texas and the Oregon Territory as campaign cornerstones.[12] Yet as Polk championed the acquisition of these vast new lands, northern Democrats grew annoyed by their southern colleagues, especially when it came to Texas.

For many observers, the debates over Texas statehood illustrated that the federal government was clearly pro-slavery. Texas president Sam Houston managed to secure a deal with Polk and gained admission to the Union for Texas in 1845. Antislavery northerners also worried about the admission of Florida, which entered the Union as a slave state in 1845. The year 1845 became a pivotal year in the memory of antislavery leaders. As Americans embraced calls to pursue their manifest destiny, antislavery voices looked at developments in Florida and Texas as signs that the sectional crisis had taken an ominous and perhaps irredeemable turn.

The 1840s opened with a number of disturbing developments for antislavery leaders. The 1842 Supreme Court case *Prigg v. Pennsylvania* ruled that the federal government's Fugitive Slave Act trumped Pennsylvania's personal liberty law.[13] Antislavery activists believed that the federal government only served southern enslavers and were trouncing the states' rights of the North. A number of northern states reacted by passing new personal liberty laws in protest in 1843.

The rising controversy over the status of freedom-seeking people swelled partly through the influence of escaped formerly enslaved people, including Frederick Douglass. Douglass's entrance into northern politics marked an important new development in the nation's coming sectional crisis. Born into slavery in 1818 at Talbot County, Maryland, Douglass grew up, like many enslaved people, barely having known his own mother or date of birth. And yet because of a range of unique privileges afforded him by the circumstances of his upbringing, as well as his own genius and determination, Douglass managed to learn how to read and write. He used these skills to escape from slavery in 1837, when he was just nineteen. By 1845, Douglass put the finishing touches on his autobiography, *Narrative of the Life of Frederick Douglass*.[14] The book launched his lifelong career as an advocate for the enslaved and helped further raise the visibility of Black politics. Other formerly enslaved people, including Sojourner Truth, joined Douglass in rousing support for antislavery, as did free Black Americans like Maria Stewart, James McCune Smith, Martin Delaney, and numerous others.[15] But Black activists did more than deliver speeches. They also attacked fugitive slave laws by helping thousands to escape. The incredible career of Harriet Tubman is one of the more dramatic examples. But the forces of slavery had powerful allies at every level of government.

The year 1846 signaled new reversals to the antislavery cause and the beginnings of a dark new era in American politics. President Polk and his Democratic allies were eager to see western lands brought into the Union and were especially anxious to see the borders of the nation extended to the shores of the Pacific Ocean. Critics of the administration blasted these efforts as little more than land grabs on behalf of enslavers. Events in early 1846 seemed to justify antislavery complaints. Since Mexico had never recognized independent Texas, it continued to lay claim to its lands, even after the United States admitted it to the Union. In January 1846, Polk ordered troops to Texas to enforce claims stemming from its border dispute along the Rio Grande. Polk asked for war on May 11, 1846, and by September 1847, the United States had invaded Mexico City. Whigs, like Abraham Lincoln, found their protests sidelined, but antislavery voices were becoming more vocal and more powerful.

After 1846, the sectional crisis raged throughout North America. Debates swirled over whether the new lands would be slave or free. The South began defending slavery as a positive good. At the same time, Congressman David Wilmot submitted his Wilmot Proviso late in 1846, banning the expansion of slavery into the territories won from Mexico. The proviso gained widespread northern support and even passed the House with bipartisan support, but it failed in the Senate.

IV. Free Soil, Free Labor, Free Men

The conclusion of the Mexican War led to the 1848 Treaty of Guadalupe Hidalgo. The treaty infuriated antislavery leaders in the United States. The spoils of war were impressive, but it was clear they would help expand slavery. Antislavery activists, who already judged the Mexican War an enslavers' plot, vowed that no new territories would be opened to slavery. But knowing that the Liberty Party was also not likely to provide a home to many moderate voters, leaders fostered a new and more competitive party, which they called the Free Soil Party. Antislavery leaders had thought that their vision of a federal government divorced from slavery might be represented by the major parties in that year's presidential election, but both the Whigs and the Democrats nominated candidates hostile to the antislavery cause. Left unrepresented, antislavery Free Soil leaders swung into action.

Demanding an alternative to the pro-slavery status quo, Free Soil leaders assembled so-called Conscience Whigs, the remnants of the Liberty Party and antislavery Democrats. The new coalition called for a national convention in August 1848 at Buffalo, New York. A number of ex-Democrats committed to the party right away, including an important group of New Yorkers loyal to Martin Van Buren. The Free Soil Party's platform bridged the eastern and western leadership together and called for an end to slavery in Washington, D.C., and a halt on slavery's expansion

Questions about the balance of free and slave states in the Union became even more fierce after the United States acquired these territories from Mexico by the 1848 in the Treaty of Guadalupe Hidalgo. *Map of the Mexican Cession*, 2008. Wikimedia. Creative Commons Attribution-Share Alike 3.0 Unported.

in the territories.[16] The Free Soil movement hardly made a dent in the 1848 presidential election, but it drew more than four times the popular vote won by the Liberty Party earlier. It was a promising start. In 1848, Free Soil leaders claimed just 10 percent of the popular vote but won over a dozen House seats and even managed to win one Senate seat in Ohio, which went to Salmon P. Chase.[17] In Congress, Free Soil members had enough votes to swing power to either the Whigs or the Democrats.

The admission of Wisconsin as a free state in May 1848 helped cool tensions after the Texas and Florida admissions. Meanwhile, news from a number of failed European revolutions alarmed American reformers, but as exiled radicals filtered into the United States, a strengthening women's rights movement also flexed its muscle at Seneca Falls, New York. Led by figures such as Elizabeth Cady Stanton and Lucretia Mott, women with deep ties to the abolitionist cause, it represented the first of such meetings ever held in U.S. history.[18] Frederick Douglass also appeared at the convention and took part in the proceedings, where participants debated the Declaration of Sentiments, Grievances, and Resolutions.[19] By August 1848, it seemed plausible that the Free Soil Movement might tap into these reforms and build a broader coalition. In some ways that is precisely what it did. But come November, the spirit of reform failed to yield much at the polls. Whig candidate Zachary Taylor bested Democrat Lewis Cass of Michigan.

The upheavals of 1848 came to a quick end. Taylor remained in office only a brief time until his unexpected death from a stomach ailment in 1850. During Taylor's brief time in office, the fruits of the Mexican War began to spoil. While Taylor was alive, his administration struggled to find a good remedy. Increased clamoring for the admission of California, New Mexico, and Utah pushed the country closer to the edge. Gold had been discovered in California, and as thousands continued to pour onto the West Coast and through the trans-Mississippi West, the admission of new states loomed. In Utah, Mormons were also making claims to an independent state they called Deseret. By 1850, California wanted admission as a free state. With so many competing dynamics under way, and with the president dead and replaced by Whig Millard Fillmore, the 1850s were off to a troubling start.

Congressional leaders like Henry Clay and newer legislators like Stephen A. Douglas of Illinois were asked to broker a compromise, but this time it was clear no compromise could bridge all the diverging interests at play in the country. Clay eventually left Washington disheartened by affairs. It fell to young Stephen Douglas, then, to shepherd the bills through Congress, which he in fact did. Legislators rallied behind the Compro-

Henry Clay ("The Great Compromiser") addresses the U.S. Senate during the debates over the Compromise of 1850. The print shows a number of incendiary personalities, like John C. Calhoun, whose increasingly sectional beliefs were pacified for a time by the Compromise. P. F. Rothermel (artist), c. 1855. Wikimedia.

mise of 1850, an assemblage of bills passed late in 1850, which managed to keep the promises of the Missouri Compromise alive.

The Compromise of 1850 tried to offer something to everyone, but in the end it only worsened the sectional crisis. For southerners, the package offered a tough new fugitive slave law that empowered the federal government to deputize regular citizens in arresting runaways. The New Mexico Territory and the Utah Territory would be allowed to determine their own fates as slave or free states based on popular sovereignty. The compromise also allowed territories to submit suits directly to the Supreme Court over the status of freedom-seeking people within their bounds.

The admission of California as the newest free state in the Union cheered many northerners, but even the admission of a vast new state full of resources and rich agricultural lands was not enough. In addition to California, northerners also gained a ban on the slave trade in Washington, D.C., but not the full emancipation abolitionists had long advocated.

Texas, which had already come into the Union as a slave state, was asked to give some of its land to New Mexico in return for the federal government absorbing some of the former republic's debt. But the compromise debates soon grew ugly.

After the Compromise of 1850, antislavery critics became increasingly certain that enslavers had co-opted the federal government, and that a southern Slave Power secretly held sway in Washington, where it hoped to make slavery a national institution. These northern complaints pointed back to how the three-fifths compromise of the Constitution gave southerners proportionally more representatives in Congress. In the 1850s, antislavery leaders increasingly argued that Washington worked on behalf of enslavers while ignoring the interests of white working men.

None of the individual measures in the Compromise of 1850 proved more troubling to antislavery Americans than the Fugitive Slave Act. In a clear bid to extend slavery's influence throughout the country, the act created special federal commissioners to determine the fate of alleged fugitives without benefit of a jury trial or even court testimony. Under its provisions, local authorities in the North could not interfere with the capture of fugitives. Northern citizens, moreover, had to assist in the arrest of fugitives when called upon by federal agents. The Fugitive Slave Act created the foundation for a massive expansion of federal power, including an alarming increase in the nation's policing powers. Many northerners were also troubled by the way the bill undermined local and state laws. The law itself fostered corruption and the enslavement of free Black northerners. The federal commissioners who heard these cases were paid $10 if they determined that the defendant was a slave and only $5 if they determined he or she was free.[20] Many Black northerners responded to the new law by heading farther north to Canada.

The 1852 presidential election gave the Whigs their most stunning defeat and effectively ended their existence as a national political party. Whigs captured just 42 of the 254 electoral votes needed to win. With the Compromise of 1850 and plenty of new lands, peaceful consensus seemed to be on the horizon. Antislavery feelings continued to run deep, however. One measure of the popularity of antislavery ideas came in 1852 when Harriet Beecher Stowe published her best-selling antislavery novel, *Uncle Tom's Cabin*. Sales for *Uncle Tom's Cabin* were astronomical, eclipsed only by sales of the Bible.[21] The book became a sensation and helped move antislavery into everyday conversation for many north-

Uncle Tom's Cabin intensified an already hot debate over slavery throughout the United States. The book revolves around Eliza (the woman holding the young boy) and Tom (standing with his wife, Chloe), each of whom takes a very different path: Eliza escapes slavery using her own two feet, but Tom endures his chains only to die by the whip of a brutish enslaver. The horrific violence that both endured melted the hearts of many Northerners and pressed some to join in the fight against slavery. Full-page illustration by Hammatt Billings for *Uncle Tom's Cabin*, 1852. Wikimedia.

erners. Despite the powerful antislavery message, Stowe's book also reinforced many racist stereotypes. Even abolitionists struggled with the deeply ingrained racism that plagued American society. While the major success of *Uncle Tom's Cabin* bolstered the abolitionist cause, the terms outlined by the Compromise of 1850 appeared strong enough to keep the peace.

Democrats by 1853 were badly splintered along sectional lines over slavery, but they also had reasons to act with confidence. Voters had returned them to office in 1852 following the bitter fights over the Compromise of 1850. Emboldened, Illinois senator Stephen A. Douglas introduced a set of additional amendments to a bill drafted in late 1853 to help organize the Nebraska Territory, the last of the Louisiana Purchase lands. In 1853, the Nebraska Territory was huge, extending from the northern end of Texas to the Canadian border. Altogether, it encompassed present-day Nebraska, Wyoming, South Dakota, North Dakota, Colorado, and Montana. Douglas's efforts to amend and introduce the bill in

1854 opened dynamics that would break the Democratic Party in two and, in the process, rip the country apart.

Douglas proposed a bold plan in 1854 to cut off a large southern chunk of Nebraska and create it separately as the Kansas Territory. Douglas had a number of goals in mind. The expansionist Democrat from Illinois wanted to organize the territory to facilitate the completion of a national railroad that would flow through Chicago. But before he had even finished introducing the bill, opposition had already mobilized. Salmon P. Chase drafted a response in northern newspapers that exposed the Kansas-Nebraska Bill as a measure to overturn the Missouri Compromise and open western lands for slavery. Kansas-Nebraska protests emerged in 1854 throughout the North, with key meetings in Wisconsin and Michigan. Kansas would become slave or free depending on the result of local elections, elections that would be greatly influenced by migrants flooding to the state to either protect or stop the spread of slavery.

Ordinary Americans in the North increasingly resisted what they believed to be a pro-slavery federal government on their own terms. The rescues and arrests of enslaved men like Anthony Burns in Boston and Joshua Glover in Milwaukee signaled the rising vehemence of resistance to the nation's 1850 fugitive slave law. The case of Anthony Burns illustrates how the Fugitive Slave Law radicalized many northerners. On May 24, 1854, twenty-year-old Burns, a preacher who worked in a Boston clothing shop, was clubbed and dragged to jail. One year earlier, Burns had escaped slavery in Virginia, and a group of slave catchers had come to return him to Richmond. Word of Burns's capture spread rapidly through Boston, and a mob gathered outside the courthouse demanding Burns's release. Two days after the arrest, the crowd stormed the courthouse and shot a deputy U.S. Marshal to death. News reached Washington, and the federal government sent soldiers. Boston was placed under martial law. Federal troops lined the streets of Boston as Burns was marched to a ship, where he was sent back to slavery in Virginia. After spending over $40,000, the U.S. government had successfully reenslaved Anthony Burns.[22] A short time later, Burns was redeemed by abolitionists who paid $1,300 to return him to freedom, but the outrage among Bostonians only grew. And Anthony Burns was only one of hundreds of highly publicized episodes of the federal government imposing the Fugitive Slave Law on rebellious northern populations. In the words of Amos Adams Lawrence, "We went to bed one night old-fashioned, conservative, compromise Union Whigs & woke up stark mad Abolitionists."[23]

Anthony Burns, the fugitive slave, appears in a portrait at the center of this 1855 print. Burns's arrest and trial, possible because of the 1850 Fugitive Slave Act, became a rallying cry. As a symbol of the injustice of the slave system, Burns's treatment spurred riots and protests by abolitionists and citizens of Boston in the spring of 1854. John Andrews (engraver), *Anthony Burns*, c. 1855. Library of Congress.

As northerners radicalized, organizations like the New England Emigrant Aid Company provided guns and other goods for pioneers willing to go to Kansas and establish the territory as antislavery through popular sovereignty. On all sides of the slavery issue, politics became increasingly militarized.

The year 1855 nearly derailed the northern antislavery coalition. A resurgent anti-immigrant movement briefly took advantage of the Whig collapse and nearly stole the energy of the anti-administration forces by channeling its frustrations into fights against the large number of mostly Catholic German and Irish immigrants in American cities. Calling themselves Know-Nothings, on account of their tendency to pretend ignorance when asked about their activities, the Know-Nothing or American Party made impressive gains in 1854 and 1855, particularly in New England and the Middle Atlantic. But the anti-immigrant movement simply could not capture the nation's attention in ways the antislavery movement already had.[24]

The antislavery political movements that started in 1854 coalesced with the formation of a new political party. Harking back to the founding fathers, its organizers named it the Republican Party. Republicans moved forward into a highly charged summer.

Following an explosive speech before Congress on May 19–20, Senator Charles Sumner of Massachusetts was violently beaten with a cane by Representative Preston Brooks of South Carolina on the floor of the Senate chamber. Among other accusations, Sumner accused Senator Andrew Butler of South Carolina, Brooks's cousin, of defending slavery so he could have sexual access to Black women.[25] Brooks felt that he had to defend his relative's honor and nearly killed Sumner as a result.

The violence in Washington pales before the many murders occurring in Kansas.[26] Pro-slavery raiders attacked Lawrence, Kansas. Radical abolitionist John Brown retaliated, murdering several pro-slavery Kansans in retribution. As all of this played out, the House failed to expel Brooks. Brooks resigned his seat anyway, only to be reelected by his constituents later in the year. He received new canes emblazoned with the words "Hit him again!"[27]

With sectional tensions at a breaking point, both parties readied for the coming presidential election. In June 1856, the newly named Republican Party held its nominating convention at Philadelphia and selected Californian John Charles Frémont. Frémont's antislavery credentials may not have pleased many abolitionists, but his dynamic and talented wife, Jessie Benton Frémont, appealed to more radical members of the coalition. The Kansas-Nebraska debate, the organization of the Republican Party, and the 1856 presidential campaign all energized a new generation of political leaders, including Abraham Lincoln. Beginning with his speech at Peoria, Illinois, in 1854, Lincoln carved out a message that

The Caning of Charles Sumner, 1856. Wikimedia.

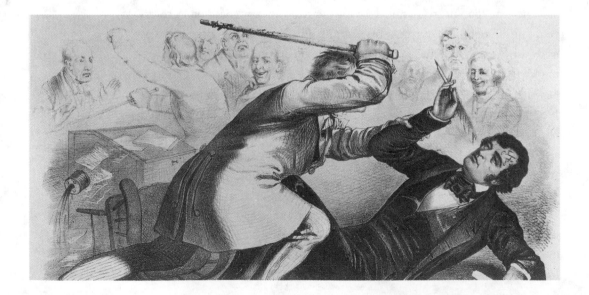

encapsulated better than anyone else the main ideas and visions of the Republican Party.[28] Lincoln himself was slow to join the coalition, yet by the summer of 1856, Lincoln had fully committed to the Frémont campaign.

Frémont lost, but Republicans celebrated that he won eleven of the sixteen free states. This showing, they urged, was truly impressive for any party making its first run at the presidency. Yet northern Democrats in crucial swing states remained unmoved by the Republican Party's appeals. Ulysses S. Grant of Missouri, for example, worried that Frémont and Republicans signaled trouble for the Union itself. Grant voted for the Democratic candidate, James Buchanan, believing a Republican victory might bring about disunion. In abolitionist and especially Black American circles, Frémont's defeat was more than a disappointment. Believing their fate had been sealed as permanent noncitizens, some African Americans would consider foreign emigration and colonization. Others began to explore the option of more radical and direct action against the Slave Power.

V. From Sectional Crisis to National Crisis

White antislavery leaders hailed Frémont's defeat as a "glorious" one and looked ahead to the party's future successes. For those still in slavery or hoping to see loved ones freed, the news was of course much harder to take. The Republican Party had promised the rise of an antislavery coalition, but voters rebuked it. The lessons seemed clear enough.

Kansas loomed large over the 1856 election, darkening the national mood. The story of voter fraud in Kansas had begun years before in 1854, when nearby Missourians first started crossing the border to tamper with the Kansas elections. Noting this, critics at the time attacked the Pierce administration for not living up to the ideals of popular sovereignty by ensuring fair elections. From there, the crisis only deepened and democratic norms collapsed. Kansas voted to come into the Union as a free state, but the federal government refused to recognize their votes and instead recognized a sham pro-slavery legislature.

The sectional crisis had at last become a national crisis. "Bleeding Kansas" was the first place to demonstrate that the sectional crisis could easily be, and in fact already was, exploding into a full-blown national crisis. As the national mood grew increasingly grim, Kansas attracted militants representing the extreme sides of the slavery debate.

In the days after the 1856 presidential election, Buchanan made his plans for his time in office clear. He talked with Chief Justice Roger Taney on inauguration day about a court decision he hoped to see handled during his time in office. Indeed, not long after the inauguration, the Supreme Court handed down a decision that would come to define Buchanan's presidency. The Dred Scott decision, *Scott v. Sandford*, ruled that Black Americans could not be citizens of the United States and therefore could be transported as chattel from any state to another regardless of state law.[29] This gave the Buchanan administration and its southern allies a direct repudiation of the Missouri Compromise. The court ruled that Scott, a Missouri slave, had no right to sue in United States courts. The Dred Scott decision signaled that the federal government was now fully committed to extending slavery as far and as wide as it might want.

The Dred Scott decision seemed to settle the sectional crisis by making slavery fully national, but in reality it just exacerbated sectional tensions further. In 1857, Buchanan sent U.S. military forces to Utah, hoping to subdue Utah's Mormon communities. This action, however, led to renewed charges, many of them leveled from within his own party, that

Dred Scott's Supreme Court case made clear that the federal government was no longer able or willing to ignore the issue of slavery. More than that, all Black Americans, Justice Taney declared, could never be citizens of the United States. Though seemingly a disastrous decision for abolitionists, this controversial ruling actually increased the ranks of the abolitionist movement. Photograph of Dred Scott, 1857. Wikimedia.

the administration was abusing its powers. Far more important than the Utah invasion, however, were the ongoing events in Kansas. It was Kansas that at last proved to many northerners that the sectional crisis would not go away unless slavery also went away.

The Illinois Senate race in 1858 put the scope of the sectional crisis on full display. Republican candidate Abraham Lincoln challenged the greatly influential Democrat Stephen Douglas. Pandering to appeals to white supremacy, Douglas hammered the Republican opposition as a "Black Republican" party bent on racial equality.[30] The Republicans, including Lincoln, fired back with warnings of divisiveness and assertions that all Americans deserved equality of opportunity. Democrats hung on as best they could, but the Republicans won the House of Representatives and picked up seats in the Senate. Lincoln actually lost his contest with Stephen Douglas but in the process firmly established himself as a leading national Republican. After the 1858 elections, all eyes turned to 1860. Given the Republican Party's successes since 1854, it was expected that the 1860 presidential election might produce the nation's first antislavery president.

In the troubled decades since the Missouri Compromise, the nation slowly tore itself apart. Congressmen clubbed each other nearly to death on the floor of Congress, and by the middle of the 1850s Americans were already at war on the Kansas and Missouri plains. Across the country, cities and towns were in various stages of revolt against federal authority. Fighting spread even farther against Native Americans in the Far West and against Mormons in Utah. The nation's militants anticipated a coming breakdown and worked to exploit it. John Brown, fresh from his actions in Kansas, moved east and planned more violence. Assembling a team from across the West, including Black radicals from Oberlin, Ohio, and throughout communities in western Canada, Brown hatched a plan to attack Harper's Ferry, a federal weapons arsenal in Virginia (now West Virginia). He would use the weapons to lead a revolt of enslaved people. Brown approached Frederick Douglass, though Douglass refused to join.

Brown's raid embarked on October 16. By October 18, a command under Robert E. Lee had crushed the revolt. Many of Brown's men, including his own sons, were killed, but Brown himself lived and was imprisoned. Brown prophesied while in prison that the nation's crimes would only be purged with blood. He went to the gallows in December 1859. Northerners made a stunning display of sympathy on the day of his execution. Southerners took their reactions to mean that the coming

The execution of John Brown made him a martyr in abolitionist circles and a confirmed traitor in Southern crowds. Both of these images continued to pervade public memory after the Civil War, but in the North especially (where so many soldiers had died to help end slavery) his name was admired. Over two decades after Brown's death, Thomas Hovenden portrayed Brown as a saint. As he is led to his execution for attempting to destroy slavery, Brown poignantly leans over a rail to kiss a Black baby. Thomas Hovenden, *The Last Moments of John Brown*, c. 1882–1884. Wikimedia.

1860 election would be, in many ways, a referendum on secession and disunion.

Republicans wanted little to do with Brown and instead tried to portray themselves as moderates opposed to both abolitionists and pro-slavery expansionists. In this climate, the parties opened their contest for the 1860 presidential election. The Democratic Party fared poorly as its southern delegates bolted its national convention at Charleston and ran their own candidate, Vice President John C. Breckenridge of Kentucky. Hoping to field a candidate who might nonetheless manage to bridge the broken party's factions, the Democrats decided to meet again at Baltimore and nominated Stephen A. Douglas of Illinois.

The Republicans, meanwhile, held their boisterous convention in Chicago. The Republican platform made the party's antislavery commitments clear, also making wide promises to its white constituents, particularly westerners, with the promise of new land, transcontinental railroads, and broad support of public schools.[31] Abraham Lincoln, a candidate few outside Illinois truly expected to win, nonetheless proved far less polarizing than the other names on the ballot. Lincoln won the

This political cartoon depicts the four candidates in the 1860 presidential election. *Dividing the National Map*. Available from the Library of Congress.

nomination, and with the Democrats in disarray, Republicans knew their candidate Lincoln had a good chance of winning.

Abraham Lincoln won the 1860 contest on November 6, gaining just 40 percent of the popular vote and not a single southern vote in the Electoral College. Within days, southern states were organizing secession conventions. John J. Crittenden of Kentucky proposed a series of compromises, but a clear pro-southern bias meant they had little chance of gaining Republican acceptance. Crittenden's plan promised renewed enforcement of the Fugitive Slave Law and offered a plan to keep slavery in the nation's capital.[32] Republicans by late 1860 knew that the voters who had just placed them in power did not want them to cave on these points, and southern states proceeded with their plans to leave the Union. On December 20, South Carolina voted to secede and issued its Declaration of the Immediate Causes.[33] The declaration highlighted failure of the federal government to enforce the Fugitive Slave Act over competing personal liberty laws in northern states. After the war many southerners claimed that secession was primarily motivated by a concern to preserve states' rights, but the primary complaint of the very first ordinance of secession listed the federal government's failure to exert its authority over the northern states.

The year 1861, then, saw the culmination of the secession crisis. Before he left for Washington, Lincoln told those who had gathered in Springfield to wish him well and that he faced a "task greater than Washington's" in the years to come. Southerners were also learning the challenges of forming a new nation. The seceded states grappled with internal divisions right away, as states with enslavers sometimes did not support the newly seceded states. In January, for example, Delaware rejected secession. But states in the Lower South adopted a different course. The state of Mississippi seceded. Later in the month, the states of Florida, Alabama, Georgia, and Louisiana also all left the Union. By early February, Texas had also joined the newly seceded states. In February, southerners drafted a constitution protecting slavery and named Jefferson Davis of Mississippi their president. Weeks after Abraham Lincoln's inauguration, rebels in the newly formed Confederate States of America opened fire on Fort Sumter in South Carolina. Within days, Abraham Lincoln would demand seventy-five thousand volunteers from the North to crush the rebellion. The American Civil War had begun.

VI. Conclusion

Slavery had long divided the politics of the United States. In time, these divisions became both sectional and irreconcilable. The first and most ominous sign of a coming sectional storm occurred over debates surrounding the admission of the state of Missouri in 1821. As westward expansion continued, these fault lines grew even more ominous, particularly as the United States managed to seize even more lands from its war with Mexico. The country seemed to teeter ever closer to a full-throated endorsement of slavery. But an antislavery coalition arose in the middle 1850s calling itself the Republican Party. Eager to cordon off slavery and confine it to where it already existed, the Republicans won the presidential election of 1860 and threw the nation on the path to war.

Throughout this period, the mainstream of the antislavery movement remained committed to a peaceful resolution of the slavery issue through efforts understood to foster the "ultimate extinction" of slavery in due time. But as the secession crisis revealed, the South could not tolerate a federal government working against the interests of slavery's expansion and decided to take a gamble on war with the United States. Secession, in the end, raised the possibility of emancipation through war, a possibility most Republicans knew, of course, had always been an option, but one they nonetheless hoped would never be necessary. By 1861 all bets were off, and the fate of slavery, and of the nation, depended on war.

VII. Reference Material

This chapter was edited by Jesse Gant, with content contributions by Jeffrey Bain-Conkin, Matthew A. Byron, Christopher Childers, Jesse Gant, Christopher Null, Ryan Poe, Michael Robinson, Nicholas Wood, Michael Woods, and Ben Wright.

Recommended citation: Jeffrey Bain-Conkin et al., "The Sectional Crisis," Jesse Gant, ed., in *The American Yawp*, eds. Joseph Locke and Ben Wright (Stanford, CA: Stanford University Press, 2019).

NOTES TO CHAPTER 13

1. David Brion Davis, *The Problem of Slavery in Western Culture* (New York: Oxford University Press, 1966).

2. David Brion Davis, *The Problem of Slavery in the Age of Revolution, 1770–1823* (New York: Oxford University Press, 1999), 164–212.

3. See "Black Founders: The Free Black Community in the Early Republic," digital exhibit, Library Company of Philadelphia, http://www.librarycompany.org/blackfounders/, accessed May 8, 2018.

4. Northwest Ordinance, July 13, 1787; Charles C. Tansill, ed., *Documents Illustrative of the Formation of the Union of the American States* (Washington, DC: U.S. Government Printing Office, 1927), House Document No. 398. http://avalon.law.yale.edu/18th_century/nworder.asp.

5. Stephen Middleton, *The Black Laws: Race and the Legal Process in Early Ohio* (Athens: Ohio University Press, 2005).

6. *The National Register: A Weekly Paper, Containing a Series of the Important Public Documents, and the Proceedings of Congress*, Volume VII (Washington City: 1819), 125.

7. Conference committee report on the Missouri Compromise, March 1, 1820; Joint Committee of Conference on the Missouri Bill, 03/01/1820–03/06/1820; Record Group 128l; Records of Joint Committees of Congress, 1789–1989; National Archives. https://www.ourdocuments.gov/doc.php?flash=true&doc=22&page=transcript.

8. William M. Wiecek, *The Sources of Antislavery Constitutionalism in America, 1760–1848* (Ithaca, NY: Cornell University Press, 1977).

9. Richard Furman, *Rev. Dr. Richard Furman's Exposition of the Views of the Baptists, Relative to the Colored Population of the United States* (Charleston, SC: Miller, 1923), 1.

10. Nicholas Wood, "'A Sacrifice on the Altar of Slavery': Doughface Politics and Black Disenfranchisement in Pennsylvania, 1837–1838," *Journal of the Early Republic* 31, no. 1 (Spring 2011): 75–106.

11. Michael F. Holt, *The Rise and Fall of the American Whig Party: Jacksonian Politics and the Onset of the Civil War* (New York: Oxford University Press, 1999).

12. James K. Polk: "Inaugural Address," March 4, 1845. Gerhard Peters and John T. Woolley, *The American Presidency Project*. http://www.presidency.ucsb.edu/ws/?pid=25814.

13. Richard Peters, *Report of the Case of Edward Prigg against the Commonwealth of Pennsylvania* (Philadelphia: Johnson, 1842).

14. Frederick Douglass, *Narrative of the Life of Frederick Douglass, an American Slave, Written by Himself* (Boston: Anti-Slavery Office, 1845). http://docsouth.unc.edu/neh/douglass/douglass.html.

15. See Sojourner Truth, *The Narrative of Sojourner Truth*, ed. Olive Gilbert (Boston: Author, 1850), http://digital.library.upenn.edu/women/truth/1850/1850.html; Maria Stewart, *Maria W. Stewart: America's First Black Woman Political Writer*, ed. Marilyn Richardson (Bloomington: Indiana University Press, 1987); James McCune Smith, *The Works of James McCune Smith: Black Intellectual and Abolitionist*, ed. John Stauffer (New York: Oxford University Press, 2007); Frank A. Rollin, *Life and Public Services of Martin R. Delaney* (Boston: Lee and Shephard, 1868), especially 313–367. https://archive.org/details/lifepublicservic00inroll.

16. Eric Foner, *Free Soil, Free Labor, Free Men: The Ideology of the Republican Party Before the Civil War* (New York: Oxford University Press, 1970).

17. Joseph Rayback, *Free Soil: The Election of 1848* (Lexington: University Press of Kentucky, 2014).

18. Eleanor Flexnor, *Century of Struggle: The Women's Rights Movement in the United States* (Cambridge, MA: Harvard University Press, 1975).

19. *Report of the Woman's Rights Convention, Held at Seneca Falls, N.Y., July 19th and 20th, 1848* (Rochester: Dick, 1848).

20. Gloria J. Browne-Marshall, *Race, Law and American Society, Second Edition* (New York: Routledge, 2013), 56.

21. Michael Winship, "Uncle Tom's Cabin: History of the Book in the 19th-Century United States" (Charlottesville: University of Virginia, 2007). http://utc.iath.virginia.edu/interpret/exhibits/winship/winship.html, accessed August 1, 2015.

22. Charles Harold Nichols, *Many Thousand Gone: The Ex-slaves' Account of Their Bondage and Freedom* (Leiden, Netherlands: Brill, 1963), 156.

23. Amos A. Lawrence to Giles Richards, June 1, 1854, quoted in Jane J. Pease and William H. Pease, eds., *The Fugitive Slave Law and Anthony Burns: A Problem in Law Enforcement* (Philadelphia: Lippincott, 1975), 43.

24. Tyler Anbinder, *Nativism and Slavery: The Northern Know Nothings and the Politics of the 1850s* (New York: Oxford University Press, 1992).

25. Charles Sumner, *The Crime Against Kansas, Speech of Hon. Charles Sumner in the Senate of the United States* (New York: Greeley and McElrath, 1856). https://www.senate.gov/artandhistory/history/resources/pdf/CrimeAgainstKSSpeech.pdf.

26. Nicole Etcheson, *Bleeding Kansas: Contested Liberty in the Civil War Era* (Lawrence: University Press of Kansas, 2004).

27. Williamjames Hull Hoffer, *The Caning of Charles Sumner: Honor, Idealism, and the Origins of the Civil War* (Baltimore: Johns Hopkins University Press, 2010), 92.

28. Abraham Lincoln, "Peoria Speech, October 16, 1854," in *Collected Works of Abraham Lincoln*, ed. Roy P. Basler (New Brunswick, NJ: Rutgers University Press, 1953), 247–283. https://www.nps.gov/liho/learn/historyculture /peoriaspeech.htm.

29. Judgment in the U.S. Supreme Court Case *Dred Scott v. John F.A. Sanford*, March 6, 1857; Case Files 1792–1995; Record Group 267; Records of the Supreme Court of the United States; National Archives. http://www.ourdocuments .gov/doc.php?flash=true&doc=29.

30. Rodney O. Davis and Douglas L. Wilson, eds., *The Lincoln Douglas Debates* (Champaign: University of Illinois Press, 2008), 68.

31. Republican Party Platforms: "Republican Party Platform of 1860," May 17, 1860. Gerhard Peters and John T. Woolley, *The American Presidency Project*. http://www.presidency.ucsb.edu/ws/?pid=29620.

32. Horace Greeley, *The American Conflict: A History of the Great Rebellion in the United States of America, 1860–1864, Volume 1* (Hartford, CT: Case, 1864), 366–367.

33. "Declaration of the Immediate Causes Which Induce and Justify the Secession of South Carolina from the Federal Union," *The Avalon Project at the Yale Law School*. http://avalon.law.yale.edu/19th_century/csa_scarsec.asp., accessed August 1, 2015.

RECOMMENDED READING

Bacon, Margaret Hope. *But One Race: The Life of Robert Purvis*. Albany: SUNY Press, 2012.

Baker, Jean H. *Affairs of Party: The Political Culture of Northern Democrats in the Mid-Nineteenth Century*. New York: Fordham University Press, 1983.

Berlin, Ira. *Generations of Captivity: A History of African-American Slaves*. Cambridge, MA: Belknap Press, 2003.

Boydston, Jeanne. *Home and Work: Housework, Wages, and the Ideology of Labor in the Early Republic*. New York: Oxford University Press, 1990.

Bracey, Christopher Alan, Paul Finkelman, and David Thomas Konig, eds. *The Dred Scott Case: Historical and Contemporary Perspectives on Race and Law*. Athens: Ohio University Press, 2010.

Cutter, Barbara. *Domestic Devils, Battlefield Angels: The Radicalization of American Womanhood, 1830–1865*. DeKalb: Northern Illinois University Press, 2003.

Engs, Robert F., and Randall M. Miller, eds. *The Birth of the Grand Old Party: The Republicans' First Generation*. Philadelphia: University of Pennsylvania Press, 2002.

Etcheson, Nicole. *Bleeding Kansas: Contested Liberty in the Civil War Era*. Lawrence: University Press of Kansas, 2004.

Flexnor, Eleanor. *Century of Struggle: The Women's Rights Movement in the United States.* Cambridge, MA: Harvard University Press, 1975.

Foner, Eric. *Free Soil, Free Labor, Free Men: The Ideology of the Republican Party Before the Civil War.* New York: Oxford University Press, 1970.

Grant, Susan-Mary. *North over South: Northern Nationalism and American Identity in the Antebellum Era.* Lawrence: University Press of Kansas, 2000.

Holt, Michael F. *The Rise and Fall of the American Whig Party: Jacksonian Politics and the Onset of the Civil War.* New York: Oxford University Press, 1999.

Howe, Daniel Walker. *The Political Culture of the American Whigs.* Chicago: University of Chicago Press, 1979.

Jeffrey, Julie Roy. *The Great Silent Army of Abolitionism: Ordinary Women in the Antislavery Movement.* Chapel Hill: University of North Carolina Press, 1998.

Jones, Martha S. *All Bound Up Together: The Woman Question in African American Public Culture, 1830–1900.* Chapel Hill: University of North Carolina Press, 2007.

Kantrowitz, Stephen. *More Than Freedom: Fighting for Black Citizenship in a White Republic, 1829–1889.* New York: Penguin, 2012.

McDaniel, W. Caleb. *The Problem of Democracy in the Age of Slavery: Garrisonian Abolitionists and Transatlantic Reform.* Baton Rouge: LSU Press, 2013.

Oakes, James. *The Scorpion's Sting: Antislavery and the Coming of the Civil War.* New York: Norton, 2014.

Potter, David M. *The Impending Crisis, 1848–1861.* New York: HarperCollins, 1976.

Quarles, Benjamin. *Allies for Freedom: Blacks and John Brown.* New York: Oxford University Press, 1974.

Robertson, Stacey. *Hearts Beating for Liberty: Women Abolitionists in the Old Northwest.* Chapel Hill: University of North Carolina Press, 2010.

Sinha, Manisha. *The Counterrevolution of Slavery: Politics and Ideology in Antebellum South Carolina.* Chapel Hill: University of North Carolina Press, 2000.

Smith, Kimberly K. *The Dominion of Voice: Riot, Reason and Romance in Antebellum American Political Thought.* Lawrence: University Press of Kansas, 1999.

Varon, Elizabeth. *Disunion! The Coming of the American Civil War, 1789–1859.* Chapel Hill: University of North Carolina Press, 2008.

Zaeske, Susan. *Signatures of Citizenship: Petitioning, Antislavery, and Women's Political Identity.* Chapel Hill: University of North Carolina Press, 2003.

14

The Civil War

I. Introduction

The American Civil War, the bloodiest in the nation's history, resulted in approximately 750,000 deaths.[1] The war touched the life of nearly every American as military mobilization reached levels never seen before or since. Most northern soldiers went to war to preserve the Union, but the war ultimately transformed into a struggle to eradicate slavery. African Americans, both enslaved and free, pressed the issue of emancipation and nurtured this transformation. Simultaneously, women thrust themselves into critical wartime roles while navigating a world without many men of military age. The Civil War was a defining event in the history of the United States and, for the Americans thrust into it, a wrenching one.

Collecting the Dead. Cold Harbor, Virginia. April, 1865. Library of Congress.

II. The Election of 1860 and Secession

The 1860 presidential election was chaotic. In April, the Democratic Party convened in Charleston, South Carolina, the bastion of secessionist thought in the South. The goal was to nominate a candidate for the party ticket, but the party was deeply divided. Northern Democrats pulled for Senator Stephen Douglas, champion of popular sovereignty, while southern Democrats were intent on endorsing someone *other* than Douglas. The parties leaders' refusal to include a pro-slavery platform resulted in southern delegates walking out of the convention, preventing Douglas from gaining the two-thirds majority required for a nomination. The Democrats ended up with two presidential candidates. A subsequent convention in Baltimore nominated Douglas, while southerners nominated the current vice president, John C. Breckinridge of Kentucky, as their presidential candidate. The nation's oldest party had split over differences in policy toward slavery.[2]

Initially, the Republicans were hardly unified around a single candidate themselves. Several leading Republican men vied for their party's nomination. A consensus emerged at the May 1860 convention that the party's nominee would need to carry all the free states—for only in that situation could a Republican nominee potentially win. New York Senator William Seward, a leading contender, was passed over. Seward's pro-immigrant position posed a potential obstacle, particularly in Pennsylvania and New Jersey. Abraham Lincoln of Illinois, as a relatively unknown but likable politician, rose from a pool of potential candidates and was selected by the delegates on the third ballot. The electoral landscape was further complicated through the emergence of a fourth candidate, Tennessee's John Bell, heading the Constitutional Union Party. The Constitutional Unionists, composed of former Whigs who teamed up with some southern Democrats, made it their mission to avoid the specter of secession while doing little else to address the issues tearing the country apart.

Abraham Lincoln's nomination proved a great windfall for the Republican Party. Lincoln carried all free states with the exception of New Jersey (which he split with Douglas). Of the voting electorate, 81.2 percent came out to vote—at that point the highest ever for a presidential election. Lincoln received less than 40 percent of the popular vote, but with the field so split, that percentage yielded 180 electoral votes. Lincoln was trailed by Breckinridge with his 72 electoral votes, carrying eleven of the fifteen slave states; Bell came in third with 39 electoral votes; and Douglas came in last, only able to garner 12 electoral votes despite carrying almost 30 percent

of the popular vote. Since the Republican platform prohibited the expansion of slavery in future western states, all future Confederate states, with the exception of Virginia, excluded Lincoln's name from their ballots.[3]

Abraham Lincoln, August 13, 1860. Library of Congress.

The election of Lincoln and the perceived threat to the institution of slavery proved too much for the deep southern states. South Carolina acted almost immediately, calling a convention to declare secession. On December 20, 1860, the South Carolina convention voted unanimously 169–0 to dissolve their union with the United States.[4] The other states across the Deep South quickly followed suit. Mississippi adopted their own resolution on January 9, 1861, Florida followed on January 10, Alabama on January 11, Georgia on January 19, Louisiana on January 26, and Texas on February 1. Texas was the only state to put the issue up for a popular vote, but secession was widely popular throughout the South.

Confederates quickly shed their American identity and adopted a new Confederate nationalism. Confederate nationalism was based on several ideals, foremost among these being slavery. As Confederate vice president Alexander Stephens stated, the Confederacy's "foundations are laid, its cornerstone rests, upon the great truth that the negro is not equal to the white man; that slavery . . . is his natural and normal condition."[5] The election of Lincoln in 1860 demonstrated that the South was politically overwhelmed. Slavery was omnipresent in the prewar South, and it served as the most common frame of reference for unequal power. To a southern man, there was no fate more terrifying than the thought of being reduced to the level of a slave. Religion likewise shaped Confederate nationalism, as southern-

The emblems of nationalism on this currency reveal much about the ideology underpinning the Confederacy: George Washington standing stately in a Roman toga indicates the belief in the South's honorable and aristocratic past; John C. Calhoun's portrait emphasizes the Confederate argument of the importance of states' rights; and, most importantly, the image of African Americans working in fields demonstrates slavery's position as foundational to the Confederacy. A five-dollar and a one-hundred-dollar Confederate States of America interest bearing banknote, c. 1861 and 1862. Wikimedia.

ers believed that the Confederacy was fulfilling God's will. The Confederacy even veered from the American constitution by explicitly invoking Christianity in their founding document. Yet in every case, all rationale for secession could be thoroughly tied to slavery. "Our position is thoroughly identified with the institution of slavery—the greatest material interest of the world," proclaimed the Mississippi statement of secession.[6] Thus for the original seven Confederate states (and the four that would subsequently join), slavery's existence was the essential core of the fledging Confederacy.

Not all southerners participated in Confederate nationalism. Unionist southerners, most common in the upcountry where slavery was weakest, retained their loyalty to the Union. These southerners joined the Union army, that is, the army of the United States of America, and worked to defeat the Confederacy.[7] Black southerners, most of whom were enslaved, overwhelmingly supported the Union, often running away from plantations and forcing the Union army to reckon with slavery.[8]

President James Buchanan would not directly address the issue of secession prior to his term's end in early March. Any effort to try to solve the issue therefore fell upon Congress, specifically a Committee of Thirteen including prominent men such as Stephen Douglas, William Seward, Robert Toombs, and John Crittenden. In what became known as "Crittenden's Compromise," Senator Crittenden proposed a series of Constitutional amendments that guaranteed slavery in southern states and territories, denied the federal government interstate slave trade regulatory power, and offered to enslavers whose enslaved people had escaped. The Committee of Thirteen ultimately voted down the measure, and it likewise failed in the full Senate vote (25–23). Reconciliation appeared impossible.[9]

The seven seceding states met in Montgomery, Alabama, on February 4 to organize a new nation. The delegates selected Jefferson Davis of Mississippi as president and established a capital in Montgomery, Alabama (it would move to Richmond in May). Whether other states of the Upper South would join the Confederacy remained uncertain. By the early spring of 1861, North Carolina and Tennessee had not held secession conventions, while voters in Virginia, Missouri, and Arkansas initially voted down secession. Despite this temporary boost to the Union, it became abundantly clear that these acts of loyalty in the Upper South were highly conditional and relied on a clear lack of intervention on the part of the federal government. This was the precarious political situation facing Abraham Lincoln following his inauguration on March 4, 1861.

III. A War for Union 1861–1863

In his inaugural address, Lincoln declared secession "legally void."[10] While he did not intend to invade southern states, he would use force to maintain possession of federal property within seceded states. Attention quickly shifted to the federal installation of Fort Sumter in Charleston, South Carolina. The fort was in need of supplies, and Lincoln intended to resupply it. South Carolina called for U.S. soldiers to evacuate the fort. Commanding officer Major Robert Anderson refused. On April 12, 1861, Confederate Brigadier General P. G. T. Beauregard fired on the fort. Anderson surrendered on April 13 and the Union troops evacuated.

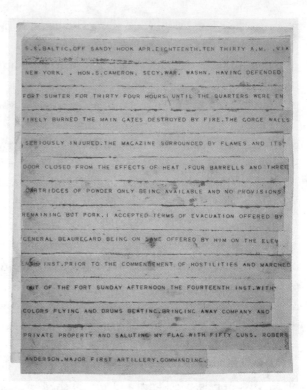

S.S.BALTIC.OFF SANDY HOOK APR.EIGHTEENTH.TEN THIRTY A.M. .VIA

NEW YORK. . HON.S.CAMERON. SECY.WAR. WASHN. HAVING DEFENDED

FORT SUMTER FOR THIRTY FOUR HOURS. UNTIL THE QUARTERS WERE EN

TIRELY BURNED THE MAIN GATES DESTROYED BY FIRE.THE GORGE WALLS

SERIOUSLY INJURED.THE MAGAZINE SURROUNDED BY FLAMES AND ITS

DOOR CLOSED FROM THE EFFECTS OF HEAT .FOUR BARRELLS AND THREE

CARTRIDGES OF POWDER ONLY BEING AVAILABLE AND NO PROVISIONS

REMAINING BUT PORK.I ACCEPTED TERMS OF EVACUATION OFFERED BY

GENERAL BEAUREGARD BEING ON SAME OFFERED BY HIM ON THE ELEV

ENTH INST.PRIOR TO THE COMMENCEMENT OF HOSTILITIES AND MARCHED

OUT OF THE FORT SUNDAY AFTERNOON THE FOURTEENTH INST.WITH

COLORS FLYING AND DRUMS BEATING.BRINGING AWAY COMPANY AND

PRIVATE PROPERTY AND SALUTING MY FLAG WITH FIFTY GUNS. ROBERT

ANDERSON.MAJOR FIRST ARTILLERY.COMMANDING.

Sent to then–Secretary of War Simon Cameron on April 13, 1861, this telegraph announced that after thirty hours of defending Fort Sumter, Major Robert Anderson had accepted the evacuation offered by Confederate General Beauregard. The Union had surrendered Fort Sumter, and the Civil War had officially begun. *Telegram from Maj. Robert Anderson to Hon. Simon Cameron, Secretary, announcing his withdrawal from Fort Sumter*, April 18, 1861; Records of the Adjutant General's Office, 1780s–1917; Record Group 94. National Archives.

In response to the attack, President Abraham Lincoln called for seventy-five thousand volunteers to serve three months to suppress the rebellion. The American Civil War had begun.

The assault on Fort Sumter and subsequent call for troops provoked several Upper South states to join the Confederacy. In total, eleven states renounced their allegiance to the United States. The new Confederate nation was predicated on the institution of slavery and the promotion of any and all interests that reinforced that objective. Some southerners couched their defense of slavery as a preservation of states' rights. But in order to protect slavery, the Confederate constitution left even less power to the states than the U.S. Constitution, an irony not lost on many.

Shortly after Lincoln's call for troops, the Union adopted General-in-Chief Winfield Scott's Anaconda Plan to suppress the rebellion. This strategy intended to strangle the Confederacy by cutting off access to coastal ports and inland waterways via a naval blockade. Ground troops would enter the interior. Like an anaconda snake, they planned to surround and squeeze the Confederacy.

The border states of Delaware, Maryland, Missouri, and Kentucky maintained geographic, social, political, and economic connections to both the North and the South. All four were immediately critical to the

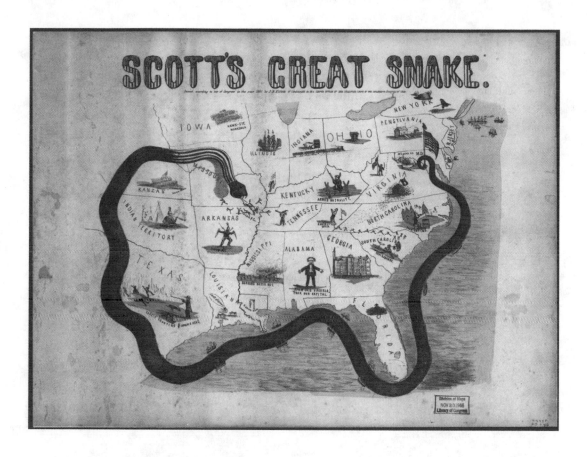

outcome of the conflict. Maryland was particularly important given its position relative to Washington, D.C. Abraham Lincoln suspended the writ of *habeas corpus* and allowed military commanders to arrest secession-friendly activists without charging them with a crime. Other border states were also important; Lincoln famously quipped, "I think to lose Kentucky is nearly the same as to lose the whole game."[11] Lincoln and his military advisors realized that the loss of the border states could mean a significant decrease in Union resources and threaten the capital in Washington. Consequently, Lincoln hoped to foster loyalty among their citizens, so Union forces could minimize their occupation. In spite of terrible guerrilla warfare in Missouri and Kentucky, the four border states remained loyal to the Union throughout the war.

Foreign countries, primarily in Europe, also watched the unfolding war with deep interest. The United States represented the greatest example of democratic thought at the time, and individuals from as far afield as Britain, France, Spain, Russia, and beyond closely followed events across the Atlantic Ocean. If the democratic experiment within the United States failed, many democratic activists in Europe wondered what

Winfield Scott's Anaconda Plan sought to slowly squeeze the South dry of its resources, blocking all coastal ports and inland waterways to prevent the importation of goods or the export of cotton. This print, while poorly drawn, does a great job of making clear the Union's plan. J. B. Elliott, *Scott's great snake. Entered according to Act of Congress in the year 1861*, 1861. Library of Congress.

hope might exist for such experiments elsewhere. Conversely, those with close ties to the cotton industry watched with other concerns. War meant the possibility of disrupting the cotton supply, and disruption could have catastrophic ramifications in commercial and financial markets abroad.

While Lincoln, his cabinet, and the War Department devised strategies to defeat the rebel insurrection, Black Americans quickly forced the issue of slavery as a primary issue in the debate. As early as 1861, Black Americans implored the Lincoln administration to serve in the army and navy.[12] Lincoln initially waged a conservative, limited war. He believed that the presence of African American troops would threaten the loyalty of slaveholding border states, and white volunteers might refuse to serve alongside Black men. However, army commanders could not ignore the growing populations of formerly enslaved people who escaped to freedom behind Union army lines. These former enslaved people took a proactive stance early in the war and forced the federal government to act. As the number of refugees ballooned, Lincoln and Congress found it harder to avoid the issue.[13]

Enslaved African Americans who took freedom into their own hands and ran to Union lines congregated in what were called contraband camps, which existed alongside Union Army camps. As is evident in the drawing, these were crude, disorganized, and dirty places. But they were still centers of freedom for those fleeing slavery. Contraband camp, Richmond, Va., 1865. The Camp of the Contrabands on the Banks of the Mississippi, Fort Pickering, Memphis, Tenn., 1862. Courtesy American Antiquarian Society.

In May 1861, General Benjamin F. Butler went over his superiors' heads and began accepting freedom-seeking escapees who came to Fort Monroe in Virginia. In order to avoid answering whether these people were free, Butler called them "contraband of war," and he had as much a right to seize them as he did to seize enemy horses or cannons.[14] Later that summer Congress affirmed Butler's policy in the First Confiscation Act. The act left "contrabands," as these runaways were called, in a state of limbo. Once an enslaved person escaped to Union lines, their enslaver's claim was nullified. The person would not be, however, a free citizen of the United States. Runaways lived in "contraband camps," where disease and malnutrition were rampant. Women and men were required to perform the drudge work of war: raising fortifications, cooking meals, and laying railroad tracks. Still, life as a contraband offered a potential path to freedom, and thousands of enslaved people seized the opportunity.

Fugitives posed a dilemma for the Union military. Soldiers were forbidden to interfere with slavery or assist runaways, but many soldiers found such a policy unchristian. Even those indifferent to slavery were reluctant to turn away potential laborers or help the enemy by returning his property. Also, enslaved people could provide useful information on the local terrain and the movements of Confederate troops. Union offi-

Photography captured the horrors of war as never before. Some Civil War photographers arranged the actors in their frames to capture the best picture, even repositioning bodies of dead soldiers for battlefield photos. Alexander Gardner, *[Antietam, Md. Confederate dead by a fence on the Hagerstown road]*, September 1862. Library of Congress.

cers became particularly reluctant to turn away freedom-seeking people when Confederate commanders began forcing enslaved laborers to work on fortifications. Every enslaved person who escaped to Union lines was a loss to the Confederate war effort.

Any hopes for a brief conflict were eradicated when Union and Confederate forces met at the Battle of Bull Run, near Manassas, Virginia. While not particularly deadly, the Confederate victory proved that the Civil War would be long and costly. Furthermore, in response to the embarrassing Union rout, Lincoln removed Brigadier General Irvin McDowell and promoted Major General George B. McClellan to commander of the newly formed Army of the Potomac. For nearly a year

New and more destructive warfare technology emerged during this time that utilized discoveries and innovations in other areas of life, like transportation. This photograph shows Robert E. Lee's railroad gun and crew used in the main eastern theater of war at the siege of Petersburg, June 1864–April 1865. *Petersburg, Va. Railroad gun and crew*, between 1864 and 1865. Library of Congress.

after the First Battle of Bull Run, the Eastern Theater remained relatively silent. Smaller engagements only resulted in a bloody stalemate.

But while the military remained quiet, the same could not be said of Republicans in Washington. The absence of fractious, stalling southerners in Congress allowed Republicans to finally pass the Whig economic package, including the Homestead Act, the Land-Grant College Act (aka the Morrill Act), and the Pacific Railroad Act.[15] The federal government also began moving toward a more nationally controlled currency system (the greenback) and the creation of banks with national characteristics. Such acts proved instrumental in the expansion of the federal government and industry.

The Democratic Party, absent its southern leaders, divided into two camps. War Democrats largely stood behind President Lincoln. Peace Democrats—also known as Copperheads—clashed frequently with both War Democrats and Republicans. Copperheads were sympathetic to the Confederacy; they exploited public antiwar sentiment (often the result of a lost battle or mounting casualties) and tried to push President Lincoln to negotiate an immediate peace, regardless of political leverage or bargaining power. Had the Copperheads succeeded in bringing about immediate peace, the Union would have been forced to recognize the Confederacy as a separate and legitimate government and the institution of slavery would have remained intact.

While Washington buzzed with political activity, military life consisted of relative monotony punctuated by brief periods of horror. Daily life for a Civil War soldier was one of routine. A typical day began around six in the morning and involved drill, marching, lunch break, and more drilling followed by policing the camp. Weapon inspection and cleaning followed, perhaps one final drill, dinner, and taps around nine or nine thirty in the evening. Soldiers in both armies grew weary of the routine. Picketing or foraging afforded welcome distractions to the monotony.

Soldiers devised clever ways of dealing with the boredom of camp life. The most common was writing. These were highly literate armies; nine out of every ten Federals and eight out of every ten Confederates could read and write.[16] Letters home served as a tether linking soldiers to their loved ones. Soldiers also read; newspapers were in high demand. News of battles, events in Europe, politics in Washington and Richmond, and local concerns were voraciously sought and traded.

While there were nurses, camp followers, and some women who disguised themselves as men, camp life was overwhelmingly male. Soldiers drank liquor, smoked tobacco, gambled, and swore. Social commentators feared that when these men returned home, with their hard-drinking and irreligious ways, all decency, faith, and temperance would depart. But not all methods of distraction were detrimental. Soldiers also organized debate societies, composed music, sang songs, wrestled, raced horses, boxed, and played sports.

Neither side could consistently provide supplies for their soldiers, so it was not uncommon, though officially forbidden, for common soldiers to trade with the enemy. Confederate soldiers prized northern newspapers and coffee. Northerners were glad to exchange these for southern tobacco. Supply shortages and poor sanitation were synonymous with Civil War armies. The close proximity of thousands of men bred disease. Lice were soldiers' daily companions.

Music was popular among the soldiers of both armies, creating a diversion from the boredom and horror of the war. As a result, soldiers often sang on fatigue duty and while in camp. Favorite songs often reminded the soldiers of home, including "Lorena," "Home, Sweet Home," and "Just Before the Battle, Mother." Dances held in camp offered another way to enjoy music. Since there were often few women nearby, soldiers would dance with one another.

When the Civil War broke out, one of the most popular songs among soldiers and civilians was "John Brown's Body," which began "John Brown's body lies a-mouldering in the grave." Started as a Union anthem praising John Brown's actions at Harper's Ferry, Virginia, then used by Confederates to vilify Brown, both sides' version of the song stressed that they were on the right side. Eventually the words to Julia Ward Howe's poem "The Battle Hymn of the Republic" were set to the melody, further implying Union success. The themes of popular songs changed over the course of the war, as feelings of inevitable success alternated with feelings of terror and despair.[17]

After an extensive delay on the part of Union commander George McClellan, his 120,000-man Army of the Potomac moved via ship to the peninsula between the York and James Rivers in Virginia. Rather than crossing overland via the former battlefield at Manassas Junction, McClellan attempted to swing around the rebel forces and enter the capital of Richmond before they knew what hit them. McClellan, however, was an overly cautious man who consistently overestimated his adversaries' numbers. This cautious approach played into the Confederates' favor on the outskirts of Richmond. Confederate General Robert E. Lee, recently appointed commander of the Army of Northern Virginia, forced McClellan to retreat from Richmond, and his Peninsular Campaign became a tremendous failure.[18]

Union forces met with little success in the East, but the Western Theater provided hope for the United States. In February 1862, men under
Union general Ulysses S. Grant captured Forts Henry and Donelson
along the Tennessee River. Fighting in the West greatly differed from that
in the East. At the First Battle of Bull Run, for example, two large armies
fought for control of the nations' capitals, while in the West, Union and
Confederate forces fought for control of the rivers, since the Mississippi
River and its tributaries were key components of the Union's Anaconda
Plan. One of the deadliest of these clashes occurred along the Tennessee
River at the Battle of Shiloh on April 6–7, 1862. This battle, lasting only
two days, was the costliest single battle in American history up to that
time. The Union victory shocked both the Union and the Confederacy
with approximately twenty-three thousand casualties, a number that ex-

The creation of Black regiments was another kind of innovation during the Civil War. Northern free Black
men and newly freed men joined together under the leadership of white officers to fight for the Union cause.
This novelty was not only beneficial for the Union war effort; it also showed the Confederacy that the
Union sought to destroy the foundational institution (slavery) upon which their nation was built. William
Morris Smith, [District of Columbia. Company E, 4th U.S. Colored Infantry, at Fort Lincoln], between
1863 and 1866. Library of Congress.

ceeded casualties from all of the United States' previous wars combined.[19] The subsequent capture of New Orleans by Union forces proved a heavy blow to the Confederacy and capped an 1862 spring of success in the Western Theater.

The Union and Confederate navies helped or hindered army movements around the many marine environments of the southern United States. Each navy employed the latest technology to outmatch the other. The Confederate navy, led by Stephen Russell Mallory, had the unenviable task of constructing a fleet from scratch and trying to fend off a vastly better equipped Union navy. Led by Gideon Welles of Connecticut, the Union navy successfully implemented General-in-Chief Winfield Scott's Anaconda Plan. The future of naval warfare also emerged in the spring of 1862 as two "ironclad" warships fought a duel at Hampton Roads, Virginia. The age of the wooden sail was gone and naval warfare would be fundamentally altered. While advances in naval technology ruled the seas, African Americans on the ground were complicating Union war aims to an even greater degree.

By the summer of 1862, the actions of Black Americans were pushing the Union toward a full-blown war of emancipation.[20] Following the First Confiscation Act, in April 1862, Congress abolished the institution of slavery in the District of Columbia. In July 1862, Congress passed the Second Confiscation Act, effectively emancipating enslaved people in land that came under Union control. Word traveled fast among enslaved people, and this legislation led to even more runaways making their way into Union lines. Abraham Lincoln's thinking began to evolve. By the summer of 1862, Lincoln first floated the idea of an Emancipation Proclamation to members of his cabinet. By August 1862, he proposed the first iteration of the Emancipation Proclamation. While his cabinet supported such an idea, secretary of state William Seward insisted that Lincoln wait for a "decisive" Union victory so the proclamation would not appear too desperate a measure on the part of a failing government.

The decisive moment that prompted the issuance of the Emancipation Proclamation occurred in the fall of 1862 along Antietam Creek in Maryland. Emboldened by their success in the previous spring and summer, Lee and Confederate president Jefferson Davis planned to win a decisive victory in Union territory and end the war. On September 17, 1862, McClellan's and Lee's forces collided at the Battle of Antietam near the town of Sharpsburg. This battle was the first major battle of the Civil War to occur on Union soil. It remains the bloodiest single day in American history: over twenty thousand soldiers were killed, wounded, or missing.

This African American family dressed in their finest clothes (including a USCT uniform) for this photograph, projecting respectability and dignity that was at odds with the southern perception of Black Americans. *[Unidentified African American soldier in Union uniform with wife and two daughters]*, between 1863 and 1865. Library of Congress.

Despite the Confederate withdrawal and the high death toll, the Battle of Antietam was not a decisive Union victory. It did, however, result in enough of a victory for Lincoln to issue the Emancipation Proclamation, which freed enslaved people in areas under Confederate control. There were significant exemptions to the Emancipation Proclamation, including the border states and parts of other states in the Confederacy. A far cry from a universal end to slavery, the Emancipation Proclamation nevertheless proved vital, shifting the war's aims from simple union to emancipation. Framing it as a war measure, Lincoln and his cabinet hoped that stripping the Confederacy of its labor force would not only debilitate the southern economy but also weaken Confederate morale. Furthermore, the Battle of Antietam and the issuance of the Emancipation Proclamation all but ensured that the Confederacy would not be recognized by European powers. Nevertheless, Confederates continued fighting. Union and Confederate forces clashed again at Fredericksburg, Virginia, in December 1862. This Confederate victory resulted in staggering Union casualties.

IV. War for Emancipation 1863–1865

As Union armies penetrated deeper into the Confederacy, politicians and generals came to understand the necessity and benefit of enlisting Black men in the army and navy. Although a few commanders began forming Black units in 1862, such as Massachusetts abolitionist Thomas Wentworth Higginson's First South Carolina Volunteers (the first regiment of Black soldiers), widespread enlistment did not occur until the Emancipation Proclamation went into effect on January 1, 1863. "And I further declare and make known," Lincoln's proclamation read, "that such persons of suitable condition, will be received into the armed service of the United States to garrison forts, positions, stations, and other places, and to man vessels of all sorts in said service."[21]

The language describing Black enlistment indicated Lincoln's implicit desire to segregate African American troops from the main campaigning armies of white soldiers. "I believe it is a resource which, if vigorously applied now, will soon close the contest. It works doubly, weakening the enemy and strengthening us," Lincoln remarked in August 1863 about Black soldiering.[22] Although more than 180,000 Black men (10 percent of the Union army) served during the war, the majority of United States Colored Troops (USCT) remained stationed behind the lines as garrison forces, often laboring and performing noncombat roles.

Black soldiers in the Union army endured rampant discrimination and earned less pay than white soldiers, while also facing the possibility of being murdered or sold into slavery if captured. James Henry Gooding, a Black corporal in the famed 54th Massachusetts Volunteers, wrote to Abraham Lincoln in September 1863, questioning why he and his fellow volunteers were paid less than white men. Gooding argued that because he and his brethren were born in the United States and selflessly left their private lives to enter the army, they should be treated "as American SOLDIERS, not as menial hirelings."[23]

African American soldiers defied the inequality of military service and used their positions in the army to reshape society, North and South. The majority of the USCT had once been enslaved, and their presence as armed, blue-clad soldiers sent shock waves throughout the Confederacy.

To their friends and families, African American soldiers symbolized the embodiment of liberation and the destruction of slavery. To white south erners, they represented the utter disruption of the Old South's racial and social hierarchy. As members of armies of occupation, Black soldiers wielded martial authority in towns and plantations. At the end of the war, as a Black soldier marched by a cluster of Confederate prisoners, he noticed his former enslaver among the group. "Hello, massa," the soldier exclaimed, "bottom rail on top dis time!"[24]

Two Brothers in Arms. Library of Congress.

The majority of the USCT occupied the South by performing garrison duty; other Black soldiers performed admirably on the battlefield, shattering white myths that docile, cowardly Black men would fold in the maelstrom of war. Black troops fought in more than four hundred battles and skirmishes, including Milliken's Bend and Port Hudson, Louisiana; Fort Wagner, South Carolina; Nashville; and the final campaigns to capture Richmond, Virginia. Fifteen Black soldiers received the Medal of Honor, the highest honor bestowed for military heroism. Through their voluntarism, service, battlefield contributions, and even death, Black soldiers laid their claims for citizenship. "Once let the Black man get upon his person the brass letter U.S." Frederick Douglass, the great Black abolitionist, proclaimed, "and there is no power on earth which can deny that he has earned the right to citizenship."[25]

Many enslaved laborers accompanied their enslavers in the Confederate army. They served their enslavers as "camp servants," cooking their meals, raising their tents, and carrying their supplies. The Confederacy also impressed enslaved laborers to perform manual labor. There are three important points to make about these enslaved "Confederates." First, their labor was almost always coerced. Second, people are complicated and have varying, often contradictory loyalties. An enslaved person could hope in general that the Confederacy would lose but at the same time be concerned for the safety of his enslaver and the Confederate soldiers he saw on a daily basis.

Finally, white Confederates did not see African Americans as their equals, much less as soldiers. There was never any doubt that Black laborers and camp servants were property. Though historians disagree on the matter, it is a stretch to claim that not a single African American ever fired a gun for the Confederacy; a camp servant whose enslaver died in battle might well pick up his dead enslaver's gun and continue firing, if for no other reason than to protect himself. But this was always on an informal basis. The Confederate government did, in an act of desperation, pass a law in March 1865 allowing for the enlistment of Black soldiers, but only a few dozen African Americans (mostly Richmond hospital workers) had enlisted by the war's end.

As 1863 dawned, Lee's Army of Northern Virginia continued its offensive strategy in the East. One of the war's major battles occurred near the village of Chancellorsville, Virginia, between April 30 and May 6, 1863. While the Battle of Chancellorsville was an outstanding Confederate victory, it also resulted in heavy casualties and the mortal wounding of Confederate major general "Stonewall" Jackson, who was killed by friendly fire.

In spite of Jackson's death, Lee continued his offensive against federal forces and invaded Pennsylvania in the summer of 1863. During the three-day battle (July 1–3) at Gettysburg, heavy casualties crippled both sides. Yet the devastating July 3 infantry assault on the Union center, also known as Pickett's Charge, caused Lee to retreat from Pennsylvania. The Gettysburg Campaign was Lee's final northern incursion and the Battle of Gettysburg remains the bloodiest battle of the war, and in American history, with fifty-one thousand casualties.

Concurrently in the West, Union forces continued their movement along the Mississippi River and its tributaries. Grant launched his campaign against Vicksburg, Mississippi, in the winter of 1862. Known as the "Gibraltar of the West," Vicksburg was the last holdout in the West, and its seizure would enable uninhibited travel for Union forces along the Mississippi River. Grant's Vicksburg Campaign, which lasted until July 4, 1863, ended with the city's surrender. The fall of Vicksburg split the Confederacy in two.

Despite Union success in the summer of 1863, discontent over the war simmered across the North. This was particularly true in the wake of the

Enrollment Act—the first effort at a draft among the northern populace during the Civil War. Working-class northerners were especially angry that the wealthy could pay $300 for substitutes, sparing themselves from the carnage of war. "A rich man's war, but a poor man's fight," was a popular refrain.[26] The Emancipation Proclamation convinced many immigrants in northern cities that freed people would soon take their jobs. These economic and racial anxieties culminated in the New York City Draft Riots in July 1863. Over the span of four days, white rioters killed some 120 citizens, including the lynching of at least eleven Black New Yorkers. Property damage was in the millions, including the complete destruction of more than fifty properties—most notably that of the Colored Orphan Asylum. It was the largest civil disturbance to date in the United States (aside from the war itself) and was only stopped by the deployment of Union soldiers, some of whom came directly from the battlefield at Gettysburg.

Elsewhere, the North produced widespread displays of unity. Sanitary fairs originated in the Old Northwest and raised millions of dollars for Union soldiers. Indeed, many women rose to take pivotal leadership roles in the sanitary fairs—a clear contribution to the northern war effort. The fairs also encouraged national unity within the North—something that became more important as the war dragged on and casualties continued

Thomas Nast, "Our Heroines, United States Sanitary Commission," in *Harper's Weekly*, April 9, 1864. Cushing/Whitney Medical Library at Yale University.

to mount. The northern homefront was complicated: overt displays of loyalty contrasted with violent dissent.

A similar situation played out in the Confederacy. The Confederate Congress passed its first conscription act in the spring of 1862, a full year before its northern counterpart. Military service was required from all able-bodied males between ages eighteen and thirty-five (eventually extended to forty-five). Notable class exemptions likewise existed in the Confederacy: those who owned twenty or more enslaved laborers could escape the draft. Popular discontent reached a boiling point in 1863. Through the spring of 1863 consistent food shortages led to "bread riots" in several Confederate cities, most notably Richmond, Virginia, and the Georgia cities of Augusta, Macon, and Columbus. Confederate women led these mobs to protest food shortages and rampant inflation within the Confederate South. Exerting their own political control, women dramatically impacted the war through violent actions in these cases, as well as constant petitions to governors for aid and the release of husbands from military service. One of these women wrote a letter to North Carolina governor Zebulon Vance, saying, "Especially for the sake of suffering women and children, do try and stop this cruel war."[27] Confederates waged a multifront struggle against Union incursion and internal dissent.

For some women, the best way to support their cause was spying on the enemy. When the war broke out, Rose O'Neal Greenhow was living in Washington, D.C., where she traveled in high social circles, gathering information for her Confederate contact. Suspecting Greenhow of espionage, Allan Pinkerton placed her under surveillance, instigated a raid on her house to gather evidence, and then placed her under house arrest, after which she was incarcerated in Old Capitol Prison. Upon her release, she was sent, under guard, to Baltimore, Maryland. From there Greenhow went to Europe to attempt to bring support to the Confederacy. Failing in her efforts, Greenhow decided to return to America, boarding the blockade runner *Condor*, which ran aground near Wilmington, North Carolina. Subsequently, she drowned after her lifeboat capsized in a storm. Greenhow gave her life for the Confederate cause, while Elizabeth "Crazy Bet" Van Lew sacrificed her social standing for the Union. Van Lew was from a prominent Richmond, Virginia, family and spied on the Confederacy, leading to her being "held in contempt & scorn by the narrow minded men and women of my city for my loyalty."[28] Indeed, when General Ulysses Grant took control of Richmond, he placed a special guard on Van Lew. In addition to her espionage activities, Van Lew also acted as a nurse to Union prisoners in Libby Prison. For pro-

Pauline Cushman was an American actress and a wartime spy. Using her guile to fraternize with Confederate officers, Cushman snuck military plans and drawings to Union officials in her shoes. She was caught, tried, and sentenced to death but was apparently saved days before her execution by the occupation of her native New Orleans by Union forces. Whether as spies, nurses, or textile workers, women were essential to the Union war effort. *Pauline Cushman*, between 1855 and 1865. Library of Congress.

Confederate southern women, there were more opportunities to show their scorn for the enemy. Some women in New Orleans took these demonstrations to the level of dumping their chamber pots onto the heads of unsuspecting federal soldiers who stood underneath their balconies, leading to Benjamin Butler's infamous General Order Number 28, which arrested all rebellious women as prostitutes.

Military strategy shifted in 1864. The new tactics of "hard war" evolved slowly, as restraint toward southern civilians and property ultimately gave way to a concerted effort to demoralize southern civilians and destroy the southern economy. Grant's successes at Vicksburg and Chattanooga, Tennessee (November 1863), and Meade's cautious pursuit of Lee after Gettysburg prompted Lincoln to promote Grant to general-in-chief of the Union army in early 1864. This change in command resulted in some of the bloodiest battles of the Eastern Theater. Grant's Overland Campaign, including the Battle of the Wilderness, the Battle of Cold Harbor, and the siege of Petersburg, demonstrated Grant's willingness to tirelessly attack the ever-dwindling Army of Northern Virginia. By June 1864, Grant's army surrounded the Confederate city of Petersburg, Virginia. Siege operations cut off Confederate forces and supplies from

Pennsylvania
Light Artillery,
Battery B, Peters-
burg, Virginia.
Photograph by
Timothy H.
O'Sullivan, 1864.
The Metropolitan
Museum of Art.

the capital of Richmond. Meanwhile out west, Union armies under the command of William Tecumseh Sherman implemented hard war strategies and slowly made their way through central Tennessee and northern Georgia, capturing the vital rail hub of Atlanta in September 1864.

Action in both theaters during 1864 caused even more casualties and furthered the devastation of disease. Disease haunted both armies, and accounted for over half of all Civil War casualties. Sometimes as many as half of the men in a company could be sick. The overwhelming majority of Civil War soldiers came from rural areas, where less exposure to diseases meant soldiers lacked immunities. Vaccines for diseases such as smallpox were largely unavailable to those outside cities or towns. Despite the common nineteenth-century tendency to see city men as weak or soft, soldiers from urban environments tended to succumb to fewer diseases than their rural counterparts. Tuberculosis, measles, rheumatism, typhoid, malaria, and smallpox spread almost unchecked among the armies.

Civil War medicine focused almost exclusively on curing the patient rather than preventing disease. Many soldiers attempted to cure themselves by concocting elixirs and medicines themselves. These ineffective home remedies were often made from various plants the men found in woods or fields. There was no understanding of germ theory, so many soldiers did things that we would consider unsanitary today.[29] They ate food that was improperly cooked and handled, and they practiced what we would consider poor personal hygiene. They did not take appropriate steps to ensure that drinking water was free from bacteria. Diarrhea and dysentery were common. These diseases were especially dangerous, as Civil War soldiers did not understand the value of replacing fluids as they were lost. As such, men affected by these conditions would weaken and become unable to fight or march, and as they became dehydrated their immune system became less effective, inviting other infections to attack the body. Through trial and error soldiers began to protect themselves from some of the more preventable sources of infection. Around 1862 both armies began to dig latrines rather than rely on the local waterways. Burying human and animal waste also cut down on exposure to diseases considerably.

Medical surgery was limited and brutal. If a soldier was wounded in the torso, throat, or head, there was little surgeons could do. Invasive procedures to repair damaged organs or stem blood loss invariably resulted in death. Luckily for soldiers, only approximately one in six combat wounds were to one of those parts. The remaining were to limbs, which was treatable by amputation. Soldiers had the highest chance of survival if the limb was removed within forty-eight hours of injury. A skilled surgeon could amputate a limb in three to five minutes from

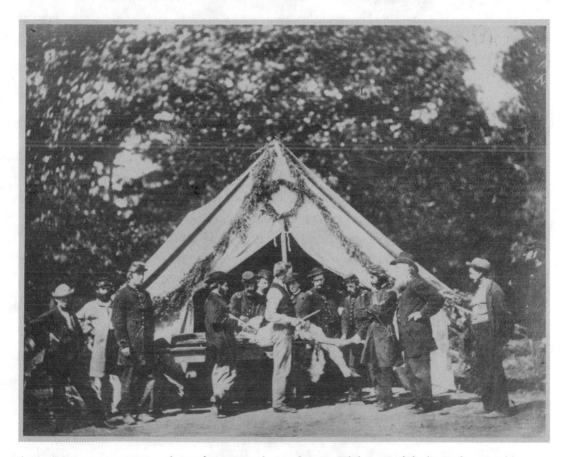

Amputations were a common form of treatment during the war. While it saved the lives of some soldiers, it was extremely painful and resulted in death in many cases. It also produced the first community of war veterans without limbs in American history. *Amputation being performed in a hospital tent, Gettysburg, July 1863.* National Archives and Records Administration.

start to finish. While the lack of germ theory again caused several unsafe practices, such as using the same tools on multiple patients, wiping hands on filthy gowns, or placing hands in communal buckets of water, there is evidence that amputation offered the best chance of survival.

It is a common misconception that amputation was done without anesthesia and against a patient's wishes. Since the 1830s, Americans understood the benefits of nitrous oxide and ether in easing pain. Chloroform and opium were also used to either render patients unconscious or dull pain during the procedure. Also, surgeons would not amputate without the patient's consent.

In the Union army alone, 2.8 million ounces of opium and over 5.2 million opium pills were administered. In 1862, William Alexander Hammon was appointed Surgeon General for the United States. He sought to regulate dosages and manage supplies of available medicines, both to prevent overdosing and to ensure that an ample supply remained for the next engagement. However, his guidelines tended to apply only to the regular federal army. Most Union soldiers were in volunteer units and organized at the state level. Their surgeons often ignored posted limits on medicines, or worse, experimented with their own concoctions made from local flora.

In the North, the conditions in hospitals were somewhat superior. This was partly due to the organizational skills of women like Dorothea Dix, who was the Union's Superintendent for Army Nurses. Additionally, many women were members of the United States Sanitary Commission and helped to staff and supply hospitals in the North.

Women took on key roles within hospitals both North and South. The publisher's notice for *Nurse and Spy in the Union Army* states, "In the opinion of many, it is the privilege of woman to minister to the sick and soothe the sorrowing—and in the present crisis of our country's history, to aid our brothers to the extent of her capacity."[30] Mary Chesnut wrote, "Every woman in the house is ready to rush into the Florence Nightingale business."[31] However, she indicated that after she visited the hospital, "I can never again shut out of view the sights that I saw there of human misery. I sit thinking, shut my eyes, and see it all."[32] Hospital conditions were often so bad that many volunteer nurses quit soon after beginning. Kate Cumming volunteered as a nurse shortly after the war began. She, and other volunteers, traveled with the Army of Tennessee. However, all but one of the women who volunteered with Cumming quit within a week.

Death came in many forms; disease, prisons, bullets, even lightning and bee stings took men slowly or suddenly. Their deaths, however, affected more than their regiments. Before the war, a wife expected to sit at her husband's bed, holding his hand, and ministering to him after a long, fulfilling life. This type of death, "the Good Death," changed during the Civil War as men died often far from home among strangers.[33] Casualty reporting was inconsistent, so a woman was often at the mercy of the men who fought alongside her husband to learn not only the details of his death but even that the death had occurred.

"Now I'm a widow. Ah! That mournful word. Little the world think of the agony it contains!" wrote Sally Randle Perry in her diary.[34] After her husband's death at Sharpsburg, Sally received the label she would share with more than two hundred thousand other women. The death of a husband and loss of financial, physical, and emotional support could shatter lives. It also had the perverse power to free women from bad marriages and open doors to financial and psychological independence.

Widows had an important role to play in the conflict. The ideal widow wore black, mourned for a minimum of two and a half years, resigned herself to God's will, focused on her children, devoted herself to her husband's memory, and brought his body home for burial. Many tried, but not all widows were able to live up to the ideal. Many were unable to purchase proper mourning garb. Black silk dresses, heavy veils, and other features of antebellum mourning were expensive and in short supply. Because most of these women were in their childbearing years, the war created an un-precedented number of widows who were pregnant or still nursing infants. In a time when the average woman gave birth to eight to ten children in her lifetime, it is perhaps not surprising that the Civil War created so many widows who were also young mothers with little free time for formal mourning. Widowhood permeated American society. But in the end, it was up to each widow to navigate her own mourning. She joined the ranks of sisters, mothers, cousins, girlfriends, and communities in mourning men.[35]

By the fall of 1864, military and social events played against the backdrop of the presidential election of 1864. While the war raged on, the presidential contest featured a transformed electorate. Three new states (West Virginia, Nevada, and Kansas) had been added since 1860, while the eleven states of the Confederacy did not participate. Lincoln and his vice presidential nominee, Andrew Johnson (Tennessee), ran on the National Union Party ticket. The main competition came from his former commander, General George B. McClellan. Though McClellan himself was a "War Democrat," the official platform of the Democratic Party in 1864 revolved around negotiating an immediate end to the Civil War. McClellan's vice presidential nominee was George H. Pendleton of Ohio—a well-known Peace Democrat.

On Election Day—November 8, 1864—Lincoln and McClellan each needed 117 electoral votes (out of a possible 233) to win the presidency. For much of the 1864 campaign season, Lincoln downplayed his chances of reelection and McClellan assumed that large numbers of Union soldiers would grant him support. However, thanks in great part to William Sherman's capture of Atlanta on September 2, 1864, and overwhelming support from Union troops, Lincoln won the election easily. Additionally, Lincoln received support from more radical Republican factions and members of the Radical Democracy Party that demanded the end of slavery.

In the popular vote, Lincoln defeated McClellan, 55.1 percent to 44.9 percent. In the Electoral College, Lincoln's victory was even more pronounced: 212 to 21. Lincoln won twenty-two states, and McClellan only carried three: New Jersey, Delaware, and Kentucky.[36]

In the wake of his reelection, Abraham Lincoln delivered his second inaugural address on March 4, 1865, in which he concluded:

With crowds of people filling every inch of ground around the U.S. Capitol, President Lincoln delivered his inaugural address on March 4, 1865. Alexander Gardner, *Lincoln's Second Inaugural*, between 1910 and 1920, from a photograph taken in 1865. Wikimedia.

With malice toward none; with charity for all; with firmness in the right, as God gives us to see the right, let us strive on to finish the work we are in; to bind up the nation's wounds; to care for him who shall have borne the battle, and for his widow, and his orphan—to do all which may achieve and cherish a just, and a lasting peace, among ourselves, and with all nations.[37]

The years 1864 and 1865 were the very definition of hard war. Incredibly deadly for both sides, the Union campaigns in both the West and the East destroyed Confederate infrastructure and demonstrated the efficacy of the Union's strategy. Following up on the successful capture of Atlanta, William Sherman conducted his March to the Sea in the fall of 1864, arriving in Savannah with time to capture it and deliver it as a Christmas present for Abraham Lincoln. Sherman's path of destruction took on an even more destructive tone as he moved into the heart of the Confederacy in South Carolina in early 1865. The burning of Columbia, South Carolina, and subsequent capture of Charleston brought the hard hand of war to the birthplace of secession. With Grant's dogged pursuit of the Army of Northern Virginia, Lee surrendered to Grant at Appomattox Court House on April 9, 1865, effectively ending major Confederate military operations.

Union soldiers pose in front of the Appomattox Court House after Lee's surrender in April 1865. Wikimedia.

To ensure the permanent legal end of slavery, Republicans drafted the Thirteenth Amendment during the war. Yet the end of legal slavery did not mean the end of racial injustice. During the war, formerly enslaved people were often segregated into disease-ridden contraband camps. After the war, the Republican Reconstruction program of guaranteeing the rights of Black Americans succumbed to persistent racism and southern white violence. Long after 1865, most Black southerners continued to labor on plantations, albeit as nominally free tenants or sharecroppers, while facing public segregation and voting discrimination. The effects of slavery endured long after emancipation.

V. Conclusion

As battlefields fell silent in 1865, the question of secession had been answered, slavery had been eradicated, and America was once again territorially united. But in many ways, the conclusion of the Civil War created more questions than answers. How would the nation become one again? Who was responsible for rebuilding the South? What role would African Americans occupy in this society? Northern and southern soldiers returned home with broken bodies, broken spirits, and broken minds. Plantation owners had land but not labor. Recently freed African Americans had their labor but no land. Formerly enslaved people faced a world of possibilities—legal marriage, family reunions, employment, and fresh starts—but also a racist world of bitterness, violence, and limited opportunity. The war may have been over, but the battles for the peace were just beginning.

VI. Reference Material

This chapter was edited by Angela Esco Elder and David Thomson, with content contributions by Thomas Balcerski, William Black, Frank Cirillo, Matthew C. Hulbert, Andrew F. Lang, John Patrick Riley, Angela Riotto, Gregory N. Stern, David Thomson, Ann Tucker, and Rebecca Zimmer.

Recommended citation: Thomas Balcerski et al., "The Civil War," Angela Esco Elder and David Thomson, eds., in *The American Yawp*, eds. Joseph Locke and Ben Wright (Stanford, CA: Stanford University Press, 2019).

NOTES TO CHAPTER 14

1. This most recent estimation of 750,000 wartime deaths was put forward by J. David Hacker, "A Census-Based Account of the Civil War Dead," *Civil War History* 57, no. 4 (December 2011): 306–347.

2. *Proceedings of the Conventions at Charleston and Baltimore: Published by Order of the National Democratic Convention* (Washington, DC: n.p., 1860).

3. William J. Cooper, *We Have the War upon Us: The Onset of the Civil War, November 1860–April 1861* (New York: Knopf, 2012), 14.

4. "A Declaration of the Immediate Causes Which Induce and Justify the Secession of South Carolina from the Federal Union," January 9, 1861, *Avalon Project at the Yale Law School*. http://avalon.law.yale.edu/19th_century/csa _scarsec.asp, accessed August 1, 2015.

5. Alexander Stephens, speech in Savannah, Georgia, delivered March 21, 1861, quoted in Henry Cleveland, *Alexander Stephens, in Public and Private. With Letters and Speeches Before, During and Since the War* (Philadelphia: National, 1866), 719.

6. "Declaration of the Immediate Causes."

7. See Jon L. Wakelyn, ed., *Southern Unionist Pamphlets and the Civil War* (Columbia: University of Missouri Press, 1999).

8. Steven Hahn, *The Political Worlds of Slavery and Freedom* (Cambridge, MA: Harvard University Press, 2009), 55–114.

9. Horace Greeley, *The American Conflict: A History of the Great Rebellion in the United States of America, 1860–1864, Volume 1* (Hartford, CT: Case, Lockwood, 1864), 366–367.

10. Abraham Lincoln, "Inaugural Address," March 4, 1861, Abraham Lincoln Papers, Library of Congress, Washington, D.C.

11. Abraham Lincoln to Orville Browning, September 22, 1861, Abraham Lincoln Papers, Library of Congress, Washington, D.C.

12. Thomas H. O'Connor, *Civil War Boston: Home Front and Battlefield* (Boston: Northeastern University Press, 1997), 67.

13. Excerpt from Benj. F. Butler to Lieutenant Genl. Scott, 27 May 1861, B-99 1861, Letters Received Irregular, Secretary of War, Record Group 107, National Archives. http://www.freedmen.umd.edu/Butler.html.

14. "THE SLAVE QUESTION.; Letter from Major-Gen. Butler on the Treatment of Fugitive Slaves," *New York Times* (August 6, 1861).

15. Heather Cox Richardson, *The Greatest Nation of the Earth: Republican Economic Policies During the Civil War* (Cambridge, MA: Harvard University Press, 1997).

16. For literacy rates within the armies, see Bell Irvin Wiley, *The Life of Billy Yank: The Common Soldier of the Union* (Indianapolis, IN: Bobbs-Merrill, 1952), 304–306; and Bell Irvin Wiley, *The Life of Johnny Reb: The Common Soldier of the Confederacy* (Indianapolis, IN: Bobbs-Merrill, 1943), 335–337.

17. For more on music in the Civil War, see Christian McWhirter, *Battle Hymns: The Power and Popularity of Music in the Civil War* (Chapel Hill: University of North Carolina Press, 2012).

18. Ethan S. Rafuse, *McClellan's War: The Failure of Moderation in the Struggle for the Union* (Bloomington: Indiana University Press, 2005).

19. Steven E. Woodworth, ed., *The Shiloh Campaign* (Carbondale: Southern Illinois University Press, 2009).

20. Glenn David Brasher, *The Peninsula Campaign and the Necessity of Emancipation: African Americans and the Fight for Freedom* (Chapel Hill: University of North Carolina Press, 2012).

21. Emancipation Proclamation, January 1, 1863, Presidential Proclamations, 1791–1991, Record Group 11, General Records of the United States Government, National Archives, Washington, D.C.

22. Abraham Lincoln to Ulysses S. Grant, August 9, 1863, Abraham Lincoln Papers, Library of Congress, Washington, D.C.

23. James Henry Gooding to Abraham Lincoln, September 28, 1863, Abraham Lincoln Papers, Library of Congress, Washington, D.C.

24. James McPherson, *Battle Cry of Freedom: The Civil War Era* (New York: Oxford University Press, 1988), 862.

25. Quoted in Allen Guelzo, *Lincoln's Emancipation Proclamation: The End of Slavery in America* (New York: Simon and Schuster, 2004), 247.

26. See Eugene C. Murdock, *One Million Men: The Civil War Draft in the North* (Madison: State Historical Society of Wisconsin, 1971).

27. Laura Edwards, *Scarlett Doesn't Live Here Anymore: Southern Women in the Civil War Era* (Champaign: University of Illinois Press, 2000), 85.

28. Quoted in Heidi Schoof, *Elizabeth Van Lew: Civil War Spy* (Minneapolis, MN: Compass Books, 2006), 85.

29. Shauna Devine, *Learning from the Wounded: The Civil War and the Rise of American Medical Science* (Chapel Hill: University of North Carolina Press, 2014), 70–71.

30. S. Emma Edwards, *Nurse and Spy in the Union Army: Comprising the Adventures and Experiences of a Woman in Hospitals, Camps, and Battle-Fields* (Hartford, CT: Williams, 1865), 6.

31. C. Vann Woodward, ed., *Mary Chesnut's Civil War* (New Haven, CT: Yale University Press, 1981), 85.

32. Ibid., 158.

33. Drew Gilpin Faust, *This Republic of Suffering: Death and the American Civil War* (New York: Knopf, 2008).

34. Sally Randle Perry, November 30, 1867, Sally Randle Perry Diary, 1867–1868, Alabama Department of Archives and History, Montgomery, Alabama.

35. LeeAnn Whites, *The Civil War as a Crisis in Gender: Augusta, Georgia, 1860–1890* (Athens: University of Georgia Press, 2000), 93–95.

36. *Presidential Elections, 1789–2008* (Washington, DC: CQ Press, 2010), 135, 225.

37. Abraham Lincoln, Second Inaugural Address; endorsed by Lincoln, April 10, 1865, March 4, 1865, General Correspondence, 1837–1897, *The Abraham Lincoln Papers*, Library of Congress, Manuscript Division, Washington, D.C.

RECOMMENDED READING

Ayers, Edward L. *In the Presence of Mine Enemies: War in the Heart of America, 1859–1863*. New York: Norton, 2003.

Berry, Stephen, ed. *Weirding the War: Stories from the Civil War's Ragged Edges*. Athens: University of Georgia Press, 2011.

Blight, David. *Race and Reunion: The Civil War in American Memory*. Cambridge, MA: Harvard University Press, 2001.

Brasher, Glenn David. *The Peninsula Campaign and the Necessity of Emancipa-*

tion: African Americans and the Fight for Freedom. Chapel Hill: University of North Carolina Press, 2012.

Clinton, Catherine, and Nina Silber, eds. *Divided Houses: Gender and the Civil War*. New York: Oxford University Press, 1992.

Devine, Shauna. *Learning from the Wounded: The Civil War and the Rise of American Medical Science*. Chapel Hill: University of North Carolina Press, 2014.

Fahs, Alice. *The Imagined Civil War: Popular Literature of the North and South, 1861–1865*. Chapel Hill: University of North Carolina Press, 2003.

Faust, Drew Gilpin. *This Republic of Suffering: Death and the American Civil War*. New York: Knopf, 2008.

Foner, Eric. *The Fiery Trial: Abraham Lincoln and American Slavery*. New York: Norton, 2011.

Gannon, Barbara A. *The Won Cause: Black and White Comradeship in the Grand Army of the Republic*. Chapel Hill: University of North Carolina Press, 2005.

Grimsley, Mark. *The Hard Hand of War: Union Military Policy Towards Southern Civilians, 1861–1865*. New York: Cambridge University Press, 1995.

Hess, Earl. *The Union Soldier in Battle: Enduring the Ordeal of Combat*. Lawrenceville: University Press of Kansas, 1997.

Hulbert, Matthew C. *The Ghosts of Guerrilla Memory: How Civil War Bushwhackers Became Gunslingers in the American West*. Athens: University of Georgia Press, 2016.

Janney, Caroline E. *Remembering The Civil War: Reunion and the Limits of Reconciliation*. Chapel Hill: University of North Carolina Press, 2013.

Jones, Howard. *Blue and Gray Diplomacy: A History of Union and Confederate Foreign Relations*. Chapel Hill: University of North Carolina Press, 2010.

Manning, Chandra. *What This Cruel War Was Over: Soldiers, Slavery, and the Civil War*. New York: Knopf, 2007.

McCurry, Stephanie. *Confederate Reckoning: Power and Politics in the Civil War South*. Cambridge, MA: Harvard University Press, 2012.

McPherson, James. *Battle Cry of Freedom: The Civil War Era*. New York: Oxford University Press, 1988.

Meier, Kathryn Shively. *Nature's Civil War: Common Soldiers and the Environment in 1862 Virginia*. Chapel Hill: University of North Carolina Press, 2013.

Neely, Mark. *The Fate of Liberty: Abraham Lincoln and Civil Liberties*. New York: Oxford University Press, 1991.

Nelson, Megan Kate. *Ruin Nation: Destruction and the American Civil War*. Athens: University of Georgia Press, 2012.

Rable, George C. *God's Almost Chosen Peoples: A Religious History of the American Civil War*. Chapel Hill: University of North Carolina Press, 2015.

Richardson, Heather Cox. *The Greatest Nation of the Earth: Republican Economic Policies During the Civil War*. Cambridge, MA: Harvard University Press, 1997.

Vorenberg, Michael. *The Civil War, the Abolition of Slavery, and the Thirteenth Amendment*. New York: Cambridge University Press, 2004.

Whites, LeeAnn. *The Civil War as a Crisis in Gender: Augusta, Georgia, 1860–1890*. Athens: University of Georgia Press, 2000.

15
Reconstruction

I. Introduction

After the Civil War, much of the South lay in ruins. "It passes my comprehension to tell what became of our railroads," one South Carolinian told a northern reporter. "We had passably good roads, on which we could reach almost any part of the State, and the next week they were all gone—not simply broken up, but gone. Some of the material was burned, I know, but miles and miles of iron have actually disappeared, gone out of existence."[1] He might as well have been talking about the entire antebellum way of life. The future of the South was uncertain. How would these states be brought back into the Union? Would they be conquered territories or equal states? How would they rebuild their governments,

Contrabands, Cumberland Landing, Virginia, 1862. Library of Congress.

economies, and social systems? What rights did freedom confer on formerly enslaved people?

The answers to many of Reconstruction's questions hinged on the concepts of citizenship and equality. The era witnessed perhaps the most open and widespread discussions of citizenship since the nation's founding. It was a moment of revolutionary possibility and violent backlash. African Americans and Radical Republicans pushed the nation to finally realize the Declaration of Independence's promises that "all men are created equal" and have "certain unalienable rights." White Democrats granted African Americans legal freedom but little more. When Black Americans and their radical allies succeeded in securing citizenship for freedpeople, a new fight commenced to determine the legal, political, and social implications of American citizenship. Resistance continued, and Reconstruction eventually collapsed. In the South, limits on human freedom endured and would stand for nearly a century more.

II. Politics of Reconstruction

Reconstruction—the effort to restore southern states to the Union and to redefine African Americans' place in American society—began before the Civil War ended. President Abraham Lincoln began planning for the reunification of the United States in the fall of 1863.[2] With a sense that Union victory was imminent and that he could turn the tide of the war by stoking Unionist support in the Confederate states, Lincoln issued a proclamation allowing southerners to take an oath of allegiance. When just 10 percent of a state's voting population had taken such an oath, loyal Unionists could then establish governments.[3] These so-called Lincoln governments sprang up in pockets where Union support existed like Louisiana, Tennessee, and Arkansas. Unsurprisingly, these were also the places that were exempted from the liberating effects of the Emancipation Proclamation.

Initially proposed as a war aim, Lincoln's Emancipation Proclamation committed the United States to the abolition of slavery. However, the proclamation freed only enslaved people in areas of rebellion and left more than seven hundred thousand in bondage in Delaware, Kentucky, Maryland, and Missouri as well as in Union-occupied areas of Louisiana, Tennessee, and Virginia.

To cement the abolition of slavery, Congress passed the Thirteenth Amendment on January 31, 1865. The amendment legally abolished slavery "except as a punishment for crime whereof the party shall have been

THE "RAIL SPLITTER" AT WORK REPAIRING THE UNION.

With the war coming to an end, the question of how to reunite the former Confederate states with the Union was a divisive one. Lincoln's Presidential Reconstruction plans were seen by many, including Radical Republicans in Congress, to be too tolerant toward what they considered to be traitors. This political cartoon reflects this viewpoint, showing Lincoln and Johnson happily stitching the Union back together with little anger toward the South. Joseph E. Baker, *The "Rail Splitter" at Work Repairing the Union*, 1865. Library of Congress.

duly convicted." Section Two of the amendment granted Congress the "power to enforce this article by appropriate legislation." State ratification followed, and by the end of the year the requisite three fourths of the states had approved the amendment, and four million people were forever free from the slavery that had existed in North America for 250 years.[4]

Lincoln's policy was lenient, conservative, and short-lived. Reconstruction changed when John Wilkes Booth shot Lincoln on April 14, 1865, during a performance of *Our American Cousin* at Ford's Theater. Treated rapidly and with all possible care, Lincoln nevertheless succumbed to his wounds the following morning, leaving a somber pall over the North and especially among African Americans.

The assassination of Abraham Lincoln propelled Vice President Andrew Johnson into the executive office in April 1865. Johnson, a states'-

rights, strict-constructionist, and unapologetic racist from Tennessee, offered southern states a quick restoration into the Union. His Reconstruction plan required provisional southern governments to void their ordinances of secession, repudiate their Confederate debts, and ratify the Thirteenth Amendment. On all other matters, the conventions could do what they wanted with no federal interference. He pardoned all southerners engaged in the rebellion with the exception of wealthy planters who possessed more than $20,000 in property.[5] The southern aristocracy would have to appeal to Johnson for individual pardons. In the meantime, Johnson hoped that a new class of southerners would replace the extremely wealthy in leadership positions.

Many southern governments enacted legislation that reestablished antebellum power relationships. South Carolina and Mississippi passed laws known as Black Codes to regulate Black behavior and impose social and economic control. Other states soon followed. These laws granted some rights to African Americans, like the right to own property, to marry, or to make contracts. But they also denied fundamental rights. White lawmakers forbade Black men from serving on juries or in state militias, refused to recognize Black testimony against white people, apprenticed orphaned children to their former enslavers, and established severe vagrancy laws. Mississippi's vagrant law required all freedmen to carry papers proving they had means of employment.[6] If they had no proof, they could be arrested and fined. If they could not pay the fine, the sheriff had the right to hire out his prisoner to anyone who was willing to pay the tax. Similar ambiguous vagrancy laws throughout the South reasserted control over Black labor in what one scholar has called "slavery by another name."[7] Black Codes effectively criminalized Black people's leisure, limited their mobility, and locked many into exploitative farming contracts. Attempts to restore the antebellum economic order largely succeeded.

These laws and outrageous mob violence against Black southerners led Republicans to call for a more dramatic Reconstruction. So when Johnson announced that the southern states had been restored, congressional Republicans refused to seat delegates from the newly reconstructed states.

Republicans in Congress responded with a spate of legislation aimed at protecting freedmen and restructuring political relations in the South. Many Republicans were keen to grant voting rights for freedmen in order to build a new powerful voting bloc. Some Republicans, like U.S. congressman Thaddeus Stevens, believed in racial equality, but the majority were motivated primarily by the interest of their political party. The only way to protect Republican interests in the South was to give the vote to

RECONSTRUCTION

While no one could agree on what the best plan for reconstructing the nation would be, Americans understood the moment as critical and perhaps revolutionary. In this magnificent visual metaphor for the reconciliation of the North and South, John Lawrence postulates what might result from reunion. Reconstruction, the print seems to argue, will form a more perfect Union that upholds the ideals of the American Revolution, most importantly (as seen on a streaming banner near the top) that "All men are born free and equal." John Giles Lawrence, *Reconstruction*, 1867. Library of Congress.

the hundreds of thousands of Black men. Republicans in Congress responded to the codes with the Civil Rights Act of 1866, the first federal attempt to constitutionally define all American-born residents (except Native peoples) as citizens. The law also prohibited any curtailment of citizens' "fundamental rights."[8]

The Fourteenth Amendment developed concurrently with the Civil Rights Act to ensure its constitutionality. The House of Representatives approved the Fourteenth Amendment on June 13, 1866. Section One granted citizenship and repealed the Taney Court's infamous *Dred Scott* (1857) decision. Moreover, it ensured that state laws could not deny due process or discriminate against particular groups of people. The Fourteenth Amendment signaled the federal government's willingness to enforce the Bill of Rights over the authority of the states.

Because he did not believe African Americans deserved equal rights, President Johnson opposed the passage of the Fourteenth Amendment and vetoed the Civil Rights Act. But after winning a two-thirds majority in the 1866 midterm elections, Republicans overrode the veto, and in 1867, they passed the first Reconstruction Act, dissolving state governments and dividing the South into five military districts. Under these new terms, states would have to ratify the Fourteenth Amendment, write new constitutions enfranchising African Americans, and abolish repressive "Black Codes" before rejoining the union. In the face of President Johnson's repeated obstructionism, the House of Representatives issued articles of impeachment against the president. Although Johnson narrowly escaped conviction in the Senate, Congress won the power to direct a new phase of Reconstruction. Six weeks later, on July 9, 1868, the states ratified the Fourteenth Amendment, guaranteeing birthright citizenship and "equal protection of the laws."

In the 1868 presidential election, former Union General Ulysses S. Grant ran on a platform that proclaimed, "Let Us Have Peace," in which he promised to protect the new status quo. On the other hand, the Democratic candidate, Horatio Seymour, promised to repeal Reconstruction. Black southern voters helped Grant win most of the former Confederacy.

In this *Harper's Weekly* print, Black men of various occupations wait patiently for their turn as the first voter submits his ballot. Unlike other contemporary images that depicted African Americans as ignorant, unkempt, and lazy, this print shows these Black men as active citizens. Three years after the publication of this print, the Fifteenth Amendment protected the right of Black Americans to vote. Alfred R. Waud, *The First Vote*, November 1867. Library of Congress.

Scalawags and carpetbaggers also buttressed Republicans in the South. *Scalawag* was the derisive term used to describe white Republicans in the South, and *carpetbaggers* was the term for northerners who traveled to the South during Reconstruction. But Black voters formed the backbone of the Republican coalition in the South.

Reconstruction brought the first moment of mass democratic participation for African Americans. In 1860, only five states in the North allowed African Americans to vote on equal terms with whites. Yet after 1867, when Congress ordered southern states to eliminate racial discrimination in voting, African Americans began to win elections across the South. In a short time, the South was transformed from an all-white, pro-slavery, Democratic stronghold to a collection of Republican-led states with African Americans in positions of power for the first time in American history.[9]

Through the provisions of the congressional Reconstruction Acts, Black men voted in large numbers and also served as delegates to the state constitutional conventions in 1868. Black delegates actively participated in revising state constitutions. One of the most significant accomplishments of these conventions was the establishment of a public school system. While public schools were virtually nonexistent in the antebellum period, by the end of Reconstruction, every southern state had established a public school system.[10] Republican officials opened state institutions like mental asylums, hospitals, orphanages, and prisons to white and Black residents, though often on a segregated basis. They actively sought industrial development, northern investment, and internal improvements.

African Americans served at every level of government during Reconstruction. At the federal level, Hiram Revels and Blanche K. Bruce were chosen as U.S. senators from Mississippi. Fourteen men served in the House of Representatives. At least 270 other African American men served in patronage positions as postmasters, customs officials, assessors, and ambassadors. At the state level, more than 1,000 African American men held offices in the South. P. B. S. Pinchback served as Louisiana's governor for thirty-four days after the previous governor was suspended during impeachment proceedings and was the only African American state governor until Virginia elected L. Douglas Wilder in 1989. Almost 800 African American men served as state legislators around the South, with African Americans at one time making up a majority in the South Carolina House of Representatives.[11]

African American officeholders came from diverse backgrounds. Many had been born free or had gained their freedom before the Civil War. Many free African Americans, particularly those in South Carolina, Virginia, and

THE FIRST COLORED SENATOR AND REPRESENTATIVES.
In the 41ˢᵗ and 42ⁿᵈ Congress of the United States.

The era of Reconstruction witnessed a few moments of true progress. One of those was the election of African Americans to local, state, and national offices, including both houses of Congress. Pictured here are Hiram Revels (the first African American senator) alongside six Black representatives, all from the former Confederate states. Currier & Ives, *First Colored Senator and Representatives in the 41st and 42nd Congress of the United States*, 1872. Library of Congress.

Louisiana, were wealthy and well educated, two facts that distinguished them from much of the white population both before and after the Civil War. Some, like Antoine Dubuclet of Louisiana and William Breedlove from Virginia, owned enslaved laborers before the Civil War. Others had helped enslaved people escape or taught them to read, like Georgia's James D. Porter.

Most African American officeholders, however, gained their freedom during the war. Among them were skilled craftsmen like Emanuel Fortune, a shoemaker from Florida; ministers such as James D. Lynch from Mississippi; and teachers like William V. Turner from Alabama. Moving into political office was a natural continuation of the leadership roles they had held in their former communities.

By the end of Reconstruction in 1877, more than two thousand African American men had served in offices ranging from local levee commissioner to U.S. senator.[12] When the end of Reconstruction returned white Democrats to power in the South, all but a few African American officeholders lost their positions. After Reconstruction, African Americans did not enter the political arena again in large numbers until well into the twentieth century.

III. The Meaning of Black Freedom

Land was one of the major desires of the freed people. Frustrated by responsibility for the growing numbers of freed people following his troops, General William T. Sherman issued Special Field Order No. 15, in which land in Georgia and South Carolina was to be set aside as a homestead for the freedpeople. Sherman lacked the authority to confiscate and distribute land, so this plan never fully took effect.[13] One of the main purposes of the Freedmen's Bureau, however, was to redistribute lands to formerly enslaved people that had been abandoned and confiscated by the federal government. Even these land grants were short-lived. In 1866, land that ex-Confederates had left behind was reinstated to them.

Freedpeople's hopes of land reform were unceremoniously dashed as Freedmen's Bureau agents held meetings with the freedmen throughout the South, telling them the promise of land was not going to be honored and that instead they should plan to go back to work for their former enslavers as wage laborers. The policy reversal came as quite a shock. In one instance, Freedmen's Bureau commissioner General Oliver O. Howard went to Edisto Island to inform the Black population there of the policy change. The Black commission's response was that "we were promised Homesteads by the government. . . . You ask us to forgive the land owners of our island. . . .The man who tied me to a tree and gave me 39 lashes and who stripped and flogged my mother and my sister . . . that man I cannot well forgive. Does it look as if he has forgiven me, seeing how he tries to keep me in a condition of helplessness?"[14]

In working to ensure that crops would be harvested, agents sometimes coerced formerly enslaved people into signing contracts with their former enslavers. However, the bureau also instituted courts where African Americans could seek redress if their employers were abusing them or not paying them. The last ember of hope for land redistribution was extinguished when Thaddeus Stevens and Charles Sumner's proposed land reform bills were tabled in Congress. Radicalism had its limits, and the Republican Party's commitment to economic stability eclipsed their interest in racial justice.

Another aspect of the pursuit of freedom was the reconstitution of families. Many freedpeople immediately left plantations in search of family members who had been sold away. Newspaper ads sought information about long-lost relatives. People placed these ads until the turn of the twentieth century, demonstrating the enduring pursuit of family reunification. Freedpeople sought to gain control over their own children or other children who had been apprenticed to white masters either during the war or as a result of the Black Codes. Above all, freedpeople wanted freedom to control their families.[15]

Many freedpeople rushed to solemnize unions with formal wedding ceremonies. Black people's desires to marry fit the government's goal to make free Black men responsible for their own households and to prevent Black women and children from becoming dependent on the government.

Freedpeople placed a great emphasis on education for their children and themselves. For many, the ability to finally read the Bible for themselves induced work-weary men and women to spend all evening or Sunday attending night school or Sunday school classes. It was not uncommon to find a one-room school with more than fifty students ranging in age from three to eighty. As Booker T. Washington famously described the situation, "it was a whole race trying to go to school. Few were too young, and none too old, to make the attempt to learn."[16]

Many churches served as schoolhouses and as a result became central to the freedom struggle. Free and freed Black southerners carried well-formed political and organizational skills into freedom. They developed anti-racist politics and organizational skills through antislavery organizations turned church associations. Liberated from white-controlled churches, Black Americans remade their religious worlds according to their own social and spiritual desires.[17]

One of the more marked transformations that took place after emancipation was the proliferation of independent Black churches and church associations. In the 1930s, nearly 40 percent of 663 Black churches surveyed had their organizational roots in the post-emancipation era.[18] Many independent Black churches emerged in the rural areas, and most of them had never been affiliated with white churches.

Many of these independent churches were quickly organized into regional, state, and even national associations, often by brigades of free Black northerners and midwesterners who went to the South to help the freedmen. Through associations like the Virginia Baptist State Convention and the Consolidated American Baptist Missionary Convention,

Baptists became the fastest growing post-emancipation denomination, building on their antislavery associational roots and carrying on the struggle for Black political participation.[19]

Tensions between northerners and southerners over styles of worship and educational requirements strained these associations. Southern, rural Black churches preferred worship services with more emphasis on inspired preaching, while Black urban northerners favored more orderly worship and an educated ministry.

Perhaps the most significant internal transformation in churches had to do with the role of women—a situation that eventually would lead to the development of independent women's conventions in Baptist, Methodist, and Pentecostal churches. Women like Nannie Helen Burroughs and Virginia Broughton, leaders of the Baptist Woman's Convention, worked to protect Black women from sexual violence from white men. Black representatives repeatedly articulated this concern in state constitutional conventions early in the Reconstruction era. In churches, women continued to fight for equal treatment and access to the pulpit as preachers, even though they were able to vote in church meetings.[20]

Black churches provided centralized leadership and organization in post-emancipation communities. Many political leaders and officeholders were ministers. Churches were often the largest building in town and served as community centers. Access to pulpits and growing congregations provided a foundation for ministers' political leadership. Groups like the Union League, militias, and fraternal organizations all used the regalia, ritual, and even hymns of churches to inform and shape their practice.

Black churches provided space for conflict over gender roles, cultural values, practices, norms, and political engagement. With the rise of Jim Crow, Black churches would enter a new phase of negotiating relationships within the community and the wider world.

IV. Reconstruction and Women

Reconstruction involved more than the meaning of emancipation. Women also sought to redefine their roles within the nation and in their local communities. The abolitionist and women's rights movements simultaneously converged and began to clash. In the South, both Black and white women struggled to make sense of a world of death and change. In Reconstruction, leading women's rights advocate Elizabeth Cady Stanton

Susan B. Anthony and Elizabeth Cady Stanton maintained a strong and productive relationship for nearly half a century as they sought to secure political rights for women. While the fight for women's rights stalled during the war, it sprung back to life as Anthony, Stanton, and others formed the American Equal Rights Association. *[Elizabeth Cady Stanton, seated, and Susan B. Anthony, standing, three-quarter length portrait]*, between 1880 and 1902. Library of Congress.

saw an unprecedented opportunity for disenfranchised groups. Women as well as Black Americans, North and South, could seize political rights. Stanton formed the Women's Loyal National League in 1863, which petitioned Congress for a constitutional amendment abolishing slavery.[21] The Thirteenth Amendment marked a victory not only for the antislavery cause but also for the Loyal League, proving women's political efficacy and the possibility for radical change. Now, as Congress debated the meanings of freedom, equality, and citizenship for formerly enslaved people, women's rights leaders saw an opening to advance transformations in women's status, too. On May 10, 1866, just one year after the war, the Eleventh National Women's Rights Convention met in New York City to discuss what many agreed was an extraordinary moment, full of promise for fundamental social change. Elizabeth Cady Stanton presided over the meeting. Also in attendance were prominent abolitionists with whom Stanton and other women's rights leaders had joined forces in the years leading up to the war. Addressing this crowd of social reformers, Stanton captured the radical spirit of the hour: "now in the reconstruction," she declared, "is the opportunity, perhaps for the century, to base our government on the broad principle of equal rights for all."[22] Stanton chose her universal language—"equal rights *for all*"—with intention, setting an agenda of universal suffrage. Thus, in 1866, the National Women's Rights Convention officially merged with the American Anti-Slavery Society to form the American Equal Rights Association (AERA). This union marked the culmination of the long-standing partnership between abolitionists and women's rights advocates.

The AERA was split over whether Black male suffrage should take precedence over universal suffrage, given the political climate of the South. Some worried that political support for freedmen would be undermined by the pursuit of women's suffrage. For example, AERA member Frederick Douglass insisted that the ballot was literally a "question of life and death" for southern Black men, but not for women.[23] Some African American women challenged white suffragists in other ways. Frances Harper, for example, a freeborn Black woman living in Ohio, urged them to consider their own privilege as white and middle class. Universal suffrage, she argued, would not so clearly address the complex difficulties posed by racial, economic, and gender inequality.[24]

These divisions came to a head early in 1867, as the AERA organized a campaign in Kansas to determine the fate of Black and woman suffrage. Elizabeth Cady Stanton and her partner in the movement, Susan B.

Elizabeth Cady Stanton, the great women's rights and abolition activist, was one of the strongest forces in the universal suffrage movement. Her name can be seen at the top of this petition to extend suffrage to all regardless of sex, which was presented to Congress on January 29, 1866. It did not pass, and women would not gain the vote for more than half a century after Stanton and others signed this petition. *Petition of E. Cady Stanton, Susan B. Anthony, Lucy Stone, Antoinette Brown Blackwell, and Others Asking for an Amendment of the Constitution that Shall Prohibit the Several States from Disfranchising Any of Their Citizens on the Ground of Sex,* 1865. National Archives and Records Administration.

Anthony, made the journey to advocate universal suffrage. Yet they soon realized that their allies were distancing themselves from women's suffrage in order to advance Black enfranchisement. Disheartened, Stanton and Anthony allied instead with white supremacists who supported women's equality. Many fellow activists were dismayed by Stanton's and Anthony's willingness to appeal to racism to advance their cause.[25]

These tensions finally erupted over conflicting views of the Fourteenth and Fifteenth Amendments. Women's rights leaders vigorously protested the Fourteenth Amendment. Although it established national citizenship for all persons born or naturalized in the United States, the amendment also introduced the word *male* into the Constitution for the first time. After the Fifteenth Amendment ignored sex as an unlawful barrier to suffrage, an omission that appalled Stanton, the AERA officially dissolved. Stanton and Anthony formed the National Woman Suffrage Association (NWSA), while suffragists who supported the Fifteenth Amendment, regardless of its limitations, founded the American Woman Suffrage Association (AWSA).

The NWSA soon rallied around a new strategy: the New Departure. This new approach interpreted the Constitution as *already* guaranteeing women the right to vote. They argued that by nationalizing citizenship for all people and protecting all rights of citizens—including the right to vote—the Fourteenth and Fifteenth Amendments guaranteed women's suffrage. Broadcasting the New Departure, the NWSA encouraged women to register to vote, which roughly seven hundred did between 1868 and 1872. Susan B. Anthony was one of them and was arrested but then acquitted in trial. In 1875, the Supreme Court addressed this constitutional argument: acknowledging women's citizenship but arguing that suffrage was not a right guaranteed to all citizens. This ruling not only defeated the New Departure but also coincided with the Court's broader reactionary interpretation of the Reconstruction amendments that significantly limited freedmen's rights. Following this defeat, many suffragists like Stanton increasingly replaced the ideal of universal suffrage with arguments about the virtue that white women would bring to the polls. These new arguments often hinged on racism and declared the necessity of white women voters to keep Black men in check.[26]

Advocates for women's suffrage were largely confined to the North, but southern women were experiencing social transformations as well. The lines between refined white womanhood and degraded enslaved Black femaleness were no longer so clearly defined. Moreover, during the war, southern white women had been called on to do traditional men's work, chopping wood and managing businesses. While white southern women decided whether and how to return to their prior status, African American women embraced new freedoms and a redefinition of womanhood.

The Civil War showed white women, especially upper-class women, life without their husbands' protection. Many did not like what they saw, especially given the possibility of racial equality. Formerly wealthy women hoped to maintain their social status by rebuilding the prewar social hierarchy. Through Ladies' Memorial Associations and other civic groups, southern women led the efforts to bury and memorialize the dead, praising and bolstering their men's masculinity through nationalist speeches and memorials. Ladies' Memorial Associations (LMAs) grew out of the Soldiers' Aid Society and became the precursor and custodian of the Lost Cause narrative. Proponents of the Lost Cause tried to rewrite the history of the antebellum South to deemphasize the brutality of slavery. They also created the myth that the Civil War was fought over states' rights instead of slavery, which was the actual cause. LMAs and their

The Fifteenth Amendment prohibited discrimination in voting rights on the basis of race, color, or previous status (i.e., slavery). While the amendment was not all-encompassing in that women were not included, it was an extremely significant ruling in affirming the liberties of African American men. This print depicts a huge parade held in Baltimore, Maryland, on May 19, 1870, surrounded by portraits of abolitionists and scenes of African Americans exercising their rights. Thomas Kelly after James C. Beard, *The 15th Amendment. Celebrated May 19th 1870*, 1870. Library of Congress.

ceremonies created new holidays during which white southerners could reaffirm their allegiance to the Confederacy and express their opposition to Black rights. For instance, some LMAs celebrated the anniversary of Stonewall Jackson's death on May 10.[27] Through these activities, southern women took on political roles in the South.

Southern Black women also sought to redefine their public and private lives. Their efforts to control their labor met the immediate opposition of southern white women. Gertrude Clanton, a plantation mistress before the war, disliked cooking and washing dishes, so she hired an African American woman to do the washing. A misunderstanding quickly developed. The laundress, nameless in Gertrude's records, performed her job and returned home. Gertrude believed that her money had purchased a day's labor, not just the load of washing, and she became quite frustrated. Meanwhile, this washerwoman and others like her set wages and hours for themselves, and in many cases began to take washing into their own homes in order to avoid the surveillance of white women and the sexual threat posed by white men.[28]

Similar conflicts raged across the South. White southerners demanded that African American women work in the plantation home and instituted apprenticeship systems to place African American children in unpaid labor positions. African American women combated these attempts by refusing to work at jobs without fair pay or fair conditions and by clinging tightly to their children.

Like white LMA members, African American women formed clubs to bury their dead, to celebrate African American masculinity, and to provide aid to their communities. On May 1, 1865, African Americans in Charleston created the precursor to the modern Memorial Day by mourning the Union dead buried hastily on a race track turned prison.[29]

Like their white counterparts, the three hundred African American women who participated had been members of the local Patriotic Association, which aided freedpeople during the war. African American women continued participating in federal Decoration Day ceremonies and, later, formed their own club organizations. Racial violence, whether city riots or rural vigilantes, continued to threaten these vulnerable households. Nevertheless, the formation and preservation of African American households became a paramount goal for African American women.

For all of their differences, white and Black southern women faced a similar challenge during Reconstruction. Southern women celebrated the return of their brothers, husbands, and sons, but couples separated for many years struggled to adjust. To make matters worse, many of these former soldiers returned with physical or mental wounds. For white families, suicide and divorce became more acceptable, while the opposite occurred for Black families. Since the entire South suffered from economic devastation, many families were impoverished and sank into debt. All southern women faced economic devastation, lasting wartime trauma, and enduring racial tensions.

V. Racial Violence in Reconstruction

Violence shattered the dream of biracial democracy. Still steeped in the violence of slavery, white southerners could scarcely imagine Black free labor. Congressional investigator Carl Schurz reported that in the summer of 1865, southerners shared a near unanimous sentiment that "You cannot make the negro work, without physical compulsion."[30] Violence had been used in the antebellum period to enforce slave labor and to define racial difference. In the post-emancipation period it was used to stifle Black advancement and return to the old order.

Much of life in the antebellum South had been premised on slavery. The social order rested on a subjugated underclass, and the labor system required unfree laborers. A notion of white supremacy and Black inferiority undergirded it all. Whites were understood as fit for freedom and citizenship, Blacks for chattel slave labor. The Confederate surrender at Appomattox Court House and the subsequent adoption by the U.S. Congress of the Thirteenth Amendment destroyed the institution of American slavery and threw southern society into disarray. The foundation of southern society had been shaken, but southern whites used Black Codes and racial terrorism to reassert control over formerly enslaved people.

The Ku Klux Klan was just one of a number of vigilante groups that arose after the war to terrorize African Americans and Republicans throughout the South. The KKK brought violence into the voting polls, the workplace, and—as seen in this *Harper's Weekly* print—the homes of Black Americans. Frank Bellew, *Visit of the Ku-Klux*, 1872. Wikimedia.

Racial violence in the Reconstruction period took three major forms: riots against Black political authority, interpersonal fights, and organized vigilante groups. There were riots in southern cities several times during Reconstruction. The most notable were the riots in Memphis and New Orleans in 1866, but other large-scale urban conflicts erupted in places including Laurens, South Carolina, in 1870; Colfax, Louisiana, in 1873; another in New Orleans in 1874; Yazoo City, Mississippi, in 1875; and Hamburg, South Carolina, in 1876. Southern cities grew rapidly after the war as migrants from the countryside—particularly freed people— flocked to urban centers. Cities became centers of Republican control. But white conservatives chafed at the influx of Black residents and the establishment of biracial politics. In nearly every conflict, white conservatives initiated violence in reaction to Republican rallies or conventions or elections in which Black men were to vote. The death tolls of these conflicts remain incalculable, and victims were overwhelmingly Black.

Even everyday violence between individuals disproportionally targeted African Americans during Reconstruction. African Americans gained citizenship rights like the ability to serve on juries as a result of the Civil Rights Act of 1866 and the Fourteenth Amendment. But southern white men were almost never prosecuted for violence against Black victims. White men beat or shot Black men with relative impunity, and did so over minor squabbles, labor disputes, long-standing grudges, and crimes of passion. These incidents sometimes were reported to local federal authorities like the army or the Freedmen's Bureau, but more often than not such violence was unreported and unprosecuted.[31]

The violence committed by organized vigilante groups, sometimes called nightriders or bushwhackers, was more often premeditated. Groups of nightriders operated under cover of darkness and wore disguises to curtail Black political involvement. Nightriders harassed and killed Black candidates and officeholders and frightened voters away from the polls. They also aimed to limit Black economic mobility by terrorizing freedpeople who tried to purchase land or otherwise become too independent from the white enslavers they used to rely on. They were terrorists and vigilantes, determined to stop the erosion of the antebellum South, and they were widespread and numerous, operating throughout the South. The Ku Klux Klan emerged in the late 1860s as the most infamous of these groups.

The Ku Klux Klan (KKK) was organized in 1866 in Pulaski, Tennessee, and had spread to nearly every state of the former Confederacy by 1868. The Klan drew heavily from the antebellum southern elite, but Klan groups sometimes overlapped with criminal gangs or former Confederate guerrilla groups. The Klan's reputation became so potent, and its violence so widespread, that many groups not formally associated with it were called Ku Kluxers, and to "Ku Klux" meant to commit vigilante violence. While it is difficult to differentiate Klan actions from those of similar groups, such as the White Line, the Knights of the White Camellia, and the White Brotherhood, the distinctions hardly matter. All such groups were part of a web of terror that spread throughout the South during Reconstruction. In Panola County, Mississippi, between August 1870 and December 1872, twenty-four Klan-style murders occurred. And nearby, in Lafayette County, Klansmen drowned thirty Black Mississippians in a single mass murder. Sometimes the violence was aimed at Black men or women who had tried to buy land or dared to be insolent toward a white southerner. Other times, as with the beating of Republican sheriff and tax collector Allen Huggins, the Klan targeted white politicians who supported freedpeople's civil rights. Numerous Republican politicians, perhaps dozens, were killed, either while in office or while campaigning. Thousands of individual citizens, men and women, white and Black, had their homes raided and were whipped, raped, or murdered.[32]

The federal government responded to southern paramilitary tactics by passing the Enforcement Acts between 1870 and 1871. The acts made it criminal to deprive African Americans of their civil rights. The acts also deemed violent Klan behavior as acts of rebellion against the United States and allowed for the use of U.S. troops to protect freedpeople. For a time, the federal government, its courts, and its troops, sought to put an end to the KKK and related groups. But the violence continued. By 1876, as southern Democrats reestablished "home rule" and "redeemed" the South from Republicans, federal opposition to the KKK weakened.

The federal government created the Freedmen's Bureau to assist freed people in securing their rights and their livelihoods. In this *Harper's Weekly* print, The Freedmen's Bureau official protecting the Black men and women from the angry and riotous mob of white Americans stood as a representation of the entire Bureau. Soon the Bureau and the federal government would recognize that they could not accomplish a fraction of what they set out to do, including keeping African Americans safe and free in the South. Alfred R. Waud, *The Freedmen's Bureau*, 1868. Library of Congress.

National attention shifted away from the South and the activities of the Klan, but African Americans remained trapped in a world of white supremacy that restricted their economic, social, and political rights.

White conservatives would assert that Republicans, in denouncing violence, were "waving a bloody shirt" for political opportunity. The violence, according to many white conservatives, was fabricated, or not as bad as it was claimed, or an unavoidable consequence of the enfranchisement of African Americans. On December 22, 1871, R. Latham of Yorkville, South Carolina, wrote to the *New York Tribune*, voicing the beliefs of many white southerners as he declared that "the same principle that prompted the white men at Boston, disguised as Indians, to board, during the darkness of night, a vessel with tea, and throw her cargo into the Bay, clothed some of our people in Ku Klux gowns, and sent them out on missions technically illegal. Did the Ku Klux do wrong? You are ready to say they did and we will not argue the point with you. . . . Under the peculiar circumstances what could the people of South Carolina do but resort to Ku Kluxing?"[33]

Victims and witnesses to the violence told a different story. Sallie Adkins of Warren County, Georgia, was traveling with her husband, Joseph, a Georgia state senator, when he was assassinated by Klansmen on May 10, 1869. She wrote President Ulysses S. Grant, asking for both physical protection and justice. "I am no Statesman," she disclaimed; "I am only a poor woman whose husband has been murdered for his devotion to his country. I may have very foolish ideas of Government, States & Constitutions. But I feel that I have claims upon my country. The Rebels imprisoned my Husband. Pardoned Rebels murdered him. There is no law for the punishment of them who do deeds of this sort. . . . I demand that you, President Grant, keep the pledge you made the nation—make it safe for any man to utter boldly and openly his devotion to the United States."[34]

The political and social consequences of the violence were as lasting as the physical and mental trauma suffered by victims and witnesses. Terrorism worked to end federal involvement in Reconstruction and helped to usher in a new era of racial repression.

African Americans actively sought ways to shed the vestiges of slavery. Many discarded the names their former enslavers had chosen for them and adopted new names like "Freeman" and "Lincoln" that affirmed their new identities as free citizens. Others resettled far from their former plantations, hoping to eventually farm their own land or run their own businesses. By the end of Reconstruction, the desire for self-definition, economic independence, and racial pride coalesced in the founding of dozens of Black towns across the South. Perhaps the most well-known of these towns was Mound Bayou, Mississippi, a Delta town established in 1887 by Isaiah Montgomery and Ben Green, formerly enslaved by Joseph and Jefferson Davis. Residents of the town took pride in the fact that African Americans owned all of the property in town, including banks, insurance companies, shops, and the surrounding farms. The town celebrated African American cultural and economic achievements during their annual festival, Mound Bayou Days. These tight-knit communities provided African Americans with spaces where they could live free from the indignities of segregation and the exploitation of sharecropping on white-owned plantations.[35]

VI. Economic Development During the Civil War and Reconstruction

The Civil War destroyed and then transformed the American economy. In 1859 and 1860, wealthy southern planters were flush after producing record cotton crops. Southern prosperity relied on over four million enslaved

George N. Barnard, *City of Atlanta, Ga., no. 1*, c. 1866. Library of Congress.

African Americans to grow cotton, along with a number of other staple crops across the region. Cotton fed the textile mills of America and Europe and brought great wealth to the region. On the eve of war, the American South enjoyed more per capita wealth than any other slave economy in the New World. To their enslavers, these people constituted their most valuable assets, worth roughly $3 billion.[36] Yet this wealth obscured the gains in infrastructure, industrial production, and financial markets that occurred north of the Mason-Dixon Line, a fact that the war would unmask for all to see.

In contrast to the slave South, northerners praised their region as a land of free labor, populated by farmers, merchants, and wage laborers. It was also home to a robust market economy. By 1860, northerners could buy clothing made in a New England factory, or light their homes with kerosene oil from Pennsylvania. The Midwest produced seas of grain that fed the country, with enough left over for export to Europe. Farther west, mining and agriculture were the mainstays of life. Along with the textile mills, shoe factories, and iron foundries, the firms that produced McCormick's wheat harvesters and Colt's firearms displayed the technical advances of northern manufacturers. Their goods crisscrossed the country on the North's growing railroad network. An extensive network of banks and financial markets helped aggregate capital that could be reinvested into further growth.

The Civil War, like all wars, interrupted the rhythms of commercial life by destroying lives and property. This was especially true in the South. From 1861 onward, the Confederate government struggled to find the guns, food, and supplies needed to field an army. Southerners did make astonishing gains in industrial production during this time, but it was never enough. The Union's blockade of the Atlantic prevented the Confederacy from financing the war with cotton sales to Europe. To pay their troops and keep the economy alive, the Confederate Congress turned to printing paper money that quickly sank in value and led to rapid inflation. In many cases, Confederate officials dispensed with taxes paid in cash and simply impressed the food and materials needed from their citizens. Perhaps most striking of all, in the vast agricultural wealth of the South, many southerners struggled to find enough to eat.

The war also pushed the U.S. government to take unprecedented steps. Congress raised tariffs and passed the first national income tax in 1862. In late 1861, Congress created the nation's first fiat currency, called *greenbacks*. At first, the expansion of the currency and the rapid rise in government spending created an uptick in business in 1862–1863.

As the war dragged on, inflation also hit the North. Workers demanded higher wages to pay rents and buy necessities, while the business community groaned under their growing tax burden. The United States, however, never embarked on a policy of impressment for food and supplies. The factories and farms of the North successfully supplied Union troops, while the federal government, with some adjustments, found the means to pay for war. None of this is to suggest that the North's superior ability to supply its war machine made the outcome of the war inevitable. Any account of the war must consider the tangled web of politics, battles, and economics that occurred between 1861 and 1865. But the aftermath of the war left portions of the Confederacy in ruins. State governments were mired in debt. White planters had most of their capital tied up in enslaved laborers, and so lost most of their wealth. Cotton remained the most significant crop, but the war changed how it was grown and sold. Planters broke up large farms into smaller plots tended by single families in exchange for a portion of the crop, a system called sharecropping. Once cotton production resumed, Americans found that their cotton now competed with new cotton plantations around the world. For the South as a whole, the war and Reconstruction marked the start of a period of deep poverty that would last until at least the New Deal of the 1930s.

War brought destruction across the South. Governmental and private buildings, communication systems, the economy, and transportation infrastructure were all debilitated. *Richmond, Va. Crippled locomotive, Richmond & Petersburg Railroad depot*, c. 1865. Library of Congress.

Emancipation was the single most important economic, social, and political outcome of the war. Freedom empowered African Americans in the South to rebuild families, make contracts, hold property, and move freely for the first time. Republicans in the South attempted to transform the region into a free-labor economy like the North. Yet the transition from slave labor to free labor was never so clear. Well into the twentieth century, white southerners used a combination of legal coercion and extralegal violence to maintain systems of bound labor. Vagrancy laws enabled law enforcement to justify the arrest of innocent Black men and women, and the convict-lease system meant that arbitrary arrests often resulted in decades of forced, uncompensated labor. But this new form of servitude, which continued until World War II, was only the most extreme example of an array of economic injustices. In the later nineteenth century, poor whites would form mobs and go "white-capping" to scare away Black job seekers.[37] Lacking the means to buy their own farms, Black farmers often turned to sharecropping. Sharecropping often led to cycles of debt that kept families bound to the land.[38]

Victory did not produce a sudden economic boom for the rest of the United States, either. The North would not regain its prewar pace of industrial and commodity output until the 1870s. But the war did prove beneficial to wealthy northern farmers who could afford new technologies. Wartime labor shortages promoted the use of mechanical reapers,

Massachusetts Agricultural College (now known as University of Massachusetts Amherst) was one of many colleges founded through the Federal Morrill-Land Grant Colleges Act. *Massachusetts Agricultural College, Amherst, Mass. 1879*, 1880. Wikimedia.

MASSACHUSETTS AGRICULTURAL COLLEGE, AMHERST, MASS.

reducing demand for labor, boosting farm yields, and sowing the seeds of inequality.

Wartime laws also transformed the relationship between the federal government and the American economy. New tariff laws sheltered northern industry from European competition. The Morrill Land Grant helped create colleges such as the University of California, the University of Illinois, and the University of Wisconsin. With the creation of the national banking system and greenbacks, Congress replaced hundreds of state bank notes with a system of federal currency that accelerated trade and exchange. This was not to say that Republican policy worked for everyone. The Homestead Act, meant to open the West to small farmers, was often frustrated by railroad corporations and speculators. The Transcontinental Railroad, launched during the war, failed to produce substantial economic gains for years.

The war years forged a close relationship between government and the business elite, a relationship that sometimes resulted in corruption and catastrophe, as it did when markets crashed on Black Friday, September 24, 1869. This new relationship created a political backlash, especially in the West and South, against Washington's perceived eastern and industrial bias. Conflicts over emancipation and civil rights quickly gave way to long political conflict over the direction of American economic development.

VII. The End of Reconstruction

Reconstruction ended when northerners abandoned the cause of formerly enslaved people and Democrats recaptured southern politics. Between 1868 and 1877, and especially after the Depression of 1873, economic issues supplanted Reconstruction as the foremost issue on the national agenda. The biggest threat to Republican power in the South had been the violence and intimidation of white Democrats. Only the presence of federal troops in key southern cities prevented Reconstruction's quick collapse. But the United States never committed the personnel required to restore order and guarantee Black southerners the rights promised by the Fourteenth Amendment.

Republicans and Democrats responded to economic uncertainty by retreating from Reconstruction. War-weary from a decade of military and political strife, so-called Stalwart Republicans turned from the idealism of civil rights to the practicality of economics and party politics. They won particular influence during Ulysses S. Grant's first term as president (1868–1872). By the early 1870s, Stalwart Republicans assumed control of Republican Party politics.

Meanwhile, New Departure Democrats—who focused on business, economics, political corruption, and trade—gained strength by distancing themselves from pro-slavery Democrats and Copperheads. In the South, they were called Redeemers. White southerners initially opposed the Redeemers and instead clung tightly to white supremacy and the Confederacy, but between 1869 and 1871, the Redeemers won support from white southerners by promising local rule by white Democrats, rather than Black or white Republicans. By 1871, Redeemers won political control and ended Reconstruction in three important states: Tennessee, Virginia, and Georgia.

In September 1873, Jay Cooke and Company declared bankruptcy, resulting in a bank run that spiraled into a six-year depression. The Depression of 1873 crushed the nation's already suffering laboring class and destroyed whatever remaining idealism northerners had about Reconstruction. In the South, where many farms were capitalized entirely through loans, sources of credit vanished, many landowners defaulted, and farmers entered an already oversaturated labor market. Wages plummeted and a growing system of debt peonage trapped workers in endless cycles of poverty. The economic turmoil enabled the Democrats to take control of the House of Representatives after the 1874 elections, blunting the legislature's capacity to any longer direct Reconstruction.

On the eve of the 1876 presidential election, the nation still reeled from depression. Scandals sapped trust in the Grant Administration. By 1875, Democrats in Mississippi hatched the Mississippi Plan, a wave of violence designed to intimidate Black activists and suppress Black voters.[39] The state's Republican governor pleaded for federal intervention, but national Republicans ignored the plea. Meanwhile, Rutherford B. Hayes, a Republican, won a landslide victory in the Ohio gubernatorial election without mentioning Reconstruction, focusing instead on fighting corruption and alcohol abuse and promoting economic recovery. His success made him a potential presidential candidate. The stage was set for an election that would end Reconstruction as a national issue.

Republicans chose Rutherford B. Hayes as their nominee; Democrats chose Samuel J. Tilden, who ran on honest politics and home rule in the South. Florida, Louisiana, and South Carolina would determine the president. Despite the enduring presence of Reconstruction in those states, white conservatives organized violence and fraud with impunity.

During the Panic of 1873, workers began demanding that the federal government help alleviate the strain on Americans. In January 1874, over seven thousand protesters congregated in New York City's Tompkins Square to insist that the government make job creation a priority. They were met with brutality as police dispersed the crowd, and consequently the unemployment movement lost much of its steam. Matt Morgen, *Print of a crowd driven from Tompkins Square by the mounted police, in the Tompkins Square Riot of 1874*, January 1874. Wikimedia.

With the election results contested, a federal special electoral commission voted along party lines—eight Republicans for, seven Democrats against—in favor of Hayes.

Democrats threatened to boycott Hayes's inauguration. Rival governments arose claiming to recognize Tilden as the rightfully elected president. Republicans, fearing another sectional crisis, reached out to Democrats. In what became known as the Compromise of 1877, Democrats conceded the presidency to Hayes on the condition that all remaining troops would be removed from the South and the South would receive special economic favors. Hayes was inaugurated in March 1877. In April, the remaining troops were ordered out of the South. The compromise allowed southern Democrats, no longer fearing reprisal from federal troops or northern politicians for their flagrant violence and intimidation of Black voters, to return to power.

After 1877, Republicans no longer had the political capital—or political will—to intervene in the South in cases of violence and electoral

Military District	State	Readmission	Conservative Takeover
District 1	Virginia	1870	1870
District 2	North Carolina	1868	1870
	South Carolina	1868	1877
District 3	Alabama	1868	1874
	Florida	1868	1877
	Georgia	1870	1871
District 4	Arkansas	1868	1874
	Mississippi	1870	1876
District 5	Texas	1870	1873
	Louisiana	1868	1877
None	Tennessee	1866	1869

This table shows the military districts of the seceded states of the South, the date the state was readmitted into the Union, and the date when conservatives recaptured the state house.

fraud. In certain locations with large populations of African Americans, such as South Carolina, freedpeople continued to hold some local offices for several years. Yet, with its most revolutionary aims thwarted by 1868, and economic depression and political turmoil taking even its most modest promises off the table by the early 1870s, most of the promises of Reconstruction were unmet.

VIII. Conclusion

Reconstruction in the United States achieved Abraham Lincoln's paramount desire: the restoration of the Union. The war and its aftermath forever ended legal slavery in the United States, but African Americans remained second-class citizens and women still struggled for full participation in the public life of the United States. The closing of Reconstruction saw North and South reunited behind the imperatives of economic growth and territorial expansion, rather than ensuring the full rights of its citizens. From the ashes of civil war, a new nation faced fresh possibilities while enduring old problems.

IX. Reference Material

This chapter was edited by Nicole Turner, with content contributions by Christopher Abernathy, Jeremiah Bauer, Michael T. Caires, Mari Crabtree, Chris Hayashida-Knight, Krista Kinslow, Ashley Mays, Keith McCall, Ryan Poe, Bradley Proctor, Emma Teitelman, Nicole Turner, and Caitlin Verboon.

Recommended citation: Christopher Abernathy et al., "Reconstruction," Nicole Turner, ed., in *The American Yawp*, eds. Joseph Locke and Ben Wright (Stanford, CA: Stanford University Press, 2019).

NOTES TO CHAPTER 15

1. Sidney Andrews, *The South Since the War: As Shown by Fourteen Weeks of Travel and Observation in Georgia and the Carolinas* (Cambridge, MA: Welch, Bigelow, 1866), 31.

2. Eric Foner, *Reconstruction: America's Unfinished Revolution, 1863–1877* (New York: HarperCollins, 1988), xxv.

3. *Statutes at Large, Treaties, and Proclamations of the United States of America*, vol. 13 (Boston: Little, Brown, 1866), 737–739. http://www.freedmen .umd.edu/procamn.htm.

4. The House Joint Resolution proposing the 13th amendment to the Constitution, January 31, 1865; Enrolled Acts and Resolutions of Congress, 1789-1999; General Records of the United States Government; Record Group 11; National Archives. https://www.ourdocuments.gov/doc.php?flash=false&doc-40& page=transcript.

5. Andrew Johnson, "Proclamation 179—Granting Full Pardon and Amnesty for the Offense of Treason Against the United States During the Late Civil War," December 25, 1868. Gerhard Peters and John T. Woolley, *The American Presidency Project*. http://www.presidency.ucsb.edu/ws/?pid=72360.

6. Edward McPherson, *The Political History of the United States of America During the Period of Reconstruction. . . .* (Washington, D.C.: Philp and Solomons, 1871), 80–82.

7. Douglas A. Blackmon, *Slavery by Another Name: The Re-enslavement of Black Americans from the Civil War to World War II* (New York: Random House, 2008).

8. *A Century of Lawmaking for a New Nation: U.S. Congressional Documents and Debates, 1774–1875*, Statutes at Large, 39th Congress, 1st Session, 27. https://memory.loc.gov/cgi-bin/ampage?collId=llsl&fileName=014/llsl014.db& recNum=58.

9. Eric Foner, *Freedom's Lawmakers: A Directory of Black Officeholders During Reconstruction* (Baton Rouge: LSU Press, 1996).

10. See Ward McAfee, *Religion, Race, and Reconstruction: The Public School in the Politics of the 1870s* (Albany: SUNY Press, 1998); and Hilary Green, *Educational Reconstruction: African American Schools in the Urban South* (New York: Fordham University Press, 2016).

11. Foner, *Freedom's Lawmakers*.

12. Ibid., xi.

13. Leslie Harris and Daina Ramey Berry, eds., *Slavery and Freedom in Savannah* (Athens: University of Georgia Press, 2014), 167.

14. Steven Hahn et al., eds., *Freedom: A Documentary History of Emancipation, 1861–1867, Series 3, Volume 1: Land and Labor, 1865* (Chapel Hill: University of North Carolina Press, 2008), 442–444.

15. Heather Andrea Williams, *Help Me to Find My People: The African American Search for Family Lost in Slavery* (Chapel Hill: University of North Carolina Press, 2012).

16. Booker T. Washington, *Up From Slavery* (New York: Doubleday, 1900), 30.

17. Henry H. Mitchell, *Black Church Beginnings: The Long-Hidden Realities of the First Years* (Grand Rapids, MI: Eerdmans, 2004), 141–174.

18. Benjamin Mays and Joseph Nicholson, *The Negro's Church* (New York: Russell and Russell, 1933), 29–30.

19. Foner, *Reconstruction: America's Unfinished Revolution*, 92.

20. See Virginia W. Broughton, *Virginia Broughton: The Life and Writings of a National Baptist Missionary*, ed. Tomeiko Ashford Carter (Knoxville: University of Tennessee Press, 2010); Shirley Wilson Logan, *We Are Coming: The Persuasive Discourse of Nineteenth-Century Black Women* (Carbondale: Southern Illinois University Press, 1999), 168; and Evelyn Brooks Higginbotham, "Religion, Politics, and Gender: The Leadership of Nannie Helen Burroughs," in *This Far by Faith: Readings in African-American Women's Religious Biography*, ed. Judith Weisenfeld and Richard Newman (New York: Routledge, 2014), 157.

21. "To the Women of the Republic," address from the Women's Loyal National League supporting the abolition of slavery, January 25, 1864, SEN 38A-H20 (Kansas folder); RG 46, Records of the U.S. Senate, National Archives. https://www.senate.gov/artandhistory/history/resources/pdf/WomensLoyal NationalLeague.pdf.

22. *Proceedings of the Eleventh National Women's Rights Convention, Held at the Church of the Puritans, New York, May 10, 1866* (New York: Johnston, 1866).

23. Frederick Douglass, "We Welcome the Fifteenth Amendment: Addresses Delivered in New York, on 12–13 May 1869," *The Frederick Douglass Papers. Series One, Speeches, Debates, and Interviews*, eds. John W. Blassingame and John R. McKivigan (New Haven, CT: Yale University Press, 1991), 213–219.

24. Faye E. Dudden, *Fighting Chance: The Struggle over Woman Suffrage and Black Suffrage in Reconstruction America* (New York: Oxford University Press, 2011).

25. Louise Michele Newman, *White Women's Rights: The Racial Origins of Feminism in the United States* (New York: Oxford University Press, 1999), 3–8.

26. Sue Davis, *The Political Thought of Elizabeth Cady Stanton: Women's Rights and the American Political Traditions* (New York: New York University Press, 2008), 158.

27. Caroline E. Janney, *Remembering the Civil War: Reunion and the Limits of Reconciliation* (Chapel Hill: University of North Carolina Press, 2013), 94.

28. Ella Gertrude Clanton Thomas, *The Secret Eye: The Journal of Ella Gertrude Clanton Thomas, 1848–1889*, ed. Virginia Ingraham Burr (Chapel Hill: University of North Carolina Press, 1990), 272–273.

29. David Blight, *Race and Reunion: The Civil War in American Memory* (Cambridge, MA: Harvard University Press, 2001), 65–71.

30. Carl Schurz, *Report on the Condition of the South*, ed. Michael Burlingame (1865; repr. New York: Arno Press, 1969), iii.

31. Douglas R. Egerton, *The Wars of Reconstruction: The Brief, Violent History of America's Most Progressive Era* (New York: Bloomsbury Press, 2014), 296.

32. Elaine Frantz Parsons, *Ku-Klux: The Birth of the Klan During Reconstruction* (Chapel Hill: University of North Carolina Press, 2015).

33. "A Defense of the Ku Klux," *Chester [S.C.] Reporter*, January 11, 1872.

34. Sallie Adkins to Ulysses S. Grant, May 20, 1869. Letters Received, Source Chronological File, Container #7, 1868–1870: President's Letters, Folder: May–December 1869, Record Group 60, General Records of the Department of Justice, National Archives and Records Administration, College Park, Maryland.

35. Nell Irvin Painter, *Creating Black Americans: African-American History and Its Meanings, 1619 to the Present* (New York: Oxford University Press, 2006), 158.

36. Leonard L. Richards, *Who Freed the Slaves? The Fight over the Thirteenth Amendment* (Chicago: University of Chicago Press, 2015), 258.

37. William Fitzhugh Brundage, *Lynching in the New South: Georgia and Virginia, 1880–1930* (Champaign: University of Illinois Press, 1993), 23.

38. Blackmon, *Slavery by Another Name*.

39. Nicholas Lemann, *Redemption: The Last Battle of the Civil War* (New York: Farrar, Straus and Giroux, 2006), 170–209.

RECOMMENDED READING

Blight, David. *Race and Reunion: The Civil War in American Memory.* Cambridge, MA: Harvard University Press, 2001.

Blum, Edward J. *Reforging the White Republic: Race, Religion, and American Nationalism, 1865–1898.* Baton Rouge: LSU Press, 2007.

Cimbala, Paul A. *Under the Guardianship of the Nation: The Freedmen's Bureau and the Reconstruction of Georgia, 1865–1870.* Athens: University of Georgia Press, 2003.

Downs, Gregory P. *After Appomattox: Military Occupation and the Ends of War.* Cambridge, MA: Harvard University Press, 2015.

———. *Declarations of Dependence: The Long Reconstruction of Popular Politics in the South, 1861–1908.* Chapel Hill: University of North Carolina Press, 2014.

Edwards, Laura F. *A Legal History of the Civil War and Reconstruction: A Nation of Rights.* New York: Cambridge University Press, 2015.

Egerton, Douglas R. *The Wars of Reconstruction: The Brief, Violent History of America's Most Progressive Era.* New York: Bloomsbury Press, 2014.

Foner, Eric. *Reconstruction: America's Unfinished Revolution, 1863–1877.* New York: HarperCollins, 1988.

Franke, Katherine M. "Becoming a Citizen: Reconstruction Era Regulation of African American Marriages." *Yale Journal of Law and Humanities* 11, no. 2 (1999): 251–310.

Hahn, Steven. *A Nation Under Our Feet: Black Political Struggles in the Rural South from Slavery to the Great Migration.* Cambridge, MA: Harvard University Press, 2003.

Higginbotham, Evelyn Brooks. *Righteous Discontent: The Women's Movement in the Black Baptist Church, 1880–1920.* Cambridge, MA: Harvard University Press, 1993.

Hunter, Tera W. *To 'Joy My Freedom: Southern Black Women's Lives and Labors After the Civil War.* Cambridge, MA: Harvard University Press, 1998.

Janney, Caroline E. *Remembering the Civil War: Reunion and the Limits of Reconciliation.* Chapel Hill: University of North Carolina Press, 2013.

Jones, Jacqueline. *Labor of Love, Labor of Sorrow: Black Women, Work, and the Family, from Slavery to the Present.* New York: Basic Books, 2010.

Kantrowitz, Stephen. *More Than Freedom: Fighting for Black Citizenship in a White Republic, 1829–1889.* New York: Penguin, 2012.

Lemann, Nicholas. *Redemption: The Last Battle of the Civil War.* New York: Farrar, Straus and Giroux, 2006.

Masur, Kate. *An Example for All the Land: Emancipation and the Struggle over Equality in Washington, D.C.* Chapel Hill: University of North Carolina Press, 2010.

Nelson, Megan Kate. *Ruin Nation: Destruction and the American Civil War.* Athens: University of Georgia Press, 2012.

Parsons, Elaine Frantz. *Ku-Klux: The Birth of the Klan During Reconstruction.* Chapel Hill: University of North Carolina Press, 2015.

Richardson, Heather Cox. *The Death of Reconstruction: Race, Labor, and Politics in the Post–Civil War North, 1865–1901.* Cambridge, MA: Harvard University Press, 2001.

———. *West from Appomattox: The Reconstruction of America After the Civil War.* New Haven, CT: Yale University Press, 2008.

Rosen, Hannah. *Terror in the Heart of Freedom: Citizenship, Sexual Violence, and the Meaning of Race in the Postemancipation South.* Chapel Hill: University of North Carolina Press, 2009.

Saville, Julie. *The Work of Reconstruction: From Slave to Wage Laborer in South Carolina 1860–1870.* New York: Cambridge University Press, 1994.

Silber, Nina. *The Romance of Reunion: Northerners and the South, 1865–1900.* Chapel Hill: University of North Carolina Press, 1997.

Wilson, Charles Reagan. *Baptized in Blood: The Religion of the Lost Cause, 1865–1920.* Athens: University of Georgia Press, 2009.

Contributors

EDITORS
Joseph Locke, University of Houston-Victoria
Ben Wright, University of Texas at Dallas

EDITORIAL ADVISORS
Edward L. Ayers, University of Richmond
Randall Balmer, Dartmouth University
Robin Blackburn, University of Essex
Edward J. Blum, San Diego State University
Christopher L. Brown, Columbia University
Jorge Cañizares-Esguerra, University of Texas
Joyce Chaplin, Harvard University
Jefferson R. Cowie, Cornell University
Hasia R. Diner, New York University
Darren Dochuk, Washington University in
    St. Louis
Ellen DuBois, University of California,
    Los Angeles
Erica Armstrong Dunbar, University of
    Delaware
Nicole Etcheson, Ball State University
María Cristina García, Cornell University
Thavolia Glymph, Duke University
Pekka Hämäläinen, University of Oxford
Leslie M. Harris, Emory University
Allyson Hobbs, Stanford University
Woody Holton, University of South Carolina
Daniel Martin HoSang, University of Oregon
Stephen Kantrowitz, University of Wisconsin
Michael Kazin, Georgetown University
David Konig, Washington University in St. Louis
Karen Kupperman, New York University
T. J. Jackson Lears, Rutgers University
Chandra M. Manning, Georgetown University
Kate Masur, Northwestern University
W. Caleb McDaniel, Rice University
James Merrell, Vassar College
Jo-Ann Morgan, Western Illinois University

Susan O'Donovan, University of Memphis
Heather C. Richardson, Boston College
Edward Rugemer, Yale University
John D. Saillant, Western Michigan University
Martha A. Sandweiss, Princeton University
Claudio Saunt, University of Georgia
Leigh Eric Schmidt, Washington University in
    St. Louis
Carole Shammas, University of Southern
    California
Richard White, Stanford University
Samuel Zipp, Brown University

DIGITAL CONTENT ADVISORS
David J. Bodenhamer, Indiana University
Christopher D. Cantwell, University of Missouri-
    Kansas City
Amy Earhart, Texas A&M University
Kathleen Fitzpatrick, Michigan State University
Tona Hangen, Worcester State University
Jason Heppler, Stanford University
Kim Gallon, Purdue University
Alex Gil Fuentes, Columbia University
Matthew K. Gold, CUNY Graduate Center
Jennifer Guiliano, University of Maryland
Cathy Moran Hajo, New York University
Lauren Klein, Georgia Tech
Jeffrey McClurken, University of Mary
    Washington
Tara McPherson, University of Southern
    California
Lincoln Mullen, George Mason University
Robert K. Nelson, University of Richmond
Bethany Nowviskie, University of Virginia
Miriam Posner, University of California,
    Los Angeles
Darren R. Reid, University of Edinburgh
Kyle Roberts, Loyola University Chicago

Jentery Sayers, University of Victoria
Kelly Schrum, George Mason University
Lisa Spiro, Rice University
Erik Steiner, Stanford University
Mark Tebeau, Arizona State University
Lauren Tilton, Yale University
Kathryn Tomasek, Wheaton College
Andrew J. Torget, University of North Texas
William J. Turkel, University of Western Ontario
Lauren Tilton, Yale University
Kathryn Tomasek, Wheaton College
Andrew J. Torget, University of North Texas
William J. Turkel, University of Western Ontario

CHAPTER EDITORS
Samuel Abramson, Rice University
Ellen Adams, Alice T. Miner Museum
Richard Anderson, Princeton University
Lauren Brand, Southern Nazarene University
Edwin Breeden, Old Exchange Building and Old
    Slave Mart Museum
Emily Conroy-Krutz, Michigan State University
Ari Cushner, San Jose State University
Matthew Downs, University of Mobile
Angela Esco Elder, Converse College
Jesse Gant, University of Wisconsin
Jane Fiegen Green, American Historical
    Association
Paula Fortier, Independent Researcher
Nathaniel Green, Northern Virginia Community
    College
Michael Hammond, Taylor University
Michael Hattem, Yale University
Mary Anne Henderson, University of
    Washington
David Hochfelder, University at Albany, SUNY
Daniel Johnson, Bilkent University
Amy Kohout, Colorado College
Gregg Lightfoot, The Girls Preparatory School
James McKay, University of Wisconsin
William Schultz, Princeton University
Nora Slonimsky, Iona College
Tara Strauch, College of Wooster
David Thomson, Sacred Heart University
Nicole Turner, Virginia Commonwealth University
Andrew Wegmann, Delta State University

Brandy Thomas Wells, Augusta College
Jonathan Wilfred Wilson, University of Scranton
    and Marywood University

IMAGE CURATORS
Erin Holmes, University of South Carolina
Katherine Lennard, Stanford University
Jo-Ann Morgan, Western Illinois University
Christina Regelski, Rice University
Amy Sopcak-Joseph, University of Connecticut
Whitney Stewart, University of Texas at Dallas
Colleen Tripp, California State University,
    Northridge

CONTRIBUTORS
Christopher L. Abernathy, University of
    Oklahoma
Gregory Ablavsky, Stanford Law School
Sam Abramson, Rice University
Ellen Adams, William and Mary
Alvita Akiboh, Northwestern University
Jim Ambuske, University of Virginia
Richard A. Anderson, Princeton University
Seth Anziska, University College London
Kelly B. Arehart, William and Mary
Carolyn Arena, Omohundro Institute of Early
    American History and Culture
Emily Arendt, Montana State University
    Billings
Jeffrey Bain-Conkin, Notre Dame University
Andrew Baker, Texas A&M University–
    Commerce
Thomas Balcerski, Eastern Connecticut State
    University
Simon Balto, Ball State University
Laila Ballout, Northwestern University
Seth Bartee, Guilford Technical Community
    College
Marco Basile, Harvard University
Jeremiah Bauer, University of Nebraska
Joshua Beatty, SUNY Plattsburgh
Amanda Bellows, The New School
Jacob Betz, Harvard University
Marsha Barrett, University of Illinois at
    Urbana-Champaign
Ian Beamish, Johns Hopkins University

Myles Beaupre, Notre Dame University

Ethan R. Bennett, Washington University in St. Louis

Daniel Birge, Boston University

William Black, Rice University

John Blanton, The City College of New York

Drew Bledsoe, Lee University

Cameron Blevins, Northeastern University

Nicholas Blood, Emory University

Eladio Bobadilla, Duke University

Lauren Brand, Southern Nazarene University

Edwin Breeden, Old Exchange Building and Old Slave Mart Museum

Michael Brenes, Yale University

Marjorie Brown, Houston Community College

Kyle Burke, Northwestern University

L. D. Burnett, Tarleton State University

Alexander Burns, Ball State University

Carole Butcher, North Dakota State University

Matthew A. Byron, Young Harris College

Michael T. Caires, University of Virginia

Christina Carrick, Boston University

Michelle Cassidy, Central Michigan University

Peter Catapano, New York City College of Technology

Steffi Cerato, Johns Hopkins University

Andrew Chadwick, University of Maryland

Tizoc Chavez, Vanderbilt University

Christopher Childers, Pittsburg State University

Micah Childress, Grand Valley State University

Mary Beth Basile Chopas, University of North Carolina

Frank Cirillo, University of Virginia

Justin Clark, Nanyang Technological University

Dana Cochran, Virginia Tech

Kristin Condotta Lee, Washington University in St. Louis

Emily Conroy-Krutz, Michigan State University

Christopher Consolino, Johns Hopkins University

Adam Constanzo, Texas A&M Corpus Christi

Wiliam Cossen, Penn State University

Aaron Cowan, Slippery Rock University

Mari Crabtree, College of Charleston

Michell Cresfield, Vanderbilt University

Ari Cushner, San Jose State University

Lori Daggar, Ursinus College

Andrew David, Boston University

Morgan Deane, Brigham Young University-Idaho

Jenifer Dodd, Vanderbilt University

Jean-Paul de Guzman, University of California, Los Angeles

Matthew Downs, University of Mobile

Jennifer Donnally, University of North Carolina

Mary Draper, Midwestern State University

Dan Du, University of Georgia

Blake Earle, Southern Methodist University

Ashton Ellett, University of Georgia

Angela Esco Elder, Converse College

Alexandra Evans, University of Virginia

Sean Fear, University of Leeds

Maggie Flamingo, University of Wisconsin

Paula Fortier, University of New Orleans

Jeff Fortnoy, University of Oklahoma

Michael Franczak, Boston College

Leif Fredrickson, University of Virginia

Zach Fredman, Dartmouth College

Stephanie Gamble, Johns Hopkins University

Jesse Gant, University of Wisconsin

Josh Garrett-Davis, Autry Museum of the American West

Zach P. Gastellum, University of Oklahoma

Jamie Goodall, Stevenson University

Jonathan Grandage, Florida State University

Larry A. Grant, The Citadel

Anne Gray Fischer, Brown University

Kori Graves, University at Albany, SUNY

Jane Fiegen Green, American Historical Association

Nathaniel Green, Northern Virginia Community College

Robert Gudmestad, Colorado State University

Joseph Haker, University of Minnesota

Blaine Hamilton, Rice University

Tracey Hanshew, Washington State University

Caroline Bunnell Harris, University of California, Los Angeles

Michael Hattem, Yale University

Karissa Haugeberg, Tulane University

Chris Hayashida-Knight, Penn State University

Richara Leona Hayward, University of Pennsylvania

Timothy C. Hemmis, Texas A&M University–Central Texas

Mary Anne Henderson, University of Washington

Mariah Hepworth, Northwestern University

Jordan Hill, Virginia Tech University

Hidetaka Hirota, Columbia University

David Hochfelder, University at Albany, SUNY

Nicolas Hoffmann, Oak Mountain Academy

Lilian Hoodes, Northwestern University

Rebecca Howard, University of Arkansas

Amanda Hughett, Duke University

Kylie A. Hulbert, Texas A&M University–Kingsville

Matthew C. Hulbert, University of Georgia

Jonathan Hunt, Stanford University

Jun Suk Hyun University of Georgia

Hendrick Isom, Brown University

Zachary Jacobson, Northwestern University

Destin Jenkins, University of Chicago

Nathan Jérémie-Brink, New Brunswick Theological Seminary

D. Andrew Johnson, Rice University

Daniel Johnson, Bilkent University

Christopher C. Jones, Brigham Young University

Matthew Kahn, Northwestern University

Suzanne Kahn, Columbia University

Micki Kaufman, CUNY Graduate Center

Lindsay Keiter, Penn State Altoona

William Kelly, Rutgers University

Brenden Kennedy, University of Montana Western

S. Wright Kennedy, Rice University

William Kerrigan, Muskingum University

Krista Kinslow, Boston University

Jonathan Koefoed, Belhaven University

Gerard Koeppel, Independent Scholar

Stephn M. Koeth, Columbia University

Amy Kohout, Colorado College

Erin Bonuso Kramer, University of Wisconsin

Dale Kretz, Texas Tech University

Matthew Kruer, University of Chicago

Mark Kukis, Keck Graduate Institute

Lucie Kyrova, Charles University

Guy Lancaster, Central Arkansas Library System

Allison Lange, Wentworth Institute of Technology

Kathryn Knowles Lasdow, Columbia University

Brooke Lamperd, Brown University

Scott Libson, Emory University

Gregg Lightfoot, The Girls Preparatory School

Matthew Linton, Brandeis University

Kyle Livie, Oholone College

Jennifer Mandel, Mount Washington College

John Garrison Marks, American Association for State and Local History

Dawn Marsh, Purdue University

Valerie A. Martinex, University of Texas

Paul Matzko, Penn State University

Ashley Mays, University of North Carolina

Lisa Mercer, University of Illinois at Urbana-Champaign

Spencer McBride, Louisiana State University

Keith D. McCall, Rice University

Charles McCrary, Florida State University

Katherine J. McGarr, University of Wisconsin

James McKay, University of Wisconsin

José Juan Pérez Meléndez, University of California, Davis

Ryan T. Menath, U.S. Air Force Academy

Samantha Miller, University of Pennsylvania

Shaul Mitelpunkt, University of York

Elisa Minoff, University of South Florida

Maria Montalvo, Tulane University

Celeste Day Moore, Hamilton College

Erik A. Moore, University of Oklahoma

Gregory Moore, Notre Dame College

Jessica Parker Moore, Texas Christian University

Joseph Moore, Gardner-Webb University

Isabella Morales, Princeton University

Felicia Moralez, University of Notre Dame

Melissa Morris, Bridgewater State University

Christen Mucher, Smith College

Andrea Nero, University at Buffalo, SUNY

Christopher Null, University of California, Los Angeles

James Owen, University of Georgia

Brooke Palmieri, University College London

R. Joseph Parrott, The Ohio State University

Adam Parsons, Syracuse University

Ryan Poe, Duke University

Matthew Pressman, Seton Hall University

Emily Alise Prifogle, Princeton University

Bradley Proctor, University of North Carolina

Ansley Quiros, University of North Alabama

Laura Redford, UCLA

Michelle Reeves, US Naval War College

Ronny Regev, The Hebrew University of
Jerusalem

Emily Remus, University of Notre Dame

Colin Reynolds, Emory University

Leah Richier, University of Georgia

Julie Richter, William and Mary

Bryan Rindfleisch, Marquette University

Angela Riotto, University of Akron

John P. Riley, Binghamton University, SUNY

James Risk, University of South Carolina

Andrew Robichaud, Stanford University

Michael Robinson, University of Mobile

Cara Rogers, Rice University

Katherine Rohrer, University of North Georgia

Emily Romeo, Depaul University

Nick Rowland, University of Texas

Brent Ruswick, West Chester University

Matthew K. Saionz, University of Florida

John Saillant, Western Michigan University

Christopher Paul Sawula, Emory University

Ian Saxine, Northwestern University

David Schley, Hong Kong Baptist University

John Schmitz, Northern Virginia Community
College

Kristopher Shields, Rutgers University

Evgenia Shnayder Shoop, University of
Pennsylvania

Cameron Shriver, Ohio State University

Matt Simmons, University of Florida

Donna Sinclair, University of Central Michigan

Phillip Luke Sinitiere, College of Biblical
Studies

William E. Skidmore, Rice University

Elizabeth Skilton, University of Louisiana at
Lafayette

Nora Slonimsky, Iona College

Katherine Smoak, Johns Hopkins University

Christopher Sparshott, Northwestern University
in Qatar

Bill Speer, American Military University

Daniel Spillman, Oklahoma Baptist University

Kate Sohasky, Johns Hopkins University

Marie Stango, California State University,
Bakersfield

Megan Stanton, University of Wisconsin

Rowan Steinecker, University of Central
Oklahoma

Colin Stephenson, Ohio State University

Gregory N. Stern, Florida State University

Whitney Stewart, University of Texas at Dallas

Tara Strauch, University of South Carolina

Joseph Super, University of West Virginia

Jordan Taylor, Indiana University

Michael Harrison Taylor, University of Georgia

Emma Teitelman, University of Pennsylvania

Chris Thomas, Reynolds Community College

Susan Thomas, University of North Carolina at
Greensboro

Robert John Thompson III, Southern Mississippi

David Thomson, Sacred Heart University

Patrick Troester, University of Akron

Ann Tucker, University of North Georgia

Nicole Turner, Virginia Commonwealth
University

Ashley Rose Young, Smithsonian Institution

Caitlin Verboon, Yale University

Alyce Vigil, Northern Oklahoma College

James Wainwright, Prince George's Community
College

Kevin Waite, Durham University

Kaylynn Washnock, University of Georgia

C. Ruth Watterson, Harvard University

Benjamin Weber, Harvard University

Kelly B. Weber, Rice University

Andrew Wegmann, Delta State University

James Wellborn, Georgia College

Brandy Thomas Wells, Augusta College

Benjamin Wetzel, University of Notre Dame

Luke Willert, Harvard University

Mason B. Williams, Williams College

Naomi R. Williams, The College at Brockport,
SUNY

Jonathan Wilfred Wilson, University of
Scranton and Marywood University

Kevin Wisniewski, University of Maryland, Baltimore County

Nicholas Wood, Spring Hill College

Michael E. Woods, Marshall University

Garrett Wright, University of North Carolina

Nathan Wuertenberg, Ball State University

Charlton Yingling, University of Louisville

Kevin Young, University of Georgia

Rebecca Zimmer, University of Southern Mississippi